EARLY HABSBURG SPAIN

D0933227

EARLY HABSBURG SPAIN
1517–1598

A. W. LOVETT

OXFORD UNIVERSITY PRESS
1986

Oxford University Press, Walton Street, Oxford OX2 6DP

Oxford New York Toronto
Delhi Bombay Calcutta Madras Karachi
Kuala Lumpur Singapore Hong Kong Tokyo
Nairobi Dar es Salaam Cape Town
Melbourne Auckland
and associated companies in
Beirut Berlin Ibadan Nicosia

Oxford is a trade mark of Oxford University Press

Published in the United States
by Oxford University Press, New York

British Library Cataloguing in Publication Data
Lovett, A. W.
Early Habsburg Spain 1517–1598.
1. Spain—History—Charles I, 1516–1556
2. Spain—History—Philip II, 1556–1598
I. Title
946'.04 DP171
ISBN 0-19-822139-8
ISBN 0-19-822138-X Pbk

Library of Congress Cataloging in Publication Data
Lovett, A. W.
Early Habsburg Spain, 1517–1598.
Bibliography: p.
Includes index.
1. Spain—History—Charles I, 1516–1556. 2. Spain—
History—Philip II, 1556–1598. I. Title.
DP172.L68 1986 946'.04 86-759
ISBN 0-19-822139-8
ISBN 0-19-822138-X (pbk.)

Typeset by Joshua Associates Limited, Oxford
Printed in Great Britain
at the University Printing House, Oxford
by David Stanford
Printer to the University

Preface

THIS book started life as an attempt to summarize recent, mainly Spanish, work on the history of the Iberian peninsula in the sixteenth century. The political changes which have taken place in Spain over the last twenty years have released a flood of talent, and nowhere is this more obvious than in the writing of history. My intention at the outset was to present the findings of this renaissance to an English-speaking audience; but I soon discovered that more was required. The admirable quality of contemporary Spanish writing rests upon foundations laid down in the nineteenth century by historians who were, for the most part, amateur. Any survey must give credit to these early pioneers, who had to contend in the course of their research with obstacles greater even than those which confront their successors. Neither can the contribution of foreign scholars be overlooked. The North Americans (and the English to a lesser extent) have done much to illuminate the way in which Castile acquired and governed her colonial empire. French students, bringing to bear their customary resources and ability, have made fundamental contributions to the understanding of both the economic and spiritual life of the peninsula. What had originally been intended as a brief résumé of the latest publications from Spanish sources developed almost immediately into a general review of existing literature.

The book is arranged as a series of lectures. This reflects its basic purpose, to serve as a teaching manual, and some conclusions drawn from personal experience. All material designed for an academic readership should first be presented before a live audience as this encourages the speaker, and subsequently the writer, to arrange his thoughts clearly. Simplicity of argument is something which the public have a right to expect from those who are paid to perform publicly. I have also used narrative as the principal technique of presentation as this is the best method of examining events and attitudes unfamiliar to the twentieth century. For the physicist time may lack all validity as a concept; for the historian it flows.

Over the years I have accumulated many debts. I would like to apologize to a number of editors at the Oxford University Press: to

David Attwooll for failing to produce a manuscript on time; to Will Sulkin for delivering the wrong one; and to Ivon Asquith for saddling him with the eventual product. I also place on record my gratitude to the librarians of University College, Dublin, who have built up an impressive collection of Continental material which could not always be justified on the strict criterion of student use. In this respect I am particularly indebted to Miss Maírín Cassidy and Mrs Clara Cullen. They have shown tolerance in the face of an apparently endless flow of recommendations for purchase and a flair for sorting out what was worth buying and what was not.

Lastly—a debt of another order—I would like to thank my parents for keeping me going through some bad moments, and to dedicate the book to them.

London, March 1985.   A. W. L.

Contents

Contents

List of maps and tables

PART ONE

CHARLES V

CHAPTER I

The geography of the Iberian peninsula

FUNDAMENTAL to any understanding of Iberian history is an appreciation of the role played by geology and climate. The folding and buckling of successive rock layers has given the peninsula its physical character, lifting up the mountain ranges which so effectively mark off one region from its neighbour. The climate, in its turn, has shaped the contours of the land through heat, cold, and water. It has also dictated the variety of agricultural usage. Not one but several weather systems prevail over the peninsula, bringing moisture in abundance to the north-west while denying it to the south-east. The farmers of the peninsula have been compelled to adapt accordingly.

If the western provinces of Russia are excluded, the Iberian peninsula represents the greatest land mass on the European continent. In all it covers some 581,000 square kilometres, of which modern Spain occupies some 85 per cent of the total and Portugal the remaining 15 per cent. The peninsula forms the most westerly projection of the main European block, registering at its furthest point, Cabo de Roca, 9 degrees 29 minutes 50 seconds of longitude from the meridian of Greenwich. It is also, after Greece, the most southerly in terms of latitude, 43 degrees 47 minutes 25 seconds from the Equator at its northernmost extremity, Cape Estaca de Bares, and 35 degrees 59 minutes 50 seconds at its southern tip, Cape Tarifa on the Straits of Gibraltar. According to one interpretation, the Iberian peninsula has acted as a land bridge between North Africa and Europe across which populations, flora, and fauna have migrated in both directions; whilst another school has seen in this rocky promontory jutting out into the Atlantic an island, virtually self-contained.

Within the overall structure of the peninsula geographers have identified four main areas. Of these, the meseta is by far and away the most important, and, perhaps, the most imposing. This granite-floored plateau extends across approximately four-sevenths of the total surface, making it the dominant feature of the peninsula. It is unusually high with an average altitude of some 650 metres above sea level, a feature which explains why Spain, after Switzerland, ranks as the highest country in Europe.

This tableland divides naturally into two halves. The northern meseta extends from the peaks of the Cantabrian Range on the bay of Biscay to another outcrop of mountains, the Central Ranges, which lie just north of the Tagus valley. The southern meseta runs on from here across a seemingly limitless horizon until meeting its southern boundary at the foot of the Sierra Morena. In historic times the northern and southern parts of the meseta have come to correspond with Old and New Castile. Considered as a single entity, the meseta is flanked by a series of mountain chains, and these have been character- ized as a separate geographical zone in their own right. The Galician Massif and the Cantabrian Range block off its northern limit, the mountains of Aragon (the Iberian Range) virtually shut off the eastern exits, whilst in the far south the Sierra Morena and the much higher Betic Ranges fix the divide between the meseta and the sea. The image of a central plateau hemmed in by a series of mountainous outcrops has suggested to some geographers a fortress defended by a curtain of walls.

Beyond the meseta and its immediate boundaries are to be found the two additional elements which complete the Iberian structure. Over millennia the waters borne by the Ebro and the Guadalquivir have created two wide basins, the Iberian and the Betic Depression respectively. These rivers differ from the others in moulding so broad an area, rather than merely cutting a channel to the sea; and for this reason have come to form a geographical zone in their own right. In the far north, removed from contact with any of the other formations, stand the Pyrenees and its spur, known as the Catalan Coastal Ranges. They serve both as a historical landmark and also, until recently, as a serious obstacle to trade.

The river systems of the Iberian peninsula have a number of special features, few of which have worked to the advantage of its inhabitants. The tectonic structure of the meseta, the manner in which geological forces have skewed and tilted it, has made it inevitable that the rivers which rise in the interior should flow down a gentle gradient into the Atlantic. The three rivers of the meseta, the Duero, the Tagus, and the Guadiana, observe the basic principle of Iberian hydrology— exorheism—in an east to west direction. The Guadalquivir, the 'great river' of the Arabs, although it does not rise in the meseta, has an action similar in most respects to its northern counterparts. From its

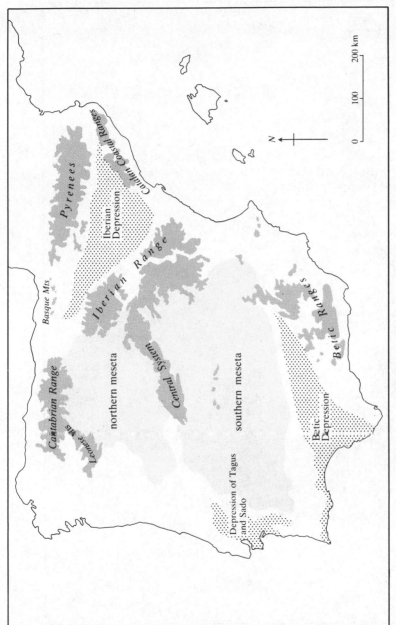

1 The Iberian peninsula: principal features

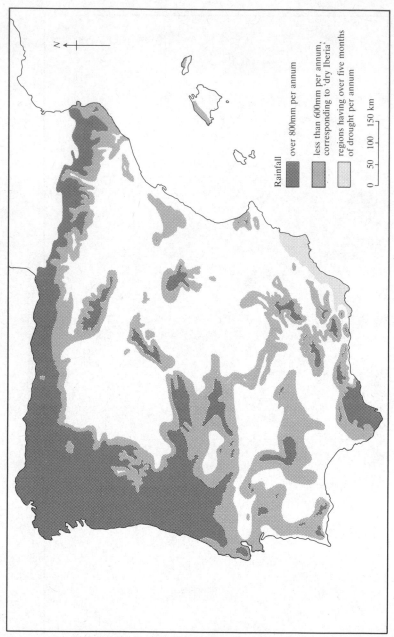

Rainfall

■ over 800mm per annum

▦ less than 600mm per annum,
corresponding to 'dry Iberia'

▢ regions having over five months
of drought per annum

0   50 100 150 km

2 The Iberian peninsula: rainfall

headwaters in the sierra of Cazorla it journeys from east to west along its broad basin until it, too, empties into the Atlantic Ocean. Of the major fluvial networks only the Ebro discharges its contents into the Mediterranean; and this fact makes it unique amongst the great rivers of the peninsula. This imbalance is further reflected in the drainage of the entire land mass. The 'Atlantic' rivers draw on a catchment area which covers 69 per cent of the total surface, while the Ebro, for its part, draws the rain and snow from the remaining 31 per cent.

By European standards, the Iberian peninsula is poorly endowed with rivers. They are far and few between, impossible to link, and navigable for relatively short distances. All too often they act as a hindrance rather than a help to communication, notably in the case of the Ebro. Secondly, their flow is irregular in the majority of examples. The 'Atlantic' rivers depend for their volume on rainfall, not snow or ice. As a consequence their flow is sluggish for much of the year; and in periods of prolonged drought this dwindles to a trickle, or dries up altogether in the higher reaches. Once again, the Ebro stands out as the exception. Through its tributaries it gathers both the rainfall and the melting snow from the Pyrenees. This combination of sources guarantees the Ebro a greater average volume of water than any other system, 615 cubic metres a second, as against 480 to 500 cubic metres a second of its nearest rival, the Tagus. Irregularity of supply has also prevented, until modern times, the harnessing of the rivers for purposes of irrigation. In summer the smaller flows often disappear for months on end; and then in the autumn the rains return, engorge the rivers, and bring the flash floods which strip the topsoil and leave barren detritus in their wake. Under such circumstances control of the water has been attempted only on a very limited scale.

The climate has also dealt harshly with the peninsula. Observers have divided the land mass into three climatic zones. The most northerly, to which the name 'humid' Iberia has been attached, includes Galicia and the mountainous fringe of the Cantabrian coast. 'Dry' Iberia is the second of these bands; and it dominates two-thirds of the peninsula; whilst in the south-eastern quarter there exists a third 'micro-climate', that of 'arid' Iberia. Mean average rainfall explains why these terms have been used. 'Humid' Iberia can expect as much, sometimes more than, 800 millimetres of rain each year. This figure falls sharply for 'dry' Iberia (the meseta, in effect) to a level which fluctuates between 600 and 300 millimetres annually. In the 'arid' pocket, the slump is even more pronounced. Rainfall in any one year seldom reaches 250 millimetres. Since so much of the peninsula is governed by a 'dry' climate, *secano* farming and transhumance have become the dominant forms of land use.

If latitude were the sole consideration, the Iberian peninsula would enjoy an Atlantic climate, that is, one marked by moisture and frequent rain. In fact this pattern is confined to the Cantabrian mountains and Galicia, 'humid' Iberia. Elsewhere the influence of the ocean has been excluded. As a result of marine and orological factors, the prevailing weather system is Mediterranean (or Continental) rather than Atlantic. This means sparse rainfall and wide variations in temperature depending on the season of the year. The Cantabrian Range and the Galician Massif prevent the moist air-streams coming in from the Atlantic from reaching the inland plateau. In the south the Betic Ranges and the Sierra Morena deny humidity to the interior in the same way.

The depth and configuration of the waters surrounding the Iberian peninsula act to confirm the predominance of a Mediterranean climate. The sill of Gibraltar, some 1,050 feet below sea level, prevents the deeper and colder currents of the Atlantic from mingling with the shallower waters of the Mediterranean. As a result the Mediterranean has a higher mean temperature than the ocean, and also a greater salinity. Weather systems which gather or pass over the inland sea draw heat from its surface; and for this reason Continental weather systems such as prevail over 'dry' Iberia record higher mean temperatures than those generated by the Atlantic.

Anticyclones sit for weeks at the centre of the weather grid; and their presence accounts for the stability, often monotony, of the climate. In summer they are responsible for the hot and cloudless days. Air is drawn down from the upper atmosphere; and as this colder mass descends it is heated, expanded, and denuded of water content. In the winter similar anticyclonic patterns maintain clear skies, with one important difference. The land retains no heat; and the biting winds sweep across 'dry' Iberia unwarmed and unimpeded.

The vegetation of a particular region is a reliable means of determining the climatic zone to which it belongs. In the north-east and along the Cantabrian coast deciduous forests thrive on the abundant rainfall. Birch, beech, and sweet chestnut flourish under these conditions. In the harsher central lands, plants and trees have adapted to the scarcity of water. The symbol of survival has become the holm oak (*Quercus ilex*), sometimes to be found on its own, at other times standing above a rough undergrowth of bushes and shrubs. This cover, the *matorral*, is often all that the poor soil of the meseta can sustain. Similar to the *maquis* or *garrigue* of other Mediterranean areas, the *matorral* contains a large number of shrubs and herbs, such as myrtle, arbutus, sweet marjoram, sage, and thyme, many of which have medicinal or culinary uses. In the extreme south, around the Cabo de la Gata, the small palm, the only type of the species to be found naturally in Spain, alone can withstand the aridity of the badlands.

CHAPTER 2

The Iberian peninsula and the Catholic Monarchs

For much of the fifteenth century it appeared highly improbable that the Spanish kingdoms, either singly or in combination, would shortly rank amongst the leading powers of western Europe. In both Castile and Aragon the aristocracy, supported by elements from within the church and by the urban oligarchs, openly disputed the authority of the crown. Their intention was to impose permanent limitations upon royal government and to convert the public treasury into a private cash-box. The factional struggles created a situation in which civil war became endemic; and this, in turn, brought on the evils of foreign intervention and, in the case of Aragon, territorial loss.

In Castile the troubles of the fifteenth century had their origins in the events of 1369. Pedro I was murdered in that year by his bastard half-brother, Henry of Trastámara, who then seized the throne for himself. With the usurper there came not only a new dynasty but also a new ruling caste, some twenty-four noble families in all, whose fortunes became inextricably linked with those of the Trastámara. Their support guaranteed the survival of the house, but it was bought at a heavy price. The Henrician aristocracy had to be placated by regular distributions of enormous grants either in the form of land or pensions chargeable to the royal purse; and these recent arrivals at the centre of power were inclined to look upon their benefactor not as a liege lord whose rights were sanctified by lineage but as one of their own number, a mere *primus inter pares*.

These ambitious and unprincipled feudatories came into their own in the time of Henry IV (1454–74). During the second half of the reign, two factions dominated the life of the court and, indeed, the country at large. One identified with the cause of Beltrán de la Cueva, the king's principal minister, the other included all those determined to drive the favourite from power and assert their own claim over royal patronage. Castilian history in this period offered a number of striking

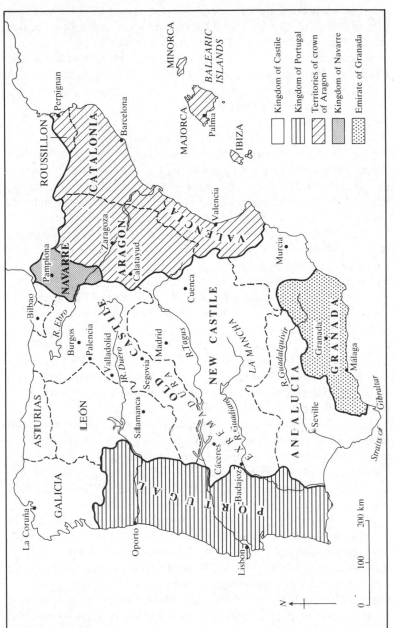

3 The Iberian peninsula *c.*1480

Kingdom of Castile
Kingdom of Portugal
Territories of crown of Aragon
Kingdom of Navarre
Emirate of Granada

MINORCA

BALEARIC ISLANDS

MAJORCA

Palma

IBIZA

ROUSSILLON
Perpignan

CATALONIA

Barcelona

ARAGON

Zaragoza

Calatayud

VALENCIA

Valencia

Murcia

NAVARRE
Pamplona

Bilbao

R. Ebro

ASTURIAS

GALICIA

La Coruña

LEÓN

Burgos

Palencia

Valladolid

OLD CASTILE

R. Duero

Salamanca

Segovia

Madrid

R. Tagus

Cuenca

NEW CASTILE

LA MANCHA

EXTREMADURA

Cáceres

Badajoz

R. Guadiana

ANDALUCIA

Seville

R. Guadalquivir

GRANADA

Granada

Málaga

Straits of Gibraltar

PORTUGAL

Oporto

Lisbon

N

0   100   200 km

parallels with contemporary events in Lancastrian England. Those who fought to replace Beltrán de la Cueva capitalized with great skill on the weaknesses of the royal party. After a promising apprenticeship as king, Henry IV became increasingly unpopular: he was accused of effeminacy (perhaps worse), and of a predilection for things Moorish and Jewish. These allegations formed the central elements in a sustained campaign of vilification against the king. But it was disloyalty within the ruling house which provided the malcontents with their most effective leverage. The previous king, John II (1406–54) had married twice during the course of a long reign. His first wife bore him a son, the future Henry IV; his second produced two children, a daughter, Isabel, born in 1451, and a son, Alfonso, who appeared two years later. The aristocracy forced Henry IV to set aside the rights of his daughter and sole heir, Juana of Castile, in favour first of his half-brother, Alfonso, and then, when Alfonso died unexpectedly in 1468, of his half-sister, Isabel. As justification for this alteration in the line of succession, the rebellious baronage maintained that Juana was not the legitimate issue of Henry IV but the daughter of the royal favourite, Beltrán de la Cueva, hence the girl's disparaging nickname, 'la Beltraneja'. Isabel the Catholic throughout her reign publicly endorsed this interpretation of events; and she rested her own claim to the throne on the accord which had been extorted from Henry IV at Toros de Guisando (19 September 1468). But there can be little doubt that, however indiscreet Henry IV's consort may have been, Juana was the lawful offspring of her father. Isabel exploited a sordid aristocratic plot for her own ends; and sanctified it by success.

The young queen was precocious in every way. Having benefited from the invention of a treasonous clique, she was determined never to allow the aristocracy to repeat the experiment. To prevent this happening, and to prepare herself for the impending civil war, she needed allies; and in 1468 this meant a husband. With little hesitation she chose her cousin, Ferdinand of Aragon, not simply because he was much younger than Afonso V of Portugal, the other candidate, but because he seemed better able to help her in the conflict that loomed. She married him, sight unseen, on 18 October 1469 in Valladolid. The spouses were still teenagers; but Ferdinand had already given signs of enterprise and vigour, having fathered two children in the previous year. For the beleaguered house of Aragon the match was nothing short of a triumph. It held out the promise that once Isabel asserted her right to the Castilian throne she would co-operate in the task of restoring the authority of the crown in Aragon. The parties to the marriage contract thought in terms of their own pressing needs not a permanent union of the Iberian kingdoms and a united Spain.

Isabel had calculated shrewdly. When Henry IV died in 1474 civil strife broke out immediately. Juana of Castile, the dispossessed daughter, made a bid for her rightful inheritance. She gathered about her a strong coalition which included Alfonso Carrillo (the archbishop of Toledo), Juan Pacheco (marquis of Villena), and, more significant than any other, Afonso V of Portugal. In 1475 the king married Juana, a union which identified him more closely with her cause while offering an alternative to that of Ferdinand and Isabel. Had the Portuguese armies triumphed, had Juana produced an heir, then the history of the peninsula would have taken a different path. But the advantage in the conflict lay with the other side. The bulk of the great families rallied to Isabel, impressed not so much by her spurious claims as by consideration of personal gain. They brought with them their clients and retainers. Ferdinand assumed command of his wife's armies, soon demonstrating that he was a far better general than any of his opponents. In the one decisive engagement of the war he defeated the Portuguese king at the battle of Toro (1 March 1476). In the aftermath of this failure, the Castilian supporters of Princess Juana started to slip away, each man making the best terms he could with the victorious party. Three years after the battle Afonso himself recognized the title of Isabel to the Castilian throne, agreeing, as part of the settlement, to put away his wife and abandon her rights. The treaty of Alcaçovas (4 September 1479) ended the civil war, settled disputes in colonial waters by specifying respective spheres of influence, and restored the traditional friendship between Castile and Portugal. Shortly after, the two ruling houses resumed their normal practice of intermarriage.

Ferdinand had given undeniable proof to his Castilian subjects that he had talent above the ordinary as a general and politician. Yet for the first years of marriage his position remained unclear. The Castilians were loath to grant him any powers above those of consort, as was made evident in the Proclamation of Segovia (13 December 1474). The civil war, and perhaps Ferdinand's pride or self-respect, made this particular arrangement unworkable; and a few weeks later a more satisfactory agreement was reached. By the terms of the Concord of Segovia (15 January 1475) Ferdinand was accorded powers in Castile equal to those enjoyed by his wife; but it was also stipulated at the

same time that the laws of succession remained as they had been
before. The right of female inheritance was safeguarded. Those who
insisted on the guarantee in 1475 could not have been aware of how
important this was to be. In 1481 Isabel acquired corresponding
powers in the lands of the Aragonese crown, although once more the
peculiarities of succession were observed. No female could succeed to
the throne of Aragon. The union of the Catholic Monarchs was very
much a working marriage, and this explains why each was authorized
to act in the kingdoms of the other. It was the harmonious co-
operation between the two spouses which accounts for their immense
success as rulers.

Although not hostile in principle to the aristocracy, the monarchs
knew that some reduction in noble power or noble excess was
essential. Royal weakness had been exploited by the great houses to
extort a whole series of grants and pensions from the exchequer, to the
extent that the yield from such patronage formed an important component of many an aristocrat's income. Inflation had brought down
the real cost of such alienations, one reason, perhaps, why the
fifteenth-century crown took a relaxed attitude to the decline in the
value of money; but the amount still outstanding represented a heavy
burden on resources. The cortes of Toledo (1480) formally approved a
scheme by which much of what had been given away by the crown was
to be resumed, that is, reincorporated into the royal domain. This act
of resumption differed in its effects from region to region. It benefited
the royal exchequer immediately by relieving it of some obligations;
and it may also, in time, have worked to the advantage of the
aristocracy itself. With the restoration of public finances, those
pensions which had been allowed to stand could expect more prompt
payment.

During the disorders of the fifteenth century the leaders of the
various factions, whether in or out of royal favour, had fought to
control the Masterships of the Military Orders. These had been
founded in the central Middle Ages to promote the reconquest of
Spain. With the great victories of the thirteenth century they emerged
amongst the principal beneficiaries of the drive south. A series of
grateful kings awarded them vast tracts of lands in Andalucía to add to
their already considerable holdings in Castile. These monks and
warriors showed commercial flair besides their other talents; and they
became some of the greatest flock-masters in the kingdom. The three
orders of Santiago, Alcántara, and Calatrava disposed of formidable

military power and wealth. They contributed approximately one-sixth of the Christian cavalry used in the protracted campaign against Granada (1482–92), and perhaps as much as one-tenth of the infantry. The Grand Master of Santiago, the richest by far of the Orders, had in his gift ninety *encomiendas*, or livings, worthy of any noble's consideration. This source of patronage gave the Grand Master of Santiago wide political influence, which he did not hesitate to employ in his private interest; and the same applied, on a more reduced scale, to the other Grand Masters. Ferdinand and his wife set about eliminating the threat to their authority by moving the Grand Masterships beyond the reach of the ambitious feudatories. This was done either by securing Ferdinand's nomination to the post or by obtaining a reversionary interest. By one or other of these methods the crown asserted its control over Calatrava in 1485, Santiago in 1492, and Alcántara in 1494. The efforts of the Catholic Monarchs to convert the Military Orders into a strength rather than a weakness reached their conclusion during the reign of their grandson, Charles V. In 1524 the papacy authorized the incorporations of all three, together with their lands, into the royal patrimony; and membership of an Order became one of the most coveted honours which the crown could bestow.

To maintain internal peace and to fight its foreign wars the Castilian monarchy required substantial armed forces. Some were available in the form of the royal bodyguard, or the followers of the royal household. But to patrol the highways and to create a national militia a more extensive organization was required. The Catholic Monarchs turned to an institution which already had a long history. Around the year 1190 four Castilian towns had joined in an association to settle commercial disputes between their respective citizens and to secure the roads from the brigands who infested them. This was the first known example of an *hermandad*, or urban alliance, in Castile, although similar organizations had sprung up elsewhere, notably Switzerland. During the Middle Ages the Castilian cities had often formed alliances for mutual protection and the settlement of trade disputes, especially in times of royal weakness, as for instance in minorities or periods of civil war. Ferdinand and Isabel revived the *hermandad* as an instrument of government, extended, and modified it.

The cortes of Madrigal (1476) affirmed the legality of the renewal; and Ferdinand lost no time in developing the Santa Hermandad into the most imposing military machine yet seen in the peninsula. A

Council of the Hermandad, appointed by the rulers, directed overall operations. Castile was zoned into a number of districts, with a junta composed of representatives drawn from the local towns placed in charge of each. The authority of the Hermandad was later extended to Galicia and Extremadura. The military significance of this body can hardly be overestimated. It contributed more in the way of men and money to the reconquest of Granada than the Military Orders; and the scale of its operations can be appreciated from the fact that during this decade, and for some years after, the ordinary revenues of the Castilian state were devoted, almost in their entirety to the upkeep of the urban militias (1480–98). So effective did they prove that the Catholic Monarchs attempted to convert them into a standing force, to be deployed, if the need arose, overseas. At this suggestion the cities bridled. They refused to continue providing the same number of troops as before. In 1498 the Catholic Monarchs, in a rare moment of conciliation, agreed to abandon the project, although the fear of its revival may have played a part in the rising of the Castilian cities in 1520–1. After 1498 the Hermandad reverted to its function of keeping the royal peace on the lonely highways of Castile.

In the assertion of their authority the Catholic Monarchs drew on the support of various groups within society. Their relations amongst the aristocracy constituted one obvious source of help; and where kinship did not exist, a noble family might identify with the cause of Isabel and her husband on the basis of interest, as happened during the critical phase of the civil war. Lower down the social scale the monarchs enlisted the unwavering adherence of the urban nobility both during the war for the succession and the reconstruction which followed. This alliance, strange at first sight, had a firm foundation. In Castile, unlike Aragon, the nobility had gravitated towards the towns in the fourteenth and fifteenth centuries. In many cases this invasion of the cities had led to the domination of the urban patriciate by the minor baronage resident within the walls. During the disturbances of Henry IV's reign, and for that matter of his immediate predecessor, the crown had transferred, under duress, authority over many of its towns to the rapacious feudatories as part of the policy of appease-ment. The new overlords were harsher and more exacting than the king; and they had little time for the pretensions of the noble patriciates over whom they now exercised authority. Faced with the prospect of permanent relegation, the urban nobility swung almost in its entirety behind the Catholic Monarchs and their campaign against aristocratic 'illegality'. They supported with equal firmness the resumption of lands which the crown had been forced to alienate in the recent past. The transfer back to the royal patrimony of towns which had been usurped was obviously to their benefit. Under the regime of Isabel and Ferdinand the lesser nobility prospered in a number of other ways. Their position in society remained unthreatened until the outbreak of the *comunero* rising in 1520, nearly forty years on. The Catholic Monarchs, as well as protecting this class, also promoted its members. They recruited many of their servants from amongst their number, men whose parents were far-sighted enough to make them attend universities, where they familiarized themselves with the rudiments of law without acquiring the arrogance of the better-born.

While aware that the towns would support them under virtually any circumstances, the Monarchs deliberately strengthened the links between the crown and the municipalities. To do this, they modified an institution which had been in existence for many years. Already by the middle of the fourteenth century the monarchy resorted to the practice of sending royal agents to administer, on a temporary basis, towns which had mismanaged their internal affairs or had fallen victim to civil strife. A similar development took place a little later in Valois France, where the inability of the municipal corporations to maintain financial order during the final stages of the Hundred Years War opened the door to royal intervention. To improve the running of the Castilian towns the Catholic Monarchs installed a number of royal judges (*corregidores*) in the principal urban centres. At the turn of the sixteenth century the total of such officials active exceeded three score. The function of the *corregidor* was to take part in the meetings of the town council in order to prevent abuse on the part of the urban oligarchs and to ensure that royal orders were obeyed.

Another motive lay behind the close supervision of the towns. In Castile seventeen cities (after 1492 eighteen, with the addition of Granada) had the right each to send two delegates (*procuradores*) to the cortes of Castile, or assembly of the realm. This gathering had the generally acknowledged right to authorize additional taxation and establish the legal framework within which the monarchy might operate. The crown intervened directly in the selection of *procuradores*, considering it to be a matter of some importance. The cortes met twice at the beginning of the reign, at Madrigal (Isabel's birthplace) in 1476, and Toledo in 1480; and then the estates of the realm were not summoned for another eighteen years. They were called together in 1498; and then continued to meet on a fairly regular basis (1499, 1502, 1504, 1506, 1510, 1512, and 1515). Dynastic considerations rather than financial demands accounted for the frequency of their convocation. The Catholic Monarchs summoned the cortes to swear allegiance to their successors, and, since these died off at an alarming rate, one cortes followed on another with surprising rapidity. In early modern Spain, as in early Tudor England, the more infrequent the summons to a cortes or parliament the more confident and effective the monarchy. The cortes, at this time, was summoned only on extraordinary occasions or to render homage to the king's heirs, to observe, as it were, the royal rites of passage.

The analogy with the Tudor dynasty can be taken a number of steps further. Both royal houses had shaky claims to their respective thrones; both showed political skills (or low cunning) of a high order; and both excelled at financial management. Of the two, the Castilian royal house emerges with the greater credit, as its commitments were more extensive. As the 'lady owner' of Castile, Isabel drew on such traditional sources of income as the internal sales tax (*alcabala*) which may have yielded as much as four-fifths of her total revenue, together with a miscellany of rights ranging from customs dues to the levies on transhumant flocks. She and her husband doubled the ordinary income of the Castilian crown in the period from 1482 to her death in 1504. This increase, from 150 million maravedís to 314 million maravedís was all the more notable in that it was achieved before the onset of inflation. It represented a doubling of real purchasing power. And the crown could employ this wealth as it saw fit.

The Catholic Monarchs are remembered principally for having fixed the boundaries of modern Spain. Whatever the ultimate significance of their actions, both Ferdinand and Isabel had inherited a number of limited objectives, each dictated by the ambitions or needs of their respective kingdoms. Highest on the agenda stood the reconquest of Granada which, given the size of the enterprise, as well as the historical antecedents, could only be undertaken by Castile.

Once the Christian forces had crossed the line of the Sierra Morena, the southern boundary of the meseta, at the beginning of the thirteenth century, the Muslim kingdoms fell in swift succession to the Christian armies. Within the space of fifty years the splendour of Islamic Spain had all but vanished. Only one native emir salvaged something from the wreckage. By acknowledging Christian overlordship, and paying handsomely for the privilege, Muḥammad I (1237–73) succeeded in establishing the Nasrid state of Granada. The refugees who flooded into his lands from adjoining regions contributed to the fertility and prosperity of this, the last of the Muslim kingdoms; and the ruggedness of the terrain provided the defenders with a natural advantage.

Although Granada flourished in the later Middle Ages, leaving behind as memorials some of the finest examples of Islamic architecture, its existence remained precarious. The Nasrid kings relied for their independence on divisions within the Christian states (or between them), their ability to pay tribute (the *parias*) to their northern neighbours, and help from time to time from their co-religionists in North Africa and Egypt. Given the delicacy of their position, it was essential that the ruling house remain united and able to present an unbroken front to the outside world. Unfortunately, from 1419 onwards the Nasri family was split continually by blood feuds; and these internal dissensions came to be reflected all too clearly in the short regnal dates of the rulers and the endless palace revolutions. The Christians seized upon the opportunity to meddle; and Ferdinand in particular exploited these disputes brilliantly, setting son against father, nephew against uncle.

There was, however, a difference in the Islamic policy of the Catholic Monarchs. They intended not to milk Granada, but end its independence. Freed in 1479 from external commitments by the treaty of Alcaçovas, they were able to bring the combined resources of Castile and Aragon to bear on the objective. They could hardly have anticipated the cost or the length of time required. In all the campaigns lasted ten years, from the siege of Alhama in 1482 to the final surrender of Granada in the first days of 1492. The Muslim emirate was steadily shorn of its territories. Between 1485 and 1487 the Christian armies destroyed the economic heartland of the realm: Ronda fell in May 1485; Loja a year later, and Málaga after a ferocious siege in 1487. By the time Boabdil (Abū ʿAbd Allāh Muḥammad) opened final negotiations with the Catholic Monarchs in 1491 he had virtually nothing left to surrender but his capital. On 6 January 1492 Ferdinand and Isabel took formal possession of the town which had not known Christian rule for nearly eight hundred years.

The military and financial effort had no parallel in the history of the peninsula. For ten years the Catholic Monarchs had kept an army of 50,000 men and 13,000 horses on a permanent footing. The crown, the towns, and the church had contributed as never before to the upkeep of the Christian armies. Losses were high, particularly in the theatres of operation. The population of the Nasrid kingdom may have declined by as much as 150,000 in the period 1482–1502 through the cumulative effects of war, pestilence, and emigration. The arrival of Christian settlers, a number put at between 35,000 and 50,000 for the years 1485–99, made good some of the civilian losses; but this still left the conquerors with a devastated kingdom.

In 1492 the Catholic Monarchs brought to a triumphant end a task which had been set in motion centuries before. But there persisted a number of other problems, of more recent origin, which required urgent attention. In 1463 Louis XI of France, exploiting the civil war then raging in the kingdom of Aragon, occupied Roussillon and Cerdagne, the two trans-Pyrenean provinces of the Aragonese crown. For John II and his son Ferdinand this was a burning humiliation. But France was no isolated emirate, lacking in resources and friends. Recovery by force of the lost territories required a European war for which Aragon, even with the full backing of Castile, was totally unprepared. Ferdinand had to await his opportunity, and, fortunately, it arrived. Charles VIII of France wished to settle outstanding differences with his neighbours in order to follow his Italian ambitions. In a moment of juvenile optimism he agreed to return the border provinces to their former suzerains (treaty of Tours–Barcelona, 8/9 January 1493), in the hope that this would buy peace with the Catholic Monarchs. Without having to strike a blow, Ferdinand was restored to Roussillon and Cerdagne; and these remained Aragonese possessions until their severance, permanent this time, at another moment of national humiliation (1659).

At the end of his life, Ferdinand, in his capacity as regent of Castile, seized an opportunity to expand the boundaries of the state over which his grandson would one day rule. The young king of Navarre committed a diplomatic blunder which furnished the pretext for the occupation of his lands south of the Pyrenees, in effect most of his kingdom. Ferdinand occupied in 1512 the area which approximates to the modern province of Navarre. Three years later the cortes of Burgos formally admitted the conquered territory into the kingdom of Castile. The dispossessed king was left with a fragment of his state across the mountains in France. The Pyrenees came to mark the frontier between France and Spain as the two states reached their natural limits.

Under the Catholic Monarchs and the regency of Ferdinand, Castile and Aragon acted as a united power only in foreign policy. In all other respects the union of Spain was an illusion. Ferdinand did, however, use Castilian resources to secure Aragonese ends both during and after the life of his spouse. He was set on extending Aragonese control from the island of Sicily to the kingdom of Naples across the straits; and to realize his ambition he employed a Castilian general, González Fernández de Córdoba (the father of the Spanish 'tercio'), recruited Castilian troops, and spent Castilian money. The military talent of González Fernández enabled Ferdinand to expel his former partners the French from Naples during the campaigning season of 1503 and to impose Aragonese rule over the entire kingdom in the following year.

Naples became a focus of Aragonese energies in much the same way as the exploration of America absorbed those of Castile. Each state continued to pursue its own interests independent of its dynastic associate. On his expulsion from Castile in 1506 Ferdinand retired for a time to Naples, to consolidate his rule there and to await the turn of events in the Iberian peninsula. If the old king had produced another family, if he could have bequeathed his lands to his younger grandson, then the union of the crowns brought about in 1469 would possibly have been judged as a temporary arrangement which had been extinguished on the death of the partners to the contract. Once the Aragonese lands had been separated from those of Castile, the two states would have been free to follow their respective destinies, one in the New World, and the other in the Mediterranean.

CHAPTER 3

The Habsburg inheritance: 1504–1517

THE dynastic alliances of its ruling houses largely determined the history of early modern Spain. In this respect the experience of the kingdoms of the Iberian peninsula did not diverge from that of other European states which pursued comparable aims and employed similar techniques. The use of marriage as an instrument of statecraft, economic and effective under most circumstances, involved one serious risk, the accidents of mortality. Barrenness or early death in an age which ignored the simplest notions of hygiene opened the way for unexpected claimants whose candidature, if successfully upheld, could bring disaster. The Spanish kingdoms provided a case in point.

In 1494 Charles VIII of France invaded Italy, thereby inaugurating a new phase in European politics. His initial success convinced many that France would become the permanent master of the Italian peninsula. The Catholic Monarchs and Maximilian of Austria, the Holy Roman Emperor (1493–1519), believing themselves mortally threatened by this turn of events, concluded an alliance designed to place a check on French expansion. A double marriage was arranged to strengthen the new friendship and give it visible expression. In 1495 Maximilian's son, Philip of Burgundy ('Philip the Fair'), took as his bride Juana of Castile, the second daughter of the Catholic Monarchs; while Philip's sister, Marguerite of Austria, became the wife of Don Juan, the only surviving son of Ferdinand and Isabel. The double betrothal, like the double-headed eagle, was a device frequently employed in royal circles. This particular alliance had only limited implications; if Don Juan and his wife produced children they would inherit Castile and Aragon. Should he die, then the older of his sisters, the Infanta Isabel, would become the lawful successor. There was little reason to suspect that Philip and Juana, or their progeny, would ever rule over the lands of the Catholic Monarchs.

Short of cash but rich in fantasy, Maximilian was a consistent exponent of the doctrine that to marry was more profitable than to make war. It was, after all, the motto of his house. In 1507 Maximilian

TABLE 1. Descent of the Spanish royal house in the fifteenth and sixteenth centuries

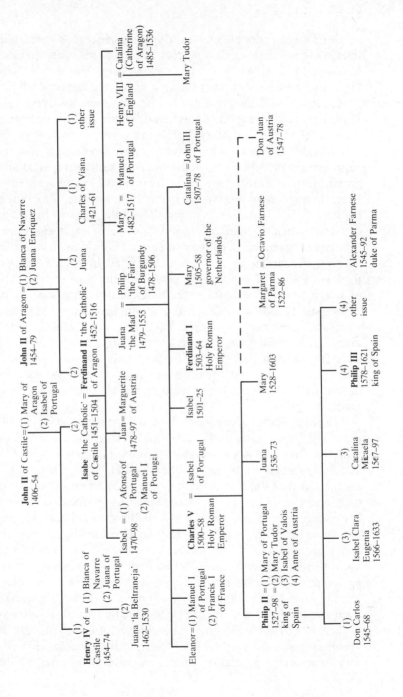

arranged another double union with consequences as far-reaching as the first. The heir to the Hungarian throne, Louis, was betrothed to his granddaughter, Mary of Habsburg; and at the same time, Anne of Hungary, Louis's sister, was promised to one or other of Maximilian's grandsons. In 1521 the provisions of the pact were observed: Anne of Hungary married Ferdinand of Austria and her brother, Louis, became the husband of Mary, Ferdinand's sister.

Through a sequence of misadventures which even the most ardent supporters of the Habsburgs could not have anticipated Maximilian's grandchildren acquired the Spanish kingdoms in 1516 and ten years later, through an even more unexpected twist of fate, the Hungarian lands, or what remained of them. The Infante Don Juan, always delicate in health, died in 1497 at the age of eighteen—from the raptures of marriage, according to some. His widow, Marguerite of Austria, gave birth to a posthumous child. Had the girl lived she would have succeeded to her father's titles, but the infant died within a matter of hours. The claim to the Spanish thrones passed to Juan's eldest sister, Isabel, wife of the Portuguese king, Manuel the Fortunate. Like her brother she lived only a few months after her marriage. She died giving birth to a son (24 August 1498). Had the boy, Dom Miguel de la Paz, survived to manhood he would have united in his person the crowns of Spain and Portugal. But he, too, succumbed to the perils of infancy before completing his second year (20 June 1500).

The shape of the succession to the Castilian throne at least could be perceived quite clearly well in advance of Isabel the Catholic's death (1504). A remorseless logic seemed to be working on behalf of Juana and the Habsburg cause. In 1505 the Castilian cortes meeting at Toro recognized Juana of Castile as the 'queen proprietress' of the kingdom; and a year later similar recognition was extended to the heirs of her body (cortes of Salamanca and Valladolid). Ferdinand of Aragon, having no longer any legal right to remain in Castile, returned to his own kingdom (13 July 1506), leaving the way clear for his daughter and his son-in-law whom he cordially detested. The government of Castile passed into the hands effectively of Philip to whom Juana was only too willing to delegate all authority. Philip's position appeared unassailable, as did that of the coterie who had schemed so patiently on his behalf both in Castile and in exile, the so-called *felipistas*. But in an age of intense emotions and brief lives the Burgundian triumph was very temporary. Mortality struck. A natural athlete, Philip of

Burgundy occupied much of his time in vigorous physical exercise. After a particularly strenuous bout on the courts he called for refreshments and was served a cold drink, something of a luxury in the heat of Castile. A few hours later he was dead (25 September 1506). Pleurisy, typhoid, or one of the many illnesses which defied the primitive diagnostic skills of the age, had once more thrown open the question of the Spanish succession.

Certain measures had to be taken immediately. Juana had long displayed signs of mental instability; and these became even more pronounced during the early days of her bereavement. She was obviously not capable of governing. The Castilian nobles, gathered together at the monastery of Guadalupe, nominated Jiménez de Cisneros, cardinal archbishop of Toledo, as the chairman of an interim council of state—in effect, the regent. Under the prompting of Cisneros, an invitation was extended to Ferdinand asking him to take over the government of Castile during the incapacity of his daughter. The care of her children became the responsibility of the grandparents: Ferdinand took charge of his namesake, Ferdinand of Austria, and his youngest granddaughter, Catalina. Both had been born in Spain. As paternal grandfather, Maximilian acted as guardian for the eldest boy, Charles of Ghent, and three of his sisters, Eleanor, Mary, and Isabel. Charles, born on 25 February 1500, had never visited the Iberian peninsula.

From 1506 until 1517 the history of the Spanish kingdoms ran in tandem with that of the Low Countries. One became an extension of the other, ever more closely linked by ties of blood, politics, and trade. The Emperor Maximilian appointed his daughter, Marguerite of Austria, as regent of the Netherlands, a post which she held from 1507 until her dismissal in 1515. A widow at eighteen and then again at twenty-five, she was a fine example of what the Habsburgs required of their womenfolk, fortitude and self-sacrifice. As part of her duties the regent supervised the upbringing of her eldest nephew, Charles, and his three orphaned sisters. Wise, fastidious, and patient, Marguerite had a profound influence over her royal charges. She took in hand Charles's formal education; and in 1512 she attached Adrian of Utrecht to his household as almoner. Charles's deficiencies in such formal disciplines as mathematics and languages were never remedied, even in later life; but Adrian did instil in the future emperor a lasting piety very much in the tradition of the Low Countries and of the principal exponent of that tradition within the Latin church,

Erasmus. The regent's court at Malines served as an international
school for the children of royalty. Maximilian Sforza, claimant to the
duchy of Milan, and John of Saxony were amongst Charles's school-
fellows.

Within the Low Countries Marguerite faced continuous opposition
from a nobility confident in its powers and clear as to its objec-
tives.The regent's policies harked back to the pro-English and anti-
French line pursued by the dukes of Burgundy. She may have had
few illusions about the recovery of ducal Burgundy with its capital of
Dijon which had been lost in 1477, but she was determined to preserve
the Low Countries against French encroachment. She may have
nurtured a personal sense of grievance against the French court where
she had spent seven years as the fiancée of the Dauphin, only to be
discarded and kept captive a further two years as a guarantee of her
father's good behaviour. From 1509 Marguerite's conduct of affairs
came under an increasing challenge. In that year Maximilian
appointed William of Croy, seigneur de Chièvres, as governor to
Charles with primary responsibility for his education. Assured in his
manner and with an easy way, Chièvres rapidly acquired a hold over
his ward's affections which was to remain unshaken until his death in
1521. The new governor represented a tradition hostile to that
followed by the regent. A spokesman of the native aristocracy, he
wished to reduce Marguerite's authority and pursue friendly relations
with France. The factional struggles at the Burgundian court soon
drew in other interests. Ferdinand of Aragon had stationed a permanent representative, Juan de Lanuza (el Viejo), at Marguerite's
court. Lanuza was under instructions to encourage the regent in her
anti-French line, if only because this might help Ferdinand retain
Navarre which he had seized in 1512. The old Aragonese king was not
given to chivalrous gestures. The Aragonese mission in the Low
Countries found itself ranged against the Burgundian nobility and the
former supporters of Philip of Burgundy (the *felipistas*), Castilian
nobles who had been denied the spoils of office by the untimely
demise of their patron and the return to power of Ferdinand the
Catholic.

Those who opposed the existing regime in the Low Countries
realized that the simplest means to supplant Marguerite and end the
regency was to have the archduke Charles declared of age. The
Estates of Brabant took a leading part in the manoeuvre. In 1514 they
informed the emperor that no money would be forthcoming until

Charles reached his majority. The impecunious Maximilian had the option of deciding when that might be. The offer by the Estates of 100,000 florins artois (with the promise of more to come) proved irresistible. On 5 January 1515, Charles was declared of age and therefore fit to rule. The seals of Maximilian and Marguerite were broken and replaced.

For the next three years a triumvirate made up of William of Croy, Jean le Sauvage, and Adrian of Utrecht directed the government. Within this group William of Croy was pre-eminent, a position readily acknowledged by his colleagues. Whatever his moral shortcomings, he was a man of tenacity and skill. Above all else he wished to secure the Iberian kingdoms for the house of Burgundy, an objective whose triumphant realization he lived to witness. This could only be brought about if a number of opposed interests were either harmonized or, at very least, rendered neutral. In terms of practical politics, such aims involved the establishment of cordial relations with France. Charles was therefore promised to a French princess first by the treaty of Paris (1515) and then by the treaty of Noyon (1516), moves which have been interpreted by some as reducing the ruler of the Netherlands to effective vassalage. Croy had furthermore to retain the ever-shifting interest of Maximilian in the design and to reconcile his daughter, Marguerite, to the abrupt loss of power. As if these goals were not enough, Croy had to win the understanding of the English court, a source, he hoped, of funds for the projected expedition to Spain. The fact that he achieved this formidable programme stands as a testimony to Croy's political ability.

Ferdinand of Aragon emerged as the principal opponent to the fulfilment of Croy's schemes. It was common knowledge that Ferdinand was appalled at the prospect of Charles's succession to the crowns of Castile and Aragon. His attitude might have sprung from a far-sighted appreciation of where such a gathering-in of states might lead, or a simple dislike for the grandson whom he had never seen. He made several attempts to deny at least his own kingdom, Aragon, to the Habsburgs. As part of his feud with Philip of Burgundy, Ferdinand married for a second time in 1506. The bride, Germaine de Foix, was seventeen at the time, the groom a sprightly fifty-three. His intention was to produce another male heir who might one day reign over the eastern kingdoms. But his old powers had sadly declined. On 1 January 1511, Germaine de Foix gave birth to their only child, a son, stillborn. Once the possibility of begetting a second family had been abandoned, Ferdinand's thoughts turned to his younger grandson, Ferdinand of Austria. Many Aragonese favoured the succession of the young archduke since he was Iberian by birth and upbringing; and he, at any rate, would not mortgage Aragon to the uncertainties of an imperial future.

It required all the capacity of Croy and the Castilian exiles in Brussels led by Juan Manuel to deflect the old king from his purpose. In 1515 Adrian of Utrecht undertook a special mission to Spain to convince Ferdinand of Aragon and Cardinal Cisneros, who probably needed less persuading, not to alter the established line of succession. Charles, not Ferdinand, should follow his grandfather when the time came. For the moment Adrian succeeded. Nothing was decided. A year later Ferdinand of Aragon was still brooding over the problem when death caught up with him at Madrigalejos, a small hamlet on the road to Seville (23 January 1516). He had outwitted all his earthly rivals; but in the end he failed to solve the only problem that really mattered—how to dispose of his kingdoms and those of his first wife for the long-term benefit of his house and subjects.

Charles's advisers moved quickly to secure the Spanish inheritance: this meant a formal announcement of the claim and an effective assertion of the right. In a ceremony lasting two days (13–14 March 1516), held in the church of St Gudule in Brussels, Charles was proclaimed king of Spain. This was tantamount to a *coup d'état*, since the rightful heir to Castile and Aragon was Juana of Castile and not her eldest son, Charles. Croy and his associates knew that the proclamation would remain so much empty form unless the archduke could present himself in Spain, quell the mutinous nobility, and arrange for the departure of his younger brother from the peninsula, an absolute necessity since his presence had so unsettling an effect. The journey, for all its urgency, required preparation, money, and not least, time.

Until the day Charles set foot on Spanish soil, a regent had to act in his name. Cardinal Jiménez de Cisneros was the natural—indeed the only—choice. Ferdinand, on his death-bed, had endorsed the nomination on the grounds that he was 'a good man, well-intentioned, without relatives, and a servant of mine and the [late] Queen'. Whatever private views he may have held, Cisneros firmly believed that Charles's installation as the lawful king of Castile and Aragon was indispensable to the welfare of both kingdoms. For that reason he persuaded the grandees of Spain to acknowledge, however unwillingly, Charles as the rightful king (31 March 1516), thereby condoning his effective usurpation of the crown. Under difficult circumstances he was able to strike up a working relationship with Croy who, in turn, was adroit enough to distance himself from the Castilian exiles in Brussels and establish links with the supporters of the late Ferdinand. Cisneros, for all his eighty years, vigorously maintained internal order. This involved the suppression of long-pent-up feuds amongst the nobility such as the attempt of Pedro Girón to settle old scores with the duke of Medina Sidonia. As part of a long-term plan to preserve the peace internally, Cisneros launched a scheme for a national militia, the *gente de ordenanza*. In spite of its merits, the project aroused bitter opposition, from the nobility who identified it with a threat to their own liberty (or licence), and from the towns who were expected to pay for the recruitment of the troops and their subsequent upkeep. In the event the trained bands were raised: and played a notable part in the disorders of 1520–1, although not in the way intended by their creator.

Cisneros displayed throughout his second regency an energy which belied his great age. Yet it is doubtful whether even this venerable patriarch could have maintained control for much longer without the physical presence of the king. On 19 September 1517, the long-awaited flotilla from the Low Countries bearing the new monarch and his entourage made landfall on the Asturian coast. Once the royal party had recovered from the ordeal of the voyage, Croy and his inner circle began to assume control over the government. Letters were dispatched to all the leading figures, including one to the cardinal thanking him for his services and dismissing him from his office. But Cisneros was denied the pleasure of reading it; he died at Roa on 8 November 1517, before the messenger could reach him.

Charles met his Castilian subjects at the cortes of Valladolid on 21 March 1518. After receiving formal recognition as king of Castile, he asked for an increase in taxation, a request which was duly granted. A few days later while on the road to Catalonia Charles met his younger brother for the very first time. When they at last stood face to face at Aranda the two brothers symbolized in their persons the choice that had been available to Spain right up until the moment of Ferdinand the Catholic's death. But Ferdinand of Austria, so beloved of his maternal grandfather, was on his way out of the peninsula never to return, while Charles was making his way slowly eastwards to receive the homage of yet more kingdoms. In the autumn of 1518 the representative institutions of the eastern kingdoms recognized each according to its own custom Charles as their liege lord; and William of Croy lived to see his life's work complete with the installation of Charles as the undisputed master of all the lands and rights which had belonged to his grandparents.

The adventure had only just begun. The court spent the winter of 1518–19 in Barcelona; and it was here that Charles learnt the news that Maximilian of Austria, the Holy Roman Emperor, had died on 12 January 1519. Charles's reaction was quick and determined; he was set on acquiring the title that had been his grandfather's. Every diplomatic nerve was strained and the formidable resources of the Fugger, already enmeshed in Habsburg affairs for over a generation, fully committed to the young archduke's election as emperor. After a campaign best remembered for its monumental jobbery, the Electoral College voted unanimously for the Habsburg candidate (28 June 1519). The worst fears of Ferdinand the Catholic had been realized. The Spanish kingdoms had become part of an empire continental in scale.

To finance his election expenses and the cost of his journey to Aachen where he was to be crowned king of the Romans, Charles had to squeeze every available resource out of his new possessions, Castile in particular. In 1520 the Castilian cortes was summoned once more. It gathered first at Santiago de Compostela, and was then unceremoniously translated to La Coruña, Charles's port of embarkation for the Low Countries. Such rough handling seemed to confirm, if, indeed, corroboration was needed, the way in which Castile had been subordinated to the priorities of an alien dynasty. The purpose behind the calling of the cortes could not have been more transparent. All the procuradores (town delegates) had been subject to intense pressure from royal officials to vote additional taxation. This they eventually did, although some paid for their unwilling generosity with their lives. Ironically, the grant which the government had so eagerly sought in the spring of 1520 was subsequently remitted.

The departure of Charles from La Coruña (20 May 1520) heralded the outbreak of a rebellion on the part of the Castilian cities. The rising of the comuneros, as the movement has sometimes been called, drew its strength from many sources. At one level the revolt had been caused by the political uncertainty which had dominated Castilian public life since the death of Isabel in 1504. Speculation, intrigue, and disloyalty had undermined respect for authority and its greatest symbol, the crown. At another level the uprising represented the indignant response of Castile to the rapacity of Charles's Flemish advisers, a greed brazenly advertised by the appointment of the twenty-year-old William of Croy, nephew of the royal favourite, to the archbishopric of Toledo. The Habsburg entourage could not resist the natural temptation to regard the new domains as a source of limitless reward. And lastly, on yet another plane, the rebellion can be seen as a struggle on the part of the Castilian towns to impose some form of constitutional check on the burgeoning powers of the state.

Social tensions which had been simmering for decades created resentments on which the insurgents drew. Towards the end of the fifteenth century the minor nobility, which had been much encouraged by the Catholic Monarchs, established a firm grip over the town councils of Castile. The merchants and artisans stood by, apparently powerless to resist the erosion of their influence over municipal government. Once installed in the towns, the urban nobility then claimed, successfully for the most part, exemption from taxation, a privilege which their fellow citizens were unable to assert, unless by some accident of noble status themselves. As elsewhere this invasion of the municipalities led to the annexation by the nobles of the right to represent the towns at the meetings of the cortes. This infiltration of noble members profoundly affected the way the cortes voted. Noble delegates showed themselves more amenable to royal wishes, and therefore granted more readily what was demanded, because they were exempt from tax. During their brief moment of power the *comuneros* attempted to curtail, if not eradicate altogether, aristocratic control over the towns; and it was this intention, taken in conjunction with others, which gave the movement its anti-seigneurial stamp.

Taxation provided a central issue in the dispute between the king and the towns of Castile. When the cortes met in the spring of 1518 to render homage to their new sovereign, the *procuradores* agreed to increase the yield of the basic tax, the *servicio*. A proposal to change the traditional method of raising the sales tax was also floated. It had been the custom for the towns to compound for the sales tax with the payment of a lump sum to royal tax-gatherers. The urban delegates, many of whom were themselves of noble status, appeared willing to sanction an innovation in the method of collection. Instead of accepting a lump sum by way of composition, the crown was to be allowed to auction the right to levy the tax to the business syndicate which lodged the highest bid. Tax-farming, as the system was known, would replace existing custom. It was popularly believed that such a

change would both increase the fiscal burden and bring 'foreigners'
into the sensitive area of tax administration. Wild rumours began to
circulate to the effect that a whole new range of levies were on the
point of introduction, such as a tax of one ducat on every married man.
All this to finance the imperial dreams of a foreign prince.

Initially the revolt, which began in June 1520, took the form of a tax
strike and sporadic acts of violence against the Flemish officials who
had remained behind. Then a blunder on the part of a royal
commander, Antonio de Fonseca, provided the incentive to create an
effective organization. On 21 August 1521, royal forces under his
command attempted to sieze the artillery park in Medina del Campo,
Isabel the Catholic's favourite town. The operation went badly wrong.
The troops set fire to the city while failing to secure the guns. A month
later delegates from thirteen cities, all represented in the Castilian
cortes, gathered in the town of Tordesillas and proclaimed their right
to govern the kingdom (26 September 1520). This provisional government declared that the Royal Council and the regent had forfeited all
authority.

Far from rallying to the cause of their new ruler, the nobility at first
observed a studied neutrality. They had been deeply offended by
Charles's apparent insensitivity to the traditions of Castile. The
appointment as regent of the king's former almoner (and later pope)
Adrian of Utrecht was the last and most serious in a series of blunders.
It outraged the leading members of the Castilian aristocracy who
naturally thought they had a better claim to the post. The nobility in
general sympathized with some, if not all, the complaints expressed by
the cities; and were in favour of reform particularly where it affected
'foreigners'. Two developments changed their attitude. The young
king heeded, at long last, sound advice. Two of Castile's premier
nobles, the Admiral and the Constable of Castile respectively, joined
Adrian of Utrecht in the government of the kingdom. The regency had
been converted into a triumvirate. The move was shrewdly judged. The
Enríquez family, hereditary Admirals of Castile, held the bulk of their
estates in the region between Valladolid and the frontier with
Portugal; while the Velascos; traditional Constables of the realm, disposed of a wide domain on the upper Ebro. The two families were, in
short, the noble houses most directly affected by the *comunero* rising.

As time progressed, the junta of Tordesillas, the governing body of
the movement, found itself increasingly the prisoner of its more
radical supporters. Many villages, particularly those in the area

around Palencia (the so-called Tierra de Campos), exploited the collapse of authority to settle old scores—the murder of bailiffs, the seizure of cattle, the wasting of land, all formed part of the pattern. Those who sat on the junta, moderates in the main with property of their own, realized all too well the implications of this rural violence. But they were powerless to act. The anti-seigneurial character of the movement became more pronounced after the *comuneros* lost control of Tordesillas (5 December 1520).

The incipient *jacquerie* made the defeat of the towns inevitable. The aristocracy rallied to the crown, determined to save their property if not their king. The Admiral and the Constable decided on a concentration of their forces as a prelude to the decisive battle. The successful junction of the two noble armies sealed the fate of the *comuneros*. Military training told over numbers or (what remained of) revolutionary fervour. The royal army with its disciplined cavalry caught up with the numerically stronger *comunero* army at Villalar (23 April 1521); and what should have been a skirmish ended as a rout. The leaders of the uprising were summarily executed in this muddy Castilian village a few kilometres on the road north from Tordesillas. Although a French invasion of Navarre provided a temporary respite, nothing could reverse the outcome of the battle. Toledo held out defiantly until the autumn of 1522 under the redoubtable María de Padilla, widow of one of those executed on the morrow of Villalar; but its resistance was more symbolic than effective.

Although marked throughout by confusion and inept leadership, the *comunero* movement revealed much about Castilian society, offering at one and the same time a gloss on recent history and a portent of what was to come. Geographically, the rising was largely confined to the lands between the Duero and the Tagus, the heartland of Old Castile, hence the need for the Constable and the Admiral, if no others. Apart from the occasional echoes and murmurs, New Castile and Andalucía failed to respond to the unrest. The inability of the *comunero* chiefs to draw in the support of these regions may be explained, at least in part, by the relative weakness of the cities south of the Tagus and the corresponding dominance of the nobility, a product of the reconquest. Within Castile economic development had produced a clash of interests. Inland towns such as Segovia and Toledo sought to promote a strong woollen industry. They would have liked to reserve part of the wool clip for domestic purchasers instead of allowing it to be sold in its entirety to foreign buyers. The great flock-masters, the Military Orders and the aristocracy, rejected such protectionist measures since, understandably, they wanted to sell their product at the best price. These upholders of unrestricted trade were joined by the town of Burgos which had a monopoly right over the transport of wool to Flanders. Economic interests coloured political attitudes. The inland towns looked to the junta of Tordesillas for a stimulus to the nascent textile industry, preferably by a limitation on the export of the country's major product; while the graziers and their urban partner, Burgos, sided with the royalists in order to preserve complete market freedom.

Ideology left a deep imprint on the *comunero* movement. The very notion of a *comunidad* reflected a mature political tradition. During the Middle Ages *comunidades* had regularly come into existence, sometimes at local, less frequently at national levels. In 1282, 1295,1313, and once more in 1317 the principal cities had banded together into General Brotherhoods for the preservation of public order. The Catholic Monarchs drew on the principle; as, for that matter, did Pero Sarmiento in 1449 for more disreputable ends. By the sixteenth century a living and long-established tradition maintained that the cities had the right to petition against misrule; and if remedy were not forthcoming, many thought that their inhabitants were authorized to take whatever action was required, including resistance to the king, or his representative. Toledo invoked these rights when it formed a *comunidad* on 21 April 1520 and expelled the royal *corregidor* ten days later. The urban oligarchs, who often stage-managed popular indignation, appealed to the surrounding cities to join with them in pursuit of common grievances. Seen in this light, the *comunidad* of 1520 can be regarded as a defensive pact, with long historical precedents, entered into by a number of like-minded Castilian towns for the remedy of outstanding abuses. Toledo and its associates objected in particular to the way in which the *procuradores* had been harassed into voting excessive taxation at the cortes of La Coruña (1520), this in addition to the plundering of Castilian offices by the Flemish advisers of Charles V.

Some amongst the inner council of the movement wished to go further than the eradication of individual abuse. The junta of Tordesillas favoured the notion that the king of Castile—he would never be in their eyes emperor, a foreign title—existed to serve the nation. As monarch, Charles was subject to restraints, those established by current law, and those to be determined by the Castilian cortes. A king under the law and obedient to the representative institution, a doctrine descended in the direct line from the creed of the medieval *comunidad*. For some on the junta even these claims were too moderate. Impressed by the constitution of Venice and Genoa, a radical minority saw a future in which the cities would rule themselves without any interference on the part of the nobility. The king, if the office remained, would enjoy powers similar to those exercised by the doge of Venice.

The ultimate significance of the *comunero* rising has provoked bitter argument. Some have detected in the attitude of the principal leaders progressive elements; others have written off the entire episode as a last, desperate, reaction against modernity, as the unwillingness of the towns to accept Castile's imperial destiny. Whatever final judgement may be cast, certain facts remain beyond dispute. The cities had carefully considered economic and political objectives. They wished to reverse what they regarded as an unwelcome trend within municipal government, that is, the encroachment of the nobility upon offices traditionally reserved for the artisan guilds and the merchants. With the notable exception of Burgos, urban spokesmen also favoured the introduction of measures designed to protect the fledgling textile industry, by imposing quotas if necessary on the export of wool. Both of these policies cut across noble interests. At the highest level, the junta of Tordesillas wanted an effective limitation on the power of the monarch, a control which the member believed could best be exercised by the cortes with its authority suitably increased. Villalar put an end to all that. The rights of the monarch, king when he left, emperor by the time he returned, emerged not merely unscathed but patently enhanced. The nobles, whose help, sparingly lent, had none the less secured the royal victory, reinforced their own standing and privileges. They also, in company with the ecclesiastical foundations, assured their own interests by insisting that Castile develop into an open economy reliant on the export of a single commodity. For the vanquished, the future was sombre. Their political aspirations were looked upon as rank treason; and their prosperity was prejudiced by the imposition of fines which were still being paid off fifty years later. The Castile of the Emperor Charles V was aristocratic and authoritarian, not urban and constitutional.

Events in the kingdom of Aragon, although not directly influenced by Castile, had followed a curiously similar course. Uncertainty over the succession once Ferdinand had died (1516) created an atmosphere of expectation on the part of the urban poor and indecision on that of

the ruling élites. Muslim piracy, a recent and, as it proved, a permanent addition to Mediterranean life, heightened the feeling of in-
security. The plague of 1518 and the flight of the rich from the towns
contributed to the breakdown of order. To this extent, Aragon and its
constituent territories suffered from the general malaise which had
overtaken the peninsula since the death of Isabel the Catholic (1504).

The subsequent rising of the *Germanías* was largely confined to the
province of Valencia. In the neighbouring region of Catalonia many
sympathized with the insurgents, or *agermanados* as they were called;
but here the crown had forestalled any open move by appointing as
governor Pero de Cardona, archbishop of Tarragona, whose ecclesiastical dignity in no way impaired his merciless efficiency. In the
traditional accounts a sermon preached by Lluis de Castelloli in the
city of Valencia (22 July 1521) on the riveting subject of sodomy
initiated the rebellion. This improving homily, with its dramatic
vision of punishment in the hereafter, electrified the faithful. Two
weeks later they, and their fellow-believers, rioted in the cathedral of
Valencia. Violence quickly spread from the pews to the streets.

Unwittingly, the crown had placed the malcontents in a position of
considerable strength. To guard the eastern coasts against the menace
of the Barbary pirates, Charles had permitted the guilds from the city
of Valencia to form themselves into an armed militia (25 November
1519). He sanctioned at the same time the creation of an emergency
administration to take charge of the city for the duration of the crisis
brought on by the plague and the flight of the municipal elders.
Elections took place for a new council on 28 December 1519; but this
was a ruling body with a difference. Membership was drawn not from
the established oligarchs, most of whom had fled, but from the guilds-
men and artisans of the city. The Valencian council, and those which
soon sprung up elsewhere in imitation, espoused what can only be
described as programmes of extreme radicalism. The Valencian committee with its thirteen plebeian members intended to make the guilds
the preponderant influence in municipal elections, if not the sole one.
Royal and nobility interference would be reduced to insignificance or
excluded altogether. The guilds of Valencia acting through their
mouthpiece, the recently elected council, provided much of the
motive power behind the insurrection.

The royal governor of Valencia handled the rising ineptly. Losing
his nerve, Diego Hurtado de Mendoza presented the *agermanados*
with a great propaganda victory when he abandoned the town of

Valencia in the summer of 1521. The urban militias, originally raised to fight pirates, secured a number of successes against the governor's troops, noticeably at Gandía (25 July 1521) and Játiva (14 August 1521). But the decisive encounter had yet to come. Everything hinged on the response of the nobility, lords of the hinterland and masters of war. To begin with the Aragonese and Valencian aristocrats had adopted a neutral stance since they too nurtured grievances against the king and the general conduct of affairs. Their attitude mirrored that of the Castilian nobility at the outbreak of the *comunero* rising. The elaboration of extreme social policies brought about a revision of opinions. By excluding the nobles from urban government and by the forcible conversion of their Islamic workforce (the moriscos), the *agermanados* threatened both the standing and the prosperity of the baronial class. Conscious, after initial equivocation, of their true interest, the nobility came out firmly for the king. Their disciplined retainers defeated the poorly led rebel army at Orihuela (30 August 1521); and thereby destroyed the *agermanado* rebellion as a serious military threat. In October 1521, Diego Hurtado de Mendoza re-entered the city of Valencia from where he was able to participate in the repression that followed. Resistance lingered on long after the main body of insurgents had been dispersed and the ringleaders executed: Játiva, the last *agermanado* stronghold and the scene of earlier success, surrendered on 5 December 1522.

The rising of the *Germanías* was a composite of many elements. Tensions within the guilds of Valencia had generated much of the energy which drove the movement. According to a recent analysis, an inner ring of wealthy masters dominated the principal guilds, the silk weavers being the example most frequently cited, and they denied opportunity quite deliberately to the mass of impoverished masters. Those who had been economically thwarted in this way were loudest in support of radical policies. Municipal debt also figured large in the agitation. The towns had incurred heavy obligations over many decades, sometimes through increased royal taxation, sometimes as a consequence of urban ostentation, and just as often through poor financial management. The plight of the towns in the eastern kingdom was similar to that of late medieval communities in France—and for the same reasons. To cover the growing urban deficits, bonds, secured against municipal income, had been floated. To meet payment of interest and principal, taxes had increased; but the burden did not fall equally. As elsewhere, the nobility who had taken up residence within the walls continued to insist on exemption from urban taxation by right of birth and status. *Agermanado* leaders speculated openly on the desirability of bringing the urban nobility within the fiscal net. Even more alarming plans were broached. Some reformers drew up projects for the conversion of debts (forcibly, if need be) on terms more favourable to the towns, whilst others suggested outright repudiation. Tax equalization schemes, or the reduction in the volume of consolidated debt doubtlessly appealed to many in the cities; but such ideas terrified the rentier class, small in number, powerful in influence.

Some historians have argued that the *Germanías* can only be understood within the broad context of the Reconquest. During the central Middle Ages the Aragonese crusaders had pushed overland with the result that they tended to settle in the interior. The newly won territories had then been parcelled out into large estates. Their partners in the Reconquest, the Catalans, used different methods: they attacked by sea; and once the victory had been secured they tended to congregate in the maritime towns where trading interests continued to dominate. Viewed in this perspective the *Germanías* can be seen in terms of sharp contrasts, the interior versus the littoral, feudal estates ranged against urban settlements, and the conservative ideology of the landlocked baronage in conflict with the mercantile spirit of the towns.

Such propositions can be endlessly debated. Yet in one respect the *Germanías* altered the nature of Valencian society by destroying an equilibrium that was never to be restored. The Islamic (or morisco) communities of Valencia, and, to a lesser extent, of Aragon, provided the rural workforce on many a baronial estate. In many inland areas agriculture depended completely on their efforts. The aristocracy protected their morisco labourers and permitted them the exercise of their faith if only to preserve the value of their lands. But the era of toleration for economic reasons was drawing to a close. Wherever the *agermanado* forces gained the upper hand, brief though that control might be, they compelled the morisco farmers to submit to Christian baptism, even administered in the course of a mass ceremony with bucket and broom. After the defeat of the rebellion, when all the acts of the insurgents had been denounced or rescinded, the conversion of the moriscos was allowed to stand. The moriscos lost their immunity to prosecution by the church; and thenceforth both they and their property fell within the jurisdiction of the Holy Office. The insurgents had added to a social (or cultural) problem that was to remain unresolved for the best part of a century.

The collapse of the *Germanía* on the mainland, and also on the Balearic Islands where it pursued an even more violent course, brought lasting political change. The urban guilds were punished severely for their part in the recent events; and the towns were saddled with indemnities which were still being paid off in the reign of Philip II (1556–98). The drain on municipal resources made their economic recovery all the more uncertain. But for the aristocracy which had restored order without help from Charles V the rewards of loyalty (or opportunism) were substantial. The agrarian character of the Valencian kingdom became even more pronounced, the noble dominance of government and society unassailable.

Both the *comunero* movement and the *Germanías* ended ingloriously; and their defeat, at almost the same moment, led to an historic compromise. Tacitly or otherwise the young king struck a bargain with his feudatories. Charles was allowed to dispose freely of his Spanish resources in the pursuit of imperial ventures; while the baronage, for its part, had its economic and social pre-eminence within the state confirmed. Spain was to become monarchical, aristocratic, and agrarian. And all three were complementary.

CHAPTER 4

The imperial career

CHARLES'S election as Holy Roman Emperor on 28 June 1519 determined the course of Iberian history for the next half century; and the
fatal complications arising from this event descended like an heirloom
to his children and their successors. In the aftermath of the electoral
contest and the euphoria at the result, there was no thought of the
long-term consequences. The most pressing need was to devise a
system of government for the Habsburg dominions, given that the new
emperor, however energetic, could only be present in one place.
Marguerite of Austria, the royal guardian, provided much of the inspiration behind the solution adopted. She had instilled in the orphans
committed to her care the conviction that service to the Habsburg
dynasty transcended any other consideration. No one believed in this
idea more firmly than Charles V. He regarded himself as the senior
partner in an enterprise whose interests were European, and ultimately global, in scale; and he demanded from the members of his
family that they should subordinate any personal feeling or ambition to
the greater good of the Habsburg cause. Assuming unqualified loyalty
on the part of his relatives, Charles distributed his many kingdoms
amongst them, and then, when the time came, their offspring. Almost
immediately (1519) he reinstated Marguerite of Austria as the regent of
the Netherlands in recognition of her steadfast devotion. Three years
later, on the eve of his return to Spain, Charles reached an understanding with his younger brother Ferdinand. As a result of negotiations conducted in Brussels in January and February 1522,
Ferdinand became the *de facto* ruler of the Austrian duchies and the
manager of Habsburg interests within the Holy Roman Empire.
Distance made the delegation of power to blood relatives unavoidable; but such methods of government corresponded to the basic
character of Habsburg rule. It was dynastic, not territorial.

When the question of the imperial succession arose in 1519,
Marguerite of Austria with her usual sagacity advised Charles not to
present himself as a candidate. She suggested that the name

Ferdinand should go forward instead, if only because a bid on his part would be less likely to awaken the fears of the European powers. Charles refused to listen. He argued that the addition of the imperial crown to his existing titles would enhance his standing amongst his fellow monarchs. Such a gain in prestige would contribute directly to his power and enable him to defend Christendom more effectively. Some historians have detected in these remarks a political programme, the implications of which, Charles, for all his youth, had understood and accepted. According to this particular reading, Charles believed that God had called him to a position of pre-eminence, shortly to be sanctified by the imperial dignity, so that he might defend Christianity from the Turks and preserve the internal unity of Europe from heresy. This simple creed, with its religious inspiration, ran through the emperor's actions, whether in war, peace, or diplomacy, like the thread of Ariadne. As a statement of political purpose it was not original. Throughout the Middle Ages the German emperors had projected themselves as the secular defenders of the church; and as the power of both the empire and the papacy waned, so each national monarchy had put forward its own version of the theme. There was even an Iberian contribution. Pedro de Quintanilla, councillor to Ferdinand the Catholic, had impressed upon his master that Aragon should concern itself primarily with the defeat of the Ottomans; and Cardinal Cisneros had likened himself to a latter-day Joshua, leading the Christian hosts against the infidel of North Africa.

Whether or not the rhetoric employed by Charles had any substance, few of his contemporaries saw him as the high-minded saviour of Christendom. They imputed more selfish motives to his actions. Many concluded that the policies of Charles V and Francis I had essentially the same objectives. Both sought the title of Holy Roman Emperor in order to strengthen their respective positions as territorial princes. The imperial title conferred upon its holder immense standing and also a number of rights in Italy which both candidates could profitably exploit. Francis I, had he been successful in his claim, would have been able to consolidate the French hold on the duchy of Milan, technically an imperial fief. As emperor he would also have been in a position to block any attempt to return the duchy of Burgundy to its Habsburg claimant whatever the fortunes of war. Charles's thoughts ran along parallel lines. Mercurino di Gattinara, the imperial chancellor from 1519 until his death in 1530, wished to revive the old Ghibelline dream of making Italy, and in particular

Milan, the centre of the Holy Roman Empire. Charles accepted the
general drift of Gattinara's ideas even if he withheld his approval on
important matters of detail. France had to be excluded from Italian
affairs, and this could only mean conflict. Charles also nursed the
hope of recovering ducal Burgundy; and here again it was important
to deny the imperial title to his rival by the simple expedient of
acquiring it for himself.

The electoral triumph of Charles in 1519 ushered in a series of wars
which outlived the emperor and were only concluded by his son,
Philip II, as he approached death. Strategic considerations, personal
animosity, and lack of realism all had a contribution to make to the
apparently endless struggle. Between 1521 and 1526 Charles and his
advisers seriously considered the dismemberment of France as a
means of guaranteeing the Habsburg position in Italy and in Europe.
The renegade, Charles of Bourbon, was looked upon by some as the
possible head of a satellite kingdom in the south of France. In the
event a feeling of monarchical solidarity persuaded the emperor to
discard the radical solution pressed on him by Gattinara. But the
damage had been done. The French court saw itself after the imperial
election hemmed in on all sides by Habsburg territory; hence the need
to break the encirclement regardless of cost. The threat of physical
extinction, which had seemed so real in the period 1521–6, meant that
Francis I and his son, Henry II, committed themselves totally to the
destruction of the Habsburg state, whatever tactical concessions they
might make from time to time.

Personal rivalries and, just as noticeable, personal obsessions,
clouded the issue. Francis I, born in 1494, and Charles V, in 1500, were
of comparable age; and both were strongly competitive. Each saw in
the other a rival to the title of Europe's foremost prince. In his earlier
years Charles held that the recovery of ducal Burgundy with its capital
at Dijon formed part of his historic mission. Only when this had been
achieved could he be certain that his mortal remains would be laid
alongside those of his ancestors in the Charterhouse of Champmol.
The restoration of Burgundy, overrun by the French in 1477, to the
descendants of Charles the Bold formed the principal objective of the
Habsburg emperor from his coronation (as king of the Romans) in
Aachen (1520) to the signing of the Ladies' Peace in 1529 and the
awakening of a maturer understanding.

Francis I had also fallen prey to hopes which were beyond realization. As a dynasty, the Valois found it impossible to resist the lure of

territorial gains in Italy. At first Naples had provided the object of French ambitions. When the kingdom passed into the more capable hands of Aragon after 1504, French energies focused on the duchy of Milan. From the strategic point of view, this shift made much greater sense; but it brought France into conflict with other powers which had interests in the region, above all the Holy Roman Empire. Louis XII held Milan from 1505 until 1512 when the French were driven out. The expulsion and the subsequent fiasco of 1513, the defeat of Novara, might have been interpreted as a useful lesson. Not so. In the year of his succession (1515) Francis I, armed with a personal claim to the duchy through a distant ancestor, proceeded to demonstrate his kingly mettle by retaking Milan. Apparently, he had discovered the remedy for previous failure. French artillery mowed down the packed ranks of the Swiss pikemen, hitherto considered invincible, at the battle of Marignano (1515). For the next six years Milan remained a French possession. Although the troops of Francis I had effectively occupied the land, the duchy was an imperial fief. It was therefore a question of time before an attempt was made to challenge the illegal occupation.

The rivalry between Charles V and Francis I extended into the realm of political theory. In order to counter the claims of a supranational monarchy, which arrogated to itself responsibility for all the Christian states, the French kings began to promote, if hesitatingly at first, the concept of the sovereign and amoral state. Such ideas were of particular value when it came to exploiting the religious and political complexities of the Holy Roman Empire. Francis I and his son, Henry II (the latter with conspicuous success), championed 'German Liberties', a potent, if at times nebulous, set of ideas which included such beliefs as the right of the imperial princes to oppose the emperor and, when thought necessary, to conclude treaties with foreign powers. The question of 'German Liberties', sedulously and cynically fostered by France, emerged as a factor of real moment under Charles V; and it was not to be resolved until the peace of Westphalia (1648)— decisively, as it turned out, in favour of the princes. French willingness to intrigue with the Lutheran princes and to conclude alliances with the Ottomans was considered by many to show a complete lack of scruple.Yet for all their dubious morality such policies might well have been unavoidable, at least in part. Victory in the imperial election allowed Charles to occupy the moral heights and pose as the defender of Christendom. Had the result gone the other way, he might well have resorted to tactics similar to those employed by his arch-rival.

Open hostility between France and the Habsburg dominions broke out in 1521. The French invaded Navarre, hoping to reconstitute a kingdom which had been dismembered by Ferdinand the Catholic in 1512. Even if the invasion prolonged the *comunero* rising, it did little for the French in Navarre and still less in Italy. Here an unfavourable situation developed rapidly. By the end of 1521 the imperial (Habsburg) nominee, Francesco Maria Sforza, was installed as duke of Milan. Swiss troops in the pay of France were defeated at Bicocca (29 April 1522), largely through their own indiscipline. A year later, a former subject of the French king, Charles of Bourbon, led an imperial army into Provence and besieged Marseilles.

In 1524 the omens appeared more encouraging. Once the challenge of the invasion led by the Constable of Bourbon had been parried and then broken, Francis I was able to pass over to the attack, a role altogether more congenial. Late in the campaigning season of 1524 he led a reconstituted army over the Alps and down into the plain of Lombardy. At first all went well. Francis re-entered Milan on 26 October 1524; and then he set about the siege of Pavia which was defended by the imperial army. Supremely confident as to the outcome, the French king detached a strong column, under the duke of Albany, and sent it southwards in the hope of gathering up the kingdom of Naples while the imperialists were occupied elsewhere. It proved a disastrous lapse of judgement. The decisive engagement of the campaign, some might say of the entire Habsburg–Valois struggle in Italy, took place on 24 February 1525. Although the details are confused, the principal developments seem clear. The French army before Pavia found itself wedged between the imperial garrison and the army marching to its relief. The odds and the terrain favoured the French army, larger in size and better dug in. What might originally have been intended by the Habsburg commanders as an attempt to run supplies into Pavia soon escalated into a generalized engagement conducted across marshy terrain through the mists of early morning. By eight Francis believed that his forces had triumphed; an hour later he was a prisoner in imperial hands. His army had been destroyed; Milan had been lost.

Francis was held captive first in Italy and was then, much to the annoyance of Gattinara, the imperial chancellor, transferred to Spain. He was held over the winter of 1525–6 under strict confinement in the Alcázar (castle) of Madrid. The experience brought him near to death. At one stage the doctors held out so little hope of his recovery from a nasal abscess that the last rites were administered. His ailments may in large part have been psychosomatic. In order to obtain his release he was prepared to grant anything and sacrifice anybody. Under the terms of the treaty of Madrid (14 January 1526) which ended his imprisonment Francis agreed to the restoration to the Habsburgs of ducal Burgundy and Tournai, to abandon his claims to Italy, and to surrender his two sons as hostages for the satisfactory discharge of his obligations. The concessions were excessive. Two imperial generals, Charles of Lannoy and the marquis of Pescara, had warned against unreasoned optimism or vindictiveness; while Francis, just before signing the treaty, had gone through an elaborate ceremony in his prison cell abjuring compliance with the terms.

Events soon confirmed the moderate view. Francis had no intention of honouring the terms of the treaty, as the charade in the cell had already shown; and even if he had, it is doubtful whether he could have restored the duchy of Burgundy to Charles without provoking a fatal crisis within France. Others, too, were seriously alarmed by the extent of the emperor's success. As if by the operation of a reciprocating mechanism, the leading European powers banded together to impose a check upon the Habsburgs. The League of Cognac (21 May 1526) undertook to expel imperial troops from Genoa and Milan. On paper the combined resources of the signatories, France, the papacy, Venice, and Florence seemed formidable, and even more so after the bilateral alliance between France and England (28 January 1528). In practice, the partners were half-hearted and their policies largely ineffectual.

A familiar sequence began anew. In 1527 a French army, commanded by Odet de Foix, seigneur de Lautrec, crossed the Alps and carried all before him. Resistance was at first slight. The imperial army, unpaid for years, had taken matters into its own hands and sacked Rome (6 May 1527) before melting away. The French entered and plundered Pavia to avenge the earlier defeat; and Lautrec marched southwards to Naples meeting little opposition on the way.

Once again the French overstretched themselves, underestimating the inherent strength of the imperialists. Lautrec began the siege of Naples. To be successful, the French army had to blockade the town by sea as well as land. For the naval operations they looked to the Genoese; but the alliance on which so much depended was badly handled. Andrea Doria, the Genoese admiral and head of a most influential house, had been passed over for command of the naval blockade in favour of the French candidate, Antoine de la Roche-foucault. Furthermore the French had revealed their intention of promoting the growth of Savona at the expense of Genoa. The ruling oligarchs of Genoa took their revenge at a critical moment; they deserted to the imperial camp during the course of the siege, taking with them their maritime skills and their financial resources (10 August 1528). Lautrec, the easy victor of a few months before, found himself trapped between Naples, now adequately provisioned, and the imperial army marching to its relief. His army, chronically under-supplied and camped on unhealthy ground, shrank from 25,000 to 4,000 men fit for service. Imperial troops under the prince of Orange had no difficulty in dispersing the French army and in hunting down those who attempted to escape. In the following year the sole surviving French force in Italy was destroyed at Landriano (21 June 1529). Nothing remained of the French position in Italy.

Throughout this monotonous calendar of initial victories and eventual defeats two women, Louise of Savoy and Marguerite of Austria, mother to the king of France and aunt to the emperor respectively, showed that they understood realities, however lacking in sense others might be. They met, with official approval, at Cambrai on 5 July 1529, each entering the town by a different gate. A month later a treaty was signed (3 August 1529). The terms of the accord recognized with a fair measure of accuracy the balance of forces. France retained ducal Burgundy and the towns of the Somme which had once belonged to the Great Duke of the West, Charles the Bold of Burgundy; she abandoned claims to Naples and Milan—a major benefit, although hardly recognized as such at the time; and the children of Francis I who had been held as hostages since 1526 were redeemed by an enormous ransom of two million écus. Charles, for his part, obtained recognition for his authority in Italy and the restoration of a number of towns along the border of the southern Netherlands. He also extracted a pledge from Francis to marry his sister, Eleanor of Habsburg, as he had in fact undertaken in 1526. Charles hoped that at last he could secure the co-operation of the French king in the imperial design, the protection of Christendom and the reform of the church, by that most tested of all Habsburg devices, a marriage alliance.

The treaty of Cambrai, or the Ladies' Peace as it is sometimes called, can claim significance on at least two counts. It acknowledged the military truth that France was in no position to challenge imperial (in the context, increasingly Spanish) control of the Italian peninsula;

and conversely, Charles could not invade France and win a victory decisive enough to force the return of Burgundy. The respective limits of military capacity had been reached. Charles was also compelled to take note of the fact that, even with the French king a prisoner in his hands, he could not extort the return of ducal Burgundy. For all his Burgundian ancestry, his bones would never rest in the Charterhouse of Champmol.

The importance of Cambrai has been partially obscured because it did not lead to a period of prolonged peace as did its restatement, the treaty of Cateau-Cambrésis (1559). Francis had little intention of abiding by the spirit of Cambrai even if military inferiority forced him to be more circumspect. His objective, the destruction of Habsburg primacy, remained as before; the role of pliant brother-in-law could not have been further from his mind. To undermine the position of the emperor Francis anticipated the actions of Cardinal Richelieu. He encouraged and, where necessary, subsidized the enemies of Charles V, but usually stopping short of outright hostility. His attention shifted to Germany where the emergence of a party proclaiming its allegiance to Lutheran doctrines offered interesting possibilities. Francis joined the League of Saalfeld in 1532; and he conducted serious negotiations with the better known Schmalkaldic League in 1535 although these came to nothing. The policy of malevolent neutrality changed in 1535 with the re-opening of the Milanese question. On 1 November 1535 Francesco Sforza, the imperial appointee to the dukedom and erstwhile schoolmate to the emperor, died. In preparation for the impending struggle, the French king moved his troops into Savoy and Piedmont (both of which were retained until 1559); and hostilities opened on 2 June 1536.

Both sides had forgotten the lessons of the previous campaigns. Charles, fresh from his triumph in Tunis, launched a two-pronged attack on France; one force struck through Picardy, the other, led by the emperor himself, marched on Provence with the objective of taking Marseilles. Imperial strategists entirely overlooked the conclusions to be drawn from Charles of Bourbon's abortive attack on the same target a decade before. In the face of an initially superior force, the French employed the tactics which had served them so well in the past. Food and provender were removed or burnt; strong points along the line of march were provisioned and fortifications put into good repair. Such precautions once again proved their worth. By mid-September Charles was in full retreat, his army wasted by disease and none of his objectives secured. In the north the other expeditionary force had little more success: Péronne held out against its imperial besiegers.

The campaign of 1536 and the inability of either side to attempt another on any scale in the following year restated a familiar lesson. Given the state of the art at that moment, the defence enjoyed the military advantage over the attack, and by a wide margin. Imperial armies disintegrated just as regularly in France as French armies in Italy. Secondly, neither the Valois king nor his apparently mightier antagonist disposed of the resources for a prolonged campaign, let alone a repetition in the following year. For want of hard cash no one side could pay its men for long enough to secure lasting gain; and this would remain a fact of political life until the last quarter of the century, if not beyond. Exhaustion compelled both camps to seek terms. The armistice of Nice and Aigues-Mortes (1538), the latter graced by a personal interview between the two monarchs, brought about a temporary lull in the hostilities. The plan to transfer Milan to a French prince through the contrivance of a marriage alliance was first mooted at Nice.

Milan haunted the imagination of Francis I. When, therefore, Charles invested his eldest son, Philip of Spain, with the duchy of Milan on 11 October 1540, this was taken as a provocative act which dispelled the possibility of a peaceful resolution to the dispute. A few months later a French envoy, Antonio Rincón, a Spanish renegade as the name indicates, was murdered in Lombardy while on his way to the Ottoman court. This careless lapse of protocol served as excuse enough for the resumption of hostilities. The Most Christian King Francis I concluded an alliance with the Turks; and their surrogates, the Barbary pirates, were given port facilities, a concession which allowed them to winter in Toulon during the closed months of 1543–4. The exemplary behaviour of the corsair squadrons caught the imagination of contemporaries as much as the arrant cynicism of the accord which brought them to France in the first place. Francis I dispatched another army down into Lombardy; and this time, better led, it had better luck. French troops under the duc d'Enghien won the battle of Cérisoles (14 April 1542), one of the comparatively rare French successes against the imperialists on Italian soil.

In the meantime, Charles showed his accustomed energy. After concluding an alliance with England, he invaded France from the Low Countries in an attempted rapid thrust against Paris. But two perennial weaknesses re-emerged: his English partner, Henry VIII, and his chronic lack of money. He was unable to advance beyond St-Dizier since his army was beginning to break up through failure to pay it. The duc d'Enghien and the young dauphin, joint commanders of the French force shadowing the imperial army, were spoiling for a decisive battle. But those better acquainted with the military realities, filth, disease, and unpaid soldiers, advised against; and Francis, himself crippled by financial shortage, followed these wiser heads. Another peace was signed, this time in the small town of Crépy-en-Laonnais (18 September 1544).

The treaty rehearsed the familiar terms, so often pledged, so often broken. Charles acknowledged an end to his claims to ducal Burgundy; Francis abandoned his rights to Artois, the free county of Burgundy (the Franche-Comté), and to Italy. The French king also pledged himself to allow his bishops to attend the universal council of the church on which the emperor had pinned his hopes for the restoration of Christian unity. The Council of Trent, the direct result of this proviso, did in fact meet in December of the following year, although French bishops did not attend its deliberations in any numbers until 1562–3. Crépy might have led to some form of lasting accommodation between the rival powers had it not been for an unexpected death.

Charles had come to appreciate over the years that France would only further his cherished designs for Christian unity and universal peace if it were associated by some direct link with the fortunes of the Habsburg house. In 1544 he put into operation a scheme which had been mentioned some years previously. By the terms of the peace of Crépy he agreed to vest a younger son of the French king, Charles duke of Orléans, with either Milan or the Low Countries on his marriage to a Habsburg princess. If the duke wedded Anne, daughter of Ferdinand of Austria, then he would receive Milan; if he took Mary, Charles's own daughter, she would bring as her dowry the Low Countries. The final combination was left to the discretion of the emperor. Potentially, he faced a historic choice.

The offer to the French court stirred up fierce arguments amongst imperial advisers, especially the Iberian ones. One group, with the cardinal of Toledo, Juan Pardo y Tavera, as its principal spokesman, came out strongly for the concession of Milan. Imperial control of the duchy had been consistently challenged by France in the past, and there was no reason to think that French attitudes would change in the future. According to this school, the Low Countries should be retained for a combination of commercial and sentimental reasons: the emperor, originally Charles of Ghent, had been born in the Netherlands and they acted as the main vent for the sale of Spanish wool. The cardinal's school preferred to see Spain concentrate on North Africa rather than squandering her wealth in the interminable Italian campaigns against a remorseless foe. This platform could be seen as a continuation of the policies pursued by Isabel the Catholic and Cardinal Cisneros.

But the views of the Milanese lobby ran into vigorous opposition led, on this occasion, by the third duke of Alba, a youthful thirty-seven at the time. He followed the path first marked out by Mercurino di Gattinara, who had not been replaced as chancellor after his death in 1530, and the most capable imperial generals of the 1520s, the marquis of Pescara and Charles de Lannoy. With his usual keen appreciation of strategy, the duke argued that the Low Countries represented nothing better than an open drain on imperial, that is, Spanish, reserves; and communications with these northern possessions could be threatened at any time should relations between England and Spain deteriorate. His later experience confirmed the wisdom of his words. Alba therefore urged that the Low Countries should be granted to the French prince. Once freed of this burden, the Habsburg monarch would be at liberty to concentrate all his resources upon building a compact block of territories in the western Mediterranean, with Milan acting as formidable *glacis* for the Spanish possessions in Naples and Sicily. In the event these discussions, so revealing about strategic perceptions, were relegated to the archives. Charles duke of Orléans died on 9 September 1545; and the emperor was not called upon publicly to indicate which of his possessions he was prepared to relinquish.

The achievement of a satisfactory religious peace in Germany remained the abiding preoccupation of the emperor throughout his adult life; and since this did represent the summit of imperial ambition and the object of such colossal expenditure it has a direct bearing on Iberian history. The creation of a confessional party within the Holy Roman Empire, armed with a defined set of beliefs and prepared to assert itself, required over a decade to reach full development. Martin Luther at first appeared as a popular agitator for the reform of the established church. Such upsurges of popular fervour, of which Luther happened to be an embodiment, punctuated the history of the

Latin church from its earliest days; and Luther could be considered part of a tradition which included ultimately orthodox figures like St Bernard of Clairvaux and St Francis of Assisi.

Internal factors, peculiar to the German agitation, transformed the movement between 1517 and 1526 and swept it into a new and unknown course. After 1521 Luther, and those who lent him aid, stood condemned by both imperial and papal authority; the established powers failed to show the lenity and flexibility which had marked the treatment of some earlier critics. Secondly, the great haeresiarch had distanced himself from those who wished to draw radical theological conclusions from his message, the Anabaptists, and those who wished to turn his teachings into a theology of liberation, the German peasants. Thus purged of social or economic implications, the Lutheran creed attracted first the Imperial Free Cities, who found the unity of believers under God an appealing and familiar concept, and then later some territorial princes, whose role in the government of the church was expanded as a result. Those who 'protested' against the religious policy of the emperor at the Diet of Speyer on 19 April 1529, and thereby gave a name to the cause, included five territorial princes, one of whom, the elector of Saxony, had a place on the Electoral College, and fourteen Imperial Free Cities from the south of Germany.

Technically the Protestants (sometimes called Lutherans, at other times Evangelicals) were under the ban of the empire and the condemnation of the pope. But it was neither Charles's purpose, nor, at the outset, within his power to coerce this group. He remained convinced that comprehension would yield better results. Far from unsympathetic himself to some ideas of the reformers, Charles, without doubt influenced by the writings of Erasmus, encouraged attempts at doctrinal reconciliation. These had little success at the Diet of Augsburg (1530) which was remembered more for Melanchthon's statement of the Protestant creed (the *Confessio Augustana*); but his promptings almost brought about the compromise so eagerly sought at the diet of Regensburg (1541).

Even if the emperor had been less conciliatory in his approach, he was hardly in a position to resort to other methods. In 1526 Ottoman armies had destroyed the Hungarian army at Mohács (29 August) and overrun much of the kingdom. This disaster, which brought the Ottoman Empire into the politics of central Europe for the next two centuries, eventually worked for the benefit of the Habsburg house;

but in the short term it put the Austrian duchies which had been committed to Ferdinand, the emperor's brother, into the front line. Ferdinand's resources were inadequate by themselves for the task. He had to turn, as in 1529 and 1532, to his brother for help—echoes of the debate over the imperial candidacy in 1519—and Charles, for all the broad sweep of his possessions, had to ask for financial assistance from his German subjects. Until the Turkish menace had been overcome, or, at very minimum, a ceasefire had been arranged, the emperor had to extend unofficial tolerance towards the Evangelical states however much it ran against the grain of his most sincerely held beliefs.

The diet of Regensburg (1541) brought a decisive change of attitude. Charles came to see that it was no longer possible to differentiate between religious and political dissent. Hitherto the emperor had treated the Lutheran problem as a purely religious question concerned with the desire to reform abuses; not as an attempt, even if only by association, to alter the political balance within the empire. He had been wrong. Philip, margrave of Hesse, and John Frederick, elector of Saxony, not merely represented the Lutheran confession within the empire, they also stood at the forefront of the movement for greater independence on the part of the territorial prince.

Over the period 1541–6, Charles began to build up a new position with patient skill. In 1544 he secured his peace with France at Crépy; and he followed this a year later by concluding a ceasefire with the Turks which was later turned into a more durable arrangement. He also won the (temporary) support of the papacy, one of the more tenacious opponents of the imperial design, in the form of a pledge to supply money and troops. Charles intended to isolate the territorial princes who had adopted Lutheranism and to destroy the League of Schmalkalden which they had set up in 1531 to defend their interests. He had reached the conclusion that the Evangelical party would only accept serious dialogue with the Latin church after it had been defeated. It must be coerced. If, furthermore, victory in battle enabled the emperor to remodel the imperial constitution to his advantage, this could be looked upon as an additional blessing.

In 1546 Charles believed that the time had come for action. He gathered a seasoned army which included both papal and Spanish contingents; and he suborned into his service one of the more prominent Lutherans of the younger generation, Maurice of Saxony, mercurial, disreputable, and yet, in his own way, brilliant. The war of the Schmalkaldic League (1546–7) began with a series of protracted manœuvres on the Danube. The campaign then shifted early in the new year (1547) to northern Germany. After the elaborate and inconclusive operations of the previous autumn, the war moved to a rapid climax. At the battle of Mühlberg (24 March 1547) Charles gained what appeared not merely to his court painter, Titian, but to the world at large, his most decisive victory. The Schmalkaldic League was destroyed, and and its two principals, the margrave of Hesse and the elector of Saxony, taken. Now at long last the real master of Germany, Charles was in a position to impose his religious and political ideas. At his insistence representatives of the Lutheran confession were in attendance when the Council of Trent opened for its second session (1551–2). It was unfortunate that some of the major doctrinal enactments designed further to distinguish the Latin church from all others had been discussed and approved during the first session (1545–7); and that the assembled fathers, or the bulk of them, no longer shared the eirenic intentions of the Holy Roman Emperor. But at least contact had been made, fleetingly and tenuously, across the confessional divide.

Religion blended with politics. To preserve the church, cleansed and revitalized by the universal council then in session, Charles proposed to refashion the imperial constitution into something which approximated more closely to that of a 'modern monarchy'. This implied the restoration of power to the executive (the emperor) at the expense of the territorial princes. To bring about this new trim, Charles suggested the formation of the sardonically named Princely League. The purpose behind this organization was to provide the funds for a federal army which would be commanded by the emperor and to which all the princes, lay and ecclesiastic, would be obliged to contribute. The League was also designed to prevent the princes, or the lesser German potentates, from contemplating, still less entering, foreign alliances. Already the princes had succumbed to this temptation, with the papacy during the Middle Ages, and were to do so again very shortly with France; but legal recognition of such action was to be withheld until the peace of Westphalia (1648) which marked, in effect, the end of all attempts to reform the imperial constitution.

Efforts to secure the acceptance of a Princely League monopolized the attention of the diet which met in Augsburg from 1 September 1547, until 30 June 1548—one of the longest on record. Resistance came from every quarter. The papacy looked on the strengthening of

Charles's position with open trepidation; the Wittelsbach dukes of Bavaria, for all their notorious devotion to the Catholic church, had no inclination to promote still further the prestige of their ancestral rivals, the Habsburgs; while in the background there lurked France, willing as always to exploit any opportunity to avenge past failures. The diet eventually made some money available for the imperial army through a levy which was paid largely by the cities. But it fought shy of any constitutional modifications which might have brought the emperor lasting gain. The victory of 1547 had unlocked few doors.

The faltering judgement of Mühlberg was cancelled out in 1551. Henry II of France (1547–59) stood eagerly by to abet any scheme to humble the Habsburgs. In his case the memory of the close confinement he had suffered in Castile (1526–9) while detained as a hostage for his father, Francis I, honed the edge of his resentment. Since the opportunities for an attack on the Habsburg position in Italy had been terminated, Henry II needed a German accomplice if anything worthwhile was to be achieved. He did not have to wait long. Maurice of Saxony, the Alcibiades who had fought for Charles in 1546–7 and contributed substantially to his success, provided the means and the partners. The renegade prince played a highly dangerous game. He continued to lead the imperial army in Germany while conducting a treasonable correspondence with his former co-religionists, the Lutherans, and with the French king. He knew that the imperial army, of which he was the field commander, acted as a guarantor of Charles's shaky pre-eminence; therefore he must set about undermining its efficiency. To do this, Maurice continued to campaign against isolated Lutheran cities which had refused to surrender after the collapse of the Schmalkaldic League, since this would drain the emperor's resources. The siege of Magdeburg, undertaken from 1550 to 1551, was intended not to reduce the town but to dissipate the imperial war chest; and this is exactly what it did. Charles, normally so worldly-wise about human motive, failed completely to uncover the purpose of Maurice's actions.

In the meantime, the German princes had been negotiating with Henry II, first at the hunting lodge of Lochau on imperial soil (October 1551); and then, more formally, at Chambord, the grandest of the hunting lodges belonging to the French royal family. At the turn of the year Maurice of Saxony and a number of Lutheran princes signed the treaty of Chambord with France (15 January 1552). By its provisions the Protestant signatories obtained the promise of funds with which to liberate the margrave of Hesse and the elector of Saxony, still held as prisoners by the emperor, and a commitment on the part of the French king to restore 'German Liberties'. As his side of the bargain, Henry II received the imperial bishoprics of Metz, Toul, and Verdun. In return for subsidies with which to recover their own position within Germany, the Lutheran princes were prepared to hand over imperial territory to the French king. An offensive alliance of great power had been forged against the Habsburgs.

The emperor in the early months of 1552 seemed totally defenceless. Maurice of Saxony had squandered all available funds on the sham siege of Magdeburg; some of his leading German subjects had entered into open alliance with the traditional enemy, France; and the papacy, whose aid had proved so valuable during the campaign of Mühlberg, had withdrawn both its subsidy and its military contingent. And worse was still to come. Charles could no longer assume the unquestioning and loyal subordination of his brother, Ferdinand, who had been crowned king of the Romans in 1531.

The roots of this estrangement reached back a long way. Charles had always regarded the Habsburg empire as a family business in which each of his blood relatives had a role to play. In the case of the Netherlands the system worked admirably. His aunt, Marguerite of Austria, had governed from 1507 until 1515 and then once more from 1519 until her death in 1530; whereupon another Habsburg widow, this time his sister, Mary of Hungary, had been appointed regent. Both women had approached the responsibilities of government with the same high sense of purpose as Elizabeth Tudor. Yet if the great ladies of the house had been forever constant to Charles, the same did not apply to Ferdinand of Austria and his numerous progeny.

Over the years the sympathies and interests of the Habsburg brothers had developed along different lines. Physical separation undoubtedly contributed to this; but the principal explanation was to be found in the changed conditions of central and eastern Europe. When first sent by his elder brother to the hereditary duchies in the east, Ferdinand had been little more than an imperial steward, whose knowledge of the Austrian lands was as minimal as Charles's for the kingdoms of Castile and Aragon. Within five years of his arrival, his position had been transformed beyond recognition. In 1526 Louis of Hungary was killed at the battle of Mohács along with most of the aristocratic and ecclesiastical élite. As the husband of the late king's sister, Anne, Ferdinand inherited part of what was left of royal

Hungary and, after the due process of election, the crown of Bohemia which Louis had once held. The foundations of the Danubian monarchy had been laid, even if its subsequent greatness could not be perceived in 1526, and Ferdinand emerged as a major figure in his own right. As king of Bohemia he automatically became a member of the Imperial Electoral College, a dignity which further added to his prestige and self-esteem.

In 1530 Pope Clement VII crowned Charles Holy Roman Emperor in the papal city of Bologna; and in the following year Ferdinand was elected king of the Romans, official recognition that he was the legal successor to his brother. The Austrian branch of the Habsburg family came to believe that they had a prescriptive right to the imperial title; and Ferdinand's children, notably his eldest son, Maximilian, looked to follow in their father's footsteps. Charles V had other ideas. He had set his heart on what became known as the 'Spanish Succession', a scheme whereby his eldest son, Philip, would one day become Holy Roman Emperor. Once news of the plan broke, acrimonious wrangling took place within the imperial family. So bitter were the arguments that Mary of Hungary felt obliged to make a winter journey from Brussels to Augsburg, Charles's residence at the time, to arbitrate in the matter (1550). Possibly as a result of her mediation, a compromise was patched up (9 March 1551). Under its terms Ferdinand of Austria was to succeed Charles as emperor, on the understanding that he would use all his influence, once installed, to bring about Philip's election as king of the Romans, and therefore, by convention, heir apparent. The arrangement, soon leaked, provoked widespread resentment and left the Austrian archdukes mortified.

The reasoning behind the Spanish Succession in 1551 followed that used by Charles in 1519 to justify his own candidacy; and in a sense it represented a maturer expression of the Imperial Idea. Charles pressed the claims of his son in the belief that a future emperor could only carry out successfully the tasks demanded of him if he disposed of both the Spanish kingdoms and the imperial title. The Spanish Succession would lock together the Holy Roman Empire and the Iberian possessions, thereby creating an indissoluble bond; and so strongly had this concept gripped his imagination that Charles continued to nurture hopes in this direction up to his death in 1558 even though it had been shown to be wholly impracticable. Ferdinand and his son, Maximilian, although they briefly acquiesced at Augsburg, had very different views on the subject. Personal ambition apart, they appreciated, as evidently Charles did not, that the German princes were hardly likely to accept Philip of Spain either for what he was or for what he represented. The next few months showed why.

Early in the spring of 1552 Maurice of Saxony, at the head of an army partly subsidized by France, swept through southern Germany. Most of the German rulers declared themselves neutral in the struggle. Maurice pushed on rapidly to Innsbruck, capital of the Tyrol, where the emperor had taken up residence. It remains an open question whether or not Maurice intended to capture his sovereign lord; but he did force Charles to make a humiliating escape from Innsbruck over the Brenner Pass to the picturesque town of Villach (19–28 May 1552). The flight ended such authority as Charles had enjoyed in Germany since 1547 and it appeared to ruin his credit with the financial community.

The collapse of 1552 compelled the emperor to face up to some unpleasant realities. Charles accepted that he must scale down (and, in the end, virtually abandon) his plans for reshaping the empire, although he was determined to fight a protracted rearguard action. In the summer of 1552 the Habsburg brothers met at Innsbruck, the last time they were ever to see one another, to concert their strategy. After negotiations with the princes who had fought the emperor and those, by far the more numerous, who had not committed themselves to either side, Ferdinand was able to secure an interim agreement at Passau (2 August 1552). The settlement prefigured the better known version signed three years later at Augsburg. Ferdinand agreed to the immediate release of Philip of Hesse and the elector of Saxony; religious toleration was extended to the princes (but not their subjects) until the question of faith could be satisfactorily resolved—in effect, until the Greek Kalends; and all outstanding political and religious issues were deferred until the next Imperial Diet. Although not mentioned, the scheme to create a Princely League designed to bolster the position of the emperor lapsed; and it, or something very similar, was not resurrected until the Thirty Years War and the peace of Prague (1635). In dealing with the various interests at Passau, Ferdinand acted not as a spokesman for one side or another but as an independent force. He mediated between the parties.

Initially, Charles conceived this retreat within the empire, conciliation in short, as a tactical measure enabling him to concentrate on what mattered to him most—the expulsion of the French from the imperial bishoprics which they had just occupied. Whilst still at Villach Charles had used all the persuasion at his command to induce Anton Fugger to provide yet more credit. The latter, yielding to the pleas of his client, made available the famous 'loan of Villach'—an advance which made no sense at all from the business point of view but merely demonstrated how even reputedly shrewd bankers could forsake their better judgement if sufficiently worked upon. The monies put up by the Fugger gave the emperor, and Ferdinand for that matter, some standing at Passau; and, just as important, imperial captains could start recruiting an army for operations against France.

In the autumn of 1552 Charles felt able to move. His recovery from the humiliation of Villach had proved remarkable and his will seemed unbroken. He marshalled his troops, some 35,000 in number with a contingent of 6,000 Spaniards and 4,000 Italians, for an all-out assault on Metz, the episcopal city which had surrendered to Henry II of France on 18 April 1552. The imperial army invested the town, defended by Francis, duke of Guise, in October. Mary of Hungary, with a fine eye for military matters, warned her brother that the season was too far advanced but the advice was scorned. Imperial commanders, Alba amongst them, gave out that the operation was feasible. Three months later the French defensive system had still to be breached; and Charles's army, so expensively gathered, was disintegrating in the rain and the squalor of the trenches. Charles lifted the siege on New Year's Day 1553. The failure before Metz completed a process set in train by the flight to Villach. At every point Charles's imperial plans had been checked; and his personal authority within the empire had been totally eclipsed, a fact which he chose to emphasize himself by moving his residence to the Netherlands and never setting foot again after 1553 on lands historically part of the empire. More significantly, recent events had sapped his confidence; Charles came to believe that he had failed in his life's mission.

Long before, in 1542, the emperor had confided in the Portuguese envoy, Lourenço Pires de Távora, that he had thought about abdication after his return from Tunis in 1535. Ten years on he was ready to put the plan into effect; but like everything concerning the emperor, the operation, as eventually carried through, was continental in scale. One last diplomatic triumph remained to be secured before the main sequence of the abdication began to unfold. The marriage between Philip of Spain and Mary Tudor, formally agreed to on 12 January 1554, represented at the very least a partial compensation for Villach, the

Spanish Succession, and Metz. If Spain and the empire were not to be joined in the person of Philip, then an alternative arrangement between England and the Iberian kingdoms had much to recommend it. The sea route from the Cantabrian ports to the weaving towns of Flanders would be safer in the future; France could be threatened on its northern flank.

Charles divested himself of his many kingdoms and titles in a series of acts which combined the functional and the ceremonial. The greatest piece of theatre took place on 25 October 1555. As hereditary ruler of the Netherlands, Charles summoned the Estates General to appear before him in the Great Hall of the Palace in Brussels. After the initial pomp, Charles, an old man with spectacles, and forced to remain seated throughout, announced his abdication as ruler of the Netherlands in favour of his son, Philip. In this the most public of all ceremonies he left an indelible impression on those present by taking his subjects into his confidence and delivering a justification of his whole life. Mary of Hungary, still the regent, had arranged beforehand that a tapestry belonging to the Order of the Golden Fleece should hang on the walls of the Great Hall. It depicted scenes from the life of Gideon, slayer of the Midianites and the hero who refused the crown.

Other acts soon followed. On 16 January 1556 Philip received formal investiture as ruler of Castile, Aragon, and Sicily. Later in the year, at a special ceremony, the Franche-Comté, that fragment of the once mighty duchy Charles had sought to restore, was made over to his son (10 June 1556), who now entered into the full Burgundian inheritance. Neither Mary of Hungary nor Ferdinand of Austria approved of the abdication, although the latter's reservations were self-interested. He doubted, with reason, whether the Electoral College would choose him automatically in place of his brother. But Charles did not listen to his brother's fears. Just before embarcation, in the small village of Souburg, three kilometres out of Flushing, the emperor made over all his imperial powers to Ferdinand (5–7 August 1556). This grant of administration (*Administratio Imperii*) was a unilateral act without any standing in law; and the electors did not endorse the fiat of the old emperor until some time later (14 March 1558).

Ferdinand had a number of immediate reasons for wishing his brother to remain. The emperor had refused to meet his subjects at the diet of Augsburg; and it was left to Ferdinand to bring about the lasting peace about which the signatories at Passau had spoken so optimistically. The settlement drawn up at Augsburg (25 September

1555) had German and European implications. The Lutheran states (but not the Calvinist or any other) acquired legal recognition for the time being; and individuals could decide which of the confessions their subjects should follow. The attempt to keep the empire faithful to a single creed had to be abandoned. With more than a premonition of what was likely to happen at Augsburg, Charles had left his brother to act as imperial plenipotentiary; but Ferdinand, worried lest his standing might be prejudiced, had withheld from the delegates the news that the emperor intended to abdicate until the day after the peace of Augsburg had been signed. The grant of legitimacy to the Lutheran states embittered the last years of Charles V and left a profound impression upon his son. The *auto de fe* on Philip's return to Spain in 1559 served notice that he had no intention of allowing his Iberian kingdoms to go the way of the empire.

Charles delayed longer than he intended in the Netherlands. It took time to collect the money with which to fit out a fleet and to pay off servants who were no longer needed. Once the funds had been gathered and arrears settled, Charles sailed from Flushing on 17 September 1556; eleven days later his flotilla touched at Laredo. Crippled with gout, the emperor was then carried six hundred kilometres south on a special litter (preserved to this day) until he reached his final destination, the Jeronimite monastery at Yuste (Cáceres). A modest set of rooms had been built on to the main structure of the building to accommodate the emperor and his suite. The monastery stood on the southern flank of the Sierra de la Vera high in the dry air, just beneath the timber line; and it was here that Charles died on 21 September 1558, in the early morning.

CHAPTER 5

The New World: Columbus and Cortés

THE discovery of America belonged as much to the history of Genoa as to that of Castile, under whose sponsorship the enterprise was officially launched. This republic perched on the Ligurian coast had a long familiarity with overseas exploration, unlike Castile which had remained throughout its historical experience for the most part land-locked. Religion may have provided some of the impulse for this out-ward drive—the Genoese had been amongst the principal architects of the crusader kingdoms in the Middle East and went on to become their main suppliers; but the consideration which outweighed all others was undoubtedly economic. The city, lacking an agricultural hinterland or a manufacturing base of any consequence, urged its sons to look to the wider world for employment and advancement. Only a steady export of manpower could relieve the pressure on the slender resources of the state. Initially the merchant community concentrated their efforts on the eastern Mediterranean where they traded, oppor-tunity permitting, with Crusader, Greek, and Muslim. The trading posts, or factories, planted in all the major ports of the Levant bore witness to the success of the attempt to expand overseas.

For much of the later Middle Ages the republic looked upon the eastern Aegean and the Black Sea as the main sources of its prosperity, but not to the total exclusion of other interests. From the thirteenth century onwards Genoese merchants found themselves heavily involved in the transport and sale of English wool. As the trade between England and Genoa required large, therefore expensive, ships, it was essential in the interests of economy that the vessels make as few calls *en route* as possible. Genoese captains received every encouragement to sail beyond the sight of land and, wherever pos-sible, by night. Such hazardous practices helped to foster navigational skills: and what served in the bay of Biscay and the Western Approaches would prove even more valuable one day in the open Atlantic.

Nor, for all their concern with the eastern Mediterranean, did the

Ligurian merchants shun other points of commercial advantage. Colonies of expatriate Genoese dotted the entire length of the Mediterranean coastline. Their presence in Seville, the principal city of southern Spain, reached back to the days of Muslim rule. After the Christian powers captured the city (1248), this Italian community continued to prosper; and by the 1470s it numbered over a hundred families. Genoese emigrants established themselves with equal success in Lisbon. At a different level of employment, Genoese admirals had for generations served with distinction in the respective navies of both Portuguese and Castilian kings.

While the eastern trade flourished, commercial activity in the Iberian peninsula or, further afield, in England, remained a subordinate consideration. Then, in 1453, circumstances changed. The Ottoman empire finally acquired possession of Constantinople and was not inclined to deal lightly with the Italian powers who had exploited the weakness of the Byzantine state. Relations between Genoa and the Ottoman conquerors grew steadily worse and trading became, as a result, more difficult and less prosperous. The merchants, sensing their peril, smartly shifted the emphasis of Genoese trade. Resources flowed westwards in increasing volume; and the Iberian peninsula profited most from this realignment of interests. Just as the supply of goods and capital sought out new destinations, so too did the human emigration from Genoa.

Christopher Columbus (1451–1506), or Cristóbal Colón in Castilian, was the son of a weaver. He did not follow in his father's trade, preferring instead to serve as a deckhand on board a Genoese merchantman which plied the route to the eastern Aegean. His ship combined commerce with piracy—the distinction had always been a fine one since Homeric times. After this apprenticeship, Columbus made his way to Portugal where he spent the best part of a decade (c.1476–c.1485). From his Portuguese years Columbus gained a wealth of experience: he certainly visited the Azores (where he married his first wife); and he was allowed to crew aboard a ship bound for São Jorge da Mina, the main Portuguese station on the West African coast. An apt and willing pupil, as well as a sturdy seaman, Columbus studied with care the latest charts while absorbing as best he could the most recent advances in navigational theory. The Portuguese sailors may also have provided their foreign shipmate with a number of insights which laid the foundations of his own achievement. The winds of the North Atlantic drive the currents in a clockwise movement, the motor gears of this slowly turning mass of water being the North East Trade Winds on the European and the Westerlies on the American side. This gyre, a combination of prevailing air-flow and currents producing a circular eddy of enormous scale, determined the course of every ship to and from the New World throughout the age of sail. In their journeys southwards along the African coast and perhaps as a result of their even less publicized voyages westwards the Portuguese mariners may have acquired a shrewd idea of how the weather system of the North Atlantic worked. These observations they may have passed on to Columbus as he toiled or drank with them; and it was left to his genius to prove what had hitherto been mere supposition and to discover how the winds and the currents might carry a man westward into the unknown and bring him home safely again.

As he grew older a thought, then an obsession, took hold of Columbus. He appreciated, as had others before him, that the sea route to the Far East which the Portuguese were currently exploring involved a laborious journey along the African coast, a voyage wasteful of time, ships, and crews. What if a shorter route existed to the Spice Islands? What if, instead of sailing on a southerly tack, an expedition should steer a westerly course? The idea of a westward route had been vigorously promoted by the Florentine Paolo dal Pozzo, better known as Toscanelli, whose theories greatly influenced Columbus. But inspired as they were, Toscanelli's beliefs rested on a fundamental misconception. The Florentine had seriously underestimated the distance between Europe and Japan (Cipangu), the nearest landfall for such a westward journey. Far from recognizing this basic error, Columbus, in his turn, compounded it. He reached the private conclusion that Toscanelli had exaggerated, not minimized, the distance between Europe and Japan. Columbus's lifelong ambition to sail westward across the uncharted sea was therefore founded on a reckoning even faultier than Toscanelli's.

In 1486 Columbus took his project to the Portuguese king, John II, who passed it on to a committee of experts for a report. After checking the calculations the junta 'of the mathematicians' rejected the scheme as unsound. Denied support by John II, Columbus moved to Castilian territory and settled in the town of Palos where relatives of his first wife lived. The decision of the Portuguese crown to withhold funds from this particular venture did not mean that it lacked interest in westward exploration. Quite the reverse. As Columbus argued his case with the Portuguese experts, another foreign seaman, the

Fleming Ferdinand van Olmen, reached an agreement with John II to explore the region west of the Azores. In the contract van Olmen spoke of a journey of forty days to discover new lands, an indication, perhaps, that he was drawing on a common pool of knowledge, even fishermen's lore. But while he may have possessed accurate notions of distance and direction he was woefully ignorant of the weather patterns. Ferdinand van Olmen left the Azores sometime during the winter of 1486–7 on a northern course which would have brought him to Newfoundland. He was never heard of again.

His disappearance prompted John II to reconsider Columbus's proposal with its emphasis on a more southerly route to the west. An invitation was extended to the Genoese mariner. He was told that if he returned to Lisbon his project would receive sympathetic consideration. Had the offer been taken up America might well have been discovered in the year 1488 and in the name of Portugal. Developments elsewhere scotched the possibilities. In December, 1488, Bartolomeu Dias returned to Lisbon with the glorious news that the Indian Ocean could be entered by rounding the tip of the African continent. The Portuguese king had his route to the east. There was no longer any need to finance the wild schemes of men like van Olmen or Columbus.

Columbus had chosen Palos as his retreat because although small it was strategically placed. Once installed he began to angle for the patronage of either the duke of Medina Sidonia or, if this were not forthcoming, that of his neighbour and rival, the duke of Medinaceli. Either sponsor could open the doors of the court. Columbus did not have to wait long for notice to be taken. Queen Isabel showed early interest; and she received the Genoese expatriate when the court settled temporarily in Córdoba (1486). Unable to judge the merits of Columbus's project for herself, she, too, referred the matter to assessors. They dismissed the plan, as had their Portuguese counterparts, on the grounds that the calculation of distance was patently false. The experts were right: Columbus was wrong; and there was nothing more to discuss.

He merely persisted; and in the end his obstinacy, or sublime self-confidence, overcame every obstacle. In 1492 the Catholic Monarchs gave their approval to the voyage. The fall of Granada had released resources for this and other ventures; and the general euphoria induced by the wonderful conclusion to the Reconquest may have affected the judgement of both Ferdinand and Isabel. The convergence of two sets of circumstances at the right moment enabled Columbus to launch an expedition for which there was little scientific justification. Columbus had realized from his many years of pleading and waiting that the fate of his plan depended on securing powerful patrons at court; and much energy went into the cultivation of the right people. His investment paid off handsomely; and he enrolled in his cause several leading figures more noted for their scepticism than their enthusiasm for dubious voyages. His backers included Luis de Santángel, treasurer to King Ferdinand, Gabriel Sánchez, treasurer of the kingdom of Aragon, and Francesco Pinelli, treasurer of the Santa Hermandad and a fellow Italian. This formidable trio, together with their clients, represented the 'new Christian' (*converso*) and Genoese element in Castilian society. Recent converts and foreigners made a fruitful combination. Columbus was also helped by the very practical consideration that his demands in terms of ships and supplies were not excessive. The ships to be used were little more than fishing vessels whose costs nowhere matched those of a deep sea merchantman out of Genoa. Nor did the stores required for the expedition compare to those taken out by the Portuguese on their lengthy voyages down the African coastline. Columbus's miscalculation of distance helped him to present a more attractive case. In short, all that Columbus needed was well within the capacity of the fishing communities of the minor Andalusian ports; and perhaps because of this his immediate associates came from the ranks not of the Genoese shipping magnates but from the masters of small trading craft who, like the Pinzón brothers, owned and sailed their boats.

Although first and foremost a seaman, Columbus shared the hope of all his fellow migrants. He wanted to become rich. Columbus always saw himself as a businessman; and he undertook the voyage of 1492 as a commercial venture, not a scientific mission. By sailing westwards he believed that he would discover a route to the Indies shorter and therefore cheaper than the existing one. Once he had proved the feasibility of his idea, he intended to benefit personally by securing for himself a privileged position from which to deal in spices, gold (dust), and slaves.

In outlook and ambition Columbus remained profoundly traditional. The accord signed by Columbus and the Catholic Monarchs on the eve of his departure demonstrates this clearly. By the terms of the Capitulations of Santa Fe (17 April 1492) Columbus received one-tenth of the produce of the lands yet to be discovered and the right to

one-eighth of the cargoes shipped from these new lands. These concessions were modelled on a similar set which the Admiral of Castile
enjoyed in Spain. Additions to the Capitulations brought out even
more strongly the archaic (or feudal) character of the privileges conferred on Columbus. He was allowed to consolidate all his possessions and rights into a strict entail (*mayorazgo*) which could pass to
his heirs. By this device Columbus was able to protect his property
and bequeath it intact to his children, just as if he had been a feudal
baron.

Columbus sailed from the harbour of Palos on 3 August 1492. Seven
and a half months later (15 March 1493) he returned to the same port
the discoverer of America. The importance, if not the exact significance, of his voyage was immediately recognized. He was lionized
wherever he went; and the seal was set on his triumph when the
Catholic Monarchs formally received him in Barcelona. He made
three subsequent journeys to the West Indies (25 September 1493–
11 June 1496; 30 May 1498–30 October 1500; 3 April 1502–7 November
1504). Whilst unique, Columbus's achievement remained limited in
scope. By courage and seamanship he discovered, or rediscovered, the
continent of America. He located, and in some cases explored, the
main islands of the West Indies; and in the process he founded the
first European settlements in the New World on the island of
Hispaniola. During the course of the later voyages he skirted the
coastline of Venezuela and went on to make landfall and temporary
camp on the isthmus of Panama. He also worked out through the
customary mixture of brilliance and error the dominant weather
system without which communications with the Americas would have
been impossible. On the outward journey he picked up the easterlies
which carried his ships to the New World; and on his way home he
discovered the prevailing trade winds which all mariners during the
age of sail sought out for the return passage to Europe. Columbus
stumbled across a new continent and was the first man since the
Vikings to come back with the tale.

Columbus was a discoverer of new worlds, not a conqueror and
administrator, as soon became painfully obvious. The Admiral of the
Ocean Seas, a title granted to him as part of the Capitulations of Santa
Fe, regarded the West Indian islands as an Atlantic version of the
Genoese trading posts in the Black Sea. On his second voyage to the
Antilles he brought with him nearly 1,500 followers, a far cry from the
ninety men who had shipped with him on his first expedition; and

these were regarded not as future settlers but as employees in Columbus's private company—and paid as such.

The Admiral's shortcomings as a colonial administrator became swiftly evident. His inability to manage the settlement on the island of Hispaniola led to a rising of his subordinates, or employees, who chose Francisco Roldán as their captain (1499). News of the unrest obliged the Catholic Monarchs to send out an official to investigate; and he saw fit to imprison Columbus and send him back to Spain in irons (1500). Yet even if the Admiral had revealed the understanding of a Cortés it is unlikely that the crown would have left him unmolested in the enjoyment of the privileges granted by the Capitulations of Santa Fe. The Catholic Monarchs, unlike Columbus, rapidly appreciated that the West Indian islands were not Genoese factories or their equivalent. They compared far more closely to the lands which had been reconquered from the Moors; and, as such, required the immediate assertion of royal control. During the lifetime of the Admiral himself, the monarchy set about whittling down his original grant just as it was to do in the case of Cortés, Pizarro, and the other conquerors of the Americas.

Columbus's difficulty in managing the first settlement stemmed from the fact that the first colonists, the bulk of whom had been recruited from the herdsmen and shepherds of southern Spain, had little intention of pursuing a sedentary life. They planned to discover gold, extract it, and then move on. How to curb such restless spirits was the first task of a royal governor—and one well beyond the capacity of the Admiral.

Nicolás de Ovando, the first governor of the Indies, arrived in Santo Domingo, the capital of Hispaniola, on 15 April 1502. In the seven years of his administration he created a flourishing colony. He subdued the natives, not difficult in view of their primitive weapons, and, more important, he subdued the Spaniards themselves. His techniques permanently influenced both Hispaniola and, later, the mainland settlements. He introduced a number of European crops and cattle which gave the colony a stable agricultural base. Ovando then divided the island into a number of municipalities (seventeen is the figure sometimes given), and thenceforth every Spaniard was considered subject to the jurisdiction of one or other of these town councils. The decision to make the town council the key element in the administrative framework left an indelible stamp on Spanish America. Colonial society became urban, not rural. To induce the individual white to remain in one place and not to decamp at a moment's notice, Ovando made each male settler a householder (*vecino*) of a particular town. As a householder each man had the right to agricultural land outside the town and a building plot within its confines. Town and country were linked together in the person of the white settler.

The device of *vecindad*, the quality of being a householder, was used in another way. The colonists had no intention of working the land themselves: rather than stoop to manual labour they preferred to starve; and during the brief supremacy of Columbus they appeared in imminent danger of doing just that. The solution to the problem was obvious—Indian labour, forced if necessary. Queen Isabel had qualms in the matter; but these were stilled. In accordance with the royal decree of 20 December 1503, Ovando began to distribute the Indian population to the 'care' of the white settlers. Technically, the Indians were required to perform labour services for the colonists in return for which the Spaniards were to provide for their spiritual welfare, that is, promote their conversion to Christianity. Ovando's assignment of native manpower served as the model for the later system, employed throughout Spanish America, of *repartimiento*. It also led in the case of the Antilles to the virtual elimination of the native population.

Once placed on a stable footing, the Spanish settlements in Hispaniola acted as the base for the exploration and occupation of the other Caribbean islands. The Greater Antilles were reconnoitred and settled in quick succession. In 1511 a son of the conqueror, Diego Colón, having recovered some of his father's rights, proposed that he should be entrusted with the conquest of Cuba; but the crown, ever mindful of the need to curb the growth of individual authority, gave the task instead to Diego Velázquez, reputedly an enemy of the Columbus family. The occupation of Cuba by Velázquez brought to an end the first cycle of conquest, often referred to as 'the Island Phase', and in so doing opened the way for the conquest of the mainland.

As part of his immediate entourage Diego Velázquez brought with him· Hernán Cortés, who was to serve the next eight years as his private secretary. Already Cortés had a long experience of colonial affairs: in 1504 Nicolás de Ovando granted him a *repartimiento* on the island of Hispaniola; and over the next few years he had patiently and shrewdly built up a private fortune. During his time in the settlements he studied the indigenous cultures of the Caribbean, then in the process of rapid disintegration, and he gained first-hand experience of native techniques of warfare. As secretary to Velázquez, Cortés came to appreciate that the timing and direction of expansion depended on the factional politics of the royal court, hence the need to cultivate powerful and reliable contacts at home. He also realized that the colonial administration already established in the New World was determined to keep tight control over the course of subsequent conquest.

Diego Velázquez had no intention of limiting himself to the island of Cuba. For one thing he wanted a command totally independent of his nominal superior, Diego Colón. In 1517 and again in the following year he fitted out and dispatched expeditions to explore the coastline of the Yucatan and the bay of Campeche. Both were designed to prepare the way for a descent in force on the mainland which he intended to lead in person. But before he could launch a full-scale military operation he needed royal authorization. While awaiting the return of his envoys bringing that consent, Velázquez decided to send out a third reconnaissance party this time led by his private secretary, Hernán Cortés. His judgement may have been sound; but his trust was misplaced. Cortés, himself a shareholder in the enterprise, gathered together his men as quickly as possible; and then, such was his haste, set sail before all the stores had been taken aboard. He feared rightly that the ever suspicious Velázquez might have second thoughts and prevent his departure.

The Aztec Confederacy, into whose life Cortés was about to intrude so brutally, stood at the end of a long line of indigenous civilizations. High within the central plateau of Middle America a number of tribes had established themselves around the lake of Mexico. These lacustrine cultures had fought and coexisted with one another until one came to assert its authority over its neighbours. In 1325 the tribe known as the Mexica began to construct their floating city of Tenochtitlán. These new lords of the lake created over the next century an order which incorporated many elements borrowed from previous societies while introducing a number of additional, and, at times, unpleasant novelties.

An arresting feature of the Aztec Confederacy, one of the names given to the state, was the emphasis placed on the cult of Huitzilopochtli, or the 'Southern Hummingbird'. This particular deity came to symbolize the superiority of the Mexica over all the other tribes; and its role as an imperial creed was actively promoted in the fifteenth century by the greatest of all Aztec warlords, Tlacaellel. The worship of the Hummingbird demanded endless human sacrifice. Military operations ceased to be exclusively territorial in purpose; they were often launched merely to enlarge the reservoir of human tribute. If there was a shortfall, the allied tribes were called upon to make good the deficit of victims through the device of mock battles staged as part of the sinister 'Flower Wars'. The preoccupation with ensuring an adequate supply of human sacrifices influenced techniques of warfare. Capture rather than the destruction of the enemy became the main concern. Such a tactic, explicable perhaps in the context of Mesoamerican societies, proved disastrous when applied against the white invaders.

Under pressure from new and unmeasured forces, the Aztec state revealed both military and psychological flaws. The official religion to which the royal family and the priestly caste were fervently attached was pessimistic in tone. The Aztec cosmology rested on a balance: the forces of darkness as represented by Huitzilopochtli and the benign influence of civilization as personified by Quetzalcoatl strove eternally for mastery of the world. The Mexica and their subjects, in common with other cultures, believed in the myth of the eternal return. It had been widely predicted that Quetzalcoatl, the light-skinned god who had gone into exile long ago, would reappear at the end of a fifty-two-year cycle; and it just so happened that the year fixed by the soothsayers for this great event was 1519.

Once he had made good his escape from Cuba, Cortés sailed the short distance to the mainland of America. His first action was to found a town with his own men providing the citizen body, along the lines of a Roman military settlement. Initially the town of Vera Cruz, whatever its subsequent history, was established as a legal device to enable Cortés to shake off the authority of Diego Velázquez, his partner and, more to the point, his superior. The town council of Vera Cruz, made up of Cortés's soldiers, duly elected him as *alcalde y justicia mayor* and captain general thereby making him independent of Velázquez. Although subsequently hailed as a master-stroke, the foundation of the Rica Villa de la Vera Cruz did not provide Cortés with an unimpeachable authority. The law was not clear on the matter; and the Spanish crown had to decide whether or not to regard the ploy as legitimate.

For the moment Cortés's luck held. He discovered ashore a

Spaniard who had been shipwrecked a few years before and had used the intervening period to learn Maya. He was also given as a present a girl, Malinche, who spoke as her mother tongue Nahuatl, the official language of the Aztecs, which she was able to translate into Maya and thus communicate with the Spanish interpreter. When Malinche, after a few months in the Spanish camp, mastered Castilian, communications became simpler. Cortés also gained as allies the Totonacs, the first tribe with whom he came into contact. These supplied him wth invaluable information about the local terrain and the policies of the Aztec empire. Just as useful, the Totonacs provided the porters and guides without whom the white men could never have contemplated the march inland to the Aztec capital.

Cortés had resolved to make his way to the very centre of Aztec power almost from the very first moment. As his army moved up country his progress was challenged at various stages by the subject cities of the Confederacy. The most formidable of these was Tlaxcala whose independence the Aztecs had tolerated as a means of supplying the victims who fed the Hummingbird. Once the Tlaxcalans had been defeated, Cortés revealed his masterly political sense by winning them over and then retaining their loyalty. The benefits of this new understanding were incalculable. Cortés's ability to win over the subject peoples almost certainly contributed more to the end of Aztec rule than his undoubted prowess as a soldier.

The Spaniards, perhaps as many as two thousand, had been monitored continuously since their first appearance off the coast. But the Aztec emperor, Montezuma II (1503–20) was uncertain how best to use the information. He dithered. Perhaps the prophecy had been fulfilled: Quetzalcoatl and his followers had returned in white tents that floated upon the sea. Well aware of the legend, Cortés exploited it for all it was worth. He reached Mexico City (Tenochtitlán) on 8 November 1519: Montezuma, in his speech of reception, appeared to acknowledge Cortés either as Quetzalcoatl in person or as his emissary and, in the Spanish versions at least, to resign his empire into his hands. A few days later, fearful that the initial awe and reverence might wear off, Cortés seized the person of Montezuma (14 November). Such a flagrant denial of the laws of hospitality marked the conquest of both the Aztec and the Inca empires. Cortés planned gradually to take over effective authority while retaining Montezuma as a figurehead for as long as he could be of use.

This scheme of peaceful annexation was soon interrupted not by the Indians but by the Spaniards. Diego Velázquez, furious at the way Cortés had flouted his authority, sent out a punitive force under Pánfilo Narváez. Narváez landed at Vera Cruz and was soon in contact with, amongst others, Montezuma. Cortés had to act quickly: he divided his forces by leaving a garrison in Mexico City while he went off with the bulk of his men to deal with the intruder. With his usual adroitness he won over Narváez's men and added them to his. But in the meantime things had gone badly wrong in Mexico City.

Cortés's lieutenant, Pedro de Alvarado, flaxen-haired and like the sun according to the natives, had been so unnerved by the rising tension within the city that he decided on a pre-emptive slaughter of the Aztec nobility who had gathered in the capital to celebrate a religious festival. The massacre sparked off a general uprising. Cortés returned with all speed to relieve the garrison penned up in the city; but he at once realized that an evacuation was imperative if the Spaniards were to escape from a death trap. The withdrawal took place on the night of 30 June 1520, a date which passed into history as the Noche Triste. In spite of careful planning and much ingenuity, what started as a retreat soon degenerated into a rout. By the time the white men got clear of the city, they were down to 440 men and twenty horses. They left behind 800 of their comrades and all the artillery. The losses amongst the Indian auxiliaries had been huge.

The moment was critical. Cortés depended entirely on his allies, the Tlaxcalans. They did not fail him. With their help he was able to rebuild his army largely through the arrival of fresh volunteers from the island settlements. His previous experience had also taught him that he must establish naval superiority on the lake of Mexico. Failure to do so accounted for the slaughter during the retreat from Tenochtitlán. With this in mind Cortés ordered the shipwright Martín López, who had fortunately survived the Noche Triste, to construct thirteen bergantines. These were assembled on Tlaxcalan soil, tested on the Zahuapan River, and then dismantled. They were carried overland and finally re-assembled on the shore of the lake of Mexico. The tackle for the flotilla came from the blocks and rigging of Cortés's ships which had landed the year before at Vera Cruz; and any other ships he had managed to get his hands on in the meantime. With the launching of his navy (some one and a half miles above sea level) and the steady influx of white recruits, Cortés felt ready to complete the task which had seemed deceptively easy the year before. The siege of Tenochtitlán began at the end of May and ended some eighty days later on 13 August, 1521. The city was eventually starved out; but before it fell, most of the buildings had been razed and a large part of the population had perished.

A number of factors besides the audacity of Cortés and the bravery of his men enabled the Spaniards to destroy the Aztec Confederacy. Technology is an obvious one. The native armies used weapons fashioned out of wood and stone. These, while capable of inflicting ugly wounds under certain circumstances, were of little use against steel and gunpowder in the hands of troops decently led. The military tactics similarly differed: the Aztec soldier aimed to capture his opponent with a view to human sacrifice; the Spaniard killed to survive. But ultimately the white man owed his triumph not so much to his own exertions or his superior equipment as to the active colla-boration on the part of the tribes subject to the Aztec Confederacy. They provided the guides, the provisions, and the porters which had made possible Cortés's initial march from the sea to the Aztec capital; their unwavering support preserved the Spaniards after the disaster of the Noche Triste; and their resources, material and military, so willingly provided, enabled Cortés to mount the decisive assault on Mexico City. Perhaps the Aztec Confederacy succumbed because it had failed to knit together either by absorption or coercion the various tribes over which it exercised suzerainty, an example of incomplete state formation; or perhaps, providentially for Cortés, the detestation felt by the subject peoples towards Tenochtitlán and the imperial cult of the Hummingbird blinded them to any consideration other than the destruction of the Aztec state.

After the violence of the conquest, Cortés demonstrated a rare understanding of native society. From the outset he grasped that it was essential to identify the new with the old, hence the need to impress upon the Indians that the white men were the legitimate heirs of their former overlords. For this reason, and against expert advice, he chose Tenochtitlán as the capital of the colony. The city had stood at the centre of the Aztec universe; and the new foundation, the hub of government and a focus of loyalty, was intended to stress the idea of unbroken continuity.

Similarly Cortés did all in his power to retain the native system of administration. The conquerors were anxious to inherit the style and privileges of the former ruling élite, not to overturn society. Nowhere was this more evident than in the case of taxation. Under the Aztecs the land had been divided up into a number of districts. Each unit had a regional capital where the local chief, who was responsible for collection, held his court. Once the Spaniards had established firm control they preserved the structure they had inherited. For much of the sixteenth century the Indian chief continued to supervise the labour force of his district and to gather the tribute in kind; but now he did so on behalf of a Spanish overlord, often an *encomendero*. It was not until the end of the century that the preconquest system of taxation started to buckle under the enormous pressures exerted upon it.

To keep the native society unchanged, however desirable in theory, was shown to be clearly impossible almost from the first days of the conquest. The white man, by his very presence, introduced a disruptive element. Cortés's followers insisted that their efforts and privations should be suitably recognized. A share of the plunder taken from the temples and palaces of Tenochtitlán was enough for some; but the more ambitious looked for something more substantial, above all an *encomienda*. Under the terms of this grant, an individual received tribute (usually in kind) and labour dues from a specific area, often a former Aztec tax district. In return, the beneficiary of an *encomienda* was expected to provide for the physical safety and spiritual well-being of those assigned to him. As an institution the *encomienda* implied no right whatsoever to the ownership of land. Fearing the establishment of an independent aristocracy in the New World, the crown had expressly forbidden the creation of *encomiendas*. The prohibition remained, for all that, a dead letter. Cortés had begun to make such grants by 1522, if not earlier, on the grounds that he had to satisfy his men and secure the colony. When he returned to Spain in 1528 he was able to argue the case in person; and, perhaps as a result of his advocacy, the crown agreed to the endorsement and continuation of the policy. Yet the sanction had been given without enthusiasm.

In 1542 the emperor, Charles V, had second thoughts. The New Laws published in that year threatened severely to curtail the *encomienda* in Mexico and abolish it altogether in Peru. The outcry was such that the crown was compelled to beat a retreat, if only to secure the loyalty of the colonists who seemed on the point of rebellion in New Spain and actually rose in the southern viceroyalty. The authorities allowed the *encomiendas* to remain but with a number of vital modifications. After 1550 the beneficiary (*encomendero*) continued to receive tribute in kind; he was not entitled to ask for labour service or to claim any other legal right. Although extensions to the life of the *encomiendas* were periodically conceded into the next century, the institution had been effectively undermined. For the permanent conquest of the soil the settlers resorted to alternative, and more effective, methods such as the landed estate and debt peonage.

The *encomienda* conferred on Hernán Cortés surpassed all others, even if it did represent a reduction in the grant the conqueror had initially awarded himself. After interminable legislation (which was not concluded until 1560) the crown settled on his family over 50,000 vassals. The marquisate in the Morelos, as the donation was called, was not only larger than any comparable grant, most had no more than 2,000 vassals, it also had civil and criminal jurisdiction, rights which the crown had carefully withheld from the normal *encomienda*. What made it virtually unique was the privilege whereby the family were to hold in perpetuity all the concessions made to them. Only the daughters of Montezuma had been shown comparable favour. In this instance, the crown treated the descendants of conqueror and conquered with an even hand.

Few of the white settlers could reasonably expect to live from the tribute and labour of the Indians. On the northern frontier there were not enough of them; and where, further south, settled communities did exist in any number they could only cover part of the white man's requirements in terms of agricultural products. The spread of plague introduced by the colonists had devastating effects on Indian settlements and made the idea of a parasitic white élite relying exclusively on the efforts of the indigenous population still more impracticable. The first colonists brought in economic forms familiar in their homeland but new to Mexico. Of these the cattle ranch was undoubtedly the most important. Geography and the pattern of human settlement favoured the importation. The Indian communities cultivated their staple crop, maize, in small plots away from the open range; while on the northern frontier the absence of a sedentary population made stock-raising both inevitable and ideal. Once horned cattle had been introduced they multiplied at an astonishing rate on land never before grazed by ruminant animals of the European type. Ranching had many advantages: it did not require extensive manpower; it produced meat in such abundance that beef, the primary product, became the staple of even the poorest white—and later, indeed, of the Indian tribes themselves; and lastly it provided the only export of consequence apart from silver, hides.

Cattle breeding also led to the development of private property in New Spain. Town councils, the majority of which were composed of stockmen, leased out, or simply assigned for a specified period, municipal lands for use as pasture. Over time these leases or temporary allocations were converted into private possessions; or, just as often, land was usurped outright with little regard for the conventions. Indian communities whose ownership of the plots they tended had been recognized by the crown were induced to part with their lands usually for cash, although royal officials fought tooth and nail to prevent such sales. On the frontier, where the crown's authority was little more than nominal, the cattle barons exercised effective control over the land whatever the law might say. The monarch himself gradually came to terms with the growth of private estates. In 1591 an ever more penurious crown agreed to pardon the illegal acquisition of land on payment of a fine. By accepting money it acknowledged the existence of private property as an institution.

The classical economy of New Spain during the colonial period rested on two activities, stock raising and mining, the two being intimately linked. The Spanish explorers came to the New World to make their fortunes; and by wealth they imagined the mounds of gold, silver, and jewels as described in the highly fanciful novels of chivalry so popular at the time. Don Quixote was not the only knight to lose his wits at the prospect. On the larger islands of the Antilles the settlers had come across alluvial gold which they had set the natives to pan. Then they located small pockets of precious minerals, mostly gold. The first miners extracted the ore by setting up a makeshift camp and sinking a primitive shaft—the process known as placer mining.

Once the Aztec empire had been overthrown, the new masters of the land set about discovering the source of the silver which had been used so lavishly in the decoration of both private and public buildings. In 1546 a small reconnaissance party set up a temporary camp at a place called Zacatecas; two years later a rich vein of silver was located nearby. It was a major strike and it guaranteed profitable working for decades to come. Zacatecas became the mining capital of the territory—a '*real de minas*'—with a permanent community to serve its needs. Subsequent prospecting led to the discovery of rich silver lodes at Fresnillo in 1554 and at Santa Bárbara, fully 1,500 kilometres distant from Mexico City, in 1567. In the case of Santa Bárbara the true potential of the region did not become apparent until the 1630s; while further north still the Parral district produced a silver bonanza in the 1650s when silver mining elsewhere had declined severely.

The mines stimulated cattle ranching and were in turn sustained by it. Mining settlements were located for the most part in the arid lands of the northern frontier. Recruitment of labour and the provision of food were major problems. To be successful, the mine owner had to become a rancher if only to keep his workforce alive and the mine in running order. The ranch produced beef; and in areas where enterprise had been shown as in the region of Santa Bárbara ranching encouraged the cultivation of fruit and vegetables. The by-products of cattle were as important as the meat. Tallow served to illuminate the undergound shafts. Animal fat lubricated axles and machinery. Leather provided material for the clothing and the sacking used by the miners. The capital costs of ranching were often, but not always, borne by successful miners who might then plough back any profits into the mines. In the seventeenth century the profitability of the silver workings slumped in many of the established mines; and this led to a slackening of the bonds between cattle herding and mining. The ranches, according to one reading, drew in on themselves and became autarkic commonwealths.

The establishment of a settled economy hinged upon the stabilization of the frontiers and the imposition of internal peace. This took the best part of a century to achieve. With the destruction of Tenochtitlán completed, Spanish expeditions spread out in all directions like so many points of a star. Cortés himself led an army into Honduras (1524–6), a mission which greatly extended geographical knowledge even if it did not produce the anticipated plunder. His lieutenant, Pedro de Alvarado, conquered the region of present-day Guatemala, another episode in the course of his eventful and violent life. Cortés's enemy, Nuño de Guzmán, president of the first *audiencia* of Mexico, retired in 1529 to conquer the Pacific coastline of Mexico, the region of New Galicia. Later in the century the 'phoenix of the conquistadores', Francisco de Ibarra, secured the north-eastern lands bordering the Gulf of Mexico, the province known as New Biscay. All these expeditions were financed and carried out in the expectation of profit; and every leader believed that another Tenochtitlán or Cuzco beckoned just beyond the horizon.

Gradually the realization dawned that there were no great kingdoms to be overthrown. All the intrepid explorer could expect to find was hardship, little spoil, and, probably, an early death. The lesson was driven home by the story of Francisco Vázquez Coronado and his fruitless quest for the Seven Cities of Cíbola. In the course of a memorable expedition (1540–1) Coronado led his men across an area now covered by Arizona, New Mexico, and Colorado. A detachment from the main force, commanded by Coronado in person, pushed on into the Kansas valley. No rich cities were discovered; and Coronado retired to Mexico to face charges of misconduct and the inescapable conclusion that his efforts had been pointless. Another expedition, undertaken at the same time as Coronado's, confirmed the message even more strikingly. Hernando de Soto, a veteran of the Peruvian campaigns, landed in Florida in May, 1539, and led his party inland. For the best part of a year (1541–2), de Soto and his men wandered on an uncertain course through Louisiana and Arkansas. They failed to locate any gold or silver, although they did, quite incidentally, discover the Mississippi. Hernando de Soto died in the late spring of 1542, of disease or mortification, and the survivors of his party struggled back to Mexico in the following year.

Between them Coronado and de Soto demonstrated a simple truth. There were no more indigenous civilizations to be plundered; the age of rapine was over. They also restated a message which was just as unwelcome. To strip New Spain of able-bodied men in pursuit of chimerical schemes was to court disaster. While the two expeditions were being planned and executed, tribes from the unconquered north had been moving southwards. One of their objectives was to persuade the southern people to rise against their white masters. Circumstances favoured a revolt. The sedentary nations of the south resented the *encomiendas*, recently imposed and as onerous as anything that had gone before. They were also in the grip of a revivalist movement which sought to expel the Christian priests and bring back the old gods. Economic and religious discontent combined to produce the Mixton War (1540–1), the most serious and widespread of the early native rebellions. At first the Spaniards thought they faced nothing more than a little local difficulty. But the death of Pedro de Alvarado soon convinced them that here was a movement that would test all the military resources of the province. Antonio de Mendoza, the first viceroy (1535–50), called on every available levy to undertake what has been termed 'the second conquest of Mexico'. Success in the Mixton War secured one part of the frontier for the colonists; stability along its entire length did not come for another sixty years.

The lure of precious minerals drew the bolder spirits into the regions beyond the borders of the viceroyalty. Mining settlements came to fulfil a dual purpose; they extracted ore and they served as advanced posts. The frontier, such as it was, hinged on the mining towns. The distance between these camps and the centres of government caused difficulties; and nowhere was this more so than in the case of Zacatecas. The link between Mexico City and Zacatecas ran through a wilderness with the descriptive name of the Empty Land (*el Despoblado*). Roving bands of Indians, their mobility increased through mastery of the horse, made the road connecting Zacatecas to the outside world anxious to receive its silver perilous at the best of times and virtually impassable at others. For half a century (*c*.1550–*c*. 1600) the colonists battled to assert their control over the no-man's-land separating the mines and the areas of secure occupation. A combination of techniques was required. Realizing that the emptiness of the land powerfully aided the marauders, the authorities inaugurated a policy of settlement. Christianized tribes from the interior, including the Tlaxcalans, were brought in and assigned plots. These Indian communities prospered and filled the land, thereby attaching it to Spain and Christianity. Royal officials working closely with the cattle barons also used a policy of selective blandishment. Some of the Indian bands were induced to accept white rule in return for grants of clothing and food, mainly beef; they were then employed on frontier duties running to earth those who refused to submit. In the domestication of the north as in the conquest of Tenochtitlán the most effective instrument at the disposal of the invader was the Indian himself. Divide and rule; one tribe was used to overcome the other; the white man orchestrated the sequence.

The church played a complex role in the initial conquest of Mexico and its subjection to Spain. At one level it acted as an agent of destruction by insisting on the elimination of the cult and shrines which had given the previous civilization its identity; at another it revealed the profound impact of the discovery of a new continent on the received notions of the old world. As the wondrous tale of America unfolded, many Europeans believed that the explorers had come across another Garden of Eden whose inhabitants had retained their primeval innocence, so many Adams before the Fall. This prelapsarian view attracted the mendicant orders in particular; and it coincided with the movement known as the Catholic Reform which sought to renew the spiritual vitality of the Latin church from within. The mendicants had supplied some of the most ardent exponents of the new trend. Cortés showed special favour towards the mendicant orders, the Franciscans even more than the others. In an act fraught with symbolism, twelve Franciscans landed in Mexico in 1524; and they were followed two years later by twelve Dominicans, and later still the Augustinians.

The mendicant orders were determined to carry into practice the ideas of Christian humanism and Catholic Reform under what seemed laboratory conditions. Cortés and his immediate successors promoted these aspirations. Before the arrival of the white man the Indian looked to his religious leaders to determine the appropriate moment for planting and reaping. The priesthood commissioned the building of the great public and religious monuments. The Indian view of the world, being more integrated than its Western equivalent, did not admit of a division between work and leisure. All human activity formed part of a ceremonial system whose regulation was entrusted to the religious authorities. They administered the sacred calendar. The mendicants, unlike the secular clergy who followed, adapted smoothly to this traditional world. They immersed themselves completely in the lives of their new congregations, anxious to shut themselves off as far as possible from the settlers and to shield their charges from contact with white society. Assuming the role of the pagan priesthood, they regulated the daily pattern of their Indian parishes down to the minutest detail. The mendicants also inherited from their predecessors a taste for building on the lavish scale, and indulged it fully. As a result their churches represented the baroque style then fashionable at its most grandiose.

The mendicant attitude towards their Indian flock was paternalist, perhaps even authoritarian. Yet by identifying so closely with existing patterns the friars softened the transition from pre- to post-Columbian society. Where the Indian communities had the good fortune to find themselves in the care of the mendicant orders the 'cultural shock' of the conquest was attenuated, at least in part. The mendicant vision of a new Jerusalem in American lands endured for a generation; then after 1550 the inspiration began to weaken. In 1572 the crown reserved all bishoprics for members of the secular clergy—the first bishop of Mexico, Juan de Zumárraga, had been a Franciscan; while the mendicant orders and the Jesuits (who arrived in that same year, 1572) settled down to a less visionary existence, identifying more with the creole society than with that of the Indians. Only on the distant frontiers, particularly in Lower California, did the friars retain their missionary zeal. The government used their proselytizing energies to Christianize the region and thereby assist in the pacification of the borderlands.

The first century of Spanish occupation was remarkable not so much for the advance of the white man as the decline of the Indian. The vertiginous descent in numbers influenced the history and development of Habsburg Mexico more profoundly than any other factor. Amidst the orgy of destruction which attended the conquest, the invaders took great pains to preserve the pictographic records on which the taxation system was based. Using these same documents, two historians, W. Borah and S. F. Cook, constructed a famous series of population estimates. They suggested that the central Mexican plateau, an area of some 200,000 square miles, may have supported as many as 25.2 million inhabitants in 1519. By 1548 this figure had dropped to 6,300,000; and by 1568, a mere twenty years later, to 2,650,000. The Indian population continued its fall for the rest of the century, although at a slower rate. It reached its floor in 1605 when it stabilized at around 1,075,000. Subsequent examination of the same pictographic records has reduced the estimate for the native population on the eve of the conquest from the improbable level of 25 million to a more acceptable range of between five and ten million. According to the latest projections, numbers fell to approximately 3.6 million by 1548; and to around 2.6 milion by 1568. The two estimates converge thereafter. Controversy over the size of Indian families, and therefore the aggregate Indian population before Cortés landed, cannot obscure the basic fact that the first hundred years of Spanish rule witnessed not so much a contraction as an implosion of Indian numbers.

The demographic collapse, startling but destined to be repeated elsewhere, can be attributed to a variety of causes. The Roman Empire in the West had fallen through a process of peaceful penetration carried on over decades, if not centuries; the Aztec Confederacy disappeared overnight in a welter of blood. Without warning a new order was imposed; and the old landmarks, political, cultural, and monumental, which had framed a way of life were violently overthrown. This 'cultural shock' undermined the resilience of native society. The principal agents of the slaughter were undoubtedly the diseases imported by the white explorers and conquerors. These included smallpox, typhus, measles, influenza, and whooping-cough, a familiar litany in any contemporary European nursery but unknown as yet to the New World.

The consequences of the demographic crisis were far-reaching. The Indian communities could no longer provide for a parasitic *encomendero* class. Against his initial instincts, the white man was driven to base his economy on something more durable than an Indian population fast approaching the point of extinction. The shrinkage in the workforce and the abandonment of land encouraged the replacement of the *encomienda* based on tribute and service by the great estate (*hacienda*) which rested on outright ownership of land and debt peonage. Miners, unable to draft in the able-bodied from amongst the natives, had to bid on the open market for the labour they needed, thereby creating a new class of free wage-earners. In the cities the slow growth of the white population and the rapid contraction of the native may have led to the breakdown of racial barriers and the emergence at the level of artisans and servants of a *mestizo* society.

CHAPTER 6

Control, convoys, and commerce

FROM the earliest days of the voyages to America the crown stood firm on the principle that royal control should be asserted as quickly as possible over all discoveries. The authorities were fully aware that, given the chance, Columbus and his successors would regard the new lands as so much free range from which to carve out their private empires. The Catholic Monarchs moved swiftly to eliminate such a possibility. To aid Columbus in the preparation of his second expedition to the Caribbean they dispatched Juan Rodríguez de Fonseca to Seville. He was confessor to the queen at the time and a man of considerable administrative talent. Fonseca had received instructions to remove all obstacles to the collection of the fleet; but this was only one of his functions, and probably not the most important. He was a royal agent with the task of preserving the monarchy's rights and of supervising Columbus to make sure that he did not infringe them.

As the number of sailings to America multiplied and it became clear that settlement would become permanent, the metropolitan government realized that a standing authority was needed to regulate the traffic and watch over the fledgling colonies. On 20 January 1503, letters patent formally established a House of Trade (Casa de Contratación) modelled closely on the institution which controlled the trade of neighbouring Portugal with the Far East. In recognition of his undoubted ability, if not his amiable character, Juan Rodríguez de Fonseca was named as the first director. As laid down by the royal orders the House of Trade was charged with the administration of the trade and navigation to the transatlantic outposts. It took cognizance of commercial cases arising out of the transport of goods to and from America; it trained and licensed the pilots who sailed the route; and it issued the charts on which they relied.

For a while the House of Trade met all the needs of the scattered settlements. But once the white man set foot on the mainland and began conquering an empire of continental scale the existing system of control soon showed itself inadequate. The changed circumstances required a body which was not commercial but gubernatorial in character. The first reference to the Royal and Supreme Council of the Indies dated from 1519; but its official foundation did not take place until 1 August 1524. As its grandiloquent title indicated, the new Council created the basic structure of government in Spanish America and directed it until the end of the colonial era. The members, acting as a body, advised the crown on appointments to the higher civil and ecclesiastical posts, in effect nominating to the upper echelons of the colonial church and administration. The Council functioned as a supreme appellate court in civil matters as well as enjoying some rights of criminal jurisdiction. And lastly it bore the responsibility for the fitting out of the fleets which sailed annually to New Spain and Tierra Firme (South America).

The Catholic Monarchs chose Seville as the location for both the House of Trade and the Council of the Indies. From the strictly maritime viewpoint, Cadiz would have been better as the anchorage was wide, deep, and relatively well protected from the elements. But Cadiz's superiority as a harbour was largely offset by its isolation from the hinterland and the difficulties of supply. Seville, on the other hand, could call easily on the agricultural surplus of the Guadalquivir basin which could provide virtually all the stores which a ship's chandler might require. This advantage more than compensated for the distance of eighty-four kilometres which separated the town from the sea. Sixteenth-century ships, even those which plied the American route, drew little water, being of reduced tonnage; and as a result were able to negotiate the Guadalquivir as far as Seville without too much difficulty. Although the American trade became identified in the popular imagination with the capital of Andalucía, several other towns, amongst them La Coruña, San Sebastián, and Cartagena, had the right to participate in the trade; but this privilege, publicly conferred in 1529, seems to have been neglected by the intended beneficiaries. Little effort was made by these other ports to develop contacts with the colonies overseas. In 1572 Philip II, acting perhaps solely in the interests of administrative order, declared Seville the only legal terminus of the American trade, a status which it retained, at least in the eyes of the law, until 1717.

At the very outset of the colonial era traders, once they had completed the necessary formalities in Seville, were at liberty to proceed on their way. But from an early date the system of individual sailing revealed itself unsatisfactory because unsafe. Seafarers from other

European countries had followed Castilian ships to the sugar islands of the Azores, Madeira, and the Canaries, often as merchants and, just as frequently, as pirates. Columbus had a brush with French corsairs on his first voyage; and this incident was to set the pattern.

The Valois kings actively encouraged piracy against Spanish colonies and shipping, regarding it as an extension of the land war against the Habsburgs. For that reason French raids reached their peak during the periods of open conflict between the two monarchies. In 1521 a squadron of ships fitted out by the naturalized Frenchman, Jean Ango, captured three caravels returning from the Americas. In the following year an employee of his, Jean Fleury, better known as Juan Florín to his victims, sailed from Dieppe on a cruise which led to the taking of the three ships which were carrying home to Spain Montezuma's treasure and much of the personal spoil amassed by Cortés and his followers. Jean Fleury had participated vicariously in the conquest of Mexico; and the exploit fired the imagination of subsequent French captains who sought to emulate what remained a unique achievement. As the French acquired greater seacraft, the scope and scale of their activities widened, so that from 1543 onwards it became possible to speak of a permanent naval war, a battle of the Caribbean waged between the two powers. During the last phase of the Habsburg—Valois struggle whole flotillas departed from French shores to wreak havoc in the West Indies. In 1554 one band led by François le Clerc, colourfully named Wooden Foot, sacked the major settlement of Santiago de Cuba; and in the following year his countryman Jacques de Sores visited the same treatment on Havana which, for good measure, was looted by another French raiding party a few weeks later. Spanish authorities had additional cause for concern at the appearance of de Sores and his kind. Jacques de Sores was a Huguenot. Simple greed no longer animated the raiders. Ideology gave naval warfare a new meaning as the idea of striking a blow for the faith began to influence the combatants.

Fortunately for Spain the French kings showed a fitful interest in the New World; and after 1562 their attentions were wholly occupied elsewhere. Yet it was precisely at the beginning of the 1560s that the French appeared to pose their gravest threat to the safety of imperial commerce. In 1562 a group of French colonists led by Jean Ribault founded a settlement at Port Royal (St Elena) in Florida; and shortly after René de Laudonnière planted another township at Fort Caroline a few miles away at the mouth of the river May. These two colonies

had a precarious life, as did most of the early foundations in the New
World; and neither was destined to flourish. For once the Spanish
crown was suitably alarmed; and it had on call just the man to deal
with the threat to its vital interests. Pedro Menéndez de Avilés had
spent a lifetime in Caribbean and European waters, sometimes as a
captain in the king's service, and sometimes, just as often, trading on
his private account, that is, as a smuggler. He realized at once the
implications of the French presence in Florida, a concern fully
reciprocated by the monarch. The two entered into a formal agreement for the expulsion of the French and the retention of the
peninsula as a Spanish colony (15 March 1565). Pedro Menéndez
proved as good as his word. He founded a permanent station at St
Agustín (8 September 1565); and twelve days later he fell upon the
unsuspecting French garrison at Fort Caroline. On 12 October 1565,
Jean Ribault, who had been absent from the scene when the Spaniards
attacked, surrendered with what remained of his starving and
demoralized band. Florida had been cleared of interlopers—and for a
long time into the future. Although he stood to gain from the
commercial development of the territory, Pedro Menéndez saw the
occupation of the peninsula, or the eastern shoreline at least, not
merely in terms of personal profit but within the context of a larger
strategic plan. During the course of his distinguished career he had
come to perceive that if the Spaniards were to make a reality out of
their high-flown claims to a trading monopoly in the Caribbean, then
royal forces must control both the entrance and the exit to this
Mediterranean of the Americas. In effect, the crown must will the
means to maintain squadrons which would regularly sweep the two
points of entry, the Windward and the Mona Passages; and it would
also have to subsidize another naval force to cruise the Florida
Channel, the point of exit. Should any intruder breach the first line of
defence he would have to run the gauntlet of the Florida patrol before
he could return to Europe to boast of his trespass. For all their
strategic insight, Pedro Menéndez's proposals were not taken up.
Protection of the Caribbean ranked low in the list of imperial priorities; lower, it has been claimed, than the upkeep of the postal service.

Yet the ideas of Pedro Menéndez and his contemporary, the
shipowner Alvaro de Bazán, did have a profound influence on another
aspect of imperial defence. Royal officials had appreciated as quickly
as others that individual merchantmen, undergunned and ponderous,
had little chance against a determined enemy. The concentration of

vessels into annual fleets went a long way towards deterring the corsairs; and this practice had the further merit of tightening government control over the flow of trade and its composition. As the crown disposed of few, if any, ships of its own, it had to lease vessels with suitably reinforced armaments to provide the necessary escorts. This took money; and there was none to spare from normal sources. To raise what was needed, the monarch imposed a tax calculated on the value of the outward-bound cargos. This levy *ad valorem*, first collected in 1521, moved within the range of 5 per cent to 10 per cent. For roughly twenty years the Castilian authorities experimented with various forms of convoys while permitting at the same time the old custom of individual voyages. Then, in 1543, something which approximated to the classic pattern of convoys emerged, probably as a response to another period of conflict with France. Yet it required another two decades before the system, which had been accepted in principle long before, acquired the form which it was to retain until the twilight of colonial rule.

The famous ordinances governing commerce with America, issued on 18 October 1564, incorporated the advice given over the previous half century by men like Pedro Menéndez and Alvaro de Bazán. The convoy became the only legitimate means through which trade could be conducted with the New World. Such a policy had been urged upon the crown by the experts; and it now received the weight of law. Two fleets carried the entire commerce of Europe with America; that, at any rate, was the intention of the ordinances. The first, the fleet of New Spain (Mexico), was expected to sail in April, a date pushed back in 1582 to May; and its complement, that of Tierra Firme (South America), was to weigh anchor in August. For much of the outward voyage the two 'flotas' followed the same route. The ships left San Lúcar de Barrameda at the mouth of the Guadalquivir and made first for the Canaries, where minor repairs were carried out and water replenished. Then the helmsmen set a westerly course as the Canaries current flowed westwards to the Americas. From the Canaries to the Lesser Antilles, the first landfall in the New World, took about four weeks. Most fleets, whatever their ultimate destination, entered the Caribbean through the Mona Passage; but once this had been negotiated safely their paths diverged. The convoy for New Spain edged its way along the coastline of the Greater Antilles, Puerto Rico, Hispaniola, and Cuba as it made its way towards Vera Cruz on the mainland of Mexico. That of Tierra Firme struck southwards towards

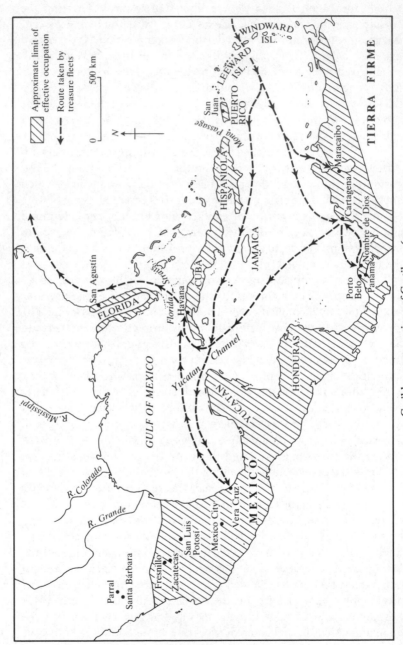

4 Caribbean possessions of Castile c.1600

Legend:
Approximate limit of effective occupation
Route taken by treasure fleets

0   500 km

N

Map labels:
WINDWARD ISL.
LEEWARD ISL.
San Juan
PUERTO RICO
Mona Passage
HISPANIOLA
JAMAICA
CUBA
Havana
Florida Straits
Yucatan Channel
FLORIDA
San Agustín
GULF OF MEXICO
R. Mississippi
R. Colorado
R. Grande
Parral
Santa Bárbara
Fresnillo
Zacatecas
San Luis Potosí
Mexico City
Vera Cruz
MEXICO
YUCATAN
HONDURAS
Panama
Porto Belo
Nombre de Dios
Cartagena
Maracaibo
TIERRA FIRME

Río de la Hacha and the towns of the Colombian coast before reaching the end of the voyage at Nombre de Dios on the isthmus of Panama. The regulations of 1564 ordered both fleets to winter in the Americas. That of New Spain rode at anchor in the deep and well-protected port of Vera Cruz; while the vessels of the southern fleet stayed just long enough on the open roadstead of Nombre de Dios to load the bullion from Peru which had been hauled laboriously across the isthmus from the town of Panama and then retreated to the safer anchorage of Cartagena de Indias (Colombia). In many respects the return of the convoys caused the authorities greater concern than the outward passage, and for a very good reason. If all had gone well, if the weather held, if the ships were undamaged, if colonial officials had shown only the normal degree of incompetence, then the fleet of New Spain left Mexican waters carrying in its holds the silver which represented the public and private profit of the viceroyalty. Its companion, the convoy of Tierra Firme, had taken aboard during its hazardous stay off the lee shore of Nombre de Dios the bullion chests which contained the taxes and personal remittances from Peru. Both fleets, therefore, set out on the return voyage with freight smaller in volume than their original cargoes but infinitely more precious in value. They offered a prize worthy of the pirate daring and skilful enough to break through the defensive screen. Fully aware of the temptation, the Council of the Indies insisted that the two convoys should rendezvous each year early in the spring at Havana; and from here, as a united force, they were to make the dangerous passage along the North American coastline before setting a fresh course for the Azores and home.

The ordinances of 1564 left little to chance and less to the initiative of the ships' masters. As well as prescribing sailing times and courses to be steered, those who drafted the regulations sought to impose a similar rigidity on the order to be observed by the vessels in transit and the tactics to be used by the escort. The duties of shepherding the merchantmen were to be shared between the flagship (the *capitana*) and the vessel commanded by the vice-admiral (the *almiranta*). The former took up station at the head of the convoy; and the individual ships astern were instructed to set their own courses either by its flag (during the day) or a great lantern hung on the stern for the purpose (by night). The *almiranta* sailed to the rear bringing up the stragglers. Needless to say, most of the regulations laid out by the armchair mariners were more frequently flouted than observed. Fleets seldom got away on time; the flags and lanterns which must have seemed so

sensible to a landlubber would not have survived for long in an
Atlantic gale; and the union of the silver argosies in the harbour of
Havana took place only in times of mortal peril. But for all the ridicule
which has been heaped on the workings of the convoys, the fact
remains that the system achieved its purpose. Very few of the
homeward-bound galleons fell prey to the corsairs. The lifeline held,
thus securing, at a high cost, the bullion on which so many commitments depended.

Crown agencies had a fair measure of success in fending off the
privateers and filibusters who haunted the sea-lanes; but they were
virtually powerless to preserve the monarchy from the depredations of
its own servants. Throughout its history the American trade was
riddled from top to bottom with fraud. The phenomenon can be
ascribed to a variety of causes. The sudden access of wealth, especially
in the portable form of ingots, unhinged the morals of those connected
with its production, transport, and registration, a situation analogous
perhaps to that created by the discovery of oil in a Third World state.
Nor did the imperial administration dispose of enough men to enforce
even basic standards. Royal officials were few in number and almost
invariably badly paid. But the main stimulus to corruption came from
the Habsburgs themselves who forced the merchants to resort to
underhand dealings if they wished to survive. Stated simply, the crown
could not resist the attraction of impounding and diverting to its own
purposes the private remittances from America. Charles V began and
then established the pernicious habit of appropriating private funds.
He resorted to the device on six occasions (1523, 1535, 1538, 1545, 1553,
1555); and his son consolidated the practice (1556, 1557, 1558, 1566,
1577, 1583, 1587, 1590, 1596). On occasions royal officials merely confiscated part of the bullion remitted on private account, and on others
the entirety. Theoretically, the merchants did not suffer loss as the
crown issued state bonds (*juros*) to cover what had been taken. Since,
in practice, the bonds depreciated from the moment of issue, they
could hardly be considered adequate compensation for the money
sequestered. In many ways, it is surprising that the American trade
survived the attentions of a monarchy which began by seizing private
monies for individual projects such as the conquest of Tunis (1535)
and then progressed to serial confiscations in the 1550s. The trading
community in Seville took great pains to see that it was informed
about the likelihood of a seizure; and when it knew that one was in the
offing it redoubled its efforts to repatriate funds illegally. This was not

difficult, although it did require planning. Success demanded resource, and confidence in the corruptibility of man. The merchants might try bribery at the highest level—the court itself. They could also come to some arrangement with the High Admiral of a returning convoy or the officers serving aboard the escort. Such understandings marked virtually every voyage; and led at times to embarrassing incidents. In 1555 a fleet returning from the New World was wrecked on the Zahara coast as it was almost within sight of home. Salvage crews working on the flagship just before it broke up discovered between its planking double the amount of silver recorded in the official registers.

If those charged with the protection of the convoys proved unaccommodating (somebody had bribed them) this could be regarded as a temporary setback. Private remittances could be safe-guarded by other ways. A vessel, even the flagship or its companion the *almiranta*, might spring a leak and find itself obliged to put into the Azores or a port on the Portuguese mainland for emergency repairs. If this strategem were considered too obvious, other methods could be employed to escape the attention of the authorities. Illegal or un-registered shipments of bullion were often transferred at sea to awaiting lighters. Cape St Vincent provided the ideal location for such clandestine operations, as indeed did most of Castile's Atlantic coastline. Should all else fail, crew members might be encouraged simply to walk off the ship with unregistered ingots in their pockets as happened in 1593, although on this occasion the customs had been tipped off and were waiting. Fraud, or, to use a more neutral descrip-tion, the determination to circumvent an arbitrary set of rules, had an all-pervasive influence on the American trade, often with unexpected consequences. Smuggling, peculation, malversation, and assorted practices seriously impaired the accuracy of the official figures relating to the volume and the value of transatlantic commerce. The statistics drawn up by such bodies as the House of Trade and the royal mint in Seville can be regarded only as rough approximations, useful as indicators of general trends but unreliable in matters of exact worth. This represented the negative aspect of frauds. It had at the same time a much more positive function. Had the merchants not disposed of means by which they could repatriate their profits intact, commercial relations would have been severely curtailed, perhaps even, at certain periods, have collapsed altogether. The ingenuity of the merchant fraternity and the venality of crown functionaries prevented this, thereby preserving a source of immense profit to the crown and more modest gain for the traders.

If the laws had been observed, the outward bound cargoes would have been of Castilian provenance. That was the main purpose behind the declaration of a trading monopoly. For nearly a century practice and regulation may well have coincided. The white colonists showed themselves reluctant to cultivate the basic essentials. Until the decade 1580–90 such Andalusian products as oil, wine, and wheat made up the bulk of the freight shipped out of Seville. The fundamental change came about during the last quarter of the sixteenth century. Spanish immigrants at last adjusted to their new surroundings: they developed a taste for such grains as maize, a native of America, and they successfully introduced to the colonial environment many of the staple European crops. Demand switched to a new range of goods. The white élite now sought the fine textiles which only the looms of northern France and the Low Countries could supply. In 1595 one contemporary, Gaitán de Ayala, claimed that goods of Flemish origin constituted the 'principal element' in the consignments for America, and that no alternative source of supply existed. The claim, although exaggerated, underlined an important truth. Foreign involvement in the American trade did not begin in the last years of the sixteenth century. The ubiquitous Genoese funded the early voyages of exploration and had subsequently advanced credit to merchants from Seville who sought to supply the American market. There was little which might be considered untoward in these activities, given the financial expertise of the Genoese bankers and their legal right to trade throughout the Habsburg dominions. The authorities had a much more justifiable cause for alarm at the changes which came about during the second half of Philip II's reign. Increasingly Castile failed to meet the import requirements of its own colonies. To sustain the trade, the government found itself obliged to condone the annexation of American commerce by foreign powers which were, as often as not, politically unfriendly. The economic consequences were profound. Castile became, whatever the law might claim, a bystander, its role confined to providing shipping agents to foreign concerns in order that the formal requirements might be satisfied. A number of European countries, in particular France and the Dutch Republic, became the main suppliers to the American trade; and they, not the subjects of His Most Catholic Majesty, reaped the benefits.

Much of the cargo space on board the outward-bound fleets was occupied by finished goods of alien manufacture; but the crown did retain control over one highly prized export, mercury. Without this fluid metal much less silver would have been recovered from the ore, to the loss of the mining entrepreneur and the royal exchequer. Tradition has credited Bartolomé de Medina, a merchant from Seville, with the introduction of the mercury amalgamation process to the New World. After 1554, the year of Bartolomé de Medina's successful experiment, the output of the Mexican mines came to depend on the supply of mercury; and the same happened in Peru when in 1572 the viceroy sponsored the new method of recovery. The crown obtained the quicksilver which it sold to the miners from three sources, namely, Almadén in southern Spain, Idria on the Dalmatian coast (although this was not a major supplier), and from Huancavélica in Peru. During the sixteenth century Almadén, supplemented by the output of the Idrian mines, satisfied the requirements of New Spain (Mexico), while Huancavélica met the needs of the Peruvian industry. This arrangement was disrupted in the seventeenth century when supplies of Peruvian mercury had to be diverted for use in Mexico. In the eighteenth century levels of output from Almadén were restored and went on to reach new heights. The production of Mexican silver soared in company thereby reaffirming the causal relationship. In all it has been calculated that Almadén provided 16,709.9 tons of mercury in the period 1561–1700. To this should be added 880.8 tons from the Idrian mines. Even when added together these European sources fell far short of the output recorded for Huancavélica which in the same period produced over 30,000 tons of mercury. This imbalance explains why Peruvian silver, not Mexican, dominated the output of the New World from the reign of Philip II to the end of the Habsburg dynasty (*c*.1570–*c*.1700).

During the first century and a half of occupation the Spaniards created what might be described as an extractive empire. The mineral wealth which was located in geological formations of comparable depth and age in the two viceroyalties provided the colonists with their chief export, and thereby the means to purchase both life and luxury. How much silver and gold was mined and smelted? Official estimates for the period 1503–1660 put the figure at approximately 181 tons of gold and 16,887 tons of silver. If the real levels of output were known, these figures would in all probability appear daringly conservative. It has been suggested recently that the official estimates should be adjusted to give a total of 300 tons of gold and 29,000 tons of silver. Not all the bullion found its way to Europe. Some the colonists retained for use as coinage, jewellery, and ornamentation. An unknown quantity drained away to the Far East which (then as now) paid higher prices for silver. In theory the trade between Mexico and the Philippine Islands should have been tightly regulated, a limited amount of silver for a specified quantity of Chinese silks and porcelain. But here, as in every branch of the administration, the rules only existed to be broken.

The exploitation of American mineral wealth falls into a number of phases. Initially, the conquerors appropriated the precious metals, notably gold, which had accumulated over the many centuries before their arrival. Montezuma's treasure and the ransom paid by Atahualpa provided dazzling examples of ancestral accumulation; and the narratives of the conquest provide many instances of how temple roofs were stripped of their precious coverings and how valuable objects were looted from desecrated sanctuaries either to be melted down or broken up. This 'robber' phase lasted from the advent of Columbus to the consolidation of Spanish control over Middle America (1492–1530); and it may have yielded between 30 and 40 tons of gold. Once the Spaniards had established themselves firmly on the mainland they quickly graduated from the theft of ancestral stocks to direct mining. This was an experience common to both Mexico and Peru. In terms of output Mexico produced the bulk of American silver from 1540 until 1575. Thereafter the southern viceroyalty overhauled it as the major supplier, a lead which it was to retain until the end of the Habsburg period (1700). The latest estimates of Spanish trade with America suggest that New Spain (Mexico) provided 36.5 per cent and Tierra Firme (in effect Colombia and Peru) 60 per cent of the total bullion received by the royal treasury in Spain for the period 1555 to 1600. In 1595 the frigate *Magdalena* safely transported the largest single cargo of bullion carried across the Atlantic in the sixteenth century. It brought to Spain precious metal worth 2,195,302 ducats, all, appropriately, from South America. From the standpoint of royal profit, Peru, and not Mexico with its more developed economic structure, was of far greater value to the Habsburg monarchy.

The impact of the New World on the European economy provoked intense debate from the middle of the sixteenth century onwards; and the controversy has never flagged since. In general terms it has been argued that the opening of the new continent and extraction of its riches boosted the level of economic activity in the Old World during the 'long' sixteenth century. Had it not been for the stimulus generated by America both as a source of additional circulating media (gold and silver) and as a market for European goods, the upswing of this period would neither have occurred so early nor lasted so long. The discovery of the New World spared Europe a lengthy depression necessary to accumulate the savings, in the form of existing bullion from European sources, required to fuel any subsequent expansion of trade. To this extent, the conquest of Middle and South America proved an uncovenanted blessing.

In the case of the Iberian peninsula, the benefits were far from obvious. On the credit side, the colonies could be acquitted of the charge that they caused inflation. Although internal prices rose four-fold during the sixteenth century, modest by the standards of contemporary Europe (not to mention South America), the increase can be attributed to factors other than bullion imports. The price index for Spanish prices recorded its steepest climb during the first half of the sixteenth century, that is, before the precious metals started to arrive in a regular flood. Population pressure within the Iberian peninsula led to a rise in the price of food which started inflation and drove it on its way.

Remittances and royal taxes from the Americas in the second half of the sixteenth century had a marginal effect on domestic (i.e. Castilian) inflation. On the commercial account, a rising percentage of the money sent back from the colonies found its way to foreign suppliers, not Castilian manufacturers. As for the crown's share, once it had been officially registered in the House of Trade, it was hurriedly transferred to awaiting galleys, Genoese usually, for shipment to Italy; and from there it was distributed throughout Europe in payment, however partial, of gigantic debts. Little of the American bullion entered the Castilian money supply; and such precious metal as did find its way into the internal circuit was frequently used for the making of jewellery or church ornaments—thesaurized, in the technical term. If Castile had shown a greater ability to satisfy colonial demand for finished goods, local industry could have flourished. If the monarchy had chosen to retain more of the profits from American taxation within the peninsula, then activities dependent on conspicuous consumption such as the building trade might have received a powerful stimulus. Neither happened. The causes of inflation are to be found elsewhere.

Although a pioneer in terms of governing overseas conquests,

Castile was unable to exploit her colonies as successfully as the Dutch
or the English. Royal administrators, and Philip II on a number of
occasions, openly voiced their intention of preserving a monopoly of
imperial trade. This proved to be little more than an empty expression since Castile could not provide what the colonies required. The
profits of the trade were not folded back into the Castilian economy.
They went, instead, to enrich others.

The Dutch and the English excluded third parties from trade with
their settlements in order to increase the power of their respective
states. They saw in such a policy the means to expand the mercantile
marine and with it the supply of trained manpower. Overseas trade
was looked upon as a 'nursery of seamen' and the creator of a deep sea
fleet. The Navigation Acts called into being the tonnage and crews on
which the English fleets of the eighteenth century relied; and they
were, therefore, instrumental in securing English naval supremacy.
Much of the thinking behind this legislation had been anticipated by
Castilian administrators; but the contrast between the Iberian and the
English performance could not have been more apparent. Far from
strengthening the state, the colonial trade placed an additional burden
on Habsburg resources. Basque shipyards consistently failed to
produce ships to the design and quantity demanded by the transatlantic crossing. Iberian builders did not hit upon an equivalent to
the Dutch fly-boat. Commerce with the New World, far from
increasing the stock of ships, diminished the supply. A recent calculation places the figure for the number of ships to make the outward
bound journey in the perid 1504 to 1650 at 10,635. Of these only 7,332
(68.9 per cent) returned. A variety of reasons account for this steady
loss. Storm damage and shipwreck claimed a high toll; while the
colonies had yet to develop, in the Habsburg period, such bulk
commodities as tobacco and sugar with which to fill the cargo space
on the homeward voyage and thereby make it profitable.

Yet a crying need existed both within the Caribbean and the
Atlantic routes for stoutly built ships. The proof of this lay in the fact
that many ships from Europe were broken up on their arrival in the
New World, their spars and tackle to be cannibalized for use on other
vessels. It was not until the end of the seventeenth century that Cuban
yards began to turn out a limited supply of fast frigates. Nor was the
shortage of raw materials a constraining factor. Colonial shipwrights
had at their disposal in the Greater Antilles, especially Cuba, stands of
timber comparable, if on a smaller scale, to the forests of New

England. The crown, however, did not make a point of encouraging the preservation of trees suitable for shipbuilding by adopting a scheme similar to that of the King's Broad Arrow. Deficiencies in organization prevented the colonial government from capitalizing upon its potential advantages.

Some have argued that the Iberian conquest of the New World represents a decisive phase in the extension of European economic control over the entire globe. The indigenous empires of the Americas had functioned without reference to European needs or methods. Indeed, the Peruvian economy had been so regulated that it operated without the invention of money. Conquest brought the new continent within the orbit of the old. The white man set about transforming native society with his own ends exclusively in mind. Mining and then ranching became the central preoccupations of the colonial economy. The primary sector was developed, virtually to the neglect of all else, to provide exports to the European market. These took the form of bullion, then, in the later colonial period, hides and sugar, both bulk commodities which complemented the silver output. The Spanish conquest inaugurated the economic subordination of Middle and South America to external markets, a condition from which neither has subsequently escaped.

The fact that the initial exploitation of the New World was carried out by Spain and Portugal contributed a key element to this dependence. The two Iberian powers were themselves primary producers, dependent on others. They exported fish, salt, and wool to their northern neighbours in return for finished goods. The industrial weakness of Spain and Portugal made the connection of the American to the European economy inevitable, since neither could meet the demands of their colonists unaided. Had the *comuneros* succeeded in building up a Castilian textile industry, the story might have differed, at least in detail. They did not; and Castile stood by, virtually powerless, as others gathered up the profits of empire, and secured colonial resources to meet their own needs.

CHAPTER 7

The conquest and settlement of Peru

IN THE century before Columbus set out on his first voyage the American continent produced two indigenous civilizations which achieved a degree of social complexity and political sophistication remarkable even by contemporary standards. The Inca state came into being at roughly the same time as the Aztec Confederacy; and the history of this South American empire can be compared profitably at many points with its Mesoamerican counterpart. Both were recent in terms of territorial composition; both failed to create internal cohesion by assimilating all the subject peoples; and each fell to a handful of Spanish adventurers.

Geography, above all else, determined the character of historic Peru. The Inca empire at its height included three broad but distinct zones: the von Humboldt current kept the arid coastal plain dry but cool; the Indian population flourished at its densest on the high plateaux of the Andes; while the prevailing easterlies were responsible for turning the slopes of the *montaña* into a tropical rain-forest. The Inca state had its origins in the Andean highlands. During the fifteenth century the tribe of that name mastered the immediate surroundings of Cuzco and then extended its authority to the valleys of the Apurimac, the Urubamba, and beyond. As their dominions expanded, the Incas drew on the techniques of government developed by previous Andean kingdoms. At the death of its last great ruler, Huayna Capac (1493–1525), 'the Land of the Four Quarters' (Tawantinsuyu), the name given to the Inca state by its native rulers, stretched from Quito in the north to the river Maule in the south. It was Andean in length and scale.

The conquest of virtually the entire southern Cordillera in less than a century attested to the military and organizational skills of the Incas. Yet the achievement, by its very rapidity, carried with it a number of penalties. The last undisputed ruler, Huayna Capac, spent much of his reign campaigning in the region of what is now Ecuador. To consolidate his hold on 'the kingdom of Quito', as the chroniclers called

N

Santa
Marta
Cartagena
Panama
Bogota
R. Orinoco
Quito
Tumbes
R. Amazon
Lima
Cuzco
Potosi
R. Pilcomayo
R. Salado
Valparaiso
R. Maule
Buenos
Aires
R. Plate
Valdivia

A N D E S

▨▨▨ Approximate extent
of Spanish control

▬ ▬ Route of fleet bringing
Peruvian bullion
to Panama

0   1000 km

5 The viceroyalty of Peru *c*.1600

it, he founded a second capital, Tumipampa—an Inca version of Constantinople. The new city, however, instead of proving a source of strength, disrupted the smooth operation of government. The imperial highways, with their system of staging-posts and teams of runners on permanent stand-by, were justly famous; but it still took time for a message to travel from Tumipampa to Cuzco and for a reply to be received. Distance, if nothing else, made it difficult to administer Cuzco and the southern provinces which still formed the heartland of the empire.

The reduction in Cuzco's standing affected the basic stability of the Inca domains. The traditional capital was far more than a political centre. According to the official religion, the cosmos divided into three different regions, the subterranean, the terrestrial, and the celestial. Cuzco, or to be more precise, the Temple of the Sun, represented the point at which the three worlds touched. Tumipampa was constructed as an exact replica of the southern capital to the extent that a new Temple of the Sun was constructed at its centre with stone blocks dragged the length of the imperial highway from Cuzco. The new city came to constitute a second nodal point for the three zones of the Inca universe; and this introduced an element of uncertainty into the religion of the state.

Of greater immediate significance, the long absences of Huayna Capac on the northern border broke the sense of unity on the part of the ruling élite, the nobles who could claim descent from the previous Incas. Whilst resident in Tumipampa the sovereign naturally turned to those in his immediate presence, thereby creating in time a new service nobility which came to identify with Tumipampa and not Cuzco. The two capitals competed for the loyalty not only of the imperial élite but for that of the subject chieftains. A fissure opened in the structure of the state.

The consequences soon showed. No clear law of imperial succession had been laid down. The Inca nominated a suitable candidate for the title, but the princes of the ruling clans made the final selection. When Huayna Capac died in 1525 (of smallpox?), one of his sons, Atahualpa, secured the backing of the royal princes in Tumipampa, while the nobility of the blood who had remained in Cuzco sided with another son, Huascar. In the ensuing civil war the ruling élite divided amongst itself on the basis of the north versus the south. Amongst the subject peoples, some like the Cañaris supported Huascar and the party of Cuzco; the bulk tried to stay aloof. After a protracted struggle, lasting perhaps as long as five years, Atahualpa emerged the victor. Unfortunately, the lapse of time between his triumph (in 1530?) and the arrival of the Spaniards did not provide sufficient to close the rifts. The invaders were well placed to exploit the smouldering resentments on the part of those members of the imperial élite who had chosen the wrong side and those amongst the subject peoples who had been unwise enough to become associated with it.

From the first moments of contact, the Spaniards registered their admiration for the visual evidence of Inca power and organization. Yet, in many ways, the most remarkable feature of the Inca state was its capacity to adapt the economy to the nature of the Andean terrain. It has been argued that the empire expanded not so much through territorial conquest or through the subjugation of foreign tribes as through the acquisition of control over the different economic systems which flourished at various altitudes of the Andean range. Reciprocal exchange, not monetary tribute or human sacrifice, formed the basis of the Inca economy. Under imperial supervision, each terrace culture, or micro-environment, traded its products and, if the occasion required, its labour with different climatic zones. The Inca genius lay in its ability to administer this gigantic system of economic exchange from the coastal plain to the high mountain valleys. Just as the monuments rose without cement, so the economy functioned without money.

The career of Francisco Pizarro, illegitimate son of an artillery officer, began in Panama. Like many others with few expectations, he had been drawn to the Indies by the lure of fame and fortune. The omens were not encouraging. Pizarro acquired an *encomienda* in Panama, a land of sweltering heat and scant prospect of gold or silver mines. More galling still, he missed out on the conquest of the Aztec Confederacy, a feat which confirmed the wildest expectations of the swordsmen who had flocked to America. But Pizarro had one other quality besides physical courage, grit.

In the 1520s Pizarro formed a partnership with three associates; the first was Fernando de Luque, a priest, who, despite his calling, was a man of substance; the second was the judge, Gaspar de Espinosa, who likewise had means at his disposal; and the third was a fellow adventurer, Diego de Almagro. Together the partners equipped a number of expeditions to explore the northern shores of South America. After several fruitless ventures, Pizarro left Panama in

January 1531, at the head of an 'army' of less than two hundred men. A year later, early in 1532, he landed at Tumbes, a frontier post on the northern border of the Inca empire. From here he made his way slowly inland, shadowed constantly by Indian scouts, until he reached the town of Cajamarca on 15 November 1532. At this point Atahualpa decided to meet the intruders from beyond the sea. He entered the Spanish camp believing Pizarro and his entourage—it could hardly be called an army—to be some diplomatic mission. Atahualpa may have calculated that the barbarians would be suitably impressed by the splendour of his attendants and intimidated by the size of his army. If so, it was a fatal mistake. During the course of the parley Pizarro had the Inca seized (18 November 1532). Whatever the morality of the act, the Spaniards had won for themselves an incalculable advantage and one they did not hestitate to exploit. The native administration, and this included the armed forces, depended for its motion on the word of its divine ruler; it ceased to function. The Spaniards gained an opportunity to reconnoitre the land and take stock of the possibilities.

During the first days of his captivity Atahualpa noticed his captors' fascination with gold and silver objects. In return for his liberty he promised to fill two rooms with precious metals and jewels. Messengers were sent the length of the empire to command that the adornments of the sacred places should be stripped to make up the ransom. By 3 May 1533 Atahualpa, true to his word, had provided 26,000 lbs of silver and 13,420 lbs of gold, with a fineness of $22\frac{1}{2}$ carat. But even if the conquerors had been honourable men, it is hardly likely that this magic hoard would have purchased the Inca's life. Atahualpa was garrotted on the ludicrous charges of apostasy and black magic (29 August 1533).

A year after the execution of the Inca, Pizarro finally entered Cuzco, the spiritual capital of the empire and the hub of the road network. Once in control of the city Pizarro took a series of measures which determined the next phase of the conquest and, as it proved, the eventual shape of the colony. His partner, Diego de Almagro, set off to discover new riches in Chile, as had been anticipated in the articles of association drawn up before the expedition left Panama. Almagro's departure southwards removed for the time being a dangerous source of rivalry between the two captains and their respective followers. To make the task of controlling the empire easier, Pizarro decided to instal a puppet regime in Cuzco with Manco Inca, a member of the royal house, as its figurehead.

The new master of the realm chose not to remain in the historic capital. Instead, he retired to the coast where, on 1 January 1535, he founded the City of the Kings, subsequently known as Lima. The choice of the new site in preference to Cuzco or Jauja, another possibility, had been prompted by strategic considerations. Pizarro needed a base on the coast to exclude Spanish interlopers hoping to repeat his achievement—or, if this was not possible, to be bought off at a price. Whatever motives determined the selection, Pizarro showed that he had less foresight than his great contemporary, Hernán Cortés. The latter appreciated, as the former did not, that it was imperative to associate the new with the old; and this could only come about with the retention of the old capital and its adoption by the invaders. Events bore out the truth of this observation. The building of Lima, a coastal town, instead of one in the high sierra, reinforced over the years the difference between the white and the native communities and with it the emergence of two quite separate 'nations'.

The last phase of the conquest began in 1536 when the Inca state, or what was left of it, made a determined bid to oust the invaders. Manco Inca, that apparently docile instrument of white rule, escaped from his Spanish guards and gathered together a force with which to retake Cuzco. The siege of the city lasted for the best part of a year (1536 to March 1537). Even though the Spanish garrison numbered little more than two hundred and the Inca had an army of 50,000, the besieged held out. The arrival of Diego de Almagro and his men on their way back after the abortive expedition to Chile compelled Manco Inca to lift the siege. The failure to capture Cuzco spelt the end of any realistic hope of reviving the Inca state.

The astonishingly rapid collapse of the empire cannot be attributed to a single cause. A number of elements must be considered; and the relative importance of each rests with the preference of the individual. Despite the ability of successive emperors, Tawantinsuyu remained unfinished as a political creation. The Incas used a variety of methods to deal with refractory tribes: sometimes they were exterminated; at other times they were forcibly resettled in different parts of the empire, a policy designed to eliminate in the course of time hostile traditions. Pizarro and his men interrupted the process at a critical moment. Profiting from the example of Cortés, they exploited the antagonisms between the ruling tribe and the subject peoples. Without the willing help of the Cañaris, Chimu, and Huancas, to name but a few, Pizarro would not have been able to march on Cuzco.

The unassimilated tribes provided the transport and local knowledge which made the conquest possible. Even after the Spaniards had given a fair indication of what they intended, Manco Inca failed to recapture Cuzco because the tribes formerly subject to the empire refused to co-operate wholeheartedly in the enterprise.

Once the invaders had taken control of the land and weathered the challenge of Manco Inca they experienced little difficulty in adapting its management to their own requirements. The Incaic state, as indeed was the case with preceding Andean empires, had been organized to provide for a ruling élite. The principal beneficiaries included the Inca and the eleven royal *ayllus*. The latter were kinship groups which claimed descent from cadet lines of the imperial house. Together the royal house and the related clans formed a group of some five hundred heads of families. Pizarro and his associates dispossessed the royal household and most of the *ayllus*, appropriating their rights in the process. As in Mexico, those amongst the conquerors who planned to remain sought their reward in the form of an *encomienda* which would entitle them to enjoy for the remainder of their lives the labour and tribute of a specified number of Indians. In all about five hundred *encomiendas* were granted by Francisco Pizarro and his successors, a number which tallies almost exactly with that of the principal officers of the Inca state. The profits of empire were thus transferred from a native élite to a similar number of white men.

For the bulk of the population the substitution had little immediate impact on their lives. The level of tribute demanded remained the same, if it did not actually increase; and the former tax system presented few problems of adaptation. Under the Incas fiscal obligations had been recorded through the use of the famous knotted strings or cords. The Spaniards had these carefully translated into Western script, thereby preserving the knowledge essential for the exploitation of their conquest. Labour dues received the same treatment. Under the Incas individual communities had been required to furnish unpaid labour for the great construction projects. The white conquerors retained this obligation, not dissimilar to existing practices in Europe, and developed it into the system which provided the workforce for the mines, the dreaded '*mita de minas*'. In broad terms it could be said that initially the Spaniards retained what they inherited. Reconstruction came later in the sixteenth century.

The division of spoils amongst the conquerors did not usher in an era of peace. In fact, the very reverse proved to be the case. The real struggle had just begun, not between the Indians and the Spaniards—this was almost peripheral—but amongst the victors themselves. The origin of the conflict lay in the compact between Pizarro and Diego de Almagro. The two had failed in their initial agreement to settle the exact limits of their respective jurisdictions, hardly surprising in view of their total ignorance of the land. If Almagro's expedition to Chile (1535–7) had resulted in the conquest of another civilization as rich as Tawantinsuyu, then a clash between partners might have been avoided. As it was, Almagro and his men found nothing but bleak terrain defended by fierce Indian tribes. If 'the men of Chile' wanted a share of spoils they had to return to Peru and stake a claim. Failure on his southern expedition made Almagro determined to gain control over Cuzco and its hinterland, even though the Inca capital fell within Pizarro's sphere of influence according to the hazy provisions set out in the articles of association.

Cuzco acted as a focal point in the struggle between Pizarro and Almagro, as it did in all subsequent disorders. The conquerors sought Indian tribute, not land. The main wealth of Peru, even after the silver mines were first located, lay in the areas of densest Indian settlement. This meant, in effect, the central highlands, the zone running from Cuzco to La Paz to Charcas; hence Almagro's interest in the region. Pizarro had little choice as to how to respond to Almagro's challenge. Gathering together his own men, he marched up from the coast and defeated his former partner at Las Salinas just outside Cuzco (6 April 1538). Hardly a benevolent man by inclination, Pizarro could not afford in this instance to show mercy. Too much was at stake. Almagro was executed later in the year on the orders of Pizarro (8 July 1538).

Violence bred violence. Almagro's *mestizo* son, of the same name but sometimes called by older historians Diego the Lad, vowed to avenge his father. Three years later he succeeded: Francisco Pizarro was assassinated in his own house on 26 June 1541. The triumph of the Almagristas was short lived. Alarmed at the turn of events, the crown sent out Vaca de Castro to restore order. With an army made up of royal supporters and the partisans of the late Francisco Pizarro the king's deputy defeated Almagro the Younger at the battle of Chupas (16 September 1542). No clemency could be expected by the losers; Almagro was immediately put to death.

The feud between the supporters of Pizarro and the followers of Almagro, sometimes seen in terms of Peru versus Chile, marked only the first phase of a protracted period of civil disturbances. In 1542 the New Laws were proclaimed in Peru as elsewhere in the Americas. Unfortunately, in the Peruvian case their implementation was left in the hands of the inept Blasco Núñez Vela who, unlike his more flexible Mexican counterpart, was intent on pressing ahead regardless. By threatening to abolish within a short time the *encomienda*, the New Laws imperilled the foundations of colonial society, while for the conquerors of the Inca realms they carried a special menace. All who had been involved in the preceding civil strife were to be deprived of their *encomiendas* forthwith. Virtually every *encomendero* was liable, since practically all had been associated with one or other of the parties. Bitterly antagonistic groups within the white community now came together to defend a common interest, the *encomienda*, and nowhere was the resistance more intense than in the areas of maximum Indian settlement (and, therefore, greatest concentration of *encomiendas*), Cuzco, Arequipa, and La Plata, the zone which had been so hotly contested by Francisco Pizarro and Diego de Almagro.

The colonists found their champion in another member of the Pizarro clan, Gonzalo, the conqueror's half-brother. Apart from a fruitless search for the Land of Cinnamon, Gonzalo Pizarro had made little impression up to that moment; but by the time of his own violent death he showed that he lacked nothing of the cruelty, drive, and imagination which had distinguished his brothers. In 1544 Blasco Núñez Vela was taken into custody on the orders of the *audiencia* in Lima; and over the next four years Gonzalo Pizarro acted as the effective ruler of the province. The murder of Núñez Vela in January 1546 bound the conspirators, in effect, the entire white community, even closer together. Gonzalo Pizarro and his principal lieutenants did not shrink from the implications of the situation. They were acting independently of the crown. Why not then regularize the position and assume complete freedom? This, in the end, became the plan. The rebel leaders proposed that the white *encomenderos* should form the new ruling caste, along the lines of the Inca *ayllus*, and Pizarro himself, by intermarrying with the Inca royal house, should create a new *mestizo* dynasty. It was a daring scheme and for a while it prospered.

In the meantime, the imperial authorities had not remained idle. In the form of the priest Pedro de Lagasca they acquired just the man to bring the rebellious colony back to its allegiance. Beneath a saintly exterior Lagasca was shrewd and utterly without illusion. For once a royal agent was carefully briefed and given powers commensurate with his task; he had the authority to issue pardons and to revoke the New Laws.

To be assured of lasting success, Gonzalo Pizarro had to control the isthmus of Panama, sometimes referred to as the 'throat' of the Peruvian colony. Lagasca first demonstrated his skill by winning over Pizarro's commander at the isthmus and acquiring in the process Pizarro's fleet. The way was open and the transport available. Once in Peru, Lagasca set about undermining the rebel position by the masterly use of coercion and corruption veiled in an other-wordly style. He promised that all who rallied to the royal cause would receive pardons and confirmations of their property rights. The *encomenderos*, believing that the king's guarantee was stronger in the long term than any pledge made by Pizarro, began to slip away; and Lagasca, that man of God, encouraged the defections right up to the hour before the final encounter. By the time he was ready to risk battle with Pizarro, Lagasca had at his command a force of two thousand white soldiers, huge by the standards of the time. Gonzalo Pizarro was defeated at Sacsahuana (8 April 1548), a site not far from Cuzco. As on previous occasions the location of the decisive battle served to underline the importance of the Inca capital and the highlands to the white colonists. The Indian population was concentrated in this region; and it was here, as a consequence, that the best *encomiendas* were to be found. Gonzalo Pizarro was executed on the spot, the by now mandatory penalty for defeated warlords. In the distribution of rewards after the battle Lagasca granted the richest prizes to those amongst Pizarro's following who had delayed their desertion until the last moment, on the grounds that precisely these betrayals had been of the greatest value. Having dealt summarily with the leaders of the revolt, Lagasca behaved generously towards the rank and file of the Pizarristas. He justified his policy of reconciliation as the only method whereby stability could be brought to white society.

The death of Gonzalo Pizarro marked the end of the civil wars which had their origins in the jealousies of Almagro and Francisco Pizarro. Disturbances continued; but none acquired the proportions of the earlier conflicts. The organization of society now became the principal task awaiting the government's attention. In this respect the crown, distracted by the problems of Charles V's later years, showed itself dilatory. The viceroy Andrés Hurtado de Mendoza, marquis of

Canete (1555–60) made a start; but the main architect of a durable colonial system was Francisco de Toledo (1569–81), the great pro-consul of the Americas.

During his term of office Toledo reduced the Peruvian viceroyalty to absolute obedience; and he imposed an administrative structure destined to last until the end of Spanish rule (1824). His first steps were directed towards eliminating the last vestiges of the Inca state. Manco Inca, having failed in his attempt on Cuzco, had retired to the remote and difficult country around Vilcabamba where he founded what has been termed a 'neo-Inca' state. This rump kingdom passed to his successors who thereby helped to preserve the traditions and memories of the conquered. Toledo decided that the enclave had to be snuffed out, to remove a rival focus of loyalty, if for no other reason. A punitive expedition was sent out against the Inca redoubt and it succeeded in hunting down Topa Amaru, the titular ruler (1572). The young man was brought to Cuzco, the city of his forefathers, where, amidst scenes of the greatest solemnity, he was decapitated in the main square, the executioner being a member of the Cañari tribe, ancestral enemies of the Incas.

Toledo's principal concern during his term was to harness the resources of the province to the needs of Spain. The Inca empire had suffered badly during the course of the initial conquest and the subsequent disputes amongst the victors. Land had been usurped by the colonists. Subject peoples settled by the Inca in different parts of the empire had returned to their place of origin. Successive plagues had reduced the Indian population, on which the whole of the colonial edifice rested, massively and permanently. The viceroy set out to shore up in some cases and to innovate in others. To gain an idea of what needed to be done, Toledo set out on a grand tour of his dominions. Abandoning the comforts of Lima, modest though they may have been, he made his way up into the highlands and spent five years (1570–5) inspecting the principal centres and the most exposed frontiers. Where he was unable to supervise the operation in person, he used a team of visitors, about sixty in number, to survey the population and resources of the districts assigned to them respectively. The viceroy and his aides hoped to complete a Domesday survey covering much of the Andean range.

Once he had acquired accurate information about the natural and human wealth of his viceroyalty, Toledo modified the existing tax structure in accordance with the needs of the new style of government. Every adult male Indian was required to pay a poll tax, an obligation which had to be met principally in the form of silver. In effect, Toledo's reform compelled the Indian workforce to enter the white man's world at some point in order to acquire specie with which to meet the poll tax, a device subsequently imitated by many other colonial powers. The bulk of the money raised through this method was made over to the Spanish *encomenderos* to whose care, if that be the word, the Indian community had been assigned. A much smaller percentage found its way into the hands of the local nobility whose services the conquerors had chosen to retain. Where tribute was paid in the form of blankets, coca, or maize, these items were disposed of on the open market and the money raised went to the crown.

The sweat and industry of the indigenous population provided one source of income for the white élite, hence Toledo's concern that an efficient taxation system be devised. He was equally interested that the mineral deposits of Peru should be profitably developed. For this to happen two conditions had to be satisfied, a better method of recovery, and a regular supply of manpower. Toledo saw to both. Under his direct supervision the mercury amalagmation process was tried and declared a success in 1572. Treatment of the ore with mercury (and salt) made it possible to extract a far higher percentage of silver than had proved the case with previous methods of smelting. Slag from old Inca workings could be profitably treated with the new technique.

For this technological advance to be exploited fully, it was necessary to expand the scope of mining. More brawn was needed to excavate the ore, and that could only mean one thing, Indian labour. The Incas had called upon the subject tribes to provide work gangs; and Francisco de Toledo decided to build upon and extend the practice. According to the famous mining code drawn up by the viceroy, Indian villages from the mining regions were to supply 13,500 men for the silver workings at Potosí and a further 1,800 for the notorious mercury deposits at Huancavélica. The draft labourers, or *mitayos*, were recruited from the *altiplano*, or high uplands of Peru. Toledo's introduction of conscript labour made the extraction of silver, and other metals for that matter, highly remunerative both to the individual entrepreneur who leased a claim and the crown which owned the mining rights. Without Toledo's innovations Potosí and other less well known sites would not have attained the levels of output which made Peru in the period from 1580 to 1615 the most important source of silver in the Americas.

No one could be oblivious for long to the dangers of mining. Dour and unfeeling as he was, Toledo insisted on protecting the Indian workers by formally stipulating the terms of their employment. Underground workers were to be paid four pesos a month; and once an Indian had served in the mines he did not become eligible again until seven years had passed. Yet whatever the intentions of this Peruvian Solon, the provisions concerning the welfare of the natives were scarcely heeded. The horrors of mining were common knowledge. Little thought was given to the safety of the miners as they toiled in the galleries, adits, and flumes of Potosí; timbering was skimped to save money and maximize profits; while the Indian labourer, often accompanied by his entire family, lived down the shafts for weeks on end. Assignment to Huancavélica represented a death sentence. A seventeenth-century administrator of the quicksilver mine, Juan de Solórzano, claimed that four years was the maximum expectation of life for those working with mercury. Death came from mercury poisoning which in its acute form ate into the very bone, asphyxia from gas which had been allowed to collect through bad ventilation, or collapsing shafts. If this were not enough, many died of exposure as a result of the sharp contrast between the heat inside the mine and the cold outside.

To tap the potential wealth of Peru with a minimum of expense and delay, Francisco de Toledo grasped from the beginning that he must preserve the native system of government where possible. The former ruling élite, the royal *ayllus*, had largely perished; but the junior ranks in the Inca administration remained, their standing and powers apparently unaffected by conquest and civil war. The viceroy decided to confirm in office this intermediate class of nobility, the *curacas*, akin in many cases to village headmen. The *curacas* acted as intermediaries between the white overlords and the Indian population. They supervised the fulfilment of labour dues, the payment of taxes, and the selection of Indians for the mines. By efficiently aiding the Spaniards to exploit the indigenous peoples the *curacas* kept their position in society, strengthened it by the hereditary principle, something which Toledo, for all his iron will, failed to prevent, and acquired in time an evil reputation for abusing their fellow Indians.

Toledo's influence upon the destiny of the southern viceroyalty extended far beyond economic matters. He intended, amongst other things, to leave a cultural stamp upon the colony. With his active encouragement, the university of San Marcos was refounded; and he personally endowed a chair of Quechua, a reflection perhaps of humanist interest in the study of language. He also revealed a passionate concern for the history of Peru; but, in this instance, altruism and scholarly curiosity were not the guiding motives.

On his great tour of the province Toledo brought with him a team of secretaries who had been instructed to collect the (oral) traditions relating to the birth of the Inca state. The pedigrees of former Inca emperors were painted onto a series of cloths which were then shown to surviving members of the royal house. The latter sometimes corrected, but most frequently verified, the painted record. Pathbreaking in their own way, these early examples of visual history had an ulterior purpose, namely, to counter an interpretation of the past favourable to the Incas. The historians patronized by Francisco de Toledo had little trouble in proving that the Incas had been neither the builders nor the first inhabitants of Cuzco. They had conquered the town and consolidated their hold on the surrounding districts by force. The Inca state had grown through the exploits of warrior chiefs such as Tupac Inca Yupanqui (1471–93), sometimes hailed as the Alexander of the Andes. The research of the Toledan school aimed partly to enlighten posterity but more to establish a legal right of conquest. Once it had been satisfactorily demonstrated that the Incas had acquired their empire through violence and oppression, then the Spaniards could justify their own occupation. The viceroy encouraged a view of history which, if not false, was certainly tendentious. His success was only partial. The philo-Incaic tradition lived on; and subsequent generations came to learn about the Peruvian past not merely from the work of Sarmiento de Gamboa with its chant of the Inca warrior but from Garcilaso de la Vega and the softer voice of an Inca princess.

In his recasting of the government and traditions of the land, Francisco de Toledo looked to the church for support. The Inquisition was introduced in 1570, a diocesan system inaugurated, and the various orders, including the Jesuits, welcomed. But the ecclesiastical establishment lacked the viceroy's energy or sense of duty; it showed marked unwillingness to leave the area of white settlement, the lowland plain. Christianity, if it penetrated to the uplands, did so in a heavily syncretized form, having to compete for its following with local religions and rural shrines, the *huacas*. Religion joined a number of other factors, geography and culture, to name but two, which brought about and made permanent the division between the creole and the Indian communities.

As in the case of Mexico, the most dramatic changes in the nature of Indian society came about through the introduction of European disease. Even before Pizarro first touched on Peruvian soil, the ailments of the invaders had gone on before, like sinister messengers of what was to follow. Indian numbers began to fall during the last years of Inca rule with the ruler himself, Huayna Capac, and his son, Ninan Cuyoche, amongst the more illustrious victims. Estimates of the pre-conquest population vary wildly. One survey proposes a total of 32 million for the empire in 1520, 16 million in 1524 as a result of the first pandemic, and 5 million in 1548 — an astonishing demographic sequence. The work of Francisco de Toledo and his visitors allows less fanciful estimates to be made. A modern writer, using Toledo's returns, had suggested a figure of 1,045,000 for the inhabitants of the Peruvian highlands in 1570 and the much lower 250,000 for the coastal plain in the same year. By 1620 the highland population had fallen to 585,000 and that of the coastal zone still more precipitously to 87,000. The Toledan records offer a reasonable basis for demographic calculations for the 1570s; but in the absence of reliable evidence for the first two decades after the conquest, the question of Indian population on the arrival of Pizarro remains open.

The decline in the indigenous peoples affected the economy in ways that were all too apparent. Labour shortages led to the curtailment of some forms of activity; and the same phenomenon prompted in some sectors the substitution of slaves for the rapidly diminishing Indian workforce. The loss of population also determined the ethnic character of the colony and the nations that emerged from it during the period of independence. The plagues, by a process of selective destruction, reinforced a trend first adumbrated by Francisco Pizarro when he moved the capital to his new creation of Lima. Diseases brought by the conquerors virtually eliminated the Indian population of the coastal strip. But in the uplands there was a different story to tell. The climate was healthier; and some illnesses, such as malaria, had little effect. Contact with the white overlords was minimal—to the lasting benefit of the Indians. As a result, numbers held up better in the mountain sierras than on the coastal plain. The highlands from Cajamarca to Lake Titicaca formed under Spanish rule, just as in Inca times, the heartland of native Peru.

The retreat to higher altitudes preserved the ethnic character of the Inca state. Its distinctive economic system did not fare so well. The delicate mechanism of a terrace economy in which each climatic zone exchanged products and manpower with its neighbour required constant attention on the part of the authorities. The conquest wrecked the work of generations and led to the introduction of a system that was radically different. The colonial economy based itself upon extraction, not exchange. Under the new dispensation the Indian population was looked upon as the source of tribute and labour for the royal government, the church and the white élite. Above all, the Indians worked the mines; and it is significant that compulsory service in this sector continued in the southern viceroyalty long after it had been replaced in Mexico by free labour. The idea that the government might use its income to alleviate the sufferings of Indian subjects was never considered.

Official policy disrupted indigenous society in another way. The viceroy, Francisco de Toledo, and the church introduced a scheme whereby the Indian tribes, scattered for the most part over a wide area, were to be settled in new townships. The civil authorities hoped that the plan would improve frontier defences with the establishment of forts. They also believed that a network of settlements in the interior would improve the chances of imposing law and order. For its part, the church supported the idea of grouping the tribes together and obliging them to remain in one place, on the grounds that it would make the task of evangelization easier. Forced assimilation had its attractions for both civil and ecclesiastical authorities. The programme of resettlement did not bring the expected results. The Indians resisted its implementation; insufficient resources were earmarked for the project; and few members of the Peruvian church had any intention of spending their lives in the remote outback. Yet even though the projected foundation of Indian towns (*doctrinas*) was soon abandoned, the initial phase of attempting to bring together the migrant tribes had imposed a further burden on Indian society.

PART TWO

PHILIP II

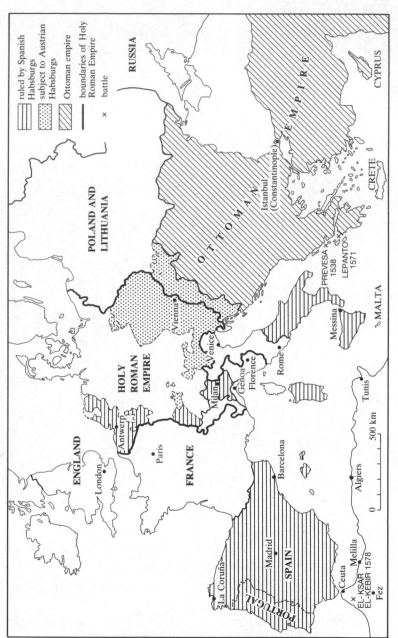

6 Europe c.1580

ruled by Spanish Habsburgs

subject to Austrian Habsburgs

Ottoman empire

boundaries of Holy Roman Empire

× battle

ENGLAND

London

FRANCE

Paris

Antwerp

HOLY
ROMAN
EMPIRE

POLAND AND
LITHUANIA

RUSSIA

Vienna

Venice

Milan

Genoa

Florence

Rome

OTTOMAN   EMPIRE

Istanbul
(Constantinople)

PREVESA × 1538

LEPANTO × 1571

Messina

MALTA

CRETE

CYPRUS

SPAIN

Madrid

Barcelona

La Coruña

PORTUGAL

EL-KSAR
EL-KEBIR 1578 ×

Fez

Ceuta

Melilla

Algiers

Tunis

0   500 km

CHAPTER 8

The character of the reign

THE Habsburgs were an alien dynasty, a fact borne out by the physical appearance of its members. Philip II did not resemble any Iberian type, even though his mother had been Portuguese. He had light skin, blond hair, and a slight build; he was also marked by a feature common to most members of his house, a protruding jaw. In terms of outward looks he could be mistaken for an Austrian archduke rather than a descendant of the Catholic Monarchs, both of whom had been swarthy and stocky. But in everything else he followed the traditions expected of a Castilian. In mature life he was frugal to the point of austerity. He drank little, and refused the heavily spiced dishes in which his father had indulged. He probably lived longer as a result. Such moderation in diet, however, did not spare the king the disorders of the stomach about which he was to complain so frequently in later years. He endured repeated bouts of typhoid and paratyphoid; and he suffered, almost certainly, from intestinal parasites. The recurrent attacks of fever to which he was subject were malarial in origin; and he may have been the victim of relapsing fever, akin to malaria in its symptoms, and carried by the tick. Gout virtually crippled him towards the end of his life, hence the need to construct a special litter in 1595. Three years later he died in the sombre magnificence of the palace he had built on a spur of the Sierra de Guadarrama, from septicaemia, gangrene, and the terminal therapy of his doctors. He had reached the age of seventy-one, respectable by the average of the modern age and remarkable by that of his.

Charles V hired the best tutors for the education of his son and heir. Of these Juan Martínez Guijarro, better known as Silíceo, left the deepest impression on his pupil. He was a demanding teacher, as well as being a good mathematician; and he insisted that the prince learn the virtues of care and hard work. The emperor showed his appreciation by nominating Silíceo to the primatial see of Toledo in 1546. But however sound as an instructor, Silíceo instilled in his royal pupil his own less commendable attributes of obstinacy, racial intolerance, and religious bigotry. Furthermore, the prince lacked any real intellectual capacity, a state of affairs which not even the adulation of fawning courtiers could conceal for very long. Barely numerate, Philip had difficulty with all but the simplest calculations; and this explains why he never mastered the intricacies of public finance and shuddered at the mysteries of borrowing in its various forms. Linguistically he revealed even greater deficiencies. Apart from his mother tongue, Castilian, he had a smattering of Latin, but no more, it was said, than might be required of a sacristan. On his visit to the Netherlands in 1549 neither he nor his companions could understand the religious plays staged for their benefit. Having failed with Flemish, the prince made even less headway in German during the course of his residence in the empire; and this, taken together with his obvious disdain for their social habits, hardened the imperial aristocracy yet further in their opposition to the idea of a 'Spanish Succession'. Even matrimony could not stimulate linguistic effort. During the ceremony which joined him in marriage to Mary Tudor, Philip addressed the bride in Spanish, a language with which she hardly understood, if at all. She attempted to speak with the groom in halting French, which he did not understand; and when all communications broke down, Latin was used. Such ignorance on the part of Philip contrasted strongly with the attainments of his Austrian cousins. Ferdinand I claimed that he and his children between them could speak German, Spanish, Latin, Czech, and Hungarian. His son, Maximilian II, boasted that he had mastered the six principal languages of Europe. There is no reason to doubt the truthfulness of either. Philip's linguistic inadequacies, pardonable in a youth, became serious burdens when he came to rule. They made the task of government more difficult by placing an obvious barrier between the king and his subjects who did not happen to live in Castile. This unwillingness to reach out into the world through the medium of foreign languages also hastened the emergence of an empire Castilian in temperament and government—with all the problems that this would bring.

The influence of Charles V upon his son has been repeatedly stressed; yet, for all that, the relationship was distant in many senses. The emperor was absent from Spain for most of Philip's childhood. Only when Charles made one of his (relatively infrequent) visits to the peninsula in 1541–3 did father and son come together for any length of time; and the relationship did not become close until the last phase of imperial rule (1554–6). Although much importance has been attached to the instructions drawn up by Charles V in 1543 for the guidance of his heir, their significance is open to question. The emperor wrote them out as he waited to take ship for Italy; and, as Charles made clear in the text, the justification for both sets of instructions, the one public, the other secret, was the possibility that he might be drowned at sea or killed during the forthcoming campaign against France. It is probable that the emperor had mentioned to his son most of the topics raised in the memoranda. Nor was what he wrote particularly startling. His comments on the structure of the court, its divisions and the dominant atmosphere of self-seeking, were a statement of the obvious, as, for that matter, was the observation that power lay at the heart of the struggle between the factions. The extent of Alba's ability as a military leader and his measureless ambition were also apparent to all those with any judgement. Charles's warning to refrain from sexual excess in the early days of matrimony is more original and interesting.

The emotional experience of childhood and early adolescence formed the prince's character. His mother's unexpected death in 1539 left him an orphan at the age of twelve. Six years later, the loss of his first wife, four days after she had given birth to a son, made him a widower. These domestic tragedies accentuated, if they did not create, his tendencies towards aloofness and withdrawal. They may account for his lack of sympathy towards his two sisters as they endured the perilous illnesses of childhood. Later in life the steady progression of wives and children to their early graves froze his emotions even harder.

But it was to require time before the king schooled himself to accept good or bad fortune without betraying any feeling. As a young man Philip showed vigour and spirit. He practised military sports even though he retained a lifelong aversion to warfare itself. He loved women passionately, both in and out of wedlock. Rumour credited him with at least three affairs, possibly more. His first mistress, Isabel Osorio, held his affections either just before, or just after, the death of Mary of Portugal; and William of Orange, in his *Apology*, was ungentlemanly enough to call the liaison bigamous. It was a lasting attachment; and long after the physical relationship had ended Philip made her a present of between 75,000 and 80,000 ducats. His father, so genial in other respects, showed himself uncaring in the provision for his mistresses, whereas the son treated his with surprising generosity. Catalina Laínez followed in the place of Isabel Osorio until she was supplanted by Eufrasia de Guzmán, the last of these illicit amours.

William of Orange, that impartial guide to the king's private life, maintained that Philip hurriedly arranged for Eufrasia de Guzmán to marry the prince of Ascoli on the eve of his own marriage to Isabel of Valois (1559), and that Eufrasia's husband subsequently died from the shame of having accepted a royal cast-off. To his third and fourth wives, Isabel of Valois (1559–68) and Anne of Austria (1570–80), Philip showed consideration and affection, although these emotions became more parental as he grew older and his wives younger.

Some idea of Philip's interests and concerns as an individual has come down to posterity as a result of a chance survival. When Philip left for Portugal in 1580 he began a correspondence with his two daughters who remained behind; and some of these letters which cover the period of his absence (1581–3) were taken by his younger daughter, Catalina Micaela, to Savoy on her marriage to Carlo Emmanuele in 1585; and there they were preserved in the royal archives in Turin. These communications of a father to his children reveal certain powers of observation and some curiosity. The king described for the benefit of his daughters the ships which rode at anchor in the estuary of the Tagus; he reported personal accidents; and he could also regret the fact that he had yet to hear the nightingale sing. He was concerned with the health of his son Don Diego (and not without reason, for he died of smallpox during the stay in Portugal). Yet these letters, although possessing a watery charm, do not show subtlety or depth of feeling; and for all the claims that have been made on their behalf they can scarcely be considered Wordsworthian in their evocation of nature. What they do reveal is a man simple, slow, and childlike.

As a king, the decisive influence on Philip II was not the advice left by his father in 1543 but rather his own experience during the negotiations for the Spanish Succession and their disastrous sequel (1550–3). During these years he served his political apprenticeship. He came to appreciate that France bore the responsibility for thwarting the plans for which his father had spent a lifetime fighting. In future the Valois must be checked either by marriage, the orthodox method, or by the promotion of civil strife, almost as traditional. The questionable attitude of his Austrian relatives during the crisis of Villach impressed on him the force of political egotism and taught him how little reliance could be placed on ties of blood or religion. But over and above everything it was the example of Maurice of Saxony which left its abiding mark on Philip's character and, in so doing, gave a particular bias to his subsequent actions. This turncoat German prince destroyed any chance of a Catholic solution to the problems of the Holy Roman Empire; and thereby denied Philip the imperial title. Later on the king saw in men like Egmont and Orange, or to take an example from another part of his dominions, Aranda and Villahermosa, the reincarnation of Maurice. Such inability to manage his subjects with a blend of firmness and understanding did not matter so much in the case of Castile or Aragon—at least in the short term: in the Low Countries it proved a calamity.

As a working ruler Philip demonstrated a number of useful qualities. He had an excellent memory coupled to a striking capacity for recall, especially in matters of detail. He showed a commendable insistence on the impartial application of the law to rich and poor without favour. He announced, or so it was reported, that he was determined that the law courts should not be like spider's webs which caught the fly while allowing the lizard to pass through. He had enough sense of theatre to put his natural timidity to good effect by projecting an image of Olympian detachment designed, in the appropriate setting of a formal audience, to overawe the foreign envoy as well as to impress the courtier. His dedication to business was legendary. He was the crowned head of his own civil service. When he left his palace for the country he would arrange for a small cloth bag full of the most urgent papers to be stowed on the coach, even though vanity prevented him from working on them while driving along. He considered the sight of a king with glasses as likely to diminish the aura of majesty. Working late into the night, he often had to give up through sheer exhaustion.

Yet just how much Philip understood of what passed across his table or what was said to him in his private office is an open question. For the most part he read the despatches of the day and his advisers' comments without taking a clear position. Perhaps he hoped that application and annotation would do service for insight and resolution, the two qualities he most obviously lacked. Only in matters of administrative minutiae did Philip show confidence in his own judgement; otherwise he dithered. He was the product of an unfortunate combination of attributes. Silíceo, and others, had left him with an unbending sense of duty without being able to inject determination and understanding. The bonding, under intense pressure, of moral calling and limited intelligence had the inevitable result. The king was high-minded, weak, and devious. These defects could be seen at their most obvious in the government of the empire. Indecision reached academic proportions. The one constant in the management of business became the fragmentation of authority either by the deliberate fostering of rivalries between various groups of officials or the employment of *ad hoc* juntas. Emotionally stunted and intellectually limited, only the physical and mental shortcomings of his descendants made Philip appear of kingly timber.

Within the structure of government, the Council of State, with its subcommittee for military affairs, occupied in terms of rank and effective power the principal position. In the course of the sixteenth century two other councils with a wide competence emerged, the Inquisition and Finance. Matters concerning the exchequer were barely understood by the king or the bulk of his servants; but even the most benighted appreciated that some direction was essential if the crown were to avoid total surrender to the bankers.

The Aragonese influence was most evident in the methods adopted by the Habsburgs to supervise their overseas dominions. In 1494 Ferdinand the Catholic set up the Council of Aragon to administer his native land. Other councils were established as the need arose, the Indies in 1524, Italy in 1559 (possibly before), Portugal in 1582, and Flanders in 1588. The membership of these bodies was drawn from those of humble origin who had graduated from one or other of the *colegios* which specialized in the teaching of law.

In the sixteenth century major policy decisions were not made within the formal councils. Charles V laid most of his plans within the small circle of his immediate entourage. His son preferred the *ad hoc* gathering or special board. As often as not the principal secretaries, men like Antonio Pérez or Mateo Vázquez, suggested the composition of these juntas, hence their authority in government. But the king was open in these matters to suggestion from any quarter. The value of the junta lay in its flexibility, and, to be fair, the possibilities it opened for the incorporation, where needed, of real experts.

This informal system flourished down to 1588. A more ordered one then replaced it. The needs of imperial defence and the levy of a new tax, the *millones*, to pay for increased expenditure brought about the transformation. Philip, who until recently had been so active in the assignment of business, delegated more and more authority to a steering committee made up of Cristóbal de Moura, Juan de Idiázquez, and the count of Chinchón. They formed what became known as the Junta of the Night, a reference not to any sinister activity but to the time at which they met. The three members helped the king to resolve the most difficult matters of state, such as the issue of peace or war with France; and their advice possibly carried more weight than any other proffered to the sovereign.

Philip instituted another board to administer the increasing volume of work. The 'large junta' (*junta grande*) had regular membership of between eight and ten, the size almost of an established council; and it, too, owed its origins to the demands generated by war and taxation. During the ten years of its existence, the last decade of Philip's reign, its competence grew steadily. It collaborated with others in co-ordinating the measures necessary to secure the vote of the *millones* in 1590; it supervised the annual fitting-out of the convoys bound for America; and it played a central role in the suppression of the Aragonese troubles (1590–2). More surprisingly, it gave detailed recommendations on how patronage should be distributed within Spain's Italian possessions. But the record of its meetings offer few indications of its participation in foreign policy, or the administration of the Low Countries, except at a purely technical level. Perhaps such items had become the preserve of the inner ring who belonged to the Junta of the Night.

The Castilian court, a mirror in this instance of society at large, was obsessed by questions of precedence. Such preoccupations, often very damaging to the efficient operation of government, could sometimes throw a revealing light on the order of priorities. At the funeral of Philip II (1598) the Royal Council took its place at the head of its respective contingent. The other councils then followed according to rank: Aragon, the Inquisition, Italy, the Indies, the Orders, Finance, and the Audit Board of the Exchequer. The Treasury, in status at least, was considered junior to all its companions. The Council of Portugal had absented itself altogether since it claimed a better position than it had been assigned.

The reign of Philip II covered nearly half a century (1556–98); and the main development to be observed during this period was the transformation of a fragment, a large one admittedly, of Charles's empire into a new imperial complex with Castile at its centre. For the first ten years after his father's abdication the young king continued the itinerant style of government inherited from the previous reign. His presence was required in the Low Countries first to defeat the French and then to secure the peace which terminated the

Habsburg–Valois conflict. Victory at St Quentin (1557) and at
Gravelinges (1558) opened the way to the treaty of Cateau-Cambrésis
(3 April 1559). After nearly forty years of warfare, Spain emerged as
the undisputed master of the Italian peninsula; and this advantage
was further improved by the outbreak of civil war in France which left
the Iberian Habsburgs free to dominate Europe for the next half
century.

In September 1559 Philip returned to Castile. Although much has
been read into this homecoming, the journey did not appear so significant at the time. Following in the manner of his peripatetic father,
the new ruler had travelled to the part of his dominions which most
required his presence at the time. Philip believed he saw the spectre of
heresy over his Iberian kingdoms; and both father and son were
adamant that they must not succumb to the menace. Even without the
seemingly precarious religious situation, there were other urgent
matters requiring attention. The attempt by the Ottoman empire to
convert the Mediterranean into a closed sea was under way. In the
spring of 1560 Spanish and Genoese ships landed a strong force on the
island of Djerba, just off the Tunisian coast. It was planned to establish an armed presence on both shores of the straits which divided
Sicily from North Africa. If successful, the Christian powers would
then be in a position to regulate the sea lanes which joined the western
and eastern basins of the Mediterranean. Strategically the concept
was sound; but the landing on Djerba was wholly mismanaged. The
Ottoman navy reacted with exemplary speed: the Christian fleet was
withdrawn; and six thousand Spanish troops were abandoned to their
fate. Turkish ships and those of their allies, the Barbary pirates, were
able to roam virtually at will in Spanish and Italian home waters. A
steady traffic in news and emigrants grew up between visiting Islamic
ships and the disaffected morisco communities of Granada and
Valencia, and many of the landings on Christian territory were quite
overt.

The Iberian kingdoms began an extensive ship-building programme to replace galleys lost in action and to increase the overall size
of the fleet. But however feverishly the Catalan yards worked to turn
out the vessels required, the brunt of defending Christendom against
the Ottoman forces fell upon others for the next few years. The resolution and endurance of the Knights of St John in preserving Malta
established a temporary balance of naval strength in the central
Mediterranean; and, thanks to this respite, Christian fleets could be

further expanded and trained in preparation for the decisive battle. In the meantime Philip had a series of difficult choices to ponder.

The clearest indication that a profound change in the character of Philip's dominions was about to take place occurred not in 1559 but in 1567. If the king had been committed to the style of government inherited from his father he should have returned to the Low Countries even without the additional incentive provided by the Iconoclastic Riots (1566). Genuine preparations were taken in hand for the transport of the king and his full entourage to the Netherlands; and if the journey had been made the decentralized form of government with which Charles had been content might have lasted a good while longer. Why, then, did it not occur?

In a word, the succession. Philip's only son and heir at the time of the proposed journey was Don Carlos, whose entry into the world cost his eighteen-year-old mother her life. From the outset the reports were unflattering. His head was disproportionately large; he was slow in learning to speak. Some observers thought he was mentally handicapped from birth. Whether this was so or not, at the age of seventeen he met with a serious accident which permanently altered his conduct. Whilst on his way to a rendezvous with the daughter of a royal gardener, he tripped on a flight of stairs and fell on his head. Only trepanning, undertaken when all else had failed, saved his life (9 May 1562).

Many assumed that one day the prince would be sent to the Netherlands to represent his father, as an introduction to the tasks he must expect to face when he succeeded to the throne. It was also widely anticipated that, before taking up his duties, he would be married off to one of his cousins, Anne of Austria most likely, but the name of his youthful aunt, Doña Juana, had surfaced in the context. Such speculations had to be dismissed rapidly when the young prince confirmed earlier impressions of instability. In his treatment of his horses and his pets he was a sadist. In company his temper could be uncontrollable; and on one occasion during a meeting of the Council of State he had drawn a knife on the duke of Alba. The relations between Don Carlos and his father were deplorable.

In the lull which followed the defence of Malta, Philip considered carefully the possibility of his return to the Netherlands and the difficulties this might present. The selection of the safest route figured high on any agenda, a land route across northern Italy and the Tyrol being favoured as it offered in addition the chance of a Habsburg reunion at Innsbruck. But the principal obstacle to any scheme was not the route, or the logistics, but the question of who should rule Castile while the king was gone. A retarded heir with a record of violence could not be left behind, and to appoint him regent could not even be contemplated. Don Carlos was becoming more unbalanced by the day as he realized that he was not to be married and not to be nominated ruler of the Low Countries. By late 1567 the prince began to make a number of inept attempts to escape to Italy, relying, foolishly and erroneously, on the assistance of his uncle, Don Juan of Austria.

Action needed to be taken, and quickly. Late in the evening of 18 January 1568, the king, armed from head to foot, led a small party to his son's bedchamber and arrested him. The prince was placed in the custody of the duke of Feria, captain of the royal guard. Many recalled the fate of another heir to the throne who had been imprisoned, the prince of Viana. In confinement Don Carlos behaved as erratically as ever. First he went on hunger strike; then he experienced a religious conversion; and lastly he reverted to gluttony combined with bizarre practices. He slept on a bed of ice. Despair and excess soon undermined his constitution. When the summer's heat was at its most oppressive, the prince ordered a highly seasoned partridge pie which he demolished in a sitting, crust and all. The meal was one of his last. He died on 24 July 1568, before dawn. He was twenty-three years and six days old.

By any measure the death of the heir apparent constituted a crisis; and it was not to be resolved until the birth, after a decade, of the son who would later become Philip III. Equally grave, the malady and imprisonment of Don Carlos provided the king with an excuse, perfectly valid in the circumstances, for not visiting the Low Countries. This was an historic refusal, and one which became irreversible with the passage of time. The monarchy took up permanent residence in the peninsula, or, to be more precise, the centre of Castile. What had been a polyglot empire administered by a migratory court now became Castilian ruled from a fixed point in the very heart of the meseta.

This change in the nature of the Habsburg domains accompanied, and may in part have prompted, another development. Charles V's government, while providing full employment for Castilian nobles, had also been open to talent from elsewhere. The career of Mercurino di Gattinara, imperial chancellor from 1521 until 1530, and a native of

Savoy, provides an example in point. After Philip's return to the peninsula (and his subsequent unwillingness to venture outside) the recruitment to high office of those not born in Castile dwindled. The closing of the bureaucracy coincided with the rise of Diego de Espinosa, in swift succession president elect of the Inquisition (1 July 1564), president of state (10 August 1565), and cardinal-bishop of Sigüenza from 1568 onwards. Cardinal Espinosa, the ablest of all his servants according to the king himself, trained a new corps of administrators who subsequently held the highest offices of state. As a group Espinosa's pupils had a number of features in common. They were Castilian to a man and they had acquired their early experience within the peninsula, often in connection with Seville and the Indies trade. For all their undoubted ability, the new generation of crown servants lacked the vision and, indeed, the knowledge of their predecessors. Their limitations contributed to the emergence of a Castilian, as distinct from a Habsburg, empire by the 1580s. Once the king himself had decided not to leave the Iberian peninsula, his civil service could only reflect and then, in turn, promote this shrinkage of horizons.

Although Philip failed to make the journey to the Low Countries his lieutenant, the duke of Alba, was able to impose order without the royal presence—and to hold out the prospect that the government of the Netherlands would become self-financing. With the duke apparently successful in the north, the king could attend to more pressing matters nearer home. The Turkish ultimatum to Venice demanding that Cyprus be handed over (February 1570) prepared the way for a grand alliance of the Christian powers. For there to be any realistic chance of meeting the Ottoman navy on equal terms, Venice, the papacy, and Spain had to combine their resources. The alliance between the distrustful partners lasted just long enough to secure the decisive victory of Lepanto (7 October 1571). The battle and its sequel established first that the Christian forces could meet and defeat their Ottoman rivals by sea—a naval superiority that would grow in the following years; and secondly, the inability to convert a naval victory into territorial gains showed that the frontiers between Islam and Christianity had reached their natural limits.

Not before time. The disengagement from the Mediterranean did not come soon enough to save the Habsburg position in the Low Countries. From 1572 onwards Castile had been obliged to finance concurrent expenditure on the Holy League, in the Mediterranean, and on Alba's army in the Netherlands. The burden led to the

financial collapse of September 1575 and the severance of credit lines
to the Low Countries for the best part of three years, a breakdown
which, on Philip's own testimony, led to the loss of at least two of the
provinces (Holland and Zeeland). Another crisis of a different type
was soon to break. From 1576 until 1579 factional struggles in Madrid
virtually paralysed royal government. Two secretaries, Antonio Pérez
and Mateo Vázquez, battled to establish a unique position in the
king's confidence; and behind them shadowy groups manœuvred for
control over policy. For all the self-seeking of the interested parties,
fundamental issues were at stake; and the way in which they were
settled would affect the character of the Habsburg state. Since the day
of Philip's return to the peninsula in the autumn of 1559, one question
above all others had to be solved. Were the king's domains to be
administered on a federal basis (a policy identified with Ruy Gómez,
the prince of Eboli), or was a more centralist and Castilian system to
be installed (a line credited to the duke of Alba, although he may not
have been the true intellectual force behind the approach)? The
solution came in stages.

The Genoese, after consideration of their position, agreed to
resume lending to the Spanish crown. The General Settlement of 1577
enabled the king to refuse the wishes of the moderate Catholics in the
Netherlands and to try instead for a solution imposed by force. The
resumption of dealings with the bankers of the Ligurian republic also
destroyed any prospect of sound financial management. The factional
struggles at court ended with the breaking of a sensational story of
deception and political murder. Antonio Pérez and his accomplice,
the princess of Eboli, were arrested (28 and 29 July 1579); and Cardinal
Granvelle, with papal and Italian experience to add to his qualifications, arrived in Madrid to direct affairs—above all, the impending
absorption by Castile of Portugal.

The 'classic' Spanish empire emerged in the decade of the 1580s. By
this stage all pretence that the king would leave the Iberian peninsula
had been abandoned. Indeed, it was hard to persuade him to journey
further than the narrow triangle based on the Escorial, Madrid, and
Aranjuez. Nor could there be any doubt that Castile was the dominant
element in the confederation of dominions ruled by the Spanish
Habsburgs. Its needs took priority over all others; and any notion of a
federalist scheme of government had been discarded long ago.

During this same period Philip's empire acquired another enduring
feature, its Atlantic or American involvement. The acquisition of

Portugal in 1580 and the assumption of new obligations in both the New World and the Far East brought on this shift of interest, at least in part. But factors internal to Castile's own colonial possessions were primarily responsible for this Atlantic 'opening'. Silver shipments from the American mines had grown beyond all expectations in scale and dependableness. By the 1580s bullion from the colonies provided the indispensable collateral without which much of Castile's fund-raising would have been impossible. Although never above one quarter of total income, the silver enabled the crown to float loan after loan, needed, in their majority, to pay the army in Flanders. At the same time, other more subtle factors encouraged this Atlantic drift. Two great viceroys, Martín Enríquez and Francisco de Toledo, had laid the groundwork of colonial government during their respective terms of office in Mexico (1568–80) and Peru (1569–81). Appointments to the new courts and the new bishoprics became one more task which Castilian administrators were expected to carry out. The government of the Americas made ever-increasing demands on the time and energy of the royal bureaucracy from the 1580s onwards, as the papers of the day confirm. If the commercial and financial bonds between Castile and her transatlantic possessions had been forged in the first half of the century, the administrative impact did not register until the last two decades.

A pioneer in the development of colonial interests, Spain remained a leading European power. Once the Genoese had promised to resume dealings with the crown (5 December 1577), and once the last chance of a compromise with the moderate Catholics in the Nether-lands at the conference of Cologne (1579) had been rejected, the reconquest of the Seventeen Provinces became the first priority of the state and the determinant of all policy. The decision to go for a mili-tary settlement led to an alarming escalation in costs and commit-ments. War broke out with England in 1585; and the hostilities outlived both Philip and Elizabeth. Support for the Catholic League as part of the policy for neutralizing France destroyed any possibility that the prince of Parma might break the resistance of Holland and Zeeland. A great opportunity was lost after the fall of Antwerp (1585); and the Dutch counter-attack which was to put any thought of re-conquest out of the question began while Farnese was campaigning in France (1590–2).

Before his death, Philip attempted to disengage, aware, perhaps, that for all the potential wealth of his kingdoms the monarchy was badly over-extended. Peace came with France in 1598 on terms that effectively re-stated Cateau-Cambrésis. In response to a long-standing plea for a ruler of the blood, Philip married his eldest daughter, Isabel Clara Eugenia, to the archduke Albert, investing the royal pair with the government of the (Southern) Netherlands. Yet even these dispositions, set in train when the king was on the edge of the grave, failed to solve the real problems facing his successor. In the Netherlands, the 'federalist' remedy had arrived at least thirty years too late. The war continued; and the Habsburgs only accepted formally in 1648 what had been apparent by 1598. Within the Iberian peninsula itself there were indications of future troubles. Portugal's ruling élite, which had accepted Habsburg rule in the hope that it might provide protection for the colonies, began to entertain doubts about Castile's real strength; and they may also have objected to attempts at introducing realistic taxation. On the other flank of the peninsula, the historic kingdoms under the crown of Aragon, neglected save for moments of crisis such as in 1591–2, came to reconsider the nature and the value of their relationship with their dominant partner, Castile.

CHAPTER 9

Islam and Habsburg Spain

THE ebb and flow of population across the straits of Gibraltar had been a constant of Mediterranean life since prehistory. The peninsula and the Mahgreb formed part of a common land mass; and the same political power had often ruled on both sides of the straits. Ferdinand and Isabel showed that, in their turn, they wished to continue a tradition which went back to the days of Carthage, if not before. Under the Catholic Monarchs, Christian forces occupied a number of strong points along the North African coast. On the death of Ferdinand (1516) Castile held Oran, Bugia, and Mers-el-Kebir; and a Christian garrison commanded the entry and the exit from Algiers through possession of an island fortress at the mouth of the port.

To an observer in 1519 it was not unreasonable to suppose that Charles of Ghent, having succeeded to the Holy Roman Empire, would go on to acquire another, this time in North Africa, dustblown and unglamorous perhaps, but certainly more relevant to the basic interests of his Spanish kingdoms than all his titles and territories in Central Europe. The prospect faded almost at once. Charles's assumption of the imperial dignity diverted attention and resources from the brush-fire campaigning needed to give Castile an unshakeable hold on the North African littoral. Spain in North Africa fell victim to Spain in Italy and Germany.

The neglect could not subsequently be made good. A number of fundamental changes had taken place in the interior which came to tilt the balance permanently against the Christian powers. During the later Middle Ages Islamic missionaries evangelized the mountain regions; and by the sixteenth century it became possible to speak of an Islamic hinterland for the first time. The success of this proselytizing drive, sometimes referred to as the maraboutic crisis, transformed the society of the uplands. The mountain tribes could never be relied upon for long by any party; but once converted to Islam they were more likely to support their co-religionists, be they Ottoman or corsair, in preference to a Christian ruler.

The failure to exploit the initial advances of the Catholic Monarchs and Cardinal Cisneros allowed the Muslim pirates to set up a loose confederation of buccaneer states which looked from the beginning for the protection of the Ottoman empire. Two brothers, Oruc and Hayreddin Barbarossa, the sons of a Greek renegade from Mytilene, founded the pirate commonwealth. Around 1514 Oruc established a base in the small port of Jijilli. In 1516 he and his brother first attracted notice when, having disposed of the Castilian client who ruled Algiers, they occupied the town, although not the Christian fort off-shore. Two years later the Turkish sultan recognized their achievement and promised the material assistance which was to stand the fraternity in good stead over the years.

Oruc (killed in 1518) and Hayreddin had a common purpose: to eliminate all Christian garrisons on African soil from the straits of Gibraltar to the gulf of Sirte. Algiers, hitherto a small fishing village, became their headquarters; and its prosperity dates from this time. Methodical and relentless in his strategy, Hayreddin winkled out the Christian force from the island which commanded the harbour of Algiers (27 May 1529); and five years later his fleet swept into the port of Tunis, capturing simultaneously the town and the fortress which guarded it, La Goleta (18 August 1534). Hayreddin also took care to regularize the nature of his relationship with Istanbul. Algiers became the administrative centre for an Ottoman province in 1525. Hayreddin, and his son after, acquired the rank of beylerbey with jurisdiction over Algiers, Tunis, and Tripoli. The arrangement worked to the equal benefit of the parties: Hayreddin had obtained formal status while the sultan acquired a new province which acted as a nursery of Ottoman admirals and sailors.

The fall of Tunis to Hayreddin convinced Charles V that he must make time from his other commitments to deal with a growing problem. Navigation in the western Mediterranean had become hazardous; and the power of the Barbary states might eventually pose a threat to Malta and Sicily. For the recapture of Tunis the imperial staff assembled a fleet of some 400 vessels and an army 32,000 strong. The cost of the operation was met in part by the bullion which Hernando Pizarro (brother of Francisco) had brought from Peru and it included the royal share of Atahualpa's ransom. The initial landing and the subsequent march on Tunis were carried out with clockwork precision. A rising of the Christian slaves within the city on the night of 20 July 1535, disrupted the planned defence; and on the following day the imperial army entered Tunis.

The amphibious operation, that most difficult of manœuvres, had been executed brilliantly. Christian forces had recovered a strategic city which restored to them control over the straits of Sicily. But for all that, the victory was incomplete. Hayreddin eluded capture, determined more than ever to continue the fight. His overlord, Suleiman the Magnificent, willingly gave him what was needed to make good his losses. The repairs and replacements did not take long. Within three years of Tunis's fall, Hayreddin fought a numerically superior imperial navy to a standstill off the coast of Epirus at the battle of Prevesa (27 September 1538); and a year later, in a daring piece of impudence, the corsair admiral sacked Gibraltar.

Painfully aware that the retaking of Tunis in 1535 had neither guaranteed Christian supremacy by sea nor inflicted a permanent check on the pirates, Charles attempted in 1541 to finish what had been left undone. As long as Algiers remained in enemy hands, Hayreddin and his successors would always have a lair to which they could retreat and recoup. The Habsburg territories were called upon to contribute in men and ships as before. But this time—and here lay the difference—the concentration of resources took much longer than anticipated. When all was ready, Andrea Doria, the senior admiral, advised against taking the offensive on the grounds that it was too late in the year. Charles V rejected his advice. On 23 October 1541 an advance guard was put ashore some five or six miles from Algiers and, at first, it met with little opposition. The landing of supplies and heavy equipment was about to begin when a storm blew up of such force that the disembarcation had to be suspended. Doria's weather eye had not failed him. It was far too late in the year to land on an open beach. Some ships ran aground; and the remainder stood out to sea to avoid the same fate. Driving rain prevented those contingents which had come ashore from attacking the city, a daunting prospect in the absence of siege artillery. The operation ended in a hastily improvised evacuation of the troops in which all supplies had to be abandoned. The Tunisian triumph had turned into the Algerian disaster.

Elated at their success, the pirates now undertook raids of greater scale and duration. Hayreddin anchored his fleet in the harbour of Marseilles during the winter of 1543–4, and was able from there to threaten a stretch of water vital to Habsburg power, the sea route linking Genoa to Barcelona. Hayreddin died in 1546; but his departure brought no relief. His post as corsair leader and Turkish admiral passed to one of his subordinates, Dragut, as he was known to the Christians. With all the ability and vigour of his predecessor, he continued the policy of eliminating the Spanish fortresses (*presidios*) along the African coast. He suffered a temporary setback in 1550 when he lost Monastir to the Christians, only to exact retribution five years later when he stormed Bugia. By the time of Charles's abdication the struggle between the Habsburg and Ottoman empire was on the point of entering its decisive phase, the battle for Sicily and the straits.

In 1560 Andrea Doria at last succeeded in trapping his old enemy, Dragut, in the shallow off the island of Djerba. The corsair fleet was bottled up in its moorings; but Dragut was resourceful. He dragged his ships across a narrow isthmus which separated them from the open sea; and once they were launched again he made good his escape to neighbouring Tripoli. The imperial admiral had allowed his quarry to slip through the net. Worse was soon to follow. The Turkish fleet, making unheard-of speed from Istanbul, surprised the Christian force as it attempted a hurried evacuation. Many of the imperial ships were lost, together with the entire expeditionary corps, some 18,000 seasoned troops.

After the calamity at Djerba, the task of holding the line against Islam fell to the Knights of St John. They had been driven out of their base on the island of Rhodes in 1522. After eight years of wandering they accepted from Charles V the island of Malta and with it Tripoli. The Knights felt unable to decline the latter even though it dangerously overstretched their resources. They established their headquarters around the Grand Harbour, leaving the rest of the island to the local Maltese nobility. From their new base the Knights continued, as before, to raid the ships of the Ottoman empire and to attack the Barbary coast. In 1551 they were expelled from Tripoli; and it became evident that an attack on Malta would not be long in coming. A former governor of Tripoli, Jean Parisot de la Valette, who had served in every capacity throughout his long career, including a spell as a galley slave on one of Dragut's ships, concluded that the arsenals and slipways clustered around the Grand Harbour must be sufficiently fortified to withstand prolonged siege. On his election as Grand Master in 1557 he began at once to convert the Grand Harbour into one of the most heavily defended fortresses in Europe. An appeal went out to the Knights scattered the length and breadth of Christendom for the necessary funds. La Valette grasped that the survival of the Order depended not only on his skills as a military engineer but on his ability to lay in adequate stores. When the siege did come, neither his men nor the civilian population cooped up within the walls suffered from lack of water, food, or munitions. His prudence was vindicated in the only way that mattered.

The Turkish fleet arrived off Malta on 18 May 1565. It comprised 180 warships; and the transports carried, in addition to the normal supplies, a special siege train which was soon to test the worth of la Valette's fortifications. Although the very sight of the Turkish force was enough to inspire fear in all, with the possible exception of the Grand Master, it was neither as strong or as well directed as it might have been. On the sultan's orders the overall command was shared between the admiral and the general. Furthermore the Turkish fleet, by anchoring on the southern side of the island, was not in a position to break Christian lines of communication with Sicily, a bare seventy miles away. With a view to securing a better anchorage the Turkish forces concentrated their attack on the fortress of St Elmo which commanded the entrance to the Grand Harbour. The defence of this strong point was widely regarded as the Order's finest hour, and with reason. It inflicted such casualties on the Turks that it may have blunted their enthusiasm for the attack on the even more heavily fortified positions.

La Valette and his followers believed that salvation could only come from Spain. Don García de Toledo, the viceroy of Sicily, had promised to send a relief force, but for much of the summer he appeared to remain inactive. He was in a difficult position. He knew that it was essential to deny the naval facilities of the Grand Harbour to the Ottomans. He was similarly well aware that if the relief operation miscarried and the Christians lost another fleet, then Sicily would be left defenceless. After a series of potentially fatal delays, the Spanish fleet made the crossing to Malta; and disembarcation of troops began on 7 September. Afraid lest his ships be caught in the autumn gales, the Turkish admiral needed little further encouragement to break camp and take off what was left of the army. Malta proved that the Ottoman forces could be stopped in their tracks by a town which was resolutely defended.

For all the undoubted courage of the Knights, the Christians had yet to show that they knew how to mount an offensive. Effective action against the Ottoman navy required the union of the Christian fleets;

and the obstacles in the way of this were formidable. The republic of Venice held the key. Under most circumstances, the Signoria avoided any action or entanglement likely to jeopardize its relations with the sultan. The spice routes which ran overland from the Far East had their western terminus in Ottoman-held territory. But the forbearance of the Venetian oligarchs was not unlimited. In 1567 the new sultan, Selim II, began laying plans for the conquest of Cyprus, a Venetian colony. Three years later the invasion started. Venice saw itself vitally threatened: the Turks were already masters of the Dalmatian coast almost in its entirety, and its most profitable possession, Cyprus, was on the point of falling into their hands. In Venice when the cock crew at sunrise it sang in Turkish, or so the humorists said. With the fall of Cyprus a foregone conclusion, the republic listened at last to the entreaties of Pope Pius V. It stifled, for the moment, its natural suspicions of Spain and entered into a military alliance with Philip II and the papacy. The Holy League, signed on 19 May 1571, made possible the concentration of Christian forces which alone offered the prospect of challenging Turkish dominance by sea.

The Ottoman navy spent much of the summer ravaging the regions of the Greek mainland which had risen against the Sultan. Such actions, in retrospect, served little purpose. They wasted the highly perishable crews which manned the galleys, slaves for the most part, condemned to toil on the great looms amidst their own sweat and excrement until released by death. In the autumn of 1571 instructions were received from Istanbul ordering the commanders to seek a general engagement with the enemy.

The Christians, in the meantime, had completed their preparations in Messina. Philip II, having provided the lion's share of the men and ships, exercised his right to appoint the supreme commander. He nominated Don Juan of Austria, twenty-three years old at the time, and his illegitimate half-brother. The papal galleys were led by the equally dashing Marc Antonio Colonna; while the Venetian galleys, more in keeping with the traditions of a staid republic, sailed under the command of the seventy-five-year-old Sebastiano Venièr (1496–1578). The heroes of several generations fought on board the Christian fleet.

Complying with their latest orders, the Turkish commanders shifted the centre of operations from Kizil Hizar on the island of Euboea to a new anchorage in the gulf of Corinth. It was from here on 7 October 1571 that the Ottoman navy set sail to meet the combined Christian detachments some miles away off the Cephalonian islands. The site of battle was one of the most historic and scenic that might have been chosen. The broad waters of the gulf flowed into the Ionian sea and the high mountains fell steeply to the shore.

The Christian admirals arranged their forces in linear formation; and the Ottomans adopted a similar disposition. Although the two fleets were roughly balanced in numbers, the Holy League could count on the surprise advantage of the Venetian galleasses. They were a primitive version of monitors capable of throwing a weight of gun metal far heavier than that of the most powerful Turkish cannon. The Turkish ships had to run the gauntlet of their enormous guns before even making contact with the Christian galleys. Before the action began, Don Juan, every inch a hero, sailed the length of the Christian line shouting to his men that the salvation of Christendom depended on their bravery. The banner of the League, blessed by His Holiness in person, was then unfurled.

Firing began just after one o'clock in the afternoon, with the main action taking place on the Christian left and the centre. The Venetians, in a display of courage which belied allegations of cowardice, prevented the Turkish squadrons from turning the left wing; while in the centre the Venetian galleasses broke the onrush of the Turkish galleys. In the main action Don Juan, after murderous hand-to-hand fighting, destroyed or disabled the ships of the Turkish centre and killed the High Admiral, Ali Pasha. On the left the beylerbey of Algiers, Uludj Ali, consistently outsailed his opponent Andrea Doria. When the battle was lost he managed to extricate thirty of his galleys and elude his pursuers by a faster turn of speed.

Even if incomplete, the victory of Lepanto was decisive. The Turkish fleet had been fought on a ground of its own choosing, and defeated. Philip publicly displayed his emotion at the news—one of the few occasions on which this happened. Venice, whose men and ships had performed so well, gave itself over a week's celebrations: notices appeared in shop windows declaring the establishment closed 'For the death of the Turk'. Elizabeth of England, although formally excommunicated and deposed by the pope, sent her congratulations to Philip and the Signoria, a graceful gesture, never to be repeated, acknowledging a common bond and a common joy at the preservation of Christendom.

But for all the carnage and the exaltation Lepanto did not lead to the territorial conquests so confidently expected. From the outset suspicions and dissensions racked the Holy League. Temporarily held in

check during the moment of supreme danger, they broke out with
renewed intensity once the crisis had passed. In the planning of future
operations, Venice and Spain adopted purely selfish attitudes. The
Habsburg court wished to exploit the naval victory to further its
ambitions in North Africa; Venice, for its part, wanted to improve its
position in the Adriatic and the Aegean. When it became obvious that
the alliance was unlikely to produce any lasting benefits, the Venetians,
encouraged by the French, opened negotiations with the Sublime
Porte. On 7 March 1573 the Signoria concluded an expensive and
humiliating peace with the sultan which at least guaranteed its trading
interests in the Levant. Spain and the papacy chose to fight on. Don
Juan captured Tunis on 11 September 1573, only to lose it a year later
on 13 September 1574. Furthermore, the military inferiority of the
Ottoman Empire could not be relied upon for any length of time. Uludj
Ali, the new High Admiral and the only Turkish commander to emerge
with credit from the disaster of 1571, set about replacing all the losses
incurred. Within less than a year he brought the navy back up to
strength; and he took especial care to improve the armament of his
ships.

Philip II continued to fret over the possibility that the Ottomans
might be contemplating a descent upon the Italian peninsula as late as
1575. His fears were groundless. Whether he knew it or not, a military
stalemate had been reached by the mid-1570s. As has often been
pointed out, the history of the two Mediterranean superpowers followed strikingly similar courses. From 1572 onwards the Habsburg
monarchy became increasingly concerned with the situation in the
Netherlands. In 1576 Don Juan was sent as governor to these northern
provinces, symbolizing in his person the transfer of interest. The
Ottoman empire found that it, too, had problems on a distant frontier.
In 1578 its armies marched against Persia in the expectation of rapid
victories. After initial success, the Turks discovered that in reality they
had committed themselves to decades of campaigning, and to no
purpose. Under Shah Abbas the Great (1587–1629) Persia recovered
most of the territory it had originally ceded in Armenia and the
Caucasus; and the frontier reverted to what it had been forty years
previously. Shah Abbas was to the sultan what Maurice of Nassau
proved to be to the king of Spain.

The analogy can be pursued further. Economic disorder at the end
of the sixteenth and the beginning of the seventeenth century undermined the position of both the Habsburg and the Ottoman empires.

The latter had not produced a satisfactory coinage of its own. Its rulers therefore permitted the free circulation of foreign currencies to compensate for this lack. Spanish silver was especially prized. But through this importation of foreign money, the empire exposed itself to the monetary ills of the Christian world, inflation above all. Faced with the consequences of a rise in prices beyond its control, the Ottoman government was driven to impose higher taxation on its people to pay for, amongst other things, the Persian adventure. At roughly the same time, Philip II had to introduce a completely new tax, the *millones*, to pay for the replacement of the Armada, another enterprise which went disastrously wrong. In the Turkish case the attempt to make up for the ravages of inflation by demanding more from the subject led to widespread unrest, particularly amongst the peasantry of Anatolia. These *Celali* rebellions, similar in nature to the tax revolts of western Europe, tied down much of the Ottoman army in the years from 1595 until 1610. Over-taxation acted as a theme common to both empires; and it had the same cause. The Habsburg monarchy attempted to suppress in the Low Countries a movement which drew its inspiration from a minority confession, Calvinism. The sultan could also justify his aggression against Persia on the grounds of a holy war. The Safavid Shahs had adopted the Shī'a tradition as the religion of the state, an act unique in the history of the Islamic world. In both the European and the Middle Eastern example defence against what was considered an external power and religious dissidence had become intertwined, and often indistinguishable. The inability of the Spanish kings and the Ottoman sultans to free themselves from the burden of distant wars so lightly undertaken meant the conversion of the temporary truce of the late 1570s into a permanent disengagement of their respective empires.

CHAPTER 10

The government of the Netherlands

THE future emperor Charles was born in the Flemish town of Ghent; and the first sixteen years of his life were spent in the Burgundian provinces which had once belonged to his father. Even after Charles of Luxemburg, to give him his first title, had acquired the Spanish and imperial thrones, the Netherlands continued to bulk large in his plans and thoughts. They made a vital contribution in terms of men and resources throughout the long years of struggle against Valois France; and they provided a useful vantage point from which to study developments in Germany. Nor can there be any doubting Charles's emotional attachment to the lands of his birth. When, at the end of his active life he set in train the various acts which signified his withdrawal from the world, he staged the first and most magnificent of the ceremonies in Brussels; and with equal consideration he chose to bestow on his heir not his Iberian possessions but his dominions in the Low Countries. It was ordained that the world empire of the Habsburgs should originate in the Netherlands and that these self-same provinces more than any others should bring about its eclipse.

In 1363 John II of France bestowed the duchy of Burgundy on his younger son Philip, later called 'the Bold'. Six years later this cadet member of the Valois house married the daughter and sole heiress of Louis de Male, count of Flanders. On his death in 1384 Philip of Burgundy entered into his wife's inheritance. He then went on to engineer a series of marriage alliances which linked his family with the neighbouring territories of Brabant, Holland, Zeeland, and Hainaut. His grandson, Philip the Good, exploiting the advantages so carefully built up by his predecessors, welded the various lordships and baronies under his control or influence into what ranked, by the standards of the age, as a centralized state. Given time, the union of ducal Burgundy in the south to the different provinces of the Low Countries in the north might have produced one of the great kingdoms of Western Europe, a makeweight perhaps to France or even the Holy Roman Empire itself. The death of Charles the Rash at the battle of

0   50   100 km

N

GRONINGEN

FRIESLAND

DRENTHE

NORTH SEA

Haarlem Amsterdam

HOLLAND

OVERIJSSEL

Leiden UTRECHT

Delft

Brill Rotterdam

GELDERLAND

ZEELAND

Flushing

BRABANT GELDERLAND

Antwerp

Brugge

FLANDERS Ghent Malines

Ypres

Brussels

BISHOPRIC OF LIÈGE

LIMBOURG

Cologne

Lille

ARTOIS Orchies

Valenciennes

NAMUR

Liège

Arras HAINAUT

Cambrai

PRINCE

St Quentin Cateau-Cambrésis

DUCHY OF LUXEMBOURG

7 The Seventeen Provinces in 1559

Nancy in 1477 put paid to this ambitious scheme; but enough was saved from the wreckage to reconstitute a new domain based this time on a fragment of the old duchy, the Free County of Burgundy, and the northern block of territories which thenceforth became by reason of population and wealth the centre of the Habsburg state. In spite of the many calls on his time and energies Charles V followed consistently in the path marked out by his Burgundian forebears. He rounded off the process of territorial conquests which former dukes had contemplated or attempted by incorporating into his existing possessions Friesland, Groningen, Drente, Overijsel, and Gelderland, thereby imposing Habsburg suzerainty over all the Seventeen Provinces of the Low Countries.

In addition to the assertion of Habsburg authority, Charles V also provided the Netherlands with a new legal identity. In 1548 the emperor, then at the height of his power, persuaded the princes of the Holy Roman Empire to sanction what became known as the Augsburg Transaction. Under its terms the Low Countries remained part of the empire, forming indeed a Burgundian 'Circle', but they no longer took part in the deliberations of the Imperial Diet, nor did they fall under the jurisdiction of the imperial courts. In effect, the links between the Habsburg Netherlands and the Holy Roman Empire had been severed; and for all intents and purposes the Seventeen Provinces came to constitute an independent state under the exclusive control of the ruler. There could be no question of extending imperial legislation to the Low Countries, a circumstance whose full significance would become apparent after the peace of Augsburg in 1555 and the religious settlement which followed. The Pragmatic Sanction proclaimed in 1549 completed the detachment from the world of imperial politics, while at the same time greatly increasing Habsburg authority over the Burgundian territories. By the terms of the Sanction all seventeen provinces were recognized as being hereditary in the house of Habsburg. Each and every one was denied the opportunity of electing its ruler or imposing conditions on the heir. The Habsburgs established in the Low Countries, even if they failed elsewhere, that basic principle of the modern monarchy, hereditary succession.

For all the advances in terms of control Habsburg rulers of the Netherlands still had to contend with a formidable series of obstacles in the way of efficient government. Diversity marked the Seventeen Provinces at almost every level. No common language existed. The southern regions, Artois, Hainaut, together with parts of Flanders and Brabant, were francophone. Further north, Holland, Zeeland, and the remainder of Flanders and Brabant spoke one German dialect, lower Franconian; while in the east their neighbours, Groningen, Gelderland, and Overijsel, spoke another, lower Saxon. Economic interests varied just as widely. Brabant and the western parts of Flanders boasted the most prosperous textile industry in Europe, whose output found buyers in the four corners of the Christian world. Already by the end of the fifteenth century Holland and Zeeland were challenging the

Hanseatic League for control of the Baltic trade; and a century later they had completely ousted their sometime rivals and established a monopoly over a region vital to the prosperity of these northern provinces. Holland and Zeeland, both under Spanish rule and during the immediate aftermath, were also busy promoting that other mainstay of the economy, the herring fisheries. While the industrial and mercantile regions looked outwards, the inland provinces of Groningen, Gelderland and Overijsel turned their energies to agriculture, the produce of which was normally sold to the local market town.

Regionalism and fierce local pride stamped even more markedly the political organization of the Netherlands. Thirteen of the provinces, including the more powerful Flanders, Brabant, Holland and Zeeland, had long enjoyed the right to hold a local assembly which reflected the lobbies and interests of the particular province. Each of these gatherings had a unique character. In Holland the principal towns dominated the proceedings of the States; while in Flanders, where the representative institution was organized along more conventional lines, the noble estate usually had the deciding voice.

In their dealings with these local assemblies, the prince or his deputy found himself obliged to secure absolute unanimity. The convention applied in all the provinces whereby, if one estate refused to contribute to a grant of money, the other estates regarded themselves absolved from further obligation. If, moreover, after the provincial assembly had voted a sum of money one estate failed to produce its quota, their colleagues considered themselves entitled to make a corresponding reduction in the amount of their respective contributions. The idea, often floated, of a majority decision binding on all the estates invariably stirred up bitter and effective opposition.

For all the annoyance and delay Charles, or, as was more often the case, his lieutenant, preferred to raise money by appealing to the wealthier provinces on an individual basis than by summoning them all as a group. Local assemblies had the reputation of being more tractable, whereas the States General of the Netherlands were generally regarded as fractious, insolent, and obsessed with local interests. But as the wars against France dragged on the Habsburgs were forced to suppress their dislike for these larger gatherings; and they became more frequent in the closing years of Charles V's rule. At the meetings of the States General, to which all seventeen provinces sent envoys after 1549, the familiar problems of management reappeared, only this time on a much larger scale. The delegates, answerable directly to their respective provinces, voted money on the strict understanding that everyone did likewise. Should a single estate from any province subsequently welch on its quota or fail to pay the full amount, then every other estate was permitted to make the corresponding adjustment. To give the principle, known as the General Clause, greater validity, it was written into the formal text of the vote. Raising money under such conditions may explain why Mary of Hungary became increasingly testy in her dealings with her loving subjects, why Philip II, more accustomed to the deferential manner of the Castilian cortes, could scarcely contain his anger at the conduct of the States General of 1558 and 1559, and why the duke of Alba would have preferred to abolish them altogether.

The Burgundian dukes and their Habsburg successors had also attempted through the meetings of the States General to foster the concept of national unity and common purpose. High hopes notwithstanding, these occasions never developed into anything more than a congress of ambassadors at which the individual envoys remained obstinately concerned with provincial affairs. The attempt to introduce majority voting here failed as resoundingly as it had done in the local assemblies. The spirit of parochial independence survived the attempts of successive rulers to break it down. Yet this same notion proved a source of both weakness and strength. It prevented the Habsburgs from imposing a uniform system of taxation upon their subjects in the Low Countries. Similarly this determination to think in terms of province rather than a larger unit prevented both the Catholic moderates and William of Orange from constructing an effective alliance against Spain.

Philip II's knowledge of government in the Low Countries came from direct experience. He had presided in person over the meetings of the States General in 1557 at Arras, and again in the following year at Valenciennes. Nothing could have more prejudiced him against the States General and the native aristocracy which played so prominent a part in the deliberations. The delegates, in a state of virtual mutiny at the repeated demands for money, and certain that the royal bankruptcy of 1557 had delivered the king into their hands, subjected the government's record to raking criticism. When they came to vote the Nine Years' Aid (3 May 1558), a substantial grant of 800,000 guilders per annum for nine years, they imposed a set of restrictions which Philip was powerless to reject. A board appointed by the States General, and not the crown, was to levy, spend, and audit the money voted. The royal treasury would see none of the funds—humiliating enough—nor could they be used as collateral for credit operations by the king's servants, little short of a disaster for a regime which seemed to live, in the Netherlands at any rate, on advances from the banking fraternity.

As he took formal leave of his Flemish subjects in Ghent, his father's birthplace, Philip had time to reflect with misgiving on the attitude of the States General and the great aristocrats, men like William of Orange (to become known as 'the Silent'), who regularly used such occasions as cover for their private manœuvres. Such problems formed the stock-in-trade of any political system, and they could normally be contained. But just as Philip was completing his preparations for departure, a new and highly unstable element was to be added to the politics of the Low Countries. In the year Philip retreated to his Castilian kingdom, Calvin founded his Academy in Geneva (1559). Its graduates and their disciples were to transform the history of the Low Countries.

Heresy was nothing new in the Netherlands. In March 1521 the authorities ordered the publication of the first of many decrees prohibiting the printing or reading of Martin Luther's works. The first Lutheran martyrs, Augustinians appropriately enough, went to the stake in Brussels two years later (1 July 1523). Charles V was determined to prevent in his Burgundian lands a repetition of what had taken place in Germany. He encouraged the Inquisition and brought out a series of ordinances of ever-increasing ferocity, culminating in the Edict of Blood (29 April 1550), with the intention of preventing the teaching or dissemination of subversive (i.e. Protestant) literature. His enthusiasm for persecution was shared and encouraged by his chief inquisitor, Erard de la Marck, prince bishop of Liège, and his successor in both offices, Corneille de Berghes (1538–44). At one time Anabaptism was identified as a major threat to church unity; but after the episode of the Anabaptist commonwealth of Münster the menace fell away. Moderates, whether Catholics or Lutherans, were hardly likely to identify with John of Leiden. Lutheranism, once an inspiration to the Anabaptist fathers, failed to prosper through the unrelenting hostility of the secular powers; and, except in such notorious hotbeds of heresy as Antwerp, the number of heretics in the Netherlands at the time of Charles's abdication may have been less than at virtually any other time during the reign.

Where Lutheranism failed, Calvinism succeeded. This new and

more virulent creed placed little if any reliance upon the legally constituted authorities, preferring instead to rely on the local community and those it attracted. Dissent like the plague normally took to the rivers; but in the case of the Low Countries its main points of entry were in the south along the French border. Calvinism, very much a product of the French cultural world, built up in the years from 1559 to 1565 a strong following in the francophone textile towns of Brabant and western Flanders; and by 1567 the English merchant Sir Thomas Gresham, not normally given to exaggeration, was reporting the existence of over 40,000 Calvinists in the golden mart of Antwerp. In the northern provinces Calvinism failed to get such a deep hold; the transformation of Holland and Zeeland into the impregnable fortresses of the faith came about as a result of later military developments. In 1561 the metrical psalms of Marot could be heard openly on the streets of Tournai and Valenciennes. Two years later this fervour had been translated into structure. By 1563 the various Calvinist communities of the southern provinces had organized a regular pattern of synods and assemblies, just as was the case in France and Scotland. Unlike the Lutherans, they had equipped themselves to do battle with the secular authorities for freedom of worship—and more, much more, if the circumstances permitted.

In drawing up his plans before his departure to Spain, Philip set out a number of priorities for his representative as ruler. He intended that the drain on Iberian resources should cease and that the Low Countries should at least cover their own running costs; he was committed to the preservation of the Catholic faith which the Council of Trent then in session was in the process of rejuvenating; and he was determined to keep the native nobility at a safe distance from the exercise of real power. In setting up the administration that was to operate during his absence from the Low Countries, which, even on the most optimistic assumptions, was certain to be prolonged, Philip observed the precedent set by his father. Provinces the size and importance of the Netherlands required a prince, or princess, of the blood to act as the symbol of royal authority. Christine of Lorraine had been considered for the post of governor but her claims had to be dismissed on the grounds that she was too closely identified with the native aristocracy. The other candidate, Margaret of Parma, seemed to have just the right qualities. She had been born to Charles V and the daughter of a tapestry weaver in the town of Oudenarde, the fruit of a temporary union in the dank months of winter. Marguerite of Austria had supervised her early upbringing, as in the case of so many others; but in 1533 the eleven-year-old-girl was sent to Italy where she had remained ever since, safely removed from any contact with the affairs of her native land and any compromising friendships. In her case the Spanish court had an additional guarantee of satisfactory conduct. The fortress of Piacenza had been occupied by Spanish troops since 1547. Margaret of Parma dearly wished to recover this possession of the Farnese house, not for her husband Octavio, whom she detested, but for her only son Alexander, on whom she doted. Origin, ancestry, vulnerability; the choice was perfect.

As governor of the Netherlands, Margaret presided over a set of 'Collateral' Councils which had been established in 1531. The most prestigious of these, the Council of State, lacked a precisely defined jurisdiction. It was called upon to offer advice on important matters of state, while its aristocratic members, the bulk of whom held high local office, were expected to represent the interests of the localities from which they were drawn. The Secret Council discharged the functions of a modern Ministry of the Interior with special responsibility for the enforcement of the religious edicts, an invidious task which may have given the institution a reputation worse than it deserved. The Council of Finance collected revenues raised locally and fought a losing battle to preserve from further depredations what little remained of royal property. Lastly the Great Council of Malines acted as the supreme court of appeal for most, but not all, of the Seventeen Provinces.

Philip had no intention of altering the outward appearance of government in the Low Countries. To obtain the effects that he required, the king believed that only a few discreet adjustments were needed. At the time of his departure the permanent membership of the Council of State stood at three, Berlaymont, Viglius, and the all-important Granvelle. Philip's original intention had been to limit the participation of the great aristocrats to occasions on which local advice was necessary or which were ceremonial in character. Within this small knot of permanent councillors the king intended that Granvelle (Antoine de Perrenot) should direct affairs. Margaret of Parma exercised a nominal sovereignty, thereby satisfying the native demand for a prince of the ruling house. Philip's purpose was to enforce strict subordination to Madrid and to minimize the influence either of local institutions such as the States General or the native aristocracy, who had always used such gatherings to further their own designs. Surprisingly, this scheme of things worked for the best part of two years, mainly thanks to Granvelle's good sense. But even his touch and delicacy could not conceal indefinitely just how fragile the system really was. A number of factors, some historic, some personal, merged to produce a force whose energy soon loosened the foundations of the state.

The diocesan structure of the Netherlands reached back into Merovingian times; and little account had been taken during the intervening centuries of political transformation or demographic change. This had led to the striking anomaly whereby most of the Low Countries fell under the spiritual authority of Rheims and Cologne, two archbishoprics neither of which was subject to the Habsburgs. From both a religious and a political standpoint the redrawing of diocesan boundaries was an urgent necessity. After years of debate, the papacy agreed to a thorough restructuring of the church in the Low Countries. The bull *Super Universas* (12 May 1559) created three new ecclesiastical provinces and designated Utrecht as the metropolitan see for the north, Malines for Brabant and Flanders, and Cambrai for the French-speaking province of the south. All three archbishoprics stood on Habsburg territory. The bull also decreed the establishment of fourteen new bishoprics within the new provinces and bestowed the right of appointment on the king. To bolster the income of the new foundations it was further provided that ten should have a neighbouring abbey incorporated into their endowment, the bishop becoming thereby an abbot *in commendam*.

The reform as laid out in *Super Universas* and its companion legislation, the bulls *Ex Injuncto* and *De Statu Ecclesiarum* (11 March 1561) was not before time. The fight against Protestantism demanded the root-and-branch reform of the diocesan administration; and the Fathers' meeting at Trent (1545–63) had laid particular stress on the role of the bishop in the revival of the Latin church. But the political risks involved in such a project were high. The idea of reform along Tridentine lines alarmed the established clergy, who thought quite rightly that it would prejudice their traditional life-style. The nobility resented a programme which, by insisting that aspirants to ecclesiastical office should hold a university degree (a touching witness to belief in education), effectively debarred their younger sons, who might otherwise have expected accommodation in the higher ranks of the church. The provinces of the north-east, the 'recent conquests' or non-patrimonial lands, regarded the whole project as an assault on provincial liberties, with the new incumbents loyal not to the locality but to the king who had appointed them. Brabant led the opposition to the 'new bishoprics' for reasons that were not hard to explain. If Malines acquired as part of its endowment the revenues from the abbey of Afflighem as had been initially proposed, the archbishop in his capacity as abbot would have the right to preside over the provincial assembly of Brabant. Such an innovation was hardly likely to pass uncontested; and when the names were added to the places the storm broke. Philip secured a cardinal's hat for his chief minister, Antoine de Perrenot (26 February 1561) and then raised him to the primatial dignity of Malines. A social parvenu, a career cleric, a man not even born in the Low Countries, was now to preside over the proudest and richest state in the land, and all were to acknowledge his pre-eminence.

Reaction was swift. The abbots, who played so prominent a part in the estates of Brabant, threatened to suspend further payment of their contribution to the Nine Years' Aid voted in 1558, thereby jeopardizing the balance still to be collected should others invoke the General Clause. They were determined to prevent the incorporation of Afflighem, a Benedictine foundation, into the arch-bishopric of Malines, on the calculation that if this took place it unduly strengthened the hand of the king and his principal minister. William of Orange and his fellow aristocrats also opposed the scheme and the man they assumed, rightly or wrongly, to be its main promoter. Up to 1561 the aristocrats on the Council of State enjoyed precedence over all others save Margaret herself. With Granvelle's elevation to the archbishopric and the cardinalate this was no longer the case. To many, even the normally level-headed William of Orange, Antoine de Perrenot had overreached himself; and this slight a socially unforgiving age was not prepared to overlook. The harmony which had prevailed at the highest levels after the king's departure began to break down.

The question of the new bishoprics and the incorporation of the abbeys contributed a further set of issues in the more general trial of strength between absent king and unruly subjects. Philip believed that such an ecclesiastical reorganization was imperative if the challenge of heresy was to be met successfully. Where Spanish arms came to prevail, his plans were largely carried out. Although the abbeys of Brabant and Flanders escaped absorption, eight sees were erected in the south after 1580. Through their work and the activities of the Jesuits, who had established their first colleges in Tournai and

Antwerp as far back as 1562, the lands south of the great rivers were thoroughly evangelized in the spirit of the Counter-Reformation. North of the divide it was a different story. The archdiocese of Utrecht and its dependent bishoprics were not given sufficient time to exert a lasting influence; and although the Catholic faith for long remained the majority religion it was looked on with disfavour, and subject to occasional persecution, by the ruling élite which emerged after 1572.

Once the aristocracy fully appreciated how Philip intended the Low Countries to be governed during his absence, they laid their plans to alter the system to their own advantage. The great magnates such as the prince of Orange, Lamoraal van Egmont, and Philip of Horne had through their membership of the Order of the Golden Fleece a convenient forum in which to meet and concert tactics. In March 1563 they withdrew from attendance at the Council of State, a serious blow to its authority and one which made it difficult to enforce the government's wishes in the localities. The absent stadholders (provincial governors) urged the calling of the States General for all the seventeen provinces, ostensibly to bring some order to the dilapidated condition of royal finance, but in reality as an opportunity to ventilate grievances against royal policy and its very incarnation, Granvelle. The aristocrats, egged on probably by William of Orange, also started to work on Margaret of Parma, neither strong nor constant, by suggesting that the cardinal, hitherto her closest adviser, was less than sincere in his efforts to persuade Philip to restore Piacenza to the Farnese. By July 1563 success lay within their grasp. Disappointed at repeated failures to recover the fortress and more than disillusioned at Philip's choice of a bride (Mary of Portugal) for her only son, Margaret turned against Granvelle. Governor and nobles combined in their efforts to bring down the king's minister. Eventually, and against the advice of a powerful lobby at the Spanish court led by the duke of Alba, Philip agreed to the cardinal's dismissal (14 December 1563).

The departure of Granvelle marked the end of direct rule from Madrid. Under pressure from the ruling classes the Spanish tercio stationed in the Low Countries had been withdrawn in 1561; and now the minister on whom Philip had relied to carry out his strict instructions had also been compelled to leave. What would now fill the vacuum? The aristocrats, organized into an informal league since 1562, had no doubts on the subject. Some suggested that business normally transacted by the Secret Council and the Council of Finance should be transferred to the Council of State, whose sessions were open to all of their rank. Others proposed that the States General be summoned and that responsibility for government finance be taken over by standing committees of this institution. Developments of these basic ideas included a project to expand the powers of the various stadholders, all aristocrats, and subject local courts to their exclusive control. These plans had a common purpose, to reverse the centralizing policies of the Habsburgs and their Burgundian predecessors and convert the Netherlands into an aristocratic commonwealth, akin in many respects to Poland and Lithuania.

In pursuit of such designs the great nobles could count on the minor nobility and the town magistrates. The former had been purchasing steadily from a penurious crown the rights of primary and middle jurisdiction. Such investments in the administration, and therefore the profits, of justice had become ever more valuable in times of rapid inflation when so many other sources of income had failed to keep pace. The attempts by Philip's ministers and, before them, by Mary of Hungary, to bring the localities under firmer control was interpreted both as a threat to regional autonomy and, less creditably, a source of baronial income. The urban patriciates, for their part, had not hesitated to benefit from the crown's financial troubles. For over a century they had been in the market steadily buying up the right to appoint to offices of justice within the city; and they were just as anxious to extend the authority of the town council to the surrounding hinterland. Over the previous decades a transfer of jurisdiction had taken place from ducal (or royal) to civic control. Like the nobles, and above them, the aristocrats, the magistrates saw themselves at risk from the agents of central government. They particularly feared the local Inquisition which, apart from its unpleasant religious function, could be looked on as a surrogate bureaucracy, an embryonic intendancy in the French style.

Within limits the king of Spain was prepared to accept tough political bargains. But once Granvelle was safely on his way 'to visit his aged mother', the magnates set forth a fresh set of demands which went (from Philip's point of view) way beyond the mark. Fully aware that Iberian resources were entirely committed to the war in the Mediterranean against the Turks and their allies, the aristocrats now required a relaxation in the 'placards', or laws, against heresy. Whatever their precise motives they were also giving expression to the majority of the population who, while remaining faithful to Rome, had never shared the enthusiasm for persecution. The connection between noble—perhaps feudal—opposition and religious dissent had at last become apparent. In the belief that Philip could be made to concede ground on both counts, Egmont was sent to Spain early in 1565. He arrived in February and remained until April.

Throughout his stay he was fêted and lionized by the court as the victor of Gravelinges (1558) and the king's good servant. Philip received him more than once in private audience; and it was on these occasions that the count was able to deliver verbally his real message. Almost certainly he stressed the need to modify the placards and associate the nobles more closely with the business of government. The king heard him out, attentive and courteous as always; and when the time came for the count to depart, he rewarded him with splendid gifts. Egmont returned to the Netherlands in the late spring of 1565 highly pleased with himself and convinced that Philip would act on what he had said. The count's prestige, as the man who, apparently, had the king's ear, never stood higher.

Others were not so optimistic. While the Low Countries awaited an official reply from Spain, a group of young men, scions for the most part of the minor gentry and strongly influenced by Calvinist teachings, met in the small German town of Spa to plot treason. Amongst the items on the informal agenda stood a proposal for the violent overthrow of the state and the seizure of ecclesiastical property which was then to be distributed for the benefit of the nobility. The schemes of Franz von Sickingen had found a delayed echo in the Low Countries. Or, if the analogy is too distant, the murky plans of these Calvinist hotheads seemed all too reminiscent of the events which had led to the Tumult of Amboise (1561).

At last Philip gave his considered reply to the demands which Egmont had brought to him. In the famous set of Letters from the Woods of Segovia (17–20 October 1565) he refused to allow any alteration in the laws against heresy; nor did he intend to change the structure of government to accommodate noble demands. Encouraged in his resolve, perhaps, by the successful defence of Malta, the king had found his authentic voice. Egmont had been duped, as, indeed, had been also those who believed that Philip could be reasoned into modifying his religious policies.

The awareness that the placards were to remain unaltered brought a fresh surge of religious and political radicalism. Towards the end of 1565 the leading nobles, this time fathers not sons, opened negotiations with the heads of the Calvinist communities on the possibilities of future co-operation. Royal intransigence and Margaret of Parma's evident inability to act firmly—in marked contrast to her illustrious predecessor, Mary of Hungary—created a dangerous situation in which two movements, one of noble opposition and the other of religious dissent, now began to make common cause. The collaboration across confessional lines soon went a stage further. In December 1565 over three hundred and fifty nobles drew up and signed a document known as the Compromise in which they pledged themselves to work for the annulment of the placards and the suspension of the Inquisition. The signatories were drawn from both Calvinist and Catholic persuasions; and the prince of Orange took a leading part in its drafting. As a document the Compromise might be considered the manifesto of the Moderates whose aim it became to hold the Netherlands together by avoiding the excesses of either religious party.

The principal opponents of the government found their way into the ranks either of the aristocratic league or the socially inferior noble union. For reasons never satisfactorily explained, the two remained separate throughout, although plans for a fusion were aired from time to time. Nevertheless, at critical moments the two did collaborate to secure common objectives. Much of the credit for this went to William of Orange who, in company with his brother, Louis of Nassau, worked continuously behind the scenes for much of 1566 co-ordinating the tactics of the main opposition parties. An early and notable example of joint planning occurred in the spring of that year. A group of noblemen who had signed the Compromise arrived in Brussels on 4 April 1566. On the following day they presented Margaret of Parma with a petition in which the usual demands for a relaxation of the heresy laws and the calling of the States General were restated. One of her advisers, Charles de Berlaymont, dismissed the petitioners as a rabble; but the governor could not afford to treat them with such contempt. After the dispatches from the Woods of Segovia had become public knowledge, the aristocrats had withdrawn from the Council of State with the intention of weakening the administration; and Margaret of Parma, already unnerved by this boycott, feared that if she turned 'the Beggars' away empty-handed her action would spark off widespread rioting. To buy time she agreed to 'moderate' the placards; and while she consulted Madrid the legislation against heresy was to remain in abeyance until orders were received to the contrary.

This tacit grant of toleration, far from restoring calm, only increased the atmosphere of tension. Margaret had shown that she was amenable to pressure; the noble opposition, both in its upper and lower reaches, had yet to extort lasting concessions; while the Calvinist communities, apparently convinced that freedom of worship had come to stay, began to act with ever-increasing daring. The message was preached openly without regard to the placards. Even more ominously, Calvinist elders held a conference at St Truiden in July 1566 to which sympathetic noblemen were invited. During this meeting the leaders of the Calvinist community asked the nobles to act as the patrons and protectors of their church, a relationship all too familiar from the examples of France, Bohemia, and the Austrian domains of the Habsburgs. Economic difficulties added a further dimension to the crisis. The Low Countries depended on the Baltic for their imports of grain. In 1565 hostilities between Sweden and Denmark led to the closing of the Sound through which all the traffic passed; supplies in the Netherlands shortened; the price of bread soared; and much of the population, especially in the textile centres, went hungry. Dearth stoked up feelings against an unpopular and irresolute government and such obvious symbols of authority as the churches and the monasteries. The task of the religious zealot became that much easier.

On 10 August 1566 an obscure clergyman, Sebastian Matte, delivered to his congregation in the small town of Steenvoorde in the Westquarter of Flanders a sermon of such passion that the audience rose and made its way to the neighbouring convent of St Lawrence. Here they destroyed the statues and any other decorations which they considered idolatrous. Their example proved contagious. Within a matter of hours similar events had taken place in the major towns of Brabant and Flanders. The movement remained very much a phenomenon of the southern provinces, losing most of its impetus the further north it travelled. Although the cleansing of the churches was subsequently portrayed as an example of widespread hooliganism, those who entered the churches did so in the majority of cases under supervision either from the local magistrates or the elders of the Calvinist communities. The intention of the so-called rioters was to secure permanent places for the exercise of their cult. Once a suitable building had been taken over, any undue ornamentation was then removed. Unfortunately, the acquisition and renovation of the churches did sometimes lead to wanton vandalism, hence the phrase applied to the episode, the Iconoclastic Riots.

To many the commandeering of the holy places signalled the total breakdown of law and order. Within a fortnight of the initial outbreak, Margaret of Parma, even when directed by the steadier hand of Peter Ernest, Count Mansfeld, had panicked into making concessions which she knew at the time would not be honoured. The Accord of 23 August 1566 sanctioned the continued practice of Protestant worship in the rural areas where it had already established itself. Margaret of Parma also promised to raise once again with Philip the question of summoning the States General. But the Accord, as with the earlier Moderation, failed to bring stability. The Calvinists, encouraged by the lack of support for the established church which the Iconoclastic Riots seemed to reveal, and elated by the concessions which had been wrung out of the government, began to recruit a private army. The principal opposition group, the Catholic and Protestant nobles who had signed the Compromise in the previous year, was badly split. This Moderate party, which the prince of Orange had done so much to foster, had been uneasy at the prospect which the conference at St Truiden had held out; and its membership was thoroughly alarmed by the religious rioting which threatened both internal security and the privileged position of the Catholic church, in which the majority continued to believe. The Moderates divided into one group which decided to collaborate with royal officials in the restoration of order, William of Orange acting as a tardy and uncertain recruit; and a much smaller faction prepared to follow the example of Hendrik of Brederode who had accepted the title Protector of the Calvinist churches, and was on the road to open rebellion.

As he sat on a hill a few miles outside Madrid by the site of old iron-workings and supervised the building of the great pantheon which would house the earthly remains of his father and his family, Philip followed the unfolding events in the Netherlands from a distance which could only magnify and distort. He had announced his intention of returning to the Low Countries in the summer of 1566 before the outbreak of the latest round of troubles. His father had made regular tours of his vast dominions, a fact to which he had proudly alluded in his speech of abdication, and it was time for his son to follow suit. But when it came for the fateful decisions to be made Philip surrounded himself with Spanish councillors, in a Spanish land, and subject to Spanish preoccupations. The discussions held at the Habsburg court in the winter of 1567 helped to determine the subsequent character of the monarchy. For the first decade of his reign

Philip ruled his inheritance very much in the style and spirit of his father. Certainly until 1559 he was prepared to regard himself as the peripatetic sovereign of numerous states, all of equal standing in his eyes and united only in their allegiance to a single dynasty. The debate over the Netherlands, and even more its upshot, revealed the slow inception of Castilianization, a process whereby every state which had fallen to Philip's inheritance was slowly subordinated to the needs, taste, and attitudes of Castile. Those who participated in the debate were also forced to contemplate the deeper implications of the unrest in the Netherlands. Would Castile govern its European territories under a system of direct rule or would a federal structure be permitted to emerge? In 1566–7 the king opted for the former, a decision foreshadowed by the career of Granvelle. Centralism was partially relaxed in the 1590s with the appointment of the archdukes. But it was not until the advent of the count-duke of Olivares (1621–43) that the failure of this policy, for economic reasons, if no others, was at last acknowledged; and a serious effort was made to create a genuine federation—by which time it was too late.

Although it was not made explicit at the time, Philip approached the problems of the Netherlands from the international and the historic context. He was determined that there would be no repetition of what had taken place in Germany during the last years of his father's reign. The Augsburg Transaction (1548) had reduced the likelihood by eliminating the jurisdiction of the Imperial Diet even if the Low Countries still remained, technically, a province of the empire. But there were those who sought to revive the connection. The mayor of Antwerp and the pensionary of Brussels both attended the Imperial Diet at Augsburg in 1562 where they had proposed that the peace to which the town had given its name (1555) should apply to the Low Countries. Coming from functionaries of middling importance such ideas could be dismissed as impudence. But that same gathering had been attended by William of Orange formerly the count of Nassau-Dillenburg and through another title a prince of the empire in his own right. The proposal to extend the Augsburg peace to the Netherlands certainly fitted in with his ideas and those of the moderate party.

Philip's judgement of the prince increasingly lacked balance as he came to discern in him the ghost of Maurice of Saxony. Yet grounds for fearing the German connection did exist. William of Orange had married the sister of the premier Lutheran ruler, the elector of Saxony. Lamoraal, count of Egmont, had close relations with the Catholic princes of the empire through his marriage to Sabine of Bavaria. Another prominent figure, almost always to the fore of noble agitation, Philip, count of Horne, had strong family ties with Germany. If Philip did opt for a policy of repression he would have to send a sizeable force to the Low Countries in order to seal the German border. And that still left the threat from France which had similar ties of blood and religion with the aristocrats of the Golden Fleece.

The king found the ideas put forward by men like William even more repugnant than their persons. He had doubtlessly heard through diplomatic channels that Sigismund II of Poland had granted freedom of worship to the Lutheran nobility of Livonia, the first Catholic sovereign to break rank over the question of toleration, in August 1561. A few months later he could contemplate a similar spectacle, and this time on Spain's very frontier. Catherine de Medici, for all her protestations of loyalty to the faith, conceded toleration to the Calvinist (Huguenot) minority in France by the Edict of January (1562); and compounded the deed by confirming the grant the following year at the peace of Amboise (1563). The Habsburgs themselves were not sound on the issue. Maximilian of Austria who inherited the imperial title in 1564 exhibited symptoms of eirenic tendencies distressingly early in his career. The worst forebodings were realized in 1568 when he permitted the nobility of Lower Austria freedom of religious practice, and again in 1575 when he extended similar privileges to Bohemia, although mercifully on this occasion the sanction was confined to a verbal promise. From Philip's standpoint, toleration was not only morally wrong, it was politically disastrous. Calvinism, unlike the more supine Lutheran creed, provided the nobility with an instrument ready-made to contest the authority of the state whether in the representative institutions or, if issues came to a head, on the battlefield. Witness Scotland, witness France, or, as Philip himself was witnessing, the Netherlands.

The monarchy reflected on the options available during a series of debates in council, a technique much favoured and which had been used in the related case of 'Milan or the Low Countries' during the previous reign. From the record of one such session, held on 29 October 1566, it is evident that the king was presented with a stark contrast of choice. One group, the nascent federalist party, if so it may be termed, advocated the return of Philip to his northern dominions accompanied by an escort of just sufficient strength to protect his person and maintain his prestige. The general tenor of the submission, prepared by Ruy Gómez and his associates, was towards conciliation. Another school of thought strongly opposed this. The proto-centralists advised the sending of an army to the Netherlands to re-establish order. Only when the provinces had been returned to peace should the king set out for the Low Countries, arriving as the long-awaited saviour of his people from heresy and perhaps even from his own forces of repression. The latter view, with its evident simplicity, became official policy.

In the Netherlands the various opposition parties knew that they were living on borrowed time. Amongst the aristocrats William of Orange and his closest colleagues tried to persuade their peers to stage a *coup d'état* in collaboration with the Calvinist communities and raise an army, a plan which foreshadowed the events of 1576. But in the winter of 1566 with fearful reports coming from Madrid including the news that the duke of Alba had been appointed Captain General, the more timid or those more strongly attached to the Catholic faith refused to take the irrevocable step. Lamoraal, count of Egmont, was amongst them. The prince of Orange, moreover, no longer enjoyed the degree of authority he once had. Margaret of Parma was strengthening the Council of State with men known for their hostility (or envy) towards William. The prince, still at this stage a Catholic and in favour of a moderate settlement in the Netherlands, was being steadily isolated.

The Calvinist churches, although willing to enter into tactical alliances, continued to follow their own line. In the autumn of 1566 they offered Philip an indemnity of three million guilders for the grant of religious toleration, a gesture analogous in some ways to the attempts of the moriscos to buy freedom of worship. When the money was declined, as the Calvinists surely knew it would be, the sum was converted into a war chest. Of all the opposition parties they were the most resolute; but they lacked at this stage the mass following and the military expertise to launch a successful resistance movement. Their militias proved no match for the train bands (*compagnies d'ordonnance*) led by aristocrats loyal to Brussels. Nor could Orange be persuaded to admit a contingent of Calvinists to enter Antwerp, or their followers within the city to come to their rescue, before they were cut down by royal troops within sight of the walls at Oosterweel (13 March 1567). That Orange should have permitted the slaughter destroyed the last chance of mounting effective resistance against the king's army then gathering in Lombardy; and it was long held against Orange himself.

Whatever the soundness of his judgement at the time, the prince guessed correctly what was in store for all those who had been prominent in the recent agitation. He advised the Calvinist preachers to leave Antwerp in April 1567, and he and his family left at the end of the month for his estates in Germany.

Such precautions were well advised. By the spring of 1567 plans for the military pacification of the Netherlands were far advanced. A small but highly professional army made up of the Spanish tercios based in the Italian peninsula was gathering in Lombardy. Philip appointed as its commander the duke of Alba, remarkable for his ability as a soldier, his contempt for bureaucratic punctilio, and his disregard of human life. The death of Suleiman the Magnificent in 1566 and the disputed succession to the Ottoman throne brought about a temporary lull on the Mediterranean front and allowed Philip to concentrate the resources needed for military operations in the north. Significantly, the king of Spain had picked to head the expeditionary force a man of unbending views, volunteered often at court on both private and public occasions; and he furnished him with virtually plenipotentiary powers to act in whatever way was required to restore the situation. Any settlement would strongly reflect the duke's ideas. Alba left Turin, the starting-point of the march, on 18 June 1567; and he entered Brussels, in person and with a small escort, on the afternoon of 22 August. While the duke arranged for his personal quarters in the capital, his troops were billeted at a number of key points, Antwerp being an obvious choice. A network of military cantonments ensured the obedience of the seventeen provinces.

The duke was quite prepared to resurrect the system of government which had obtained in the time of Granvelle, as, no doubt, was Philip, whose authorization such a scheme would have required. Margaret of Parma was to remain in office while the duke decided and carried out policy. But the daughter of Charles V refused to be a party to such a plan. She presented her resignation on 8 September 1567; and she was out of the capital with her entourage by the end of the year. The duke then became the ruler of the Netherlands both in name and in fact. The symbolism of the change did not go unnoticed: for the first time the highest office in the land had been vested in one not of royal family. The Burgundian inheritance no longer merited a prince of the blood.

Alba set to work unhampered by any restraining influence, setting up a strongly authoritarian system of government. Within a few days of arrival he nominated a special tribunal charged with enforcing the placards and ferreting out those involved in the religious disturbances of the previous year. The Council of Troubles, rapidly rechristened the Council of Blood, began its operations on 5 September 1567. During the course of its existence it heard well over ten thousand cases. About eleven hundred of those arraigned were executed, while the goods of a further nine thousand were confiscated. Alba also intended to show equal severity to the ringleaders of the disturbances. Some of the principal agitators had already died, or were about to. Another, Montigny, was in Spain, held at first in honourable detention, then strict confinement, until in 1571 he was quietly strangled. That still left two of the foremost nobles at large, Egmont and Horne. They were arrested on 9 September 1567; and nine months later, contrary to an earlier promise of clemency, they went to the scaffold (5 June 1568). The ceremony, magnificently staged in the most public place in all the land, the Great Square of Brussels, served as a warning to all and a portent of things to come.

   Philip chose the duke of Alba as his representative in the Netherlands not merely for his belief in firmness but because Alba was the best general of the day. The elimination of so many leading aristocrats invited some form of military challenge whether from within the Netherlands, or, more likely, the surrounding states. In 1568 Alba vindicated his selection with an astounding display of military judgement. William of Orange, now the undisputed head of the noble opposition after the liquidation of his associates, pawned all his goods to raise an army and appealed to his sympathizers for additional funds. Once the campaigning season opened he planned to attack the Low Countries in a four-pronged movement. The ambitious operation failed dismally through poor co-ordination and lack of finance. Orange was unable to get his main force into the field until late on: he crossed the Maas at Stokken on 5 October 1568, but was unable to make contact with the enemy. The duke prudently avoided a general engagement, confident that without pay the opposing army would disintegrate, as it did. Alba's tactical sense contributed greatly to the royal victory in that *annus mirabilis* of 1568; but there was another, perhaps more profound, reason for this success. The bulk of the population, moderate Catholics overwhelmingly, still remembered the Iconoclastic excesses of 1566. Not a single city rose for the prince of Orange when he launched his forlorn venture. At this stage William appeared as little more than an aristocratic frondeur with a sense of self-preservation superior to that of his colleagues. Only blunders on the part of the royal administration could create for the prince a mass following.

After his military triumph Alba enjoyed a freedom of action denied to any governor of the Netherlands either before or after. Yet even he found himself obliged to operate within a number of constraints. It had been made clear to the duke before he left the Spanish court that he was required, once the army had taken up permanent quarters in the Netherlands, to cover all the costs of administration from local sources. In the Mediterranean, Ottoman naval units were astir; and a major blow was expected in the near future. The crown was not in a position to underwrite warfare against the Turks and the pacification of the Low Countries, a fact which was spelt out to the duke in 1569 in case he had forgotten. As the head of Philip's cabinet (Cardinal Espinosa) expressed the point 'The amount of money which the Castilian Exchequer has had to provide for the Netherlands does not cease to cause grave concern. And, indeed, if you [sc. Alba] do not arrange things so that the outlay stops, I am convinced that it will be impossible to go on any longer.'

The Netherlands were amongst the most prosperous regions in Europe, with an enormous fiscal potential. Once all attempts at resistance had been crushed, Alba decided to introduce a number of taxes modelled on those traditionally levied in Castile itself. He laid his plans before the States General convoked for an extraordinary session, in which the element of coercion was underlined by the brevity of the meeting (20–1 March 1569). The duke required the assent of the delegates to three impositions: firstly, a tax of 1 per cent on all capital assets (land mostly) to be levied on a once-off basis; secondly, a recurrent tax of 5 per cent to be raised from the sale of land; and lastly the notorious 10 per cent turnover tax to be paid whenever an item changed hands. Contemporaries referred to these as the Hundredth, Twentieth, and Tenth Penny respectively. In spite of Alba's minatory attitude, the States General voted only the non-permanent levy of 1 per cent and refused point-blank to concede the other demands. As a placatory gesture they offered the duke a further non-recurrent grant of four million florins to be spread over the next four years. Containing his rage, Alba accepted, in the hope that the States General would prove more amenable in two years' time. But when they showed themselves equally obdurate in 1571, the duke, his vestigial patience long exhausted, announced that he intended to raise the Tenth and Twentieth Penny with or without consent (31 July

1571). If Alba's measures had taken effect, if the new taxation had been granted (or successfully extorted), then the king's government would have become self-financing; and, as a consequence, the Habsburgs might have preserved their control over the undivided Netherlands.

The moderate Catholics had been petrified by the excesses of the Iconoclastic bands in 1566. They were therefore unwilling to help the prince of Orange when he invaded in 1568, as he was thought to be an intimate of the Calvinists. The duke's fiscal intentions changed their minds. Alba's ultimate goal, financial independence for the crown, threatened provincial liberty and commercial prosperity. Had success crowned his efforts, royal power would have increased to an unacceptable degree. To prevent this happening, the Catholic majority was ready to ally with Calvinist rebels. Philip himself conceded the point when he, in effect, annulled the levy of the Tenth Penny on 26 June 1572. Unfortunately, the damage had already been done. Local observers, and subsequently most Spanish commentators, agreed that the duke's tax innovations provoked the popular rebellion of 1572.

Ever since the fiasco of 1568 the prince of Orange had spent his time attempting to raise another army. He looked to his father-in-law, the elector of Saxony for help; but the latter, while keen to oblige, was subject to intense diplomatic pressure from the Holy Roman Emperor, Maximilian II, who was adamantly opposed to such involvement. William's younger brother John VI (1536–1606), count of Nassau-Dillenburg, made Herculean efforts on his behalf. On the security of his small German state he ran up debts of 400,000 guilders, managing all the while to avoid bankruptcy. The States General belatedly started to repay this loan in 1594, long after the struggle for independence had been won. For all the goodwill and the endeavours of his German relatives, Orange knew that if he had to depend on them alone he stood little real chance of improving on his previous performance. Something must change. And it had. In the period 1566–72 over fifty thousand inhabitants of the Netherlands chose exile rather than endure Alba's rule. About half this number emigrated to England, while the other half scattered amongst the various German principalities. In all perhaps 2 per cent of the population made its way abroad in this period. Although like all such communities bitterly divided amongst themselves, the exiles could be looked upon as a valuable new source of men and money if only they could be induced to unite. Delegates from the emigré communities met in the German town of Emden in the autumn of 1571 (4–13 October); and here they agreed upon a common statement of faith, the *Confessio Belgica*. They also debated the possibilities of an imminent return to their native land, and the means whereby this might best be achieved. Orange disliked the doctrinaire tone of the Calvinist divines gathered at the Synod of Emden; but he was realistic enough to appreciate that he needed their support.

The prince also maintained relations with another group which shared a common purpose. Unemployment in the fishing industry, particularly as it affected Holland and Zeeland, religious persecution throughout the Low Countries, and factional struggles within the urban oligarchies, had produced a motley horde of freebooters who preyed indiscriminately on shipping in the Channel and the bay of Biscay. The Huguenots of La Rochelle had made their port available to these Sea Beggars, as they were called; and Queen Elizabeth had opened up England's harbours to the marauders, although she became increasingly restive at their presence. The prince of Orange had issued letters of marque to the Sea Beggars, thereby clothing their activities with a semblance of legality. All three groups, prince, emigrés, and privateers awaited the moment of return. It came in 1572.

The Sea Beggars moved first. Worried by the thought of international complications, Elizabeth ordered their leader, Willem van der Marck, lord of Lumey, out of all English ports by 1 March 1572. As ejected tenants Lumey and his crews, some eleven hundred men in all, found themselves in urgent need of alternative accommodation. Within a month they had new premises. On 1 April 1572, the Beggars entered Brill, a choice of target which although hasty was not random. One of Lumey's captains, Willem Blois van Treslong, came from the town where he was related to a number of leading families. From Brill the Sea Beggars extended their control to the neighbouring towns. By the summer of that year they were master of Holland with the important exception of Amsterdam. The rebellion initiated by the Beggars received enthusiastic support from the towns of Friesland, Overijsel, and Gelderland. Further south the reaction was less positive. Brabant retained a clear memory of Iconoclastic outrages; and the proximity of Alba with the bulk of his army may have dampened the first surges of revolutionary fervour.

Under normal circumstances events such as the taking of Brill would have brought swift and merciless retribution. But the times were not normal. Orange's great design, although poorly co-ordinated as usual, had lumbered into action at long last. His brother Louis of

Nassau seized Mons (24 May 1572) in the far south, intending to await the arrival of an expeditionary corps sent by the French Calvinists (Huguenots). Gaspar de Coligny, Admiral of France, was exploiting his new-found ascendancy at the French court to urge that France should aid the insurgents. Such action, once taken, would provoke open conflict with Spain which, in turn, would remind his fellow countrymen that they were French first and Catholic or Protestant second. Alba, his strategic sense unimpaired, realized that the main threat to his position came not from the Sea Beggars with their as yet slender reserves but from the southern border. The Massacre of St Bartholomew's Night (23–4 August 1572), by removing the Huguenot party from a position of influence at the French court, relieved the pressure; and it led directly to the surrender of Mons on terms by Louis of Nassau (21 September 1572). Alba was free at last to turn to the unfinished business in the north.

The duke never wavered in his belief that vigorous repression offered the only means to put down the rebellion. Those towns which had opened their gates to the enemy must face the consequences. Malines was sacked for three days (1–4 October 1572); and similar treatment was accorded to Zutphen and Naardem. Fearful of equally brutal treatment, Haarlem refused to surrender at the duke's summons (11 December 1572); seven months later it too was taken and the garrison massacred (12 July 1573). Such brutality did not produce the anticipated effect; it merely hardened the determination of the remaining towns to hold out. The citizens of Leiden might not have fought so stubbornly—and ultimately so successfully—had it not been for the awful warning of Haarlem. Time, moreover, was against the duke. In anticipation of war on two fronts he had raised a large number of German and Walloon regiments to supplement his Spanish tercios. The financial liabilities thereby incurred destroyed any prospect of balancing the books; and the accumulating arrears prepared the war for the mutinies of both Spanish and 'foreign' troops which more than any other event led to the independence of the Seven Provinces. Even Philip, so firm a believer in rigour, began to have doubts about the sack of Malines and the indiscriminate application of such a policy. The theories of government advanced by the proto-centralist school of thought, even when applied by the high priest of the doctrine, appeared politically flawed and morally dubious.

In the autumn of 1573 Philip recalled Alba, choosing as his replacement a Catalan nobleman, Luis de Requesens. Although obviously not of royal blood, a serious mistake in itself, the new governor brought with him a reputation for humanity. He was also in close contact with Cardinal Granvelle, a family friend, who offered sound advice throughout his brief term of office. The new governorship began with a brisk determination to tear out by the roots all reminders of the previous regime. Requesens shared the view that the current difficulties were attributable in large measure to the misconduct of royal, and particularly Spanish, troops. He also understood, even before taking up his post, that a military reconquest of Holland and Zeeland, the two provinces which had successfully withstood the duke, was a financial impossibility, the more so since the States General refused to contribute a penny towards the running costs of the army or the administration. Negotiations offered the only practical solution.

After a year of informal contacts serious discussions began at Breda on 3 March 1575. The representatives of the two provinces demanded the summoning of the States General and the withdrawal of foreign troops. These two items might have been accommodated. But the conference broke down over the religious issue. Neither Holland nor Zeeland were prepared to restore Catholicism to its exclusive position. The talks were finally abandoned in July; but they had served a purpose if only to establish the basic issues around which successive attempts to bring about a peace settlement would ebb and flow.

The opportunity of resolving the stalemate came in the following year through a series of disasters. Requesens died suddenly during the night of 4–5 March 1576. Authority passed into the hands of a Council of State, weak and bitterly divided. The Spanish troops spent part of the summer besieging Zierikzee; but when this fell (30 June 1576) they mutinied. Arrears of pay went back for years; and the tercios were determined to take what they believed was due to them. On 4 November 1576 they entered and sacked Antwerp, possibly the only prize rich enough to satisfy their greed and their pent-up resentment. The collapse of royal authority, both civil and military, offered the provinces the chance to reassert their own presence. Without awaiting royal authorization, which would not, in any case, have been granted, the estates of Brabant convened in the summer of 1576 and then proceeded to summon the States General representing fifteen of the provinces. The States General, dominated by the Moderate party, had a clear policy: they were resolved that the foreign troops must be withdrawn from the Netherlands and that some form of religious accommodation be reached with Holland and Zeeland. These objectives found formal expression in the Pacification of Ghent (8 November 1576), a document which owed much to the various proposals which had been made at Breda in the previous year. The States General then in session in Brussels did not include representatives from Holland and Zeeland. It was overwhelmingly, if not exclusively, Catholic in composition; but it was determined to make the religious concessions advocated by the moderates and then to present Philip II with a *fait accompli*.

Could the middle party succeed? Would their programme be accepted? Don Juan of Austria, the hero of Lepanto, was forced to agree to part of their demands, the evacuation of Spanish troops, before he was formally accepted as the legitimate governor of the Netherlands (12 May 1577). Although Don Juan had sworn to uphold the Perpetual Edict (17 February 1577), he was irked by the restrictions it imposed on him. Temperamentally incapable of playing the waiting game, the new governor finally reverted to his true self by seizing the citadel of Namur (24 July 1577) even though he had no military force with which to build on this success. The States General refused any further dealings with him; and the delegates turned, instead, to another prince of the blood, this time from the other branch of the Habsburg family, Archduke Matthias, a fresh face but hardly a better character. The deposition of Don Juan as governor (7 December 1577) and the induction of the archduke strengthened the hand of the middle party and the prince of Orange who was assigned to his staff as a 'political adviser'.

The real threat to the prospects of the middle party now lay not in the danger from Don Juan but from the internal tensions within the seventeen provinces. A number of provincial governors, men like Boussu, Aerschot, de Farners, and Rassenghien, objected to the privileged position enjoyed by the prince of Orange, their motives being in part envy and in part genuine distrust. Holland and Zeeland added to the difficulties of the moderates. Both provinces never disguised the fact that they would not allow the Catholic faith to be restored to its monopoly position. In point of fact, practice of the Catholic faith had been difficult if not impossible in these two provinces since 1572. But it was developments in the south which undermined the moderate position and made a mockery of the intentions so solemnly professed in the Pacification of Ghent. Calvinist cadres seized control of some of the major towns in Flanders and Brabant. These takeovers resulted in the establishment of Genevanstyle commonwealths and, very often, a much greater influence on the part of the guilds in the management of the city. The failure of the prince of Orange to restrain Calvinist agitators and prevent the seizure of Ghent (18 May 1578) by a radical clique persuaded a growing number that no lasting accommodation could be reached with Holland and Zeeland. In the absence of such an accord, the more Catholic-minded provinces began to think of reopening contacts with Spain. The reconquest of the Netherlands which throughout 1577 had seemed little more than a pipe-dream began to seem a distinct possibility.

Don Juan, reinforced by detachments brought north under the command of Alexander of Farnese, his nephew, began the task with an unexpected victory over the troops of the States General at Gembloers (31 January 1578) which enabled him to break out from his limited area of operations around Namur. When Don Juan died that autumn (1 October 1578) Alexander Farnese became the interim, then the permanent, governor of the Netherlands; and it was with him that the real business of reconquest commenced. Farnese had all the military skill of his late uncle, and, more important, a political understanding totally lacking in his predecessor. He appreciated that with the right management some of the provinces in the south might be detached from the rest. He began to woo a number of southern noblemen known to be alarmed about religious developments, in particular the Calvinist assaults on the principal towns. This group, to be given the name of Malcontents, added their prestige and influence, and that of their respective families, to the movement which finally sought reconciliation with Spain in 1579.

The moderates, still the dominant party in the States General which continued to sit in Brussels, made one last effort to hold the provinces together. A delegation made up of six Catholics and four non-Catholics was sent in the spring of 1579 to Cologne where they met representatives of the Spanish crown. Negotiations lasted until November, 1579, the envoys discussing every avenue, every possibility, however remote, of an accord. As before, religion acted as the insuperable barrier. Philip II would not concede a special religious status to Holland and Zeeland.

Even before the abandonment of the talks, other parties had drawn their own conclusions. In the south the provinces of Artois, Hainaut, and Douai had come together in the Union of Arras (6 January 1579) with the express intention of entering into negotiation with Spain.

They wished to preserve their faith, hardly a matter of dispute, to obtain formal acknowledgement of their provincial liberties, and to receive a solemn pledge that foreign (i.e. Spanish) troops would not be quartered on them. The prince of Parma conceded all three points; and the reconciliation was proclaimed officially in the peace of Arras (17 May 1579). Through diplomacy Farnese had recovered part of the south; through warfare he would come near to completing the conquest of the north.

   The determination on the part of the strongly Catholic provinces to break away from the States General had its counterpart in the regions north of the great rivers. At least two of the northern provinces, Holland and Zeeland, had developed political traditions which differed markedly from those of their colleagues in the south. Nor did they share the enthusiasm of the southern aristocracy for foreign princelings, French or Austrian, who were invariably Catholic, feckless, and penniless. The two states which had inaugurated the struggle against Spanish rule, Holland and Zeeland, entered into their own defensive alliance with their immediate neighbours, Friesland, Utrecht, Gelderland, and Ommelanden. The Union of Utrecht (23 January 1579) was technically open to all; but it soon developed into a kernel of states increasingly Calvinist in character and anti-Spanish in policy. The States General continued to sit first in Brussels and then in Antwerp. Its meetings, however, ceased to possess much relevance. As Farnese began his great campaigns, resistance became northern and Calvinist. The moderate ideal of a united Netherlands, Catholic in religion but with toleration for a minority, disappeared; and in its place two unbending ideologies battled for conquest or survival.

CHAPTER II

Portugal and the Habsburgs

THE ties between Portugal and its more powerful neighbour had long been close, although not always cordial. Manuel the Fortunate (1495–1521)—the Grocer King to some of his spiteful contemporaries—had married into the family of the Catholic Monarchs on three occasions; and papal dispensations permitting such unions within the forbidden degree flowed regularly from Rome to Lisbon. The Portuguese ruling family had furnished, in its turn, a steady supply of daughters to the Habsburg house. The Emperor Charles V married Isabel of Portugal in Seville on 11 March 1526. Her brother, John III (1521–57) took as his bride Catalina, sister to Charles V and the only one of Juana the Mad's children to have lived with the queen in her lugubrious confinement. The Habsburgs favoured these double matrimonial arrangements as offering greater security for their diplomatic alliances; and, given the quirks of mortality, they sometimes led to unexpected territorial gains.

Nearly twenty years later, as part of his grand design to isolate France, the emperor arranged for two of his children to marry Portuguese spouses. In 1543 Mary of Portugal became the first of Philip's four wives. Two years later, and barely turned eighteen, she died (12 July 1545) having just given birth (8 July) to a son, Don Carlos. Her brother, when his time came, proved even more frail. At the ripe age of fifteen and a half, the Infante John Manuel married Juana of Castile, Philip's sister, in January 1552. Within two years he too was dead (2 January 1554), burnt up, so it was related, by the unbridled passions of wedlock. A son was born posthumously on St Sebastian's Day (20 January 1554), hence the infant's name, Dom Sebastian, and his sobriquet, O Desejado. The young widow, Juana of Castile, responded to her bereavement in a way which recalled the conduct of her demented grandmother and namesake. Four months after giving birth, she returned to Castile, abandoning her son to the care of his paternal grandmother, Queen Catalina. Portuguese independence rested on the life of this child. If he died in infancy or without issue, a struggle for the throne would surely follow; and the most powerful contestant would be his uncle, Philip II of Spain, himself the son of a Portuguese princess.

The Queen Mother ruled Portugal from 1557 until 1562. She was succeeded as regent by her brother-in-law, Cardinal Henry, who governed in the name of the king until he came of age on his fourteenth birthday in 1568. The economic condition of the kingdom in mid-century gave cause for unease. Under John III expenditure had risen uncontrollably with the result that by 1543 the government's obligations stood at 1,946,920 cruzados and it was compelled to pay rates of 25 per cent on additional borrowing. The exchequer could not rely on revenue buoyancy to cover these liabilities. By the middle of the sixteenth century the Italian republics had re-established their positions as major purchasers and distributors of spice from the Far East. The recovery cut into the profits of the sea route to the Indies first pioneered and then jealously guarded by the Portuguese. Signs of impending commercial difficulties could be found elsewhere. Trade with China had been suspended completely between 1548 and 1553; while in 1549 the Portuguese depot in Antwerp, then the mercantile hub of the world, closed for good. A fundamental alteration in the character of the Portuguese empire was taking place. The East Indies no longer guaranteed the huge profits of earlier days as the cost of defending the Portuguese stations overseas and the toll of natural disasters ate continually into commercial gains. And it was merely a question of time before European interlopers, principally the Dutch, better financed and more powerfully armed, began their assault on the Portuguese factories.

Yet as the advantages of an Indian empire began to diminish, other regions beckoned. In the northern captaincies of Brazil sugar cane, after many setbacks, became a profitable cash crop. Some perceptive observers saw the possibility of transforming the empire from an Indian to an Atlantic concern. One historian has attached significance to the programme of a group which acted vigorously and vocally in the cortes of 1562. This lobby, or embryonic party, recommended that the forts once held by Portugal along the Moroccan coast, and then abandoned by John III in the interests of economy, should be recovered. This plan represented an element in a wider design. Its advocates wished to see a reconstructed empire in which grain, leather, and gold were imported from North Africa, and sugar, the replacement for the dwindling stock of Far Eastern spice, from Brazil. If this policy were accepted, then, in time, the Atlantic and not the Indian Ocean would become the true pathway of empire.

Queen Catalina and Cardinal Henry showed realism in confronting the economic situation. They understood that, with the limit on available resources, colonial entanglements had to be kept to a minimum. Neither felt much enthusiasm for the reoccupation of the North African forts abandoned by John III. Unfortunately, this prudence did not flow over into their domestic affairs. In her continuous feuds against Cardinal Henry, the queen appealed time and again for moral support from her nephew, Philip of Spain; and the cardinal did exactly the same. Dom Antonio, prior of Crato, a possible claimant to the throne in spite of his illegitimate birth, also looked to the Spanish king for comfort and encouragement. Philip, without a move on his part, became the acknowledged arbiter of disputes within the Portuguese royal house. When the prior of Crato sought sanctuary in Castile for eighteen months (1565–6), Philip resolved the problem by sending to Lisbon a confidential agent, Cristóbal de Moura, Portuguese by birth and a man whose name would soon become intertwined with the affairs of the kingdom. Philip acquired an almost prescriptive right of intervention.

On his fourteenth birthday, Sebastian assumed effective power. He has sometimes been compared to his cousin, the Spanish Infante Don Carlos. They had an ancestor in common, Juana the Mad; and each was unstable from early childhood. One thought dominated Sebastian's mind—a crusade against the state of Fez, culminating in a joust to the death between himself and the infidel king. Attempts have been made to see this obsession as a rational plan which reflected the undoubted changes taking place within the economy of the empire. But to attribute a subtle understanding of shifting economic forces to the wilful Sebastian seems far-fetched. He was an unpleasant young man who never grew up.

The king set foot on North African soil for the first time in 1574. The purpose of his reconnaissance was to inspect the Portuguese enclaves of Tangiers and Ceuta. Two years later he met his uncle at the monastery of Guadalupe, scene of so many historic encounters. Over a series of formal discussions (22 December 1576 to 1 January 1577) Sebastian asked Philip to grant him two things, the hand of his eldest daughter, to which a firm commitment was politely denied, and support for a crusade in North Africa. To enlist Spanish help he

conjured up the prospect of an Ottoman attack on the Atlantic ports of
Arzila and Larache. Philip, in his reply, was long on advice and short
on aid. He knew that the Turkish armies were tied down by operations
in the Caucasus; and he appreciated that nothing was to be gained by
offering provocation at a time when Spain itself was deeply embroiled
in the Netherlands. Philip's main adviser, the duke of Alba, an old
soldier who showed little sign of dying, took an equally sceptical view.
He pointed out that the Portuguese army had not faced a properly
equipped and competently led force for almost a century; if the ill-
conceived venture were to proceed, and given Dom Sebastian's temperament anything was possible, foreign mercenaries would have to
be recruited to provide some military stiffening.

The king of Portugal had originally planned to sail for Africa in
1577. His optimism outran his resources. Additional taxes had to be
levied; and it was not until the following year that preparations were at
last deemed complete. The Portuguese army disembarked at Arzila on
the North African coast without encountering any opposition (14 July
1578). The stated objective of the expedition was the port of Larache,
due south of the spot where the landing had been made. As the
transports which had carried the army from Portugal were still
serviceable, the troops could have been re-embarked and ferried to
Larache which could then have been attacked from the sea. But
Sebastian was not interested in prudent generalship. He was determined to seek out the enemy as soon as possible; and he chose to disregard the fact that his opponents were superior in number and had
been reinforced by morisco emigrés from Andalucía who were familiar
with Christian tactics and thirsted for vengeance. The Portuguese
force marched inland. At the battle of El-Ksar el-Kebir (4 August
1578) it was totally destroyed, its leaders captured, and its impetuous
commander killed.

The annihilation of the Portuguese army brought on a crisis whose
effects can hardly be overstated. The country had been drained of men
and money. After the battle most of the ruling class was either dead or
in captivity. The country faced the very real prospect that it would
pass under alien rule. When the news of Dom Sebastian's death was
confirmed, Cardinal Henry, the late king's great-uncle, succeeded to
the throne. Suggestions were made that he should be dispensed at
once from Holy Orders so that he could marry and beget an heir. But
the proposal bordered on the absurd, if not the indecent. At the time of
his coronation, the cardinal was sixty-six years of age, deaf, half-blind,

without teeth, and in bad health. Even if he had been mechanically capable, and someone prepared for a heroic act of self-sacrifice had been found, there was little realistic hope of continuing the line of Avis.

Philip of Spain sent a special delegation to Lisbon with instructions to hold a watching brief. It was led officially by the duke of Osuna. His sister had married the duke of Aveiro, a leading Portuguese nobleman and a traditional enemy, usefully enough, of the other principal noble dynasty, the Bragança. But the real brains were provided by Cristóbal de Moura. It was he who conducted with exemplary discretion the murky diplomacy of the mission and arranged, where necessary, for the outright bribery. A nephew of Lourenço Pires de Távora, he had been sent as a boy to Spain to serve in the household of Doña Juana, the mother of King Sebastian. When she returned to Spain in 1554, Cristóbal de Moura followed; and he eventually joined Philip II's inner circle of officials.

The strength of the Habsburg claim to the Portuguese throne rested on hereditary right—Philip's mother was a princess of the royal house—and on the threat of force. But there were at least two other candidates to be considered. The prior of Crato, Dom Antonio, was born in 1531 from the tempestuous union between the Infante Luis (1506–55) and Violante Gomes, the daughter of a *converso* family. Their son was compelled at an early age to enter the church. Dissolute, spendthrift, and highly popular, the prior spent much of his time petitioning the pope for his release from Holy Orders. Unluckily for Dom Antonio, he had incurred the lasting hatred of Cardinal Henry, who disapproved of his loose morals and blocked all attempts to legitimize his kinsman.

If strict succession in the male line had been enforced, the crown should have gone by rights to Catarina, duchess of Bragança. She descended in the male line from Manuel the Fortunate, whereas all the other claimants, Philip included, had to base their cases on descent in the female line. Vivacious and spirited, she enjoyed widespread support, even, it was reliably reported, that of the cardinal himself.

To help him decide the succession, the aged cardinal-king summoned a cortes to meet in the town of Almeirim on 11 January 1580. The lobbies campaigned furiously on behalf of their respective patrons, each hoping to sway the sovereign one way or another. Weak-willed and indecisive, he could not bring himself to state a clear preference; and he was soon spared the choice. He died on 31 January 1580. His throne became a prize for the strongest. In a much-cited letter, Cristóbal de Moura analysed the state of the parties at the accession of Cardinal Henry; and the picture he presented probably holds good for the end of the reign. According to Philip's envoy, one group, powerfully supported by the upper clergy, argued that resistance to the Habsburg contender was impossible; and that everything therefore should be done to settle with him on the best possible terms. Another element favoured the duchess of Bragança. She had rallied to her cause not only the ducal retainers, but also the Jesuits and the lower nobility. A third faction, drawn primarily from the lower clergy and the poor, gave their loyalty to the prior of Crato.

From the outset circumstances worked to the benefit of the Spanish contender. Cristóbal de Moura negotiated patiently to build up an interest. To the urban oligarchs of Lisbon he stressed the commercial advantages to be derived from a Habsburg victory. The case almost argued itself. In their trade with the Far East, still a matter of prime concern, the Portuguese required silver. Much of this they obtained through contraband trade with Castile's American colonies. Settlements in Brazil ran supplies of food and clothing up the river Plate and its tributaries to the Spanish colonies in Chile and Upper Peru. Payment was made in silver, the only significant export of the region. As they pondered where to bestow their loyalty in 1580, the merchants of Lisbon knew better than anyone that the maintenance of their precarious trading position in the Far East depended on access to the American silver controlled by the king of Spain.

In his negotiations with the Portuguese nobility, Philip held a number of trumps; and these were played in masterly fashion. The disaster of the North African venture was a case in point. Motivated partly by genuine philanthropy, partly by self-interest, the Spanish king paid out of his own pocket for the ransom of some of the nobles who had been taken prisoner. He exercised diplomatic pressure to secure the release of the duke of Barcelos, heir to the house of Bragança. Once freed, the young duke was brought to Castile, fêted by his kinsman, the duke of Medinaceli, and refused permission to return home. Cristóbal de Moura extracted the maximum political advantage from such actions.

Opposition to the Spanish candidacy might have proved more effective if the two Portuguese contenders, the prior of Crato and the duchess of Bragança, had reached an understanding. In 1580 such unity eluded the Portuguese. Philip bought off the duke of Bragança and his wife by granting some of their less outrageous demands. A series of lands and titles, including that of Constable, were incorporated into the ducal house. The ducal pair, in accepting Philip's generosity (June 1580), withdrew their claim, thereby enriching their house and preserving it for another day.

The prior of Crato wanted even more than his cousins. Or perhaps he possessed greater determination. On 19 June 1580 the prior proclaimed himself king in his stronghold of Santarem. Without some unexpected twist of fate, his bid for the crown had no chance. Of the five governors appointed by Cardinal Henry to rule Portugal after his death only one came out unequivocally in favour of Dom Antonio. His personal resources were negligible.

On 13 June 1580 almost a week before Dom Antonio's proclamation, the Habsburg army, under the command of the duke of Alba, began to march. Everything went according to plan. The towns on the main road from Badajoz to Lisbon fell in quick succession. The prior's attempt to halt the invasion force on the outskirts of Lisbon at the bridge of Alcântara turned out to be little more than a glorified brawl (25 August 1580); and his levies were dispersed after an action lasting two hours. Dom Antonio fled north, hoping to convert Oporto into a centre for organized resistance; but he was soon dislodged by a flying column under the command of another Flemish veteran, Sancho de Avila. At the time there was some talk of the prior carrying the struggle to Brazil, an early example of the New World redressing the balance of the Old, but nothing came of it.

Resistance to the Spanish takeover continued in the Azores long after it had ceased on the mainland. The partisans of Dom Antonio gained control of the largest islands; and they received substantial aid from France. An attempt by the Spaniards to take the island of Terceira in the summer of 1581 failed (25 July); but the prior's victory was isolated and misleading. In 1582 a Spanish fleet commanded by Alvaro de Bazán, familiar with these waters since early manhood, encountered a strong French squadron off the Portuguese coast. The defeat of the French in the course of the two-day battle of Vila Franca do Campo (25–6 July 1582) decided the fate of the Azores. Although in the following year the French were able to run supplies into their base on the island of Terceira, they could not prevent a Spanish landing (24 July 1583). Within a week the French garrison capitulated, thus ending all opposition. Philip of Spain, thanks to the excellence of his servants and the divisions of his enemies, had become the undisputed master of Portugal and its empire.

Philip II was formally presented to the representatives of the Portuguese nation at the cortes of Tomar (16 April 1581). The king met his new subjects in the convent which overlooked the small town, a building famous throughout the land for its nautical motifs in the Manueline style. Here Philip solemnly pledged himself to observe the customs of Portugal, her laws, and her statutes. He bound himself to appoint only natives to offices of profit and honour, an undertaking which he carried out to the letter. He further promised that taxes would be spent on Portuguese needs and not on behalf of Castilian objectives, a commitment which again Philip and his descendants respected. The Portuguese gained an additional concession which could not be acknowledged publicly. Castilian authorities turned a blind eye to the activities of Portuguese interlopers who used the forbidden route of the river Plate to bring goods from Portuguese settlements in Brazil to the silver mines in the viceroyalty of Peru. This indulgence lasted until the 1630s. The notables gathered at Tomar hoped that their new sovereign would apply the naval power of Castile to the defence of the overseas empire. The assumption was not unreasonable; and Philip was willing to acknowledge his obligations. Unfortunately, neither he nor they could have anticipated the phenomenal growth of the Dutch mercantile marine which, before the century was out, had come to threaten the Iberian monopolies in both Far Eastern and American waters.

The Portuguese made it clear in the Capitulations of Tomar that they expected to be ruled, in the king's absence, by a prince of the blood. They had in mind the Infante Don Diego. But when Philip left the Portuguese capital early in 1583 he appointed as his representative a nephew, the cardinal archduke Albert of Austria. Little is known about the history of the archducal regime. The outbreak of hostilities against the English in 1585, and the permanent danger from the Dutch rebels, led to the stationing of mainly Castilian troops in the strategic towns of Porto, Cascais, and Setubal. In 1591 the cardinal archduke tried to raise a special tax to meet the cost of coastal defence and the upkeep of a flotilla to protect the deep sea fleet from the depredations of the corsairs. Although eventually conceded, the tax did little to diminish the threat from piracy. Many complained that the country had been placed under a form of government tantamount to martial law. But the image of the Habsburg administration as an oppressor was almost certainly false. In the Castilian budget for 1594 a sum of 510,000 ducats was set aside for the maintenance of garrisons both in

Portugal and her colonies and the support of galleys to patrol the coastline. The figure represented 8.3 per cent of total imperial expenditure. The Lusitanian kingdom may well, in fact, have constituted another drain, and a substantial one, on Habsburg resources.

After the cardinal archduke's recall in 1593, the government was placed in commission. Four leading Portuguese notables, each distinguished for the part he had played in the Castilian succession, sat on this executive board. The device, unusual in terms of Habsburg practice, satisfied two requirements: it rewarded Philip's most stalwart followers amongst the ruling élite; and it gave Portugal government by her own nationals. When the experiment ended in 1599, the principle of nationality was still maintained. Cristóbal de Moura, marquis of Castel Rodrigo since 1594, was sent to Lisbon as part of a manœuvre honourably to exile him from the Castilian court. He had left his native land forty-five years before as a page. He now returned as its viceroy.

Philip II's reign in Portugal ushered in a long period of stability after the weak government of Queen Catalina and the folly of her grandson. Whatever criticism might have been levelled at the time or later, the first Habsburg king did his utmost to respect the liberties and rights of his subjects. A Dual Monarchy came into being at Tomar in which the junior partner enjoyed many advantages. The bargain, for all that, soon showed itself unsatisfactory, mainly because the assumptions on which it had been based were unjustified. Before long Portugal was involved in protracted warfare against the English and, far more damaging to her trading interests, the Dutch. For all the efforts of the Habsburg dynasty, Portugal watched its Far Eastern possessions being steadily overrun by the men and ships of the Seven Provinces; and these events seemed likely to repeat themselves in the South Atlantic. When in the 1630s the Castilian authorities sought to tighten the bonds of association by the levy of an imperial as distinct from an exclusively national tax, and when in the same period the king's ministers decided to enforce the Castilian trading monopoly throughout the American possessions by closing, amongst other measures, the river Plate to contraband, then the Portuguese discovered cause enough to reconsider their links with their neighbour. This time the house of Bragança, after due prodding, placed itself at the head of an undivided opposition; and in Cardinal Richelieu the conspirators discovered a more reliable patron than Catherine de Medici and her unstable court.

CHAPTER 12

The Grand Design

IN THE autumn of 1578 Don Juan of Austria died of typhoid in his camp at Namur (1 October). The outlook for the Habsburg cause had never appeared so bleak. Its prestige was virtually extinct; only Luxemburg, Namur, and a narrow band of territory in the south-western corner of the Low Countries answered to royal commands; and the recently concluded pact between the crown and its Genoese bankers on which the restitution of authority depended had yet to prove its worth. No formal provision had been made for the replacement of the late governor. Time was needed to select and groom a prince of the blood for the task. Philip's own children were still too young; and of the Austrian candidates, the most suitable in terms of age, Matthias, had already disgraced himself. For the time being Alexander Farnese (1545–92) assumed command, if only to prevent the chaos which had led to the military indiscipline of 1576. He was the son of Margaret of Parma, and, therefore, the nephew of Philip II, though not in the legitimate line. He had served with Don Juan, another uncle, during the campaign of Lepanto and had been with him when he died. Although considered by the court as a temporary replacement, the prince of Parma rapidly emerged as the saviour of the Catholic faith and Spanish power in the Netherlands. He devised and put into effect the strategy which led to the recovery of all the lands south of the great rivers; and his conquests in the eastern states of Gelderland, Overijssel, and Drenthe sealed off the frontier with Germany, thereby denying the rebels supplies by the land route from sympathizers in the Holy Roman Empire. Under Farnese the re-assertion of Habsburg suzerainty over all the provinces which had at one time sworn allegiance to Philip II became, if only for a short period, a feasible proposition.

In the first years, from 1578 until 1581, Farnese concentrated his attention upon winning over the French-speaking (Walloon) provinces. Deeply Catholic, they were alarmed at what they considered to be the Calvinist excesses of the northern states, Holland and Zeeland were uppermost in their minds, and those religious enthusiasts who sought to import the example into the south. The Walloon nobility, furthermore, envied William of Orange as a person and disliked the general drift of his policies. Whether it was the clergy of Artois or the nobility of Hainaut, Farnese played deftly on the hopes and fears of the ruling class. He put the full weight of his authority behind the Union of Arras (1579); and once it had been concluded, he abided scrupulously by its terms. The hated Spanish tercios were withdrawn in 1580, as demanded by the native signatories; and for the next two years Farnese had to rely on the troops raised and led by the southern nobility, often called the Malcontents, who had broken with the States General. The prince chose his advisers from amongst those who had been born in the Low Countries; there was no seedy inner coterie of Iberians as in the time of Alba; and the local (Catholic) nobility supplied his officer corps. Unlike his more rigid predecessors, the new governor was also prepared to respect provincial jurisdictions. By leaving these local rights undisturbed, he ensured the loyalty of the town oligarchs and rural élites of the areas he controlled. Farnese's sympathetic approach to the question of government stemmed from the fact that he was not a Spaniard by birth, even if he had been educated in the peninsula, and he listened to the advice of Cardinal Granvelle, another 'foreigner' capable of understanding provincial aspirations.

The prince adapted his policies to the circumstances of the Walloon provinces; and he showed the same flexibility in his conduct of military operations. Initially, the forces at his disposal were small, too small to be used in a frontal assault on a well-defended target; and he lacked a heavy siege train. His objectives had to be correspondingly modest. Parma set about reducing the principal cities of the south one by one; and to do this he adopted what became a standard procedure. First he destroyed the harvest, and then he blocked off the supply lines to the outside world. Starvation completed the work. Parma's tactics called for an appreciation of local terrain, the skill of an engineer, and the patience of a great commander. He had also concluded from his earlier experiences that the brutal sacking of towns only stiffened the resolve of others to hold out. In a striking reversal of traditional policy he offered terms even to those which had stood siege; and this moderation in the long run gained time and saved lives. From 1580 until 1584 he followed his chosen course, slowly and methodically picking off one city after another. The process reached a climax in the

Areas held by
Spanish in 1579

Lands conquered
by Parma

0   50   100 km

N

Steenwijk

Deventer

Zutphen

Nijmegen

Breda

Sluis

Ostend

Brugge

Antwerp

Dunkirk

Ghent

Louvain

Maastricht

Brussels

Namur

8 The conquests of the prince of Parma 1579–88

campaigns of 1584–5 which provided the crowning vindication of
Parma's methods and, with it, the possibility of total reconquest.

On 17 September 1584 Ghent, the citadel of Calvinism in the south,
opened its gates to the royal army. The city was a prize in its own right;
but the surrender had a yet greater significance for the progress of the
war. Farnese turned Ghent into the headquarters and arsenal for the
largest operation he had ever undertaken or ever would. Antwerp was
the commercial hub of the Netherlands; and it had become the seat of
government once the States General had decided to abandon
Brussels. As the city could not be taken by storm, it had to be starved
into submission. On the landward side Parma dug regular siege works
to prevent food supplies from entering; but the main problem, from
his point of view, was the river Scheldt which linked the town to the
sea. Throughout the winter of 1584 and the spring of 1585 his sappers

toiled to construct a fortified boom across the Scheldt to close this sole remaining link with the outside world. Two forts, one on either bank of the river, acted as protective piers. The completion of the barrage was hailed, rightly, as one of the sixteenth century's most astounding feats of military engineering. Its preparation had required the use of over 10,000 tree-trunks and the pile-driving of 1,500 ships' masts—imported from the Baltic and almost without doubt supplied by rebel merchants—to anchor the structure. The capitulation of Brussels to Farnese on 10 March 1585 released more troops which were immediately thrown into the blockade of the metropolis. The States General and the Antwerp garrison made frantic attempts to halt the construction, and then to destroy it once it was finished. But not even the use of fireships against the boom could open the vital maritime link to the relief convoy downstream. As one sortie after another failed and provisions within the beleaguered city dwindled, confidence ebbed away. The States General were incapable of meeting Parma's resources, matching his talent, or breaking his grip. Antwerp surrendered on 17 August 1585.

Philip had good reason to wake his daughter in the middle of the night with the news. Both he and his great commander thought that they had secured the decisive victory of the war. There were military and political grounds for believing so. The States General had yet to show that they had the means to stop the apparently inexorable advance of Parma's army. Their lack of success could be attributed in part to the policy advocated by William of Orange, the incarnation of resistance to Spain and the most influential of his contemporaries. He remained convinced throughout his career that the rebellious provinces could only survive with external help, and that meant France. Neither he nor the moderate leadership of the cause could imagine Holland and Zeeland defying the Habsburgs unaided. As a result of his advocacy, a tentative approach was made to France in 1578. The duke of Anjou, a younger brother of the French king, Henry III, was offered and accepted the title of 'Defender of the Liberties of the Netherlands'; and although this title lacked real substance Anjou was to flit in and out of Dutch politics for the next six years, with results that were uniformly disastrous.

Undaunted by the duke's failure materially to assist them, the States General, once more at the prompting of William, conferred upon Anjou the higher-sounding honour of 'prince and lord of the Netherlands' (23 January 1581). That summer the States General renounced the authority of Philip II (26 July 1581). The abjuration was in part a response to the public condemnation of the prince, by Philip, as a traitor (1580); and to that extent it represented an episode in the formal trading of insults between William of Orange and his erstwhile liege. The act of abjuration was buried amongst numerous other items of legislation; and its approval by the States aroused little comment at the time. Although the duke of Anjou had accepted his new dignity at the beginning of 1581, and with it the appearance of sovereignty, he did not make his entry into Antwerp, the provisional capital, until February 1582. From the outset his relations with his new 'subjects' were deplorable. He looked upon the lordship of the Netherlands as an interlude in his career. The land, he confidently expected, would provide him with a luxurious court as he awaited the death of his brother, Henry III, who had acted the same way in the case of the Polish crown. When he discovered that the States General were not prepared to keep him in the style to which he aspired, Anjou decided to carve out his own patrimony. His attempt on Antwerp itself was bungled (the 'French Fury', 17 January 1583); but his servants had more success elsewhere, occupying a number of strategic towns, amongst them Dunkirk, Vilvoorde, and Dendermonde. Even after this display of treachery and incompetence, Orange still persisted in urging on his fellows that the French link be maintained. In 1584 the States General, turning a blind eye to all that had so recently passed, offered even wider authority to the duke of Anjou. But the charade progressed no further. In the last stages of consumption, he was no longer a factor to be reckoned with—or a pawn to be manipulated. When he died on 10 June 1584, his troops, despairing of their pay, surrendered to Parma the towns they had occupied during the 'French Fury'. The loss of such strong points as Dunkirk, coming in the midst of other reverses, was serious enough; but it was shortly eclipsed by another disaster. As the provinces with which he had become totally identified braced themselves for the military onslaught, William of Orange fell to an assassin (10 July 1584). Philip and Alexander Farnese had cause enough to be optimistic.

But even if the final victory lay only a fingertip away, how could it be secured? How could Holland and Zeeland be broken? At the court two schools pressed their respective solutions. Ever since his naval victories off the Azores (1582–3) Alvaro de Baźan, the marquis of Santa Cruz, believed that the conquest of England held the key to the Dutch problem. This island kingdom, with its hybrid Protestant church, had long been a favourite bolt-hole for rebel ships and had rendered invaluable, if at times erratic, support to their cause. Without the installation of a friendly regime in England, one pro-Spanish and Catholic as in the days of Mary Tudor, the final reduction of the rebellious provinces might never be achieved. Santa Cruz had been working on the project for a number of years. His first drafts, composed in 1586, called for a task force of some 556 ships, more than the mercantile marine of Spain and Portugal put together. Anticipating the imminent struggle against England, he had incorporated lessons learnt from recent Atlantic warfare into the design of the king's ships. The latest models were more seaworthy, had cleaner lines, and carried heavier guns. Emphasis was placed on manœuvrability and firepower. The prince of Parma argued for a totally different strategy. He pleaded that the land campaign in the Netherlands should take priority over all else, and his small following at court took up the theme. He pointed out that after the fall of Antwerp the royal army stood poised to cross the great rivers in the south, or to mount an attack on Holland and Zeeland from its bases in the eastern provinces. Farnese wanted pressure against the Dutch to be maintained at all points; and he begged the king to allocate his rising income from the Americas for the purpose. The prince appreciated as well as the next man the value of English support to the rebels; but he regarded the idea of a maritime invasion of England as a foolhardy diversion of resources and one not likely to succeed.

Philip had reasons of his own for listening to those amongst his servants who advocated firm action. For approximately twenty years Elizabeth of England had followed a cautious foreign policy. She wished to avoid involvement in any European alliance. To preserve her neutrality she insisted that no offence be given to the major powers. True, she had invested in Francis Drake's circumnavigation of the world (1577–80), a piratical venture paid for by raiding Spanish colonies. Fortunately for diplomatic relations between Spain and England, Philip had chosen not to consider the act as serious provocation. Correct relations survived a little longer. But circumstances were changing in ways that neither country could disregard. As a result of Farnese's triumphs in the Low Countries and the success of the Guise in France the entire coastline from Brittany to the estuary of the Rhine had come under Catholic control. Elizabeth and her Privy Council considered that this development threatened English security. Even the queen accepted the need for action. Three days after the fall of

Antwerp she signed the treaty of Nonsuch with the emissaries of the nascent Dutch Republic (20 August 1585). England agreed to pay the rebels an annual subsidy of £126,000 and received in return a number of cautionary towns. Elizabeth became not merely a public accomplice of the Dutch in their fight against Spain; but in garrisoning Flushing, Brill, and the fort of Rammekens, she was invading Habsburg territory, a fact which no king, however prudent, could overlook.

In 1586 Philip consented to the plan for a naval attack on England. Preparations began immediately for the assembly in the Tagus estuary of the largest military convoy ever to sail in Atlantic waters during the sixteenth century. Gathering the transports, provisioning them, and keeping the crews fed throughout taxed the royal commissariat to the very limit; and the whole process was vulnerable to disruption as Francis Drake proved when he raided Cádiz (19–20 April 1587). For all the delays and shortages, Spanish officials had the fleet ready for sea by the early summer of 1588. The achievement spoke well for the competence of the administration. Much attention has been paid to the bad tack and unseasoned barrel staves which the quartermasters shipped aboard; but these were recurrent difficulties and easy to overrate. The real threat to the venture came from another direction. As on so many other occasions, Philip, or his closest advisers, were unable to produce a definite plan and, equally important, communicate it unambiguously to those entrusted with the execution. At one stage the court appeared to favour two separate operations against England: Santa Cruz (after his death, Medina Sidonia) would use the fleet to capture the Isle of Wight. His action would draw off the bulk of the English ships thereby permitting Farnese to cross the Channel with his army virtually unopposed. Later this operation was discarded in favour of a single operation in which Spanish naval units would sweep up the Channel and land marine contingents, together with Farnese's troops if these could be safely embarked, somewhere at the mouth of the Thames. But doubts about the final plan and Medina Sidonia's secret instructions, if any, persisted even after the Armada had set sail. Parma continued to think that the duke would take the Isle of Wight and convert it into a secure anchorage before proceeding any further.

In the event, the Enterprise of England did take the form of two uncoordinated operations, but not in the way at one time imagined. The lookout on Medina Sidonia's ship first sighted the Lizard on 29 July 1588. For the next ten days the Habsburg fleet, some hundred and thirty vessels in all, fought a running battle up the Channel. Most of the English vessels were, like their counterparts, merchantmen which had been specially strengthened for the purpose; but amongst them were to be found twenty-two ships belonging to the queen. These had been designed to incorporate the latest advances in naval architecture. The top hamper had been reduced, the sails flattened, and the batteries uprated by the inclusion of heavier guns, the famous culverins. But for all its nimbleness and superior armament, the English fleet made little impression on their opponents until the night of 8 August. The Spanish vessels had anchored off Gravelinges while the duke of Medina Sidonia frantically sought to replenish his store of victuals and shot from a prince of Parma who was powerless to help. As the Spaniards waited, the English decided to use fireships; and whereas the device had failed against Farnese's boom, this time it succeeded brilliantly against Medina Sidonia's fleet. Cables were cut in the desperate attempt to escape with the result that the Spanish ships lost the order which had hitherto preserved them. The English fleet pursued their quarry the length of the northern coastline; and contact was only lost when a certain Harris left the survivors west of the Orkneys flying into a raging sea.

Sceptical though he might be about the soundness of the project, Parma had played a full part in the preliminaries. As instructed, he had broken off his intended offensive against Holland and Zeeland in the north to concentrate all his resources on the capture of a port which might serve as a base for the Spanish fleet. Ostend could not be taken, as the prince discovered after initial probing; but he was able to take Sluys instead (5 August 1587). Having secured a harbour on the North Sea from which his invasion barges could sail, Farnese held 16,000 of his best troops in readiness. They never left port. The Dutch under the command of Justin of Nassau patrolled the waters just outside the harbour mouth, ready to pounce on the frail barks the moment they put to sea; and the Spanish fleet, harassed all the time by the English and almost out of munitions, could not even contemplate an action against the Sea Beggars and their offspring. The capacity of the Dutch rebels to bottle up the prince of Parma and interdict the seaways to him was as striking as the naval victory of Elizabeth's makeshift fleet. It was achieved in total independence of the English queen. Indeed, no communications had passed between the Protestant fleets during the course of the action. The Dutch already had grounds for questioning the value of their association with a monarch who continued to negotiate with the enemy in spite of solemn treaty obligations and whose representative in the Low Countries, the earl of Leicester, behaved more like a duke of Anjou than a long-awaited Protestant saviour. From the standpoint of Habsburg commitment on the European continent, the Armada had a double significance. It deflected Parma from completing the reconquest of the Netherlands in the years, perhaps months, after the capture of Antwerp when the window of possibility slid open; and it demonstrated the growth of Dutch seapower and all that this heralded for the course of Spanish imperial history.

At the news of the disaster Philip II exercised the restraint for which a lifetime's discipline had prepared him; but even he could not long remain oblivious to the fact that the defeat led to a reversal of priorities which was to have serious consequences. For much of his reign the king and his advisers had looked upon France as a theatre subordinate to the main concern of the dynasty, namely, the reconquest of the Seventeen Provinces. For success this operation required that the border with France be open only to friendly traffic, or, and this would have been preferable, sealed altogether. For over a quarter of a century (*c*.1560–*c*.1585) domestic conditions in the Valois state had favoured Habsburg designs. France had been in no position to help the insurgents in the Low Countries or to challenge Spain in the traditional areas of conflict. Parma's inability to cross the Channel and the scattering of the king's ships before the Protestant winds brought to an end this period of prosperity. After 1588 France became the major concern of Spanish policy-makers and the principal drain on resources.

The eclipse and re-emergence of France as a European power depended on the authority of the monarchy; and to this extent French internal politics impinged directly on the success or failure of Habsburg plans. The creation of a unified state on the part of the Valois house was a recent achievement. Brittany, Normandy, and Burgundy were gathered into the royal patrimony during the fifteenth century; and the process continued well into the sixteenth century with the addition of Angoulême, the lands of the constable of Bourbon, and the kingdom of Navarre. These provinces, and others besides, cherished a lively sense of former independence and an equally strong feeling of resentment against their Valois overlord. In the sixteenth century religion added a fresh complexity to the problems of regionalism. Determined action on the part of Francis I contained the diffusion of the Lutheran faith; but Calvinism proved a much hardier import. During the 1550s it recruited widely from amongst the nobles, the lawyers, and the artisans. As a creed it was able to fuse in such regions as Provence and Languedoc with older traditions of dissent. So rapid was the spread of Calvinism, and so influential its party at court, that by the early 1560s it began openly to bid for power.

If Henry II had lived, the French monarchy might have met the challenge of Calvinism, and the dangers associated with it, thereby preserving France's status as a leading power on the international scene. While taking part in a tournament to celebrate the marriage of his daughter, Isabel 'of the Peace', to Philip II, Henry was mortally wounded. A sliver of wood from a shattered lance penetrated his eye and pierced the brain. He died on 10 July 1559; and his widow, Catherine de Medici, became the effective ruler of France for the next thirty years. Although her three sons, Francis II, Charles IX, and Henry III each ruled in turn, it was she who provided the element of continuity, sometimes as the officially recognized regent, sometimes merely as the king's closest adviser. For all the twists and turns in her policies, Catherine had two clear objectives: she wished to reduce, if possible eliminate completely, the religious element in contemporary politics, making them instead a matter of pure self-interest; and she fought to preserve the kingdom undivided for her children and those who should follow them in the legitimate order of succession.

A combination of factors peculiar to the times made her task immeasurably complex. The leading aristocratic clans identified with one or other of the confessions, the house of Bourbon with the Huguenots, their rivals, the Guise, with the Catholics. The blend of confessional loyalty with baronial ambition did not represent the full extent of the danger. The opposing groups built up their support on a regional basis. Thus religion became an aspect of particularism, and the converse. The Catholic party drew its strongest support from eastern France, where the Guise held their principal fiefs, and the provinces of Normandy and Brittany, where much of the territory was in the hands of their clients. The Protestants created a similar network in the south and south-west based, like its counterpart, on feudal and sectarian allegiance. From the Spanish viewpoint such a distribution had merits and demerits. The Guise helped to reduce the flow of support from the Huguenots to their co-religionists in the Low Countries; whereas the kingdom of Navarre, the very cradle of French heresy, abutted on to Aragon. Subversive material and general undesirables could pass to and fro over the mountain tracks, almost with impunity.

The civil wars which raged in France throughout the 1560s and 1570s meant that the Habsburgs could pursue their own projects un-hindered by their traditional rivals. Occasionally it seemed that this separation of interests might be abandoned. In June 1565, the Spanish queen, Isabel of Valois, met her mother, Catherine de Medici, at Bayonne. The presence of the duke of Alba at the reunion, but not, it should be stressed, Philip, gave rise to the suspicion that the Catholic powers were planning a broad offensive against Protestant Europe; but even if such a scheme had been floated, it had no practical con-sequences. There had been a more serious alarm in 1572. Gaspar de Coligny, a leading Huguenot and the favourite of Charles IX, per-suaded his master to lend substantial help to William of Orange. In effect he was proposing to solve France's internal difficulties by an aggressive foreign policy. Catherine de Medici, fearful of an open con-frontation with Spain, attempted to forestall this by arranging for Coligny to be eliminated quietly. When the attempt failed, she con-doned, tacitly or explicitly, the murder of the Protestant notables gathered in Paris for the wedding of her daughter to Henry of Navarre. The massacre of St Bartholomew's Night (23–4 August 1572) directly benefited the duke of Alba who was able to redeploy his troops once the threat from France had disappeared. It also meant that any chance of subsequent French involvement in the Netherlands had been put back a good ten years.

To preserve the weakness of its natural rival, the Spanish court had merely to promote domestic unrest; and in the house of Guise and the Catholic party it disposed of ready-made surrogates. Henry, duke of Guise, had received a subsidy of 10,000 écus in 1582; and his Spanish patrons progressively stepped up the amount until by 1585 he was drawing 350,000 écus, a king's ransom indeed. Unfortunately, what had started out as a *douceur* to a greedy nobleman soon developed into the permanent funding of a national cause. A series of unexpected deaths which changed the succession to the French throne explained this alarming escalation of cost, and, eventually, commitment.

In actuarial terms the last Valois represented 'bad' lives. Francis II, always sickly as a child, failed to survive adolescence. His brother Charles IX (1560–74) enjoyed little better health, and ruined an already unsound constitution by debauchery. On his death, at the age of twenty-two, the throne passed to Henry, at the time king of Poland.

Although it soon became apparent that Henry III was unlikely to have children (sterility or homosexuality may have been the reason), the succession created no problem as his surviving brother, Hercule-François, duke of Anjou, was both of age and a Catholic. But when the latter died in 1584, wasted by the family disease of tuberculosis, Henry de Bourbon-Vendôme, king of Navarre, inherited his claim provided, that is, the Salic Law could still be enforced. The emergence of a Protestant heir appalled the Catholic party and its foreign sponsor, Philip II. The house of Guise-Lorraine could add another justification for its ancestral feud against the Bourbons; and it was determined to stop at nothing to prevent the accession of Henry of Navarre, even if this meant rejecting the provisions of the Salic Law.

The Catholic party, coached by the Guise, decided that Henry III must be coerced into setting aside the normal rules of succession. The Guise had tried once before to create a confessional body that might bring pressure to bear on the monarch. In 1576 they promoted the first Holy League, often called the League of Péronne, after one of the towns deep in Guise territory. On this occasion Henry III outwitted his overmighty subjects by having himself declared the head of the organization (1577). Eight years later a decision was taken to revive the Holy League; and this time the lawful king discovered that all escape routes had been blocked. The Guise and their confederates had planned well. They took the precaution of negotiating a formal agreement with the king of Spain, an indication in itself of how far the authority of the French crown had sunk. Juan Bautista de Tassis and Juan Moreo, a serving officer and a spy-master respectively, acted on behalf of the Habsburgs. the duke of Guise, his brother the duke of Mayenne, and a clutch of Guise relatives spoke for the Catholic party, the distinction between family and cause being a fine one. By the treaty of Joinville (31 December 1584), Philip promised the Holy League a monthly subsidy of 50,000 écus; and, in return, he extracted pledges that Cambrai would be returned to Spain, that Protestantism be eliminated from French soil, and that the rights of the Huguenot claimant to the throne be disregarded in favour of the Catholic, Cardinal Charles of Bourbon. The Holy League and its directors, the Guise, had assumed sovereign powers.

Joinville marked only the beginnings of Valois tribulations. Within a few months of its signing, the Holy League, originally based on Paris but gaining adherents all the time from other French towns, found itself in a position to dictate terms to Henry III. Catherine de Medici, in one of the last services she rendered to her family, pleaded with her son to bow before the inevitable and accede to the demands, no matter how disastrous they appeared at the time. Henry III gave way and bound himself by the treaty of Nemours (7 July 1585). Under its provisions the Protestants were denied any form of toleration, Henry of Navarre was excluded from the succession, and the Leaguers were permitted to fortify a number of towns. The French king had become a cipher in his own realm; and internal strife promised to become both endemic and eternal.

Such a state of affairs suited the Habsburgs admirably; and three years later, as the Invincible Armada was being prepared for sea, they had an even greater stroke of luck. On 9 May 1588 the duke of Guise entered Paris in defiance of an express order from the king. Henry III's attempt to reassert his authority on 12 May only led to fresh calamities. The royal guard which had been ordered into the city soon found itself trapped by a maze of barricades which had sprung up everywhere; and the killing started. Catherine de Medici had to be carried in a chair across the road-blocks to the duke's headquarters where she pleaded with Henry of Guise to use the magic of his name to stop the massacre of the troops; and this he graciously condescended to do. On 13 May Henry III left the city in which he counted for so little, never to return. Guise and his confederates, who had ruled most of France since 1585, were now installed in its principal town as the undisputed master. Henry III prepared to answer the monstrous insult to his dignity with force; but once again Catherine persuaded her son that he was powerless to act in the circumstances. By endorsing the Edict of Union (21 June 1588) the crown confirmed the terms agreed at Nemours, further promising to summon the Estates General in which the Catholics and Guisards were sure to have the dominant voice. Whether by design or accident, the state of France could not have been more propitious for the commencement of the operation intended to solve Spain's northern problems once and for all.

The sweeping victories of the Holy League and the humiliation of the Valois seemed to mark the permanent disqualification of France as a great power. But, in fact, the year 1588 signalled the high point of Catholic (and Spanish) fortunes. The defeat of the Armada gave renewed hope to Henry III, the moderate Catholics who had not lost their heads to the Guise, and the outcast pretender, Henry of Navarre. The position of the Holy League might not be impregnable, nor the influence of the Guise unassailable. As the year drew to its close, the duke and his brother foolishly answered a summons of the king to the royal château at Blois; and here in the council chamber, with its low ceiling and sombre panelling, Guise was struck down early in the morning (23 December 1588). Although the deed has often been held up as another example of Valois folly, Spain was the real loser. None of the Guise who came after could match the duke's swagger and bluster, charm the mob in the same way, or intimidate the crown so effectively. After the murder at Blois, French affairs deteriorated rapidly; and the Habsburgs found themselves with a liability of ever-growing proportions.

From 1589 onwards Spain kept alive the Catholic cause in France to the prejudice of objectives elsewhere. The inability of the Holy League to sustain itself without massive outside help resulted from its grave structural flaws. Too many irreconcilable elements had been forced together under intense but short-lived pressures. The inner core of the party was made up of the Guisards and the Catholic zealots willing to put religion before all else. Around this nucleus circled less stable elements. The cities who joined the Holy League after 1585 had done so through fear that law and order might break down completely. At the time association offered the only means of protection, although the municipalities were prepared to reconsider their decision the moment this became feasible. The virtual abdication of power by Henry III to the Holy League also prompted the desertion of another class who under normal circumstances could be looked on as firm supporters of the crown. As a group the *parlementaires* represented the judges who sat both in the regional courts of appeal and on the most prestigious of these bodies, the parlement of Paris itself. They exercised wide powers of administration in addition to their legal functions; and the *parlementaire* families had acquired over the course of time enormous landed wealth. Hereditary tenure, purchased from the monarch at a price, buttressed their splendid social position. When it became clear that Henry III could no longer shield them from the attacks of their critics and rivals, the *parlementaire* class made common cause with the Guise and their friends. But the alliance was never easy, and the judges longed for a return to the more congenial relationship with the monarchy.

The history of Paris and its government during the years of the Holy League laid bare the stresses and fractures within a seemingly monolithic cause. From the time of Anjou's death onwards the committed

Catholics in the capital had been constructing an urban organization based on the sixteen quarters of Paris. Its executive body, the Council of the Sixteen, first appeared publicly in March, 1585; and its role had increased steadily. After the assassination of the duke of Guise, the Council of the Sixteen had assumed effective power within the capital. But this sovereign committee did not confine its activities to the defence of the Catholic religion. It attempted to introduce genuine democracy into the government of the city, a programme with which the oligarchs and aristocrats who also made up the League were hardly likely to sympathize. Relations between the council and the parlement became increasingly strained. On 15 November 1591, the Sixteen ordered the arrest of the president of the parlement and two others. All three were tried, sentenced, and executed on the same day. This example of summary justice forced the duke of Mayenne, brother to the late duke of Guise, and titular head of the Holy League, to act. He punished the instigators of the trial and broke the power of their organization. The League was purged of urban radicals, but by the same token fatally weakened.

Throughout the turmoil of the 1580s a small party had managed to remain aloof from the general hysteria and sudden panics. These were the *politiques*, a term which, according to de Thou, first appeared in 1568. This group included men like the moderate Catholic Henry de Montmorency-Damville, the governor of Languedoc, who believed that the political integrity of the state took precedence over confessional allegiance. As the Holy League became more radical in its demands, and more openly dependent on Spain for its survival, the views of Montmorency-Damville gained a wider following. The *politiques*, like the *parlementaires*, may have been few in number; but they had wealth and standing in the community. They awaited the appearance of a natural leader who knew how to reintegrate the interests and loyalties which had formerly given the monarchy such authority. In 1589 Henry III and his namesake, the king of Navarre, united their forces and prepared to besiege Paris. The assassination of the last Valois (1 August) on the eve of the general assault put an end to this example of collaboration across religious lines; but it made Henry of Navarre the rightful king in the eyes of the legitimists. France had a ruler who was personally attractive, politically astute, and lucky in battle. The *politiques*, the *parlementaires*, and the municipal oligarchs had found their man.

Philip II was determined to contest this accident of destiny. In one of the more fateful directives of the Eighty Years War he instructed the prince of Parma to make the survival of the Holy League, not the conquest of Holland and Zeeland, his prime concern (26 November 1589). Farnese, already terminally ill, appreciated better than anyone the full significance of this switch in priorities. Yet he set in train the necessary preparations; and in carrying out the new policy he proved once more that he was the foremost captain of the age. When the campaigning season opened in 1590 Henry of Navarre laid siege to Paris hoping to achieve the victory which had eluded him in the previous year. Aware that the fall of the capital would mean the end of the Catholic cause, Farnese gathered a scratch force and marched south to link up with Mayenne on 25 August 1590, at Meaux. In a series of brilliantly executed manœuvres he drew Henry's army away from Paris, refused the formal offer of battle, and ran provisions into the city (30 August).

A year later Henry of Navarre attempted to surprise Rouen, another Leaguer stronghold and one that blocked his lines of communication with England. Responding with exemplary swiftness, Parma crossed the frontier on 18 December 1591, with another hastily composed army. The town of Caudebec held the key to the relief. Like Rouen it stood on the Seine; some way downstream, it had been held by Henry's army which had thereby been able to prevent the movement of supplies into the city by river. By marching and counter-marching, the prince took Caudebec on 17 April 1592, and broke the blockade of Rouen. By another masterly ploy he managed to transfer his army with its artillery across the Seine and escape a numerically superior force which was closing in on him (16 May 1592). Parma had provided the League with a short respite and he had saved his men; but in the process he had brought forward his own death. Just before the capture of Caudebec a musket ball had struck him immediately below the elbow (14 April); and he never fully recovered. Parma returned to France later in 1592 on his third expedition to shore up the Holy League. He reached Amiens; and here he died on 3 December 1592, apparently still ignorant of the fact that he had been relieved of his command.

Whatever other effect they might have had, the campaigns of Farnese ensured that Henry of Navarre could not end the war as the leader of the Protestant party. Paris was worth a Mass; and the prince had driven home the lesson. Henry III had urged Navarre to abjure the Protestant faith as early as 1584; but to have done so at this early date would have destroyed his credit. He refused. By 1589 he had modified his attitude considerably, promising the adherents of the late king, Henry III, that Catholicism would remain the religion of the state. After his defeats before Paris and Rouen the king of Navarre accepted the inescapable truth that only a Catholic could rule France. The recently elected pope, Clement VIII, was anxious to encourage this realism, in part wishing the carnage to be halted and in part hoping to restore France as a counter-balance to Spain. On 25 July, 1593, Henry of Navarre officially proclaimed his conversion to Catholicism (the experience was not a new one for him); and on 27 February 1594 his coronation took place in the cathedral of Chartres. The crown did not threaten to slip off his head, as had happened twice during the ceremony with Henry III. Philip II had tried to negate the consequences of the conversion which he knew to be imminent by offering his daughter, Isabel Clara Eugenia, as the queen of France. From the hereditary view she had an excellent claim; but politically her candidature had little chance. The Estates General of 1593, rabid Catholic though they may have been, refused to give their loyalty to a Spanish princess; and the parlement of Paris, for once speaking with the genuine voice of the people, reaffirmed the validity of the Salic Law. The Protestant Henry of Navarre became the Catholic Henry IV, founder of the Bourbon dynasty.

The implications of Philip's intervention in French affairs can be measured partly in financial terms and partly in loss of territory. Between 1590 and 1594 Philip sent greater sums than ever to the Netherlands. The Military Treasury in the Low Countries acknowledged receipt of 60.7 million guilders; but of this sum about three-quarters was spent on the French expeditions and subsidies to the Holy League. The figures spoke eloquently of the rearrangement of priorities which had taken place. Equally seriously, they demonstrated how Philip was prepared to weaken his position in Flanders at a time when the rebellious provinces, heartened by their success during the crisis of 1588, were poised to take the offensive. While Parma was absent in France, Maurice of Nassau inaugurated a series of campaigns at the head of an army which had been thoroughly re-organized on new principles. His first success came with the capture of Breda in 1590. Over the next decade Maurice and his brother, William Louis, cleared the eastern provinces north of the great rivers of Spanish garrisons, commencing with Zutphen and Deventer in 1591, then Groningen in 1594, and ending with Grave in 1602. The recovery of Drenthe, Overijssel, and Gelderland secured the Dutch

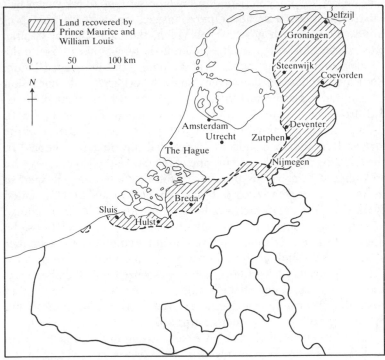

9 The conquests of Prince Maurice and Prince William Louis, 1588–98

Republic since the Habsburgs could no longer mount the pincer operation against Holland and Zeeland on which Farnese, and others, had relied to bring about a lasting reconquest. By the same token, the States General, now that individual provinces no longer felt threatened by royal garrisons in close proximity, were willing to release forces to Maurice of Nassau for a thrust across the rivers into the Catholic south. In the long run, Spain might not have preserved the eastern lands secured by Alexander Farnese; but had it not been for the French imbroglio Habsburg commanders might have been better placed militarily to withstand the Dutch offensives of the 1590s.

Nor was the Spanish crown able to shake itself free from the attempt to deny Henry of Navarre his inheritance. The first Bourbon, once he had entered Paris as the lawful king (22 March 1594) and asserted his control over most of France, formally declared war on Spain

(17 January 1595), regularizing, in effect, a state of affairs which had existed for at least a decade. Operations commenced on a number of fronts. The Spanish governor of Milan, the Constable of Castile, crossed the Alps with a small expeditionary force, linked up with the forces commanded by the duke of Mayenne, and threatened Dijon. For a moment it seemed possible that the Habsburgs, in the confusion of civil war and domestic strife, might recover the Burgundian lands, the dream of Charles V and, in an attenuated form, of Philip II. Prompt action on the part of Henry IV prevented the capture of the former Burgundian capital and dispelled any lingering hopes. In Brittany, the duke of Mercœur, one of the few Catholic grandees who still refused to make his peace with the new king, helped Spanish troops to become masters of le Blavet; but both he and his allies failed against Brest, a port which would have provided an ideal anchorage for convoys en route to Flanders. In the main theatre of operations, the Flemish frontier, Habsburg generals taught their opponents a number of hard lessons and confirmed once more the superiority of Spanish arms in conventional warfare. Calais was seized on 7 October 1595; and it remained under Spanish military occupation until the end of hostilities. Worse followed. On 11 March 1597, the enterprising Spanish governor of Doullens surprised Amiens, a city which, by reason of its site alone, occupied a key position in the French system of defence. Henry IV, convinced that his own survival hung in the balance, spent an entire campaigning season and all his reserves in the recovery of the town. The Spanish garrison, deprived of supplies from the Netherlands, at length surrendered with the full honours of war (25 September 1597) at the end of what was to prove the last major engagement of the conflict.

Both sides had pushed their subjects to the limits of endurance. The Assembly of the Notables gathered at Rouen (4 November 1596–29 January 1597) told Henry IV that additional taxation on the scale needed to win a decisive victory would not be voted. In the Habsburg case, the money markets delivered a similar message. The third bankruptcy of Philip's reign took place on 29 November 1596. Even though the remittances from the Americas stood at a record high, the Spanish crown had committed itself to expenditure far in excess of its resources, and credit was simply not forthcoming.

Many parties worked towards the conclusion of a general peace between France and Spain; and the settlement at Vervins can be seen more as the cumulative result of previous missions and private initiatives than as the product of a single conference. Since 1595 the papacy had been urging that the two Catholic monarchies should come to terms, if only so that Christendom could unite against a common foe, the Turk. Charles III of Lorraine, although at one time high in the governing circles of the Holy League, lent his good offices to the peace movement in order to spare his own lands the ravages of successive armies. After the Spanish failure to retain Amiens, the recently appointed ruler of the Habsburg Netherlands, Archduke Albert, recognized the futility of prolonging the war and advised Philip to settle with France as speedily as possible. The king, bowing to the force of the arguments and aware that his days were numbered, gave his consent to negotiations. The terms agreed upon were formally embodied in the peace of Vervins (2 May 1598).

The treaty marked the close rather than the opening of an era. By agreeing to its provisions, Philip recognized a series of basic truths. He was not in a position to secure the French crown for his elder daughter, Isabel Clara Eugenia, however excellent her claim might be. He was also forced to realize that although temporary gains might be secured at France's expense while she was torn by internal dissensions, these could not be retained once French unity had been restored. The English had made a similar discovery during the course of the Hundred Years War.

The territorial settlement of Vervins was essentially a re-statement of the one concluded at Cateau-Cambrésis a generation before (1559). All conquests were returned; and the frontiers, with the exception of the marquisate of Saluzzo, reverted to the lines of 1559. Philip also confirmed that any idea of reviving the duchy of Burgundy in all its glory had been abandoned. Within the traditional frontiers of the French kingdom, the Habsburgs retained the Free County of Burgundy and the county of Charolais, the latter as a vassal of the French monarch. These were fragments of a once great inheritance.

The Spanish court had every reason to celebrate the conclusion of peace, and the Castilian taxpayer even more so. Peace with France indicated an eventual settlement with her allies, the Dutch and the English. Yet amidst the festivities, the far-sighted amongst the royal counsellors had reason to be apprehensive. By 1598 it was obvious that seven out of the original seventeen provinces in the Netherlands were lost to Spain. For all the enormous resources at the disposal of the Castilian monarchs, their recovery was beyond the capacity of the Habsburg kings. This basic fact did not prevent the prolongation of

the war for another fifty years. These same perceptive members of
Castilian government might have reflected on a further disturbing
question. If France had preserved her unity in spite of eight civil wars,
what might she not achieve in the hands of a capable ruler? Once the
Bourbons had re-established order within their own house, might
they not bid for the position in Europe which their Valois predecessors had sought? Cardinal Richelieu and the count-duke of Olivares
addressed these same problems and gave the answers.

CHAPTER 13

The eastern kingdoms

DURING the sixteenth century Aragon, in company with the other Iberian kingdoms, experienced a steady and at times rapid demographic growth. Recent estimates have suggested that during this period the population rose from 230,000 inhabitants at the beginning to a possible 356,000 by the end of the century. The conversion of land from dry-farming (*secano*) to irrigation led to more intensive agriculture which in turn made it possible to support greater numbers. In this respect, Aragon shared the common experience of the Iberian peninsula under the first Habsburgs; but the comparison is of restricted use.

The outstanding feature of Aragonese history in the early modern period was its virtual irrelevance to the main course of events. The region counted for little in terms of royal, later imperial calculations, a marginal kingdom in every sense. Ferdinand the Catholic chose to spend less than three and a half years out of a reign which spanned thirty-seven within the borders of his natal state; and he slighted it even in death by electing to be buried in the city of Granada and not in one of the traditional pantheons of his ancestors. A number of factors accounted for the decline in Aragon's significance. The land was poor, and the climate harsh. In the summer the heat lifts the scent of wild herbs from the mountain-side; but in winter the freezing temperatures crack the earth and shatter the rock. Part of the population lived from the sheep flocks; while the transit trade which passed through Zaragoza on its way to Jaca and the French frontier generated another, and more substantial, source of wealth. Landlocked, virtually without industry, and barren for the most part, Aragon was the least endowed of the territories which made up the kingdom of that name.

Constitutional developments also went some way towards explaining the neglect into which Aragon fell during the sixteenth century. In the course of the later Middle Ages its rulers had bartered away many of their regalian rights for financial assistance. Their subjects, taking advantage of royal penury, had created a number of defensive institutions which made change, of any sort, almost impossible to achieve. The cortes, or representative body, emerged as one of the principal beneficiaries from the erosion of monarchical authority. Four estates, the clergy, the aristocracy, the gentry, and the towns made up this assembly; and together they were in a position to dictate government policy, something which their Castilian counterparts had never been able to do. Before a measure received the formal approval of the cortes, it had to obtain the assent of every member. The power of a single delegate to block legislation accounted for the infrequent summons of the Aragonese cortes, since the crown did not consider the effort to cajole the delegates into unanimity worth the often derisory sums voted. But even when not in session the representative institution was quite capable of making its presence felt. Since 1436 the cortes had appointed a standing committee or Diputación, to meet on a permanent basis during the often prolonged intervals between one cortes and the next. Eight deputies, two from each estate, composed the membership; and their term of office ran for three years. The Diputación, more important for practical purposes than its parent body, enjoyed a standing equal to, and perhaps above, that of the Inquisition. It was overwhelmingly aristocratic in number and spirit as three out of the four *brazos* (estates) either came from the higher nobility or aped its conduct; and the aristocratic tone was preserved by the useful (and simple) device of co-option. Automatic access to the revenues of the state assured its financial viability; and any grant made by the kingdom to the monarch normally had a sum deducted for the upkeep of the Diputación.

The power of the nobility found expression in another way. After 1348 the king appointed a Justiciar to defend the constitutional rights of the subject. In 1442 the prestige of the office was further increased by the grant of life tenure; and, as a further concession, the incumbent could only be removed once he had been successfully impeached before the cortes—that is, for all practical purposes, he could not be ejected. The office of Justiciar, hereditary in the house of Lanuza from the mid-fifteenth century until 1591, occupied a place of extraordinary prominence in public life. At his coronation each king of Aragon swore before the Justiciar to observe the privileges (*fueros*) of the realm; and it was left to the Justiciar to determine if and when a contravention had occurred. To advise him in these and similar matters, the Justiciar had on hand a court, or consistory, made up of five judges learned in the law. His authority could be invoked in both civil and criminal cases; and he was also called upon to adjudicate in disputes between the crown and the nobility. The protection of his court was available to all, except those legally bound in serfdom, through two legal devices, the right of remonstrance (*firma de manifestación*) and the right of redress (*firma de derecho* or *Jurisfirma*). If an appellant called on the first he was held in the Justiciar's prison—the gaol of the *manifestados*—until his case had been heard and judged by the competent authorities. If the latter right were invoked by a fugitive or defendant, the Justiciar had to issue an injunction preventing royal officials from carrying out an arrest or confiscating goods until it had been decided whether or not a case existed. Originally both privileges were intended to protect the subject from arbitrary imprisonment or distraint at the hands of crown agents; but each was abused to such an extent that the law became almost unenforceable.

The aristocratic nature of society found its reflection in the composition of the Diputación, recruitment to the upper ranks of the clergy, and, of course, the Justiciarship itself. Yet its most obvious indication could be seen in the power wielded by the nobles over their tenantry, a dominance which in terms of severity both matched and preceded the 'second enserfment' of eastern Europe. The Aragonese baronage extracted the customary range of leases, rents, milling rights and ancillary dues made familiar by French rural history. They could also discipline their subordinates in the most direct physical way by invoking the *ius maltractandi*, which allowed execution without any process of law. In 1599 the duke of Híjar felt little compunction in ordering without a trial the hanging of two mayors and two aldermen of Belchite—and this in a climate supposedly changed after the cortes of Tarazona (1592). In fact the Aragonese nobility retained the power of life and death over their subjects until the abolition of such traditional privileges in 1707. To enforce respect for their rights the nobles recruited private armies. The magnates often used their morisco subjects for this purpose, their cultural and religious alienation providing an additional guarantee of loyalty. But anyone with funds could recruit the necessary muscle from amongst the bully-boys and brigands who infested the uplands.

The town of Zaragoza alone could balance the noble estate in terms of wealth and influence, its role akin perhaps to that of Danzig or Koenigsberg in the Baltic region. By right it nominated one of the two urban representatives who sat on the Diputación; and it was therefore well able to argue its cause on the most significant body in the land.

Apart from its role as a staging post for goods on the road to France, the city developed extensive cattle- and sheep-rearing interests. As early as 1127 its inhabitants acquired the right to graze and water their livestock on all the mountain pasture in the kingdom. This led to clashes with the stockmen from other towns such as Daroca, Calatayud, and Teruel. In spite of these disputes, the kings of Aragon saw fit to extend rather than limit the privileges of the city. In 1235 James I directed that the flocks belonging to its inhabitants should be permitted to graze freely on all royal lands. To assert and preserve its grazing rights, Zaragoza was then awarded a further concession which had a profound bearing on the relationship between the city and the rest of Aragon, the notorious Privilege of the Twenty. As the title indicated, a tribunal of twenty men drawn from the citizen body assumed responsibility for the preservation of the city and its rights, concepts which were ever more liberally interpreted. The Twenty had formidable powers by any standards. If they considered the circumstances appropriate, they could call out the urban militia to enforce a ruling of the magistrates. Once they had arrogated to themselves competence, a right permitted to them under the Privilege of the Twenty, the tribunal acted as party and judge in all cases over which they presided. They feared no one; and they had little hesitation in passing the death penalty. In 1589 the archbishop of Zaragoza, acting under orders from Madrid, persuaded the outlaw, Antonio Martón, to leave the Justiciar's prison where he had sought sanctuary pending his trial, and return to the royal gaol where he had originally been housed. As both buildings stood within the city, the Twenty soon came to hear of the transfer. They immediately issued secret instructions for Antonio Martón to be removed from royal custody. At the dead of night he was rowed to the other bank of the Ebro and garrotted (10 September). The Aragonese nobility nursed a particular resentment against the Privilege as they were frequent victims of its exercise; but for all its arbitrary application, the monarchy permitted it to stand unaltered as a check on the baronage and an instrument, one of the very few, with which to combat rural lawlessness.

The lack of effective order on which so many contemporaries remarked had a variety of causes. One was the attempt made by the tenants of many fiefs to change their legal status in order to escape from the arbitrary authority of their overlords. The longest running dispute involved the family of Palafox y Rebolledo and the town of Monreal de Ariza. The inhabitants claimed that Ariza had been alienated from the crown domain illegally and that they could not, in law, be regarded as of servile condition. Partially successful in 1493 when the Palafox were deprived of their *dominio directo*, the house-holders of Ariza were not able to advance further on the road to personal freedom. Petitions to the cortes of Aragon in 1519 and again in 1585 failed to secure a clear ruling in their favour. Litigation through the courts in 1572 and 1576 proved equally unproductive. Confident of his rights, Juan de Palafox imposed a new duty, payable in corn, on his reluctant vassals from Ariza in 1556. Far from bowing to superior authority the inhabitants, enraged by what they considered to be an unwarranted demand, killed him in 1561. The cycle of violence began. The heirs of the murdered man executed the ringleaders and burnt down their houses, thus adding to the store of hate. At the cortes of Monzón (1585) Philip confirmed the rights of the Palafox; but their unwilling subjects from Ariza contested the decision right into the seventeenth century.

The barony of Monclús was sold by the king of Aragon in 1465 to Rodrigo Rebolledo; and the validity of the sale was confirmed in 1507 and again in 1519. But the inhabitants and their descendants were determined not to accept their reduction to serfdom brought about by the transfer. They contested the alienation, first through the courts, and, when that failed, by open rebellion in 1575. Ten years later the crown agreed to the reincorporation of the fief into the royal patrimony. This victory, famous in every way, gave encouragement to the men of Ariza and all like them who hoped to escape from personal bondage.

The most celebrated case of disputed lordship involved the county of Ribagorza. It drew in the largest number of disparate elements; and it provided, in miniature, a picture of every ill to afflict Aragon in the sixteenth century. Ribagorza, a narrow wedge of territory whose northern edge adjoined the French frontier, had a population of about four thousand and belonged in name to the dukes of Villahermosa. The county yielded small returns by way of income, some four to five thousand ducats annually. Ducal officials at the best of times faced a hard task in governing the mountainous terrain, a series of high peaks and narrow valleys with torrential, poplar-lined, streams; and the obstacles were increased by the reluctance of the inhabitants to observe ducal law. Servile status had not been imposed on Ribágorza, hardly possible in a land where men lived isolated on the upland pastures breathing the pure air of liberty; and the population had wrested from their titular overlords important legal and personal rights. Every year, on 22 January, the inhabitants converged on the town of Benabarre to hold a rupestrian parliament, comparable to the Icelandic assembly of the Viking Age, which discussed and delivered judgement on matters of common interest. During the gathering two *síndicos* (representatives) were elected; and it was their obligation to watch over the rights of the county during the interim between the dissolution of one assembly and the calling of the next.

Relations in the county between subject and overlord had steadily worsened over the decades. In the second half of Philip's reign the anti-seigneurial movement gathered momentum; and a virtual civil war raged from 1578 until 1589. Don Martín de Gurrea, whose title over Ribagorza the king had confirmed in 1567, complained bitterly to Madrid that his authority was merely nominal. In 1582 the viceroy of Aragon informed the king that the *síndicos* had in effect taken over the administration of justice and the collection of taxes. The Holy Office, called in at the same time to discover if the duke of Villahermosa had allowed Gascon heretics (i.e. French Huguenots) to enter the region, expressed amazement at the lawlessness which had flourished unchecked for years. When in 1589 action was at last taken to restore order to the county, it produced startling confirmation of what many had long suspected. The governor of Aragon led a column on Benabarre, the regional capital which the brigands had made their headquarters. On entering the town, he found that it had been turned into one large warehouse for the storage of loot.

On the death of Don Martín de Gurrea in 1581 Philip hesitated before confirming his successor, Don Hernando, as the rightful heir to Ribagorza, a delay which could only prompt further disorders. The youthful claimant had to wait four years before he was enfeoffed at the cortes of Monzón (1585). Once installed, the duke, realizing that only violent methods would work, recruited a gang, or, a more graceful term, a private army, to fight the brigands who had usurped power in the county. In 1586 his retainers stormed Benabarre, killing during the assault Juan de Ager, one of the two *síndicos* and the master spirit behind the resistance. This should have ended effective opposition. But the duke chose to stay his hand instead of hunting down the fugitives. Shortly after, for very special reasons of its own, the court in Madrid urged the survivors to re-group. In their anxiety to prevent the collapse of the insurgent cause, royal officials connived at, if they did not actually arrange, the hire of new leaders, amongst them the native

Luis de Bardaji, and a foreign expert, the Catalan bandit, Minyó de Montellà, on secondment, as it were, from his normal duties. The ruffians and bandoleros from either side fought a number of running battles and conducted regular sieges; and during the course of hostilities the two principal towns of the county, Graus and Benabarre, were sacked. Anarchy descended on the region as the inhabitants, egged on and supported by powerful elements at court, proved well able to hold themselves against those in the pay of Villahermosa. The conflict ceased only when Madrid decided that the scandal could no longer be tolerated. On 15 April 1588 the duke received a summons to present himself in person before the king. Royal garrisons were quartered on the towns of Ribagorza, ostensibly to deter any French invasion, in reality to intimidate the duke and his supporters. Under such pressure the talks between the house of Villahermosa and the king's ministers did not take long. The duke agreed to the sale of his troublesome fief for 30,000 ducats cash down and the annual payment of 5,000 ducats. On 6 March 1591, the crown took formal possession; and Ribagorza, fractious and strategic, passed into the royal domain.

The quarrels over jurisdiction throw much light on the operation of government in Aragon, or, to be more precise, its malfunction. Where no limitations had been introduced, the baronage and the ecclesiastical foundations enjoyed almost absolute power over their tenantry, to the exclusion of all external authority, including the king's. It proved impossible to insist on a uniform and universal system of justice. If an individual chose to mistreat his subordinates or to ally with the local banditti, the crown had little chance of interfering. Only by resorting to the methods used by the seigneurs, brigandage and intimidation, could it make its own presence felt, a situation which in turn added to the unrest and promoted banditry.

In the particular instance of Ribagorza, the monarch unwisely allowed faction at court to spill over into regional affairs, with results that cast discredit on his administration and brought disaster to the region. Contemporaries spoke openly about the animosity which had sprung up between the house of Chinchón and that of Villahermosa. The plot was worthy of grand opera. In 1564 Juan de Aragón, count of Ribagorza, married Doña Luisa de Pacheco, whose sister was the wife of the count of Chinchón, already a rising man at court. The marriage was not successful, Juan de Aragón suspecting, with good reason, adultery on the part of his wife. The pair moved back from Toledo, where they had been living, to one of the family estates in Aragon; and here Doña Luisa was murdered by her husband's servants. Chinchón, far from seeing the count of Ribagorza as the doctor of his honour, was determined that he should pay for the crime with his life. Juan de Aragón had sense enough to escape to Italy after the deed; but, in a moment of reckless confidence, he crossed Spanish-held territory, although aware that a warrant was out for his arrest. He was caught, shipped back to Spain, and garrotted at Torrejón de Velasco. The execution of the murderer did not atone for the crime. From that day onwards the count of Chinchón conducted a relentless feud against the house of Villahermosa. The shadow of his anger lay across all subsequent events. Chinchón's brother became archbishop of Zaragoza in 1585, and he himself came to exercise increasing influence over the king. Chinchón stood behind the policy of inciting the inhabitants of Ribagorza to resist the authority of their overlord; and he also had a voice, perhaps a decisive one, in deciding Villahermosa's fate in the reckoning which followed the troubles of 1591.

As the question of Ribagorza approached a final settlement, another problem, of much longer standing, surfaced once more. 'The war of the mountainmen and the moriscos', as the episode has been described, had its origins in a quarrel over grazing rights. Although the various accounts differ on important points of detail, they agree that winter transhumance provoked the 'war'. As the cold season drew on, the flock-masters of the Pyrenees, Old Christians to a man, or so they claimed, brought their herds down to graze on the banks of the Ebro. One version maintains that in 1585 a certain Pedro Pérez, native of Escarilla high in the Pyrenees, led his flock to winter pasture on the Ebro near the town of Codo. The choice was dangerous, since Codo was a morisco village subject to the monastery of Rueda. Within a few days he was killed by unknown assailants almost certainly from the village. A variant narrative holds that the murder of an Old Christian shepherd by the men of Codo took place in 1586; and the victim's name was Oliván. The struggle for winter grazing, that classic point of friction between the mountain and the plain, acquired a further dimension, sectarian hatred. In the first days of November 1586, a party of four who had trekked down from the Pyrenees to Codo set upon a group of moriscos as they worked in the fields, killing two of them. A few weeks later, the moriscos, taking justice into their own hands, retaliated by murdering two shepherds, both Old Christians, and mutilating their bodies. This was only a beginning. The mountaineers, led by Antonio Martón who, some claimed, was the brother of Pedro Pérez, the first casualty of the range war, attacked Codo in force, only to find that it had been evacuated (April 1588). Martón and his associates then marched on another morisco village, Pina, which they took, and then proceeded to massacre its three hundred inhabitants. The moriscos, with fewer resources at their disposal, responded on a more limited scale. A group of terrorists, 'the moriscos of vengeance', operated on the stretch of road between Zaragoza and Calatayud, murdering travellers at random.

As the spectre of complete anarchy loomed, the Aragonese authorities resolved to deal with the brigands of Ribagorza, the shepherds of the Pyrenees, and the moriscos of the lowlands. A punitive column was sent out against Benabarre to eject the banditti from their stronghold; and another was dispatched at the same time (1589) to take the morisco village of Pleitas, thought to be the hiding-place of 'the moriscos of vengeance'. Once Pleitas had been secured, the royal commander ordered twenty-nine adult males to be garrotted for suspected complicity. The leader of the gang, 'el Focero', was run to earth a little later, and shot as he tried to escape from a blazing house. The mountain men were able to melt back into the glens and distant mountains from where they had emerged, but not so their leader who had a distinguished criminal record. With the full, if tacit, approval of the crown, the city of Zaragoza was grimly resolved to settle the account with Antonio Martón, not on the count of bigotry but for brigandage; and this meant resort to the Privilege of the Twenty in all its rigour.

The settlement of Ribagorza and the damping-down, for the time being, of communal antagonisms did not bring peace to the region. They acted, instead, as a prelude to much greater events which compelled the crown to consider the very foundations of royal government in Aragon.

In 1590 the former royal secretary, Antonio Pérez, realizing his execution for complicity in the murder of Juan de Escobedo to be imminent, fled from Castile to Aragon. His choice of refuge, as might be expected from one who had been at the centre of power for many years, was neither accidental nor unpremeditated. Aragon held out the promise of shelter for a distant son—his paternal grandfather had come from Monreal de Ariza, already famous from another context; and the kingdom had a set of privileges which could give effective protection to one who showed himself able to manipulate them. With luck, and with the *fueros*, Pérez might be able to strike a bargain, or (who could tell?) work his way back to favour. France was a last resort.

Pérez was undoubtedly aware that circumstances favoured him in another way. Resentment had been steadily mounting against the king and what appeared his chosen instrument, the Inquisition. For decades the town of Teruel had claimed the privileges of Aragon. These the crown had steadfastly refused to grant; and during the course of the dispute royal troops had occupied the town (1570). In 1571 Antonio Gamir, a citizen of Teruel, lodged a formal complaint before the viceroy of Aragon, alleging that the town's (Aragonese) rights had been violated. The charge was rejected; and Gamir was sentenced to a year's exile for his temerity. Some have seen in the figure of Antonio Gamir a precursor to Antonio Pérez from the manner in which the privileges of Aragon were initially invoked (only to be dismissed) and the use made during the earlier case, as in the later, of the Inquisition to bring about a result satisfactory to the crown. At the cortes of Monzón (1585) Philip made amends by conceding to Teruel inclusion in the general privileges of the realm; but the good impression this might have caused was immediately dispelled by another incident. The authorities sent a small force, some two hundred men, to occupy Albarracín in 1585, even though it too had just been given the protection of Aragonese privilege. The feeling that the crown rode roughshod over the rights of the kingdom and that it was ready to make improper use of the Holy Office to secure its ends worked powerfully in favour of Antonio Pérez and gave him a popular following in his hour of need.

On crossing the Aragonese border Pérez made for Calatayud where, calling on the right of remonstrance, he appealed to the Justiciar's court for protection. The validity of the claim once recognized, he was taken under escort to Zaragoza and lodged in the prison of the *manifestados*, not an agreeable experience for one of his luxurious tastes, but infinitely preferable to the alternatives—and much less secure. During his years in captivity, Pérez had cultivated his connections with the Aragonese nobility; and the count of Aranda was commonly believed to have had knowledge of his plans to escape from Castile. When sentence of death was formally passed on Antonio Pérez (1 July 1590) many of the secretary's aristocratic patrons discreetly withdrew; but his popularity remained high amongst the urban mob of Zaragoza. Pérez had wit enough to retain their sympathy by a clever programme of propaganda and misinformation.

In Madrid a small committee had been constituted to monitor events. On 15 September, 1590, officials acting on behalf of the crown inaugurated the *proceso de enquesta*, an attempt to bring Pérez to book through the Aragonese courts. The scheme had to be abandoned rapidly as the king was reliably assured that no court would convict on the evidence the crown intended to present. Acting on the advice of his expert committee, or his own instinct, or, perhaps, a combination of both, Philip concluded by the spring of 1591 that his former servant could not be left to Aragonese justice. If all the niceties of the *fueros* were observed, if the due legal process were allowed to take its course, sentence could be postponed for years; and the longer Pérez remained alive, the greater the threat he represented. It was time for the Inquisition to take a hand.

Charges of heresy were preferred against Antonio Pérez on 4 May 1591; and nine days later the Supreme Council of the Inquisition sitting in Madrid instructed the Tribunal in Zaragoza to bring the accused from the Justiciar's prison to the safer custody of the Tribunal's cells, the distance between the two not being great. The reverend fathers clearly intended to have Pérez abducted and spirited over the border. On 24 May 1591 the translation was carried out; and the prisoner found himself in the Aljafería, home of the Tribunal and its interrogation chambers. In no doubt that his life hung on a thread, Pérez called out his supporters; and Gil de Mesa, his loyal henchman, did yeoman work amongst the urban rabble urging them to rise in defence of liberty and freedom, concepts they barely understood. The mob poured into the streets. One group of rioters converged on the house of the marquis of Almenara, in Zaragoza on special business for the crown and widely regarded as the inspiration behind royal policy in Aragon, while another set off for the dungeons of the Inquisition to rescue their idol and return him to the Justiciar's prison. In the fracas that followed the marquis of Almenara was so badly beaten up that he died fourteen days later, the first notable victim of the troubles, but not the last. For Antonio Pérez the day ended in triumph. He was escorted back to the prison of the *manifestados*, accompanied in his coach by the viceroy and other leading worthies.

Throughout the summer of 1591 the Aragonese authorities who between them had the necessary armed force with which to impose order dithered over a suitable line to adopt. In the meantime a furious pamphlet war broke out. The friends of the disgraced secretary spared no efforts in portraying him as a martyr to the sinister machinations of the evil politicians in Madrid and their collaborators in Aragon, who were willing to betray ancestral liberties for contemptible royal favour. Antonio Pérez spent his summer filing away at the bars of his cell in the Justiciar's prison, only to be discovered when he was within a few millimetres of success. The situation could not be allowed to drift indefinitely. The king's right to govern had been impugned, and his representative beaten to death. The Inquisition had suffered a serious blow; and if it were to retain its awesome prestige, punishment, swift and condign, must be inflicted. Pérez was still alive, and very active.

The crown had taken a number of precautionary measures. From August 1591 onwards recruits began to make their way to the Castilian town of Agreda, just across the border from Aragon. Some officials thought that the use of armed force, or even the threat, might drive Aragon into the arms of 'Vandoma', Henry of Navarre; but the counter-argument that sooner or later the king would have to intervene to end the turmoil carried the day. As Philip seriously pondered the invasion and its consequences, the wiser heads amongst the Aragonese ruling class concluded that Antonio Pérez must be handed back to the Inquisition. His sojourn in the prison of the *manifestados* was becoming an embarrassment, and the longer he stayed there, the more likely the king was to resort to force. The *fueros* no longer exerted their appeal on the leading aristocratic families, most of whom were more interested in proving their loyalty to their Habsburg overlords. Aranda and Villahermosa alone cherished the older ideals. The date for Pérez's return to the Aljafería was set for 24 September 1591.

At the appointed hour several coaches drew up before the Justiciar's palace which housed both his court and his prison. Pérez had been bound ready for delivery. A few more steps down a flight of stairs and he would have been in the power of the Inquisition. Once more the mob, answering to obscure and turbid reasons, rioted to save their unlikely hero. They fell on the coaches sent by the Holy Office and overturned them. In the ensuing pandemonium Pérez escaped at last, although it was to take him a further two months to cross into France and safety.

Pérez's friends, or those who had risen in his name, controlled Zaragoza for the next few weeks; but the secretary became less important as the city and the crown moved into open conflict. The collapse of recognized authority decided royal policy. Early in October 1591 the royal commander, Alonso de Vargas, received orders to march his troops from Agreda to Zaragoza, instructions formally announced in an official communiqué of 15 October. The Diputación, now completely in the hands of the rebel faction, called for support from all the estates, corporations, and cities of the land; and on 1 November it took the final step of declaring war on the king. The Justiciar, Juan de Lanuza, who had just succeeded to the title, showed his immaturity by allowing himself to be swept along by the momentary elation. He declared that the *fueros* had been contravened; and he called on his fellow Aragonese to defend them thereby providing a cloak of legitimacy for what would be interpreted, after its failure, as an act of high treason.

Events did not follow the course anticipated by the Diputación or the Justiciar. Outside Zaragoza no one rose in defence of the *fueros*. Catalonia and Aragon, while perhaps sympathetic, did not stir. On 8 November Alonso de Vargas crossed the Aragonese frontier at the head of an élite corps of Flemish veterans. He continued his march on Zaragoza along roads and across bridges which were left undefended and intact. On 12 November royal troops entered the city after what could only be described as a military promenade.

The ease of the victory and the indifference of the country at large to the cause of the *fueros* were arguments for a show of clemency on the part of the king. A number of complications made such an act difficult for one who was slow and then implacable. The duke of Villahermosa and the count of Aranda, their position gravely compromised by their association with the Diputación, had retreated to the town of Epila on hearing that Vargas had set out. From here they issued on 11 November a manifesto calling on the kingdom to resist the invasion. The appeal was ill-timed and ill-considered; and had fatal consequences for those who composed it. The junta of Epila, as the group was called, did not stay together for long. On 24 November both Aranda and Villahermosa returned to Zaragoza, where they were joined two days later by the Justiciar. All three had a touching faith in their rights and the king's mercy.

Another band of *foralistas* with less trust and more resolution sought refuge in Béarn. Early in 1592 these emigrés launched an expedition in the hope of rekindling the spirit of Aragonese independence. The invasion force, under the command of Martín Lanuza, a brave and resourceful man, occupied the hamlet of Biescas for ten days (9–19 February 1592). But they discovered that their fellow countrymen, far from welcoming them with open arms, used the invasion as an opportunity to demonstrate their loyalty to Philip II. The exiles and their

'Gascon' (French) allies were driven back across the mountain passes with loss.

Before this forlorn enterprise took place the king had already carried out part of his plan for the pacification of the kingdom. This required one act of terror to overawe those who had been so willing to riot, and two imprisonments with extreme prejudice to remove the natural leadership of any secessionist movement in the future. Juan de Lanuza, the Justiciar, went to the scaffold without a trial. His youth, his bearing, and the black clothes he wore in memory of his late father, heightened the dramatic impact of his public execution. Aranda and Villahermosa were imprisoned and taken to Castile, where both died in the following year, the first at Coca (4 August 1592) and the second at Miranda del Ebro (6 November 1592). Contemporaries did not miss the striking analogy with the Flemish troubles of the 1560s; and, indeed, the comparison was more than superficial. The leaders of the two aristocratic Frondes had met fates that were either terrifying or mysterious. There was even in Martín Lanuza a potential William of Orange, or at least a Louis of Nassau. But here the resemblance ended. Philip II, although visibly ailing, did what he had baulked at doing in the Flemish case. He made the journey to Aragon.

Intent on eliminating the provisions of the Aragonese constitution most open to abuse, Philip was careful at the same time to observe the constitutional proprieties. The estates of Aragon (but not of Catalonia or Valencia) were summoned to meet at Tarazona where the cortes opened on 15 June 1592. The real business of the gathering was conducted in private between a royal delegation led by the archbishop of Zaragoza and leading members of the four estates. The king arrived just before the formal closure, like a rainbow, according to one description, at the end of a storm, the harbinger of peace and concord. The analogy with what had been planned for the Low Countries, but had failed to take place, holds good once again.

The cortes agreed to a number of constitutional modifications which affected the representative institution itself and the future administration of justice. The delegates conceded the majority principle (8 August 1592): henceforth each of the four estates would give or withhold its consent to a proposal on the basis of a numerical vote; and no individual would be permitted to exercise the right of veto. From a constitutional viewpoint the reform was long overdue. In diminishing the power of the member, it enhanced that of the estate and therefore the institution. Secondly, the Diputación, that instrument of oligarchic dominance, found that it could no longer make free with the tax revenues of the state. It had to content itself, in the first instance, with a fixed income of three thousand Aragonese pounds which could be supplemented by recourse to the Justiciar and then, if more were needed, to a royal official, the Procurator Fiscal. The legal amendments had as their primary design the abolition of privileges which had enabled Antonio Pérez and, before him, lesser fry to elude justice. The rights of prisoners to be set free on a legal technicality arising out of the circumstances of their arrest were swept away. Similarly, a fugitive from justice who sought sanctuary in Aragon from some other part of the Habsburg dominions could be extradited back to the place where he was originally to stand trial. On the general problems of law and its enforcement, the cortes conceded a number of important points. The king gained greater say in the appointment of the senior judges in a move designed, perhaps, to render them less amenable to aristocratic pressure. At a lower level, royal judges were authorized to intervene more directly than had hitherto been the case in the dispensing of seigneurial justice, although this had little practical consequence in terms of curbing arbitrary conduct. The formal concessions granted by the cortes and enshrined in what became known as the *fueros* of Tarazona represented the legal changes which the popular tumults of 1590 and 1591 had brought about. This alteration in the status of the kingdom found expression in two supplementary acts, one symbolic, the other patently visual. After 1591 the office of Justiciar ceased to be hereditary in one family: from that date onwards the incumbent held the honour at the king's pleasure and could be dismissed accordingly. As if to serve notice that a new era had dawned, the king insisted, although he was moderation itself in comparison to some of his advisers, that a fort, manned by royal troops, should be built in the Aljafería as testimony, in stone, to the symbiotic relationship between the crown and the Holy Office. The fort was not removed until 1626.

CHAPTER 14

The principality of Catalonia

AT THE end of a civil war which had lasted ten years (1462–72) John II pledged to his Catalan subjects that he would observe all their rights and privileges that had existed before the outbreak of hostilities. The Capitulation of Pedralbes (24 October 1472) reaffirmed a constitutional order that was to endure until the eighteenth century. The great age of the king, John II, and the prostration of Catalonia may have encouraged the acceptance of such eminently moderate terms; while at the same time Ferdinand II was more anxious to turn his attention to the affairs of his wife's kingdom.

The Habsburgs imitated Ferdinand's neglect. As their attention was invariably engaged elsewhere, they revived what was a Catalan (or more correctly, Aragonese) precedent. In peacetime a viceroy ruled the principality in the king's name; and in wartime he might be assisted, or replaced, by a Captain General. The Council of Catalonia acted as the supreme court of appeal, in the same way as a Castilian audiencia. In 1494 the Catholic Monarchs set up the Council of Aragon which followed the royal household wherever it went. It provided the link between the court and the lands subject to the Aragonese crown, amongst them Catalonia.

The Catalan corts comprised three estates, the ecclesiastical, the military, and the urban. Formal sessions of this representative assembly were very infrequent during the sixteeenth century, normally being reserved for the formal act of homage to the new sovereign. The corts did not need to be summoned regularly to defend what were considered to be traditional Catalan rights. The Diputació did this for them. This all-powerful body included a representative nominated by each of the three estates. Although small in number and renewed only on the death of a member, the Diputació did more than any other organization to preserve the political identity of Catalonia through the reigns of successive Habsburg kings until it became during the ministry of the count-duke of Olivares (1621–43) the embodiment of resistance to royal, that is Castilian, demands.

The fortunes of Catalonia in the sixteenth century could not have differed more starkly from those of its Castilian neighbour. From an economic and political standpoint, Catalonia represented the dark side of the moon. The events of the fifteenth century were responsible for this. During the Black Death and its aftermath land became available in abundance through the operation of what has been termed 'inverse Malthusianism'. Population contracted faster than the food supply. Those fortunate enough to survive the plague, and its sequels, were able to add the abandoned holdings (*masos rònecs*) to their own farms, improving thereby their own living standards. In 'Old' Catalonia, where the feudal system was at its most developed, the baronage had tolerated these incorporations as a means of keeping the land in use. Once, however, the shortage of manpower was over, and once the feudal overlords began to feel the financial pressure of greater personal expenditure, they made a determined effort to impose the obligations of feudal tenure on all those who had taken over land previously held on that basis. The baronage sought to reimpose 'the six bad uses' and the *ius maltractandi*. Had they succeeded in imposing the last-named, this in itself would have reduced the *remensa* class, as it came to be known, to serfdom. The *ius maltractandi* allowed the landlord to imprison tenants and confiscate their goods without showing due cause. On this occasion the intended victims of the return to old customs showed that they were well able to fight for themselves. Agrarian violence became widespread after 1454; and it merged into the general civil war which took place between 1462–72. The *remensa* class provided constant and powerful support for the royal cause throughout, one of its leaders, Francesc de Verntallat, receiving a marquisate for his service. Their claims, notwithstanding, remained unsatisfied on the death of John II in 1479.

After a renewed outbreak of the land war (1482–4) Ferdinand acknowledged that the crown must resolve the *remensa* problem once and for all. A judicious balancing of interests brought this about. Under the terms of the Sentence of Guadalupe (1486) the 'bad uses' and the levy of unreasonable payments were declared illegal. In turn, the occupants of the *masos rònecs* were obliged to pay a redemption fee to the overlord. It was further stipulated that in the future relations between the tenant and the landlord would be based on contract, and the tenant once his contractual obligations had been fulfilled could leave when he wished. Principally as a result of the Sentence the structure of Catalan agriculture underwent profound change in the course of the next century. Denied the supplementary income which service at the royal court might have provided, the minor gentry found itself squeezed progressively harder; whereas the substantial farmer, now assured of legal tenure, exploited his opportunities and prospered. Stability came to the land; and the improvement in conditions for those who worked it led to a modest increase in output during the second half of the sixteenth century.

The depression of the later Middle Ages hit Catalonia's overseas trade even more severely than it did farming. In the thirteenth and fourteenth centuries Catalan merchants developed a commercial empire in North Africa and the eastern Mediterranean; in the fifteenth century this all but vanished. The process began in 1408 when trading relations were broken off with Egypt. The crusading zeal of Alfonso the Magnanimous (1416–58) accelerated the loss. He failed to save Constantinople from the Turks but his aggressive policies did lead to the exclusion of his subjects from their traditional markets in the Aegean. While the resources of the principality were overcommitted (or misdirected) in the east, merchants from the Italian city states were busy annexing the trade of Andalucía, a region which, given geographical proximity, should have been the preserve of the Catalans. The inability of the principality's trading community to maintain itself in southern Spain had an immediate impact; and in the longer perspective it explained much about the character of overseas exploration and the trade patterns which emerged once the New World had been discovered.

After 1430 the decline in exports became acute. The contraction in trade brought latent tensions in Barcelona out into the open. Within the city one group, the Busca, made up of the weaving masters and the exporters, wished to see the crown adopt a number of measures designed to encourage the productive sector. These policies included the debasement of the currency and the introduction of protection. Their opponents, the Biga, represented the interest of the city fathers and the large importers who were anxious to keep 'sound' money and free trade. Such policies worked to the advantage of those who had switched their resources away from trade and into municipal bonds. This phenomenon, a Catalan variant, perhaps, on 'the treason of the bourgeoisie', had become all too common in the fifteenth century. During the civil war (1462–72) the Biga party held the city for the anti-monarchist faction, thereby bringing upon Barcelona the twin disasters of isolation from its hinterland and siege by its king. In 1468 the municipal bank, the Taula de Canvi, which managed the city's debts, suspended all payment. But the damage ran much deeper than that. The finances of the city were not restored to any semblance of order until 1507.

Nor did the export trade of Catalonia show clear signs of recovery until well into the second half of the sixteenth century. After the battle of Lepanto (1571) trading in the Mediterranean became less of a hazard, a fact which encouraged the reopening of long-neglected markets. The transfer in bullion shipments from the Biscay route to the Mediterranean at the outbreak of the Dutch Revolt (1567) provided a stimulus to the principality's economy, as did a similar switch in the export of Castilian wool from its traditional outlet in the Low Countries to northern Italy. At about this time the Catalan textile industry may, at last, have succeeded in breaking into the American market. Rough cloth produced on Catalan looms was sold to Seville; and from here it was probably shipped out to the New World. In this way, and belatedly, Catalonia derived some benefit from the overseas possessions of its Habsburg masters.

Somnolence is often the description applied to the principality in the sixteenth century; but this term would hardly have been employed by Philip II or his advisers. In the 1560s the line of the Pyrenees became the frontier between not only two countries, France and Spain, but two confessions, Catholic and Calvinist. According to one account, the Habsburg government was set upon ending the unregulated movement of men, cattle, and contraband across the mountains. The Pyrenees were to become an impenetrable barrier. The policy was first entrusted to Diego Hurtado de Mendoza, viceroy of Catalonia from 1564 until 1571; and it remained the official line throughout Philip's reign. Catalan historians have interpreted this sealing of the border as a detail in the wider plan to isolate the entire peninsula from external (and undesirable) ideas, in particular heresy.

The alarming increase in brigandage prompted in part the anxiety to prevent all contact between France and Catalonia. Whenever they needed to go to earth, the outlaws slipped across the Pyrenees; and once in Béarn or Languedoc they could not avoid exposure to Calvinism in its most virulent form. Official reports make frequent mention of the 'Gascons' (Frenchmen) who were recruited over the border and returned with the gangs as soon as the hue and cry had died down. Various factors contributed to the endemic phenomenon of banditry. Rural poverty was a fundamental cause: a land unable to employ all its sons drove the more violent and energetic into this agrarian version of theft. The brigands, moreover, could always count on the support not only of the dispossessed but those who were better placed in society. Excluded from the royal court and denied an outlet for their talents, the nobility threw itself into private feuds with a passion. As in the case of neighbouring Aragon, they frequently recruited the rural gangs into their private armies. The king's agents were virtually powerless to track down the banditti and bring them to book. Much of Catalonia was covered by baronial and ecclesiastical immunities where the king's writ did not run. A brigand chief had only to place himself under the protection of a local noble (perhaps even a local abbot), reach some arrangement about the divison of the spoils, and he could reckon on escaping from the short arm of the law.

The daring of the bandits grew with the passing of every year. In 1573 the royal authorites decided to provide the bullion train from Madrid to Barcelona with an armed escort. Fourteen years later the inevitable happened. Minyó de Montellà, probably tipped off by somebody in high places and with ample resources at his disposal, intercepted the silver convoy on its way overland to Barcelona. His was the first successful assault, but not the last, or the most lucrative. A seventeenth-century counterpart to Minyó called Perot Roca Guinarda achieved literary immortality. Don Quijote spent three days and nights with him, admiring all the while his style of life. With exquisite courtesy the brigand then escorted the knight and his squire to the beach just outside Barcelona, remembering just before he left to give Sancho Panza ten escudos, as he had promised. But behind the manners lay another reality. Roca Guinarda never slept in the same camp as his men, for fear of betrayal.

Throughout the sixteenth century Catalonia remained unaffected by the commotions which shook the adjacent kingdoms. It did not participate in the rising of the *comuneros* or the coetaneous revolt of the *Germanías*. Nor did it respond in any way to the discontent fanned and promoted by Antonio Pérez. But this lack of involvement did not indicate a change in the nature of the principality. Catalan institutions, laws, and currency remained unaltered, and the country's sense of identity unimpaired. Catalonia was no nearer adapting to Castilian ways in 1598 than it had been in 1469.

CHAPTER 15

The financial system of the Habsburg empire

W HEN Charles of Ghent inherited the thrones of Castile and Aragon a new chapter opened in the history of the Iberian kingdoms. The dimension and direction of this transformation can be nowhere better studied than in the fiscal and credit policies which the new dynasty was compelled to adopt. To pay for their ambitious projects the Catholic Monarchs had dug into the pockets of their subjects, lay and ecclesiastical; and, where necessary, they had resorted to extensive borrowing, generally on the inland market. But their Habsburg successors both taxed more severely and raised loans on a scale which dwarfed all that had gone before. After 1519 the financial needs of the monarchy began to exert a pressure which at first impeded, then arrested, and finally, under Charles's son and grandson, drained the Castilian economy on which everything had come to depend.

The Habsburgs, both as rulers of the Austrian duchies and as Holy Roman Emperors, relied heavily on the banking families of southern Germany. The Fugger of Augsburg ranked as the leaders of this select community. In return for their extensive financial assistance, they had been granted control over the silver mines of the Tyrol which formed the most valuable asset of the Austrian dukes to whom they belonged. The links between the Fugger and the Habsburgs were at their closest during the first quarter of the sixteenth century, the period, as it happened, of greatest prosperity for the dynasts of Augsburg. Without the timely intervention of the Fugger the early success of Charles—or, for that matter, his later survival—would be hard to explain. Jakob Fugger, patriarch and a genius with money, contributed the lion's share of Charles's electoral expenses (i.e. bribery) in 1519, putting up 530,000 florins out of the 850,000 florins needed to square the electors. The Genoese appeared on the financial stage for the first time in 1519, but their role was one of subcontractor in the business of electoral jobbery. The Fugger played a prominant and at times dominant role in imperial affairs up to the abdication of 1555. Charles V required their services even more than had his Austrian forebears, to the extent that his reign became synonymous with the age of the Fugger. In 1531 the principals of their bank helped to engineer the nomination of Ferdinand, Charles's brother, as king of the Romans, an operation even more costly than the imperial election itself. Two decades later Anton Fugger, the less astute son of Jakob, was amongst the few to accompany the emperor on his flight from Innsbruck to Villach in the spring of 1552. Here, against all the dictates of financial sense, he entered into the *asiento* of Villach (28 May 1552), whereby he opened a credit line of 400,000 ducats, one hundred thousand to be paid in cash on the spot, and the balance to be delivered part in Italy, part in the Low Countries. This advance and a number of equally unsound ones concluded shortly afterwards on the Antwerp bourse left the family dangerously exposed. At the end of 1560 the Spanish Habsburgs on a contemporary calculation owed the house three million ducats, the bulk of which was not likely to be repaid in cash. Poor judgement, bad debts, and perhaps a general shift in trading patterns prompted the Fugger, and the south German banks in general, to disengage from royal finance and head for the calmer waters of commerce. Their departure left the way open to a new breed, the oligarchs of Genoa, who brought to their chosen speciality greater knowledge, daring, and resource.

In the history of public finance, the era of the Fugger contributed a number of distinctive features. The funds which they and their German consorts placed at the emperor's disposal sprang from personal fortunes, namely, their own. The sale of shares in government debt (*juros*) to the general public had yet to take place. Up to 1540 the Netherlands paid for the bulk of imperial loans. As a result, the Spanish kingdoms remained for the most part outside the circuit of credit and settlement. Charles's Iberian subjects might resent the presence of foreign bankers in the peninsula and the abuses they were alleged to perpetrate; but until the second half of the reign they had little cause to complain.

After 1540 circumstances changed swiftly and permanently. To defray the cost of war against Francis I in the 1540s and then the even more expensive campaigns against his son Henry II, imperial agents borrowed more and more on the principal European markets; and this time they stipulated that repayment should take place in the peninsula. The burden of empire was being shifted from the Burgundian to the Iberian inheritance of the Habsburgs. The Netherlands continued to be an important source of funds; but Castile had the doubtful privilege of acting as imperial paymaster from the 1540s onwards.

At the outset the effective exploitation of Castilian riches ran into a number of problems. Since 1268 the export of bullion from Castile had been strictly prohibited, a regulation which Charles, for political if no other reasons, would have been unwise to flout until he had proved himself not a foreign but a true king of Castile. How, then, could imperial creditors be repaid? Those who wished to do business with the crown had to accept not precious metal but commodities. Imperial bankers took payment for their loans at the Castilian fairs of Medina del Campo or Villalón, invested the money in the purchase of primary produce, and then sent what they had bought legally out of the country. Alum sometimes figured among the purchases; but the bankers preferred to repatriate their funds by acquiring the wool clip—good for the flock-masters (amongst these the aristocrats) who saw a welcome boost to prices, less good for the weavers who found that their costs had risen. In short, foreign creditors accepted payment and interest for their loans in the form of wool or some other disposable product. Before the 1550s it could be argued that imperial borrowing did not inflict permanent injury upon the Castilian economy. Repayment kept domestic prices up; and, since there was a limit to the value of the wool clip, or the output of the alum mines, it checked the growth of debt. After 1550 this restraint disappeared.

Although the Iberian kingdoms did not assume responsibility for the bulk of imperial costs until after 1540, foreign bankers made an early appearance in the peninsula. After 1521 the Fugger took in part payment of their loans trading and mining concessions in the peninsula even if Jakob Fugger had grave misgivings on the subject. His firm drew a substantial income from the lands of the Military Orders, the so-called *Maestrazgo* lease; and they also administered, generally at a profit, the mercury mines of Almadén. Another south German group, the Welsers, showed a much greater willingness to accept risk by sponsoring the exploration and early settlement of Venezuela. The alienation of public income and the grant of trading concessions was relatively modest under Charles V. For all that, it was an omen—and a bad one.

In the history of the state warfare inevitably meant debt; and the outcome of most conflicts turned on the ability of one or other of the contestants to borrow more. The Habsburg–Valois struggle illustrated this simple point. Imperial debt grew steadily from 1521 to 1529, with a brief dip from 1525–7; it lifted once again between 1536–7, responded in a similar way to the hostilities which lasted from 1542–4, and ballooned after 1552.

A number of technical developments permitted the Habsburgs, in company with their fellow monarchs, to borrow on an unprecedented scale. In the early 1540s two financial experts, a Frenchman, the cardinal de Tournon, and an Italian, Gaspar Ducci, pioneered a new means of raising credit on behalf of their respective employers, the king of France and the Holy Roman Emperor. They discovered that merchants trading at the great fairs of Antwerp and Lyons were willing to buy shares in government loans just as if they were investing in ordinary commercial ventures. It became possible to monetize royal debt. Thenceforth European monarchs could satisfy their credit requirements by drawing not just on the private fortunes of rich individuals but increasingly on the apparently limitless resources of the investing public. Such an innovation undoubtedly marked an important step in the growth of public credit. It also offered the crowned profligates of the day an opportunity for abuse which they were not slow to take advantage of.

Charles's determination to retake Metz in 1552 signalled the point of no return. To finance a level of expenditure breathtaking even by imperial standards, Charles and his kindred sought out every device or malpractice within reach. The Treasury had just received a timely windfall in the shape of wealth confiscated from the Pizarro brothers and their followers; and it supplemented this by seizing the remittances sent from the Americas to the merchants who supplied the trade. But the real gold-mine from this period proved to be not the new-found lands but the exchange of Antwerp. The Habsburgs floated a series of loans on the market which outdid in scale all previous borrowing. The mercantile and banking consortia, loath to leave cash balances idle and lured on by the high interest rates, answered the siren call by lending money as never before. Leading the rush to destruction was Matthias Oertel, agent of the Fugger in Antwerp. He was sacked in 1557 by his employers for involving the house in loans which imperilled its very survival.

The belief that a day of reckoning would never come affected all levels of public life. The city of Antwerp as a corporation stood surety for a number of imperial loans (almost certainly in imitation of the role played by Paris in the French system), oblivious to the fact that even the richest city had finite resources. Habsburg officials, once more in the Netherlands, discovered that additional sums could be raised on the security of local revenues administered by provincial treasurers. Prudently managed, borrowing on such collateral would have brought stability. Recklessly misused, it merely hastened the inevitable crash. In 1557 the crown suspended repayment on its debts, thereby triggering off a whole series of defaults on the part of the merchants, the city of Antwerp, and the provincial treasurers.

As a period in political and financial history the last phase of the Habsburg–Valois struggle merits particular attention. After 1552 the crown showed itself incapable of containing the growth of debt. Periodic defaults, like those of 1557 and its sequel in 1560, brought temporary stability, but the drift continued upwards throughout the sixteenth and well into the seventeenth century. It was Castile, moreover, and not the Netherlands, still less the Italian possessions, which bore exclusive responsibility after 1552 for the payment of this burgeoning debt. This chronic burden, like the Seventeen Provinces with which it was to become so intimately associated, formed part of the fateful inheritance bequeathed by Charles to his son.

After Charles had retired to Yuste and the German houses had abandoned their role as bankers to empire, the new king resorted to the services of another banking community. The Genoese had been established in the Iberian peninsula since the later Middle Ages. Their moment came when in 1528 the 'old nobility' of Genoa concluded a treaty with the emperor which gave its citizens, along with other privileges, unrestricted access to Habsburg possessions in the old and the new world. The 'old nobility' had come to specialize in loans, or banking to use the modern term, while their fellow citizens and mortal rivals, the 'new nobility', continued to trade in commodities. As a group the 'old nobility' built up a financial network which far surpassed that of the Fugger; and they also managed by means as yet not satisfactorily described to draw on the savings of a much wider circle of depositors. From a symbolic point of view, the Genoese reinforced the Mediterranean and Counter-Reformation aspects of Philip II's empire.

In general terms it could be said that the bankers of this Ligurian republic were the architects of the financial system which made possible and sustained Castile's position as a first-rate power. The institution which served as the embodiment of all their resource and skill was the fair of Piacenza. Charles V had wished to create a rival to the market at Lyons where his Valois enemy arranged for most of his funding. Besançon in the Franche-Comté had been chosen as the site for the experiment; but eventually the fair acquired its permanent home in Piacenza. In its new location the financial market entered its most glorious days after 1579. Contemporaries admired it both for the volume of traffic and the sophistication of techniques used. Between 1579 and 1627, the date of its eclipse as a major banking centre, the fair at Piacenza raised annually for its Spanish clients never less than five and sometimes as much as ten million ducats, most of which was earmarked for the pay of the Spanish army in Flanders. The Genoese, who dominated the fair, had a mysterious skill which in itself would have made them indispensable to the Habsburgs. They had developed the art of receiving silver in Genoa while paying the army of Flanders in gold. Presumably the Genoese bankers used American silver to purchase existing stocks of European gold, a factor which may explain the appreciation of the latter in terms of the former.

The fair at Piacenza lasted eight days, each day, or session, having a specific function reserved for it. In the course of dealings an artificial unit of account was used based on a basket of the five soundest currencies. This was designed to minimize the effects of coin clipping or monetary fluctuations. During the fair little cash changed hands. Instead book transfer became the order of the day, an economic method of operation which led to notable savings in terms of transport and insurance. At the end of the fair those who had been licensed to deal compared credits and liabilities, and then settled outstanding balances in cash. It was strictly forbidden to postpone payment or to roll over contracts, a regulation which greatly enhanced the standing of the fair itself.

Although a landmark in the history of public credit, the facilities which the Genoese provided did not come free of charge. There was a heavy price which Castile, and Castile alone, was called upon to pay. Operating on a far wider scale than their south German predecessors, the Genoese in time succeeded in rewriting the rules of engagement. They, and their depositors, were no longer content with the purchase of the wool clip or its equivalent. For one thing, commodities could no longer absorb the amounts which the crown owed. The bankers wanted more; and given the needs of the monarchy, they were able to insist. As a preliminary, they demanded the right to export bullion from the peninsula. Under Charles V these 'licences to export' had been sparingly granted: Philip II came to agree to such concessions as a matter of form. Much of the gold and silver landed in Seville remained in Castile just long enough to be registered before it was dispatched post-haste to Italy. The Genoese also set about the systematic exploitation of Castile itself. These quick-witted financiers devised a number of methods whereby the money needed by the monarchy to cover its permanent over-spending came from the peninsula. Their principal technique was the sale of state bonds (*juros*) to the investing public of Castile. Those with money to spare, notably the ecclesiastical foundations, the lawyers, and some aristocratic houses, snapped up the government paper, to the gratification and reward of the Genoese. State bonds had come into existence long before the sixteenth century, sometimes in the form of a grant to a loyal (on occasions, disloyal) subject, or as a straightforward acknowledgement of debt on the part of the government. But their real importance dates from the reign of Philip II. After 1560 the state began to compete vigorously on the internal market for available funds through the offer of *juros*. It could outbid those who required capital for agricultural or industrial purposes by offering a higher rate of interest. Thus from the beginning of Philip's rule surplus funds attracted by better returns found their way into royal debt rather than productive enterprises; and this undoubtedly contributed to the increasing difficulties encountered by the Castilian economy after 1575.

The Genoese were in large part responsible for developing the general sale of state bonds. This would have been enough to explain their unpopularity; but they acquired a particularly unsavoury reputation through the number and character of the additional privileges they were able to extort. During the 1550s royal bankers, worried by the credit rating of their imperial client, had stipulated on a number of occasions that in addition to the normal terms of contract whereby the monarchy pledged itself to the repayment of principal and interest some form of collateral should be made over to them as an extra guarantee. This security took the form of lands or a lien on a particular tax, and was returned to the crown once the terms of the loan had been completed satisfactorily—that is, the bankers recovered their money with interest. After 1566 these *juros de caución* gave way to a form of security which proved far more insidious. The Genoese, with their customary inventiveness, brought in the *juros de resguardo*. These, like their predecessors, involved the surrender to royal creditors, in this case the bankers themselves, of lands or rents which were to be returned on completion of the contract. But there was one important addition. When the crown became really desperate for funds, as in the period 1573–5, the Genoese obtained royal consent to the sale of this collateral on the open market, the sum realized to be offset against the value of the initial loan. In this way, the Genoese, and all those who could extract similar concessions, insulated themselves from the worst effects of a bankruptcy by the simple device of selling the securities (*resguardos*) as quickly as posible.

The Genoese also safeguarded their long-term position by requiring of the government another concession which only men of real force could have obtained. After a bankruptcy had been declared, as in 1575 and 1596, a period of time elapsed, usually between one or two years, before a general settlement (*medio general*) was reached between the crown and its creditors. When these accords were formally agreed, the Genoese insisted on a clause whereby if they accepted state bonds which had, in fact, depreciated, then they in turn were allowed to insist on a similar form of settlement with their own creditors. To express it in a slightly different way, if the Genoese, for the sake of restoring business relations, were willing to take from the crown *juros* calculated at par when, in fact, they only fetched half that value in the open market, then the creditors of the Genoese must submit to the same kind of treatment. As long as the 'old aristocracy' had the power to write this clause—'*de la misma moneda*' (of the same coin) as it was known—into the text of the formal agreement ending a bankruptcy, they had little reason to fear, since their depositors bore the true cost of the royal default.

For all their notoriety—Quevedo, no less, hymned their vices—the Genoese never lacked for willing investors. They earned this trust because they understood the workings of Castilian finance much better than the bureaucrats and theologians nominally in charge. The investing public sought to place its money where it would bring in a safe and steady return. The Genoese and their pupils were able, for a time at least, to satisfy these demands. When the crown floated a loan, the official contract specified the rent or tax which had been set aside to meet the interest. In theory the provision of dividends should have presented few problems; but in reality a series of formidable obstacles stood between the rentier and his money. Some royal rents were small or irregular in yield. Others were already encumbered, although this was no barrier to 'overloading'. The Genoese owed their high reputation to their ability to pick their way through the wasteland of royal finance and still find sources to pay the interest on state bonds. Acting Virgil to Dante became more difficult as Philip II—not to mention his successors—pawned away his patrimony, leaving virtually no tax or right unencumbered.

One further hazard awaited all those who invested in state paper. The exchequer in Madrid carried few cash balances. Generally income from royal taxes—the salt tax, to take a random example—flowed into the chests of a provincial treasury. Whenever a bond holder wished to collect his dividend he had to apply to the regional treasurer within whose jurisdiction the source appointed for the payment of that particular loan happened to fall. If, by ill luck, this source of revenue had dried up in the meantime, or if the source had been 'overloaded' and the money had been paid over to somebody else, the regional treasurer had no obligation to satisfy the demands of those who presented themselves before him. Collection of interest came to depend on luck, speed, and connection. On all three counts the Genoese scored through their superior intelligence and their influence in both high and low places.

The merchant princes of Genoa came to dominate Castilian public finance as a consequence of overcommitment on the part of the Habsburgs. Yet on occasions not even they could appease the crown's hunger for credits. It proved difficult, and then impossible, to keep up interest payments on past loans, still less to amortize the principal. Liquid funds evaporated, interest rates soared into the blue. The king, in the final moments of indigence, lacked the money to pay his menials. Physical survival depended on the suspension of all repayment and with it the admission of bankruptcy. These solemn, if embarrassing, occasions acted as important signposts to both the political and economic trends of the era.

By announcing publicly that it was unable to honour its obligations, the crown gave notice that it intended to restructure its debts. The forced conversion carried out in 1557 and completed in 1560 served as a model for subsequent developments. At the beginning of the new reign the government carried out a forced conversion of its short-term debts into state bonds. Investors lost all possibility of recovering the principal of their loans but received by way of compensation a yearly interest payment of 5 per cent. The state, lacking resources to honour the original terms of contract, transmuted its debts into a series of annuities. The innovations of 1560 offered a number of possibilities which, if properly exploited, might have led to the creation of a national debt along lines similar to those devised by English (or Scots) promoters in the 1690s. To pay the 5 per cent on the consolidated debt, the crown set aside the revenues of the Casa de Contratación—the taxes on the American trade. Had the scheme been well managed the new bonds might have retained most, if not all, of their value, thereby providing a particularly safe haven for widows' mites and young girls' dowries—an early version of the eighteenth-century 'consols'. Nothing of the sort happened. The officials of the Casa misunderstood the system, some said they were corrupt; and the crown took to raiding the American revenues for its own purposes, such as the levying of Alba's army in 1566. The bonds attached to the Casa de Contratación depreciated rapidly, spurned by all especially the Genoese who insisted on sounder rents for their clients.

In the period between the first and second defaults (1560–75) the debts of the crown assumed a formal structure. The funded obligations represented an element both constant in size and stable in cost. The other component went by the name of the 'floating' debt, that is, recent loans contracted since 1560. These carried a fairly high rate of interest and they were regarded as purely commercial loans demanding the repayment of principal. Thus the Castilian exchequer had to manage two accounts, the first a consolidated debt on which it disbursed 5 per cent p.a., the second, and far more volatile, a growing body of unfunded liabilities on which the authorities paid varying rates of interest. The 'floating' and the funded debt acted as the blades of a financial scissors, one which the crown was always trying to tug open.

The periodic suspension of repayment marked off the reign of Philip II into three sections each of roughly twenty years (1557, 1575, 1596). A bankruptcy took place when the crown borrowed so much short-term that it was unable even to meet the interest on its loans. An unpleasant, often acrimonious, interlude then followed in the relationship between the monarch and his creditors until an understanding was reached. The crown was ever penurious while the banking community could scarcely restrain its eagerness to make a profit, however short-lived, from the accumulated savings of domestic and overseas depositors.

Once the temporary difficulties had been smoothed over, the king of Castile could revert to his former addictions. Confidence returned; money poured in; and the crown began to run up short-term obligations, mainly in the form of the notorious *asientos* which supplied the life-blood of the armies in Flanders. These fresh liabilities formed the new 'floating' debt on which the exchequer had to pay high rates of interest and, sometimes, to make special concessions. For a while the investing public, skilfully shepherded by the ubiquitous Genoese, flocked to subscribe. Then, once more, the volume of short-term debt began to swell; shafts of lucidity broke through the clouds of optimism; the financiers took fright. The crown, over-extended as always, lacked the cash to meet its most basic needs. Another forced funding of short-term debt loomed.

In the short term a bankruptcy did not lead to the dire consequences which the term might imply. When the crown and its major creditors resumed their dealings, special provision was made in the general settlement for the consolidation of the 'floating' debt. All short-term liabilities incurred up to the moment the crown suspended repayment were converted into fixed-interest bonds, almost certainly non-redeemable. As before, specific items of royal revenue were set aside to cover the new charge; while the interest and inducements offered on the new flotations hardly ever failed to pull in an enthusiastic public. But in the long term few could remain oblivious to the impact of repeated bankruptcies and, indeed, the whole tenor of financial management. Repeated forays on to the trading fairs of Castile, Medina del Campo and Villalón in particular, drained off funds. The delays in repayment, in themselves often merely a prelude to an official default, destroyed the fairs and damaged the system for settling purely commercial debts. But it was the accumulation of dishonoured liabilities which revealed the true extent of the harm wrought. The consolidated debt, as if created through a process of sedimentation, acquired many layers. The older obligations were pushed deeper and deeper, whilst above each successive bankruptcy deposited a new stratum of liabilities. When viewed in section, the consolidated debt which first saw life under Philip II represented the collective savings of a kingdom poorly endowed by nature, a surplus which its rulers had chosen to squander on ends that were sterile and unattainable.

Where a bankruptcy had its most visible as well as its most drastic effect was in terms of military consequences. Defaults usually occurred at the end of protracted warfare as their timing (1557–60, 1575, and 1596) indicates. Once the crown had declared a moratorium on the repayment of its debts, it could no longer remit money to Italy or Flanders as the bankers, who normally handled such transactions, withdrew their services either in retaliation or through incapacity. The absence of funds prevented the Habsburgs from exploiting their success at St Quentin in 1557 and their equally decisive victory at Gravelinges in the following year, campaigns full of military glory but barren of lasting gain. The collapse of 1575–7, far more serious than its predecessor, prevented the reassertion of royal control in the Netherlands and allowed Holland and Zeeland to build up a position that in the end proved unassailable. Two decades later the suspension of payments in 1596 confirmed the plain truth that Castile, for all the wealth of the Americas or the endurance of its taxpayers, did not have resources sufficient to fight the Dutch rebels, their English allies, and the new Bourbon dynasty in France. To this extent the bankruptcies acted as sharp reminders of the line separating the possible from the impossible.

The role of Castile in imperial finance became predominant after 1540. As a kingdom it owed this dubious eminence to its relative wealth, superior to that of all Habsburg possession with the exception of the Low Countries, and to its fiscal vulnerability. The representative institution, the cortes, although far from subservient, could not shelter behind the formidable breastwork of rights which rendered the neighbouring kingdoms virtually impregnable to royal demands. From the viewpoint of the Treasury the richest source of revenue controlled by the cortes was the sales tax, or *alcabala*, first granted to the kings of Castile in 1342. Islamic in origin and designed as a temporary measure, this levy quickly established itself as the most profitable and most reliable of all sources, the sum of which was periodically adjusted by the cortes. Technically the *alcabala* was a duty of 10 per cent to be applied every time an item changed hands. In practice the rate was much lower.

After various experiments in the system of collection, the sales tax acquired its classic form in 1534. Charles V consented to a scheme whereby the cortes purchased the farm of the *alcabala*. The eighteen cities acquired exclusive rights of collection in return for a guarantee to the crown of a fixed sum every year of the lease—six, ten years, in some cases more, depending on the particular contract. By securing such rights the cortes 'compounded' for the tax, in the contemporary phrase. The arrangement brought mutual benefits: the crown could rely on a steady income for the life of the farm, useful knowledge when conducting credit operations; while the cities profited from a heavy discount in that the rate they levied on their respective provinces seldom rose above 5 and never reached the theoretical 10 per cent. Compounding for the sales tax had the additional merit of shutting out the foreign bankers who would certainly have moved in given the opportunity.

The yield of the sales tax, even when expressed in nominal terms, pointed to a familiar trend, the upward swing of government expenditure which became especially noticeable in the 1570s. In terms of ducats, the unit of account, the *alcabala* produced per annum:

1504	800,000
1534	848,000
1562–74	1,277,000
1576–7	3,715,000
1578–87	2,715,000
1588–1610	2,755,000

The sudden jump in the sales tax during the early part of the 1570s resulted from the cumulative expenditure first on the Holy League then on the Netherlands after 1572. In the cortes of 1573–5 the king alluded to these specific problems in his attempt to secure a threefold increase in the *alcabala*. Although the sum was conceded, widespread shortfalls in the quotas of the individual cities forced the king to scale down his original demands. After 1577 the price on the farm of the sales tax remained stable, having effectively reached its maximum. In the 1590s, when faced with a crisis comparable to the 1570s, the crown used different methods to cover the additional needs.

In addition to the sales tax, the king could count on another tax granted by the cortes, the *servicio*. This came in two forms, the ordinary and the extraordinary; and as a levy it fell exclusively upon the shoulders of the non-privileged, the *pecheros*. By Philip II's time the cortes voted at the beginning of its sessions an ordinary and an extraordinary *servicio*, the collection to be spread over three years. In the second half of the sixteenth century the exchequer reckoned on an annual income from the amalgamated *servicios* of 1,200,000 ducats.

Perhaps the best known of all the secular revenues on which the Spanish Habsburgs relied were those drawn from the American colonies. In the year of Charles V's abdication (1556) the Indies contributed some 372,350 ducats to the Castilian treasury. This amount increased unsteadily to reach the figure of 921,288 ducats in 1566 and 1,209,905 ducats two years later. Revenues dipped in the early 1570s, falling to 700,208 ducats in 1574, a year of particular stringency. Then the upward climb resumed and was not to be broken until the end of the century. In 1577 the Indies provided the Castilian exchequer with 2,168,334 ducats, nearly double the previous record; and this, taken in conjunction with the General Settlement of 1577, may have encouraged Philip to opt for 'power projection' in the Netherlands. This high was in turn surpassed in 1583 when 3,200,273 ducats were landed in Seville for the benefit of the crown—and, almost certainly, as end-user, the prince of Parma. Four years later, as the Invincible Armada gathered, the tax remittances from the Indies touched a new high of 4,472,260 ducats. The figure declined in the years immediately following; and then sprang back in 1595 to reach 5,737,737 ducats, a maximum which the next century would equal but never surpass. The Castilian exchequer drew its American income from a variety of sources. The crown received one-fifth of all precious metals and stones produced in the New World, an automatic right, that is, to the output of the mines and pearl fisheries. Commodities shipped to and fro across the Atlantic were also subject to tax, the *almojarifazgo de Indias*. As patron of the church in America, the kings of Castile had the right to levy the tithes of the church there and, once provision had been made for the establishment and maintenance of the ecclesiastical system, to enjoy any surplus. In return for the benefits of white rule, such as they were, the indigenous population of the New World found itself obliged to pay a yearly tribute; and here again, once the necessary deductions had been made, the balance was remitted to the Iberian peninsula.

The wealth of the Indies dazzled contemporaries in Spain and elsewhere. Many thought that it was the main pillar of Castilian greatness. But this was a delusion, and a pernicious one. Several other sources of revenue yielded a higher and more reliable output. Ecclesiastical taxation provides a notable example. The pope had conceded the right to tax church property as early as 1219, on the understanding that it should be regarded as a temporary grant. Like the sales tax it did not take long to establish itself as a regular source. In 1494 Alexander VI, himself of Iberian extraction, regularized the practice by granting the monarchy the right to enjoy two-ninths of the tithe in perpetuity. Further concessions were made in 1569 (the tithe and first-fruit of newly ploughed land) and again in 1572 (permission to appropriate the tithe of the third-richest parishioner). Ecclesiastical taxation entered the account books of the exchequer under the heading of The Three Graces, the reference being to the three separate levies known as *cruzada*, the *subsidio*, and the *escusado*.

The Habsburgs exploited the religious endowments of previous generations in another way. Ferdinand the Catholic appropriated the lands and patronage of the Military Orders by securing his own nomination as Master of all three (Calatrava, Santiago, and Alcántara). Adrian VI obliged his former pupil Charles V by allowing the permanent incorporation of these foundations into the royal patrimony (1523). The property of the Aragonese Order of Montesa was absorbed in a similar way in 1558.

In all it has been calculated that by the end of the sixteenth century the church regularly contributed, in one form or another, 1,400,000 ducats annually to imperial revenues; and to this figure should be added a further 370,000 ducats brought in by the lands of the Military Orders. Even without the inclusion of supplementary levies such as the sale of church property, the Castilian church produced over the years of imperial dominance a more regular income than that derived from the Indies and one which the latter only surpassed for a brief period.

Castile's role as chief provider to the Habsburg monarchy was affirmed once again when the cortes met in the autumn of 1588. The defeat of the Armada left Philip II with a shattered navy; and he feared that the English and the Dutch would follow their recent success by a full-scale assault on the Caribbean. The safety of the maritime empire hung in the balance, or so he thought. To cover the cost of imperial defence, the king turned to the cortes of Castile for an extraordinary vote which was to be levied in addition to existing taxes. At the end of a difficult session which tested the managerial skills of the crown to the limit, the eighteen towns authorized to send representatives granted the *millones* (4 April 1590). The monarchy was to receive eight million ducats spread over six years. Although intended as an emergency measure, never to be repeated, the *millones* immediately became the central element in the financial system, renewed unfailingly whenever the grant expired, and sometimes before.

As a levy it incorporated several original features. The urban representatives had insisted throughout the course of their preliminary debates that there should be no exemptions. All were liable, privileged and non-privileged, rich and poor, laity and clergy. This condition was written into the formal vote (the *otorgamiento*); and the crown gave its willing assent. At first each city chose the method by which its quota was raised; and many did so by taxing basic necessities of life. In 1596, with the extension of the *millones*, the various techniques were standardized. Thenceforth wine, oil, vinegar, and meat were taxed at the point of sale to make up the contributions. This might have represented an important step towards a more equitable system, in that whenever foodstuffs were purchased the buyer, irrespective of legal status, paid the levy. But whether the privileged, with their own source of supply from their estates, contributed as much as the poor and unprivileged is open to question. It is far more likely that those exempt from taxation before 1590 lived on undisturbed by the *millones*.

The vote of 1590 heralded a sharp deterioration in the economic position of the non-privileged orders. According to a recent estimate, a Castilian householder unable to plead exemption from tax paid in 1594 some 135 maravedís a year as his contribution to the ordinary and extraordinary *servicio* and the sales tax. These were traditional revenues granted by the cortes to the sovereign. But the householder now found himself obliged to provide an additional 337 maravedís to meet his liability by way of the *millones*. Fiscal increases of this magnitude explain the growing disquiet felt over the economic state of Castile, and the even more common belief in the 'decay' of agriculture.

The poor and those unable to shuffle off their obligations on to others were the first to suffer from the *millones*. In the long term, royal penury brought about not merely the oppression of the weak—that was historic—but a reduction in monarchical authority. To bring in money the crown consented to a range of *arbitrios* (expedients), each more complex than the last. These included the alienation of royal income to satisfy foreign bankers and the sale of wheat stored in municipal granaries—a favourite device of the towns in 1590. Neither of these innovations had produced more than a fraction of the money needed by the administration. The king and his advisers were forced to sanction the sale of municipal office—and even this was not enough. In effect, the shortage of funds compelled the crown to relinquish its hold over the localities to the benefit of the urban oligarchs who had the money to snap up what had been placed on offer.

The new era ushered in by the grant of the *millones* profoundly affected the history of Castile. The non-privileged were pushed to, and then beyond, the level of endurance, a phenomenon which accelerated, if it did not initiate, the demographic decline of the kingdom. Furthermore, the crown traded short-term gains for long-term penalties. Devolved government emerged from the ruin of imperial finance. By the mid-seventeenth century the municipal oligarchies had purchased so many local offices that they were well able to resist royal demands and, on occasions, to dictate the policy of the state, confident in the knowledge that they were the effective rulers of the land.

PART THREE

SOCIETY

CHAPTER 16

The economic life of the peninsula

TRADITIONALLY the Iberian peninsula has sold its primary produce to the more developed regions of Europe. Wool provided during the early modern period the single most important export. The raising of sheep on a large scale was well established in prehistoric times, as the archaeological evidence clearly reveals; and successive generations of invaders came quickly to appreciate the suitability of this type of pastoral economy to the conditions of the land they had conquered. The Romans, with their own experience of the Italian peninsula, favoured the extension of sheep-rearing; the Arabs transformed the character of the industry by the introduction of at least one new strain (and a complete vocabulary); while the Christian states regarded the flocks as a major source of wealth and protected them accordingly.

Sheep-raising on any scale created a number of problems. Rights to land and the return of strays were amongst the most frequent cause of dispute. To avoid a range war over such issues the shepherds adopted from early on the habit of gathering periodically in the largest town of the region. Here they decided on who could claim rightful ownership of strays and who should be granted access to pasture. These local associations acquired the name of *mesta*, a term possibly derived from the word for stray, *mezclado*. During the earlier phases of the Reconquest most of the flocks travelled relatively short distances, if they moved at all. But even before the final advance of the frontier, the shepherds had become more adventurous. The flock-masters from the province of Cuenca were already leading their herds southwards in search of winter grazing in 1208; and this is only the earliest reference to their activity.

Transhumance, the movement of flocks over hundreds of miles, began in the first half of the thirteenth century after the Christian victories over the Islamic kingdoms opened up the southern ranges. The herds were able to move from their summer grazing in the north to winter pastures on the banks of the Guadiana and the Guadalquivir, the newly liberated territories. Something akin to a land rush took place. When the graziers of New Castile arrived to winter in the south, they discovered that others had staked a claim before them. The Military Orders, with thousands of head of cattle, attempted to exclude all others from this winter grazing by appealing to the lavish privileges granted to them by successive monarchs. In order to defend, by force if need be, their own rights the shepherds from the sierra de Guadalupe and the area known as the *montes* of Toledo organized themselves into a special association. This may well have provided the nucleus for what became a national body, the Honourable Assembly of the Shepherds, set up in 1273 under royal sponsorship.

Whatever its origins, the Mesta, as it swiftly became known, had a number of features which distinguished it from the outset. The Mesta's jurisdiction covered virtually the whole of Castile; and the organization was democratic in terms of its government. The Honourable Assembly had two principal functions, to protect the interests of its members at court and to supervise the movement of the flocks to and from the grazing lands.

In their migrations the herds followed a special network of tracks which had been in existence for centuries. The transhumant flocks reached winter pasture by making their way south along three principal routes. The more westerly sheep walk, or *cañada*, began in León, drew in the herds from Zamora and Béjar, and ended in the vicinity of Badajoz (Extremadura). The central and most heavily used of these routes started on the upper reaches of the Ebro and then split immediately into two branches: the first, winding its way around Burgos and Palencia, travelled south until it linked up at Béjar with the sheep walk from León; the second meandered past Soria and Sigüenza, crossed the Tagus, and continued right across the Mancha before terminating on the Guadalquivir. Yet another system, possibly the first to be developed, joined the summer pastures in the region of Cuenca to the abundance of winter feed to be found on the banks of the Guadalquivir, or, an equal attraction, the grazing provided by the river Segura in the province of Murcia.

The Mesta appointed a number of roving officials to see that its rights were respected and that no encroachments on the sheep walks took place. If a town along one of the routes used by the migrating herds attempted to enclose a section, then the *alcalde entregador*, as the itinerant judge was called, had the right to compel the municipality (or individual, for that matter) to restore the land to its original purpose. The determination of the Mesta to cling to all its privileges drew down upon it the wrath of eighteenth-century improvers such as Gaspar Melchor de Jovellanos. Recent historians, however, have tended to absolve it from responsibility for the decline of Castilian agriculture.

The flocks divided into three categories. The bulk of the herds which participated in the annual migrations came from the north of Castile, and these were referred to as *serranos*. Many of these herds belonged to ecclesiastical corporations such as the archbishopric of Burgos. Not all the sheep which used the *cañadas* travelled the entire distance along the network. Some flocks were moved by their owners only a few miles and were called *riberiegos*. As the name indicates, these herds were normally pastured in the vicinity of a town and its river; and they belonged, in the main, to the urban patriciates. A third type of flock did not take part in transhumance at all. Many small-holders kept a few head of sheep either on their own property or, more frequently, on communal lands. Although these sheep remained in the same place throughout the year (a fact which gave them their name *estantes*), they provided an important component in the overall size of Castile's sheep flock. Traditionally, the owners of the *estantes* had been considered full members of the Mesta; but in 1603 they were excluded from its privileges, an indication of the increasingly oligarchic character of the organization.

The different types of herds have to be borne in mind if the history of the industry is to be understood. In terms of overall numbers, the flock size averaged in the sixteenth century around four and a half million, all three categories included. In the seventeenth century the figure declined to around three and a half million. The migratory flocks which took part in transhumance, a group referred to as the *cabaña real*, oscillated in numbers between 2.5 and 3 million in the sixteenth, and 1.7 and 2 million in the seventeenth century. The figures illustrate the simple point that the *cabaña real* did not include all the sheep in the kingdom of Castile.

The Mesta concerned itself primarily with the interests of the transhumant flocks; and as a lobby it enjoyed prolonged success. Although the *cabaña real* reached its maximum size in 1519 with a total of 3,177,699 head, the era of real prosperity had yet to dawn. In 1563 the Mesta obtained from the crown, in return for a hefty payment, a pledge that the tax levied on the herds would not be increased; and subsequently the privilege was reaffirmed on a number of occasions. The Honourable Assembly benefited enormously from the stabilization of its tax liability in a period of rapid inflation; and its affairs were managed with thrift and good sense. In financial terms the golden age of the Mesta lasted from 1563 until 1684, when the immunities which had shielded it were at last withdrawn.

Recent research has identified two phases in the internal development of the sheep industry during the early modern period. The period from 1467 until 1526 witnessed a rapid increase in the size of the *estante* flocks. Communal grazing remained plentiful; and the small masters, reacting to the economic optimism of the times, kept more sheep. This period of expansion continued up to the middle decades of the sixteenth century. Circumstances then began to change, partly as a result of government policy. The crown sanctioned the enclosure of communal lands in its efforts to raise money. The town magistrates, many of whom had invested heavily in *riberiego* sheep, were amongst the principal purchasers. As their position improved, that of the small masters who owned the sedentary flocks deteriorated with the loss of access to common pasture.

After 1566 the *riberiegò* class also gained at the expense of the noble houses and the ecclesiastical foundations whose wealth lay in the *serrano* herds. Government policy, once again, was responsible. In 1566 foreign bankers won the right to export specie as settlement for debt. They were no longer obliged to accept payment in commodities. Hitherto royal creditors had been major purchasers of the wool clip. Now they were no longer in the market and the price declined accordingly. The income of noble and ecclesiastical flock-masters was badly hit, and adjustment proved difficult. The urban particiates, on the other hand, showed that they knew how to exploit falling prices, and they moved in on what had become a bargain. In the later sixteenth century the town magistrates expanded the size of their own herds and purchased much of the wool produced by the trans-humant, principally *serrano*, flocks. The *riberiego* element probably increased its influence within the management of the Honourable Assembly; but a number of factors prevented the town magistrates from dominating completely its proceedings. The pastoral sector of the economy was too fragmented for any single group to impose effective control, let alone a monopoly, over its organization. In some regions, moreover, the small flock-masters continued to prosper. In the seventeenth century those who owned less than five hundred head apiece contributed a third of the migratory sheep which regularly used the eastern *cañada* to the winter grazing in Murcia.

Sheep provided Castile with its main source of foreign income. During the first half of the sixteenth century much of the clip was dispatched via Burgos to the looms of Flanders and Brabant. The Low Countries acted as the principal market for Castilian wool until the 1560s, when a combination of religious and commercial factors brought about a shift in the direction of the trade. Antwerp's days as the mart of Christendom were approaching an end; and the outbreak of the Dutch revolt (1567) created uncertain conditions in the major weaving centres of the southern provinces and made communications by sea increasingly hazardous. In the 1570s a new vent for Castilian wool opened up in France. At the same time a more fundamental re-direction of the trade was taking place. Much of the wool produced in the regions of Granada, Cuenca, and Toledo was forwarded to the ports on Spain's eastern coast from where it was sent to the workshops of northern Italy. An obvious logic lay behind the new trading relationship, in that it followed the lines of the bullion shipment. Exports to Italy remained at a high level for the last three decades of the sixteenth century; and the prosperity of this particular trade may well have run on into the seventeenth.

The wool trade touched every aspect of the Spanish economy by reason of its size; and it has figured prominently in the search for the causes of the economic malaise already visible by the end of Philip II's reign. The sale of communal lands provides a link between sheep raising and general agricultural developments. The first auctions of open pasture began significantly in 1557, the year in which the crown declared itself bankrupt. During the 1560s the Council of Finance administered a pilot scheme in Granada where communal lands were sold off, frequently at prices way below the market rate. Sales took off in the 1570s and 1580s, to reach their peak in 1590. Philip II promised each successive cortes, almost by way of ritual, that he would abandon the practice, but he never did. The urban oligarchs, who had often already established illegal ownership, were the most active buyers of communal lands. By permitting these sales, the monarchy alleviated its wants for a brief period, but the cumulative effects were serious for the population at large. The smaller flock-masters were denied pasture for their herds, which led to a reduction in the number of sheep. The enclosure of common lands also contributed to rural depopulation. This was certainly the view of Caja de Leruela whose famous tract on the subject first appeared in 1631. He argued that the recent past had witnessed an alarming decline in the size of the sedentary flocks, a phenomenon which had led to a sharp rise in the cost of meat and wool. Keeping men on the land had become harder. With the disappearance of so many herds the land could no longer be maintained in good heart. He suggested as a remedy, therefore, that the lands which had been sold off should be recovered and restored to their original use, a move which should form part of the general plan for the restoration of abundance.

The shortage of public grazing lands may or may not have acted as a principal cause of Spain's economic difficulties at the turn of the seventeenth century. Whatever weight is attached to this development, one fact is beyond dispute. It reflected population pressure. The importance of demographic factors is borne out by the testimony of another source, the movement of Spanish prices. Although the correct 'weighting' of a price index has provoked heated controversy, the general direction of prices during the sixteenth century is clear at least in outline. The rate of inflation was higher in the period 1501–62 than in the years from 1562 to 1600: in the first phase the average annual rate stood at 2.8 per cent, in the second it fell back to 1.3 per cent. Prices went up quicker in the period before the arrival of American bullion in quantity. Inflation in the sixteenth century was attributable primarily to non-monetary factors, and of these population increase was the most likely cause.

CHAPTER 17

Demographic change in the sixteenth century

IN COMMON with other monarchs, the Habsburg rulers of Spain showed a persistent determination to secure more accurate information about the resources at their disposal. As a result they commissioned a number of surveys for the various provinces and kingdoms under their control. At least five such inquiries were carried out during the sixteenth century in the lands directly administered by Castile. These early versions of a modern census took place in 1528–36, 1541, 1571, 1587, and 1591. They varied considerably from one another in terms of completeness and, inevitably, the value of their information. Yet their basic purpose remained the same, namely, to assess the tax liability of each town and rural district. This was done by calculating the number of households (*vecinos*) in any one area. These enquiries, although prompted by fiscal considerations, have provided an excellent source for the study of population once certain technical difficulties have been overcome. The main problem in the use of tax returns for demographic purposes is the conversion of the household, a fiscal unit, into a number. Many historians have given the term a value of 4.5; but Felipe Ruiz Martín, the leading authority in these matters, has opted for the higher coefficient of 5. It is on the basis of five individuals for every household that he has presented a set of estimates both for the population of Castile and for the other kingdoms of the peninsula.

By employing the results of the tax survey carried out between the years 1528–36 Ruiz Martín has estimated that the laity of Castile may have numbered some 4,485,389. The mendicant orders contributed a further 28,054 to this total. According to Ruiz Martín the second and third decades of the sixteenth century in Castile may have witnessed a period of relative stagnation in terms of population growth. By contrast, the period from 1530 to 1570 saw a period of vigorous expansion which, measured in terms of the rate of increase, would not be

TABLE 2. Regional growth 1530–91, as a percentage of the total population

	1530	%	1591	%
Castile	4,485,389	78.39	6,617,251	81.48
Aragon	289,776	5.06	348,533	4.29
Catalonia	312,227	5.45	373,490	4.59
Valencia	(300,000)	5.24	409,979	5.04
Guipúzcoa	(67,000)	1.17	(75,000)	0.92
Biscay	(65,000)	1.13	(72,500)	0.89
Alava	50,093	0.87	65,604	0.80
Navarre	151,885	2.65	157,980	1.94

Figures in parentheses are estimated.
Source: Felipe Ruiz Martín: 'La Población española al comienzo de los tiempos modernos' (*Cuadernos de Historia* 1, Madrid, 1967, 199).

TABLE 3. Population figures for individual towns (in *vecinos*)

	Cáceres	Murcia	Valladolid	Córdoba
c.1500				5,500–6,000
1530		2,595	6,750	6,222
1557	1,401			
1561	1,471	2,956	6,644	8,889–9,333
1570			5,258	
1571				11,111–12,000
1584	1,540*			
1586	1,547	2,996		
1587			6,941	10,000–10,667
1591		3,370	8,112	9,556–10,000
1595	1,674			
1608	1,571			
1618				6,889–7,556
1626–33				6,889–8,000
1646	1,370			

* Variant: 1,463.
Sources: Cáceres: Angel Rodríguez Sánchez: *Cáceres ... en el Siglo XVI*; Murcia: Francisco Chacón Jiménez: *Murcia en la centuria del quinientos*; Valladolid: Bartolomé Bennassar: *Valladolid au siècle d'or*; Córdoba: J.I. Fortea Pérez: *Córdoba en el Siglo XVI*, part I.

matched until well into the eighteenth century. The middle decades of the sixteenth century represented, demographically speaking, a golden age. After 1575 the momentum of growth began to falter but the population continued to edge upwards until it reached its maximum, in the Castilian case, sometime during the 1590s. By the time of the last and most detailed of the fiscal inquiries, that prepared in 1591 as a preliminary for the imposition of the *millones* tax, Castile's population may have numbered as many as 6,617,251. Between 1530 and 1591 some 2,131,862 inhabitants had been added to the population of Castile, an increase of 34.4 per cent.

Surveys carried out elsewhere, and with exactly the same ends in mind, reveal that the rate of population increase was even higher than that registered in Castile. The census taken for Aragon in 1495 returned a figure of 257,000 for the population of this particular region (that is, not the kingdom as a whole): just over a century later in 1603 the figure may have reached 354,920. The neighbouring kingdom of Valencia, which formed part of the patrimony of the Aragonese crown, grew from 320,375 in the years 1565–72 to some 483,655 by the turn of the seventeenth century.

For all their obvious shortcomings, the most obvious being incomplete returns and uncertainties as to the coefficient, the fiscal surveys can be used to provide a picture of the broad demographic trend. They can be exploited to reinforce conclusions, or impressions, drawn from non-statistical sources. Within the overall framework thus provided it has become possible to present an interpretation of population movement both in terms of the individual kingdoms which made up the Habsburg inheritance and of specific regions.

In the case of Castile, population growth can be traced back to the early fifteenth century. The kingdom was not as badly affected by the Black Death as its neighbours; and its recovery was not impeded to the same degree by the recurrence of plague. Although official documents and parish registers, another invaluable source for demographic history, do not become abundant before the Habsburg period, the population expansion, unaffected to all appearances by the civil disturbances of the period, was gathering momentum well before the turn of the sixteenth century. By the time of the Habsburg succession sources for the study of local history start to become plentiful, continuous, and within certain limitations, reliable. Ideally, an account of Castile's demographic history should begin with a discussion of Burgos, important as a seat of government and even more so as a centre of trade. But in the absence of figures for the early history of Burgos, the development of Castile has to be studied through the records of other towns. Medina del Campo, much favoured by Queen Isabel and a major banking centre throughout the period of the early Habsburgs, had at the beginning of the sixteenth century on one estimate a population in the region of 20,000. If the figure is accurate—and there are strong reasons for doubt—then Medina del Campo ranked as one of the principal cities of Castile, indeed of Europe as a whole. By 1561, even though a few more good years remained to the town, the number of inhabitants had fallen to 14,836, still a remarkable figure by the standards of the age. Thereafter the decline became even more precipitous. In 1591 the town numbered 8,536, a loss of 42.5 per cent on the level of 1561. Special circumstances partly accounted for this story of precocious expansion followed by a fall as dramatic as it was prolonged. Much of the town's prosperity depended on its position as an international fair. The crown's defaults in 1575 and again in 1596 shattered the confidence of the banking community which had dealt both in loans to the king and international trade. Medina del Campo also failed to recapture the royal favour which had generated so much prosperity. None of Isabel's descendants chose to make it a royal residence for any length of time.

Valladolid, another town of the central Castilian meseta, could boast of a more fortunate experience. Strategically placed, well supplied, and on more than one occasion a capital city, Valladolid was larger in size and numbers than either Segovia or Burgos. This town of the Duero basin expanded rapidly in the period 1500 to 1560. For both town and its hinterland the years from 1543 until 1559 witnessed an exceptional growth-rate on the part of the population. In 1530 the number of households for the town was recorded as 6,750, a figure which might represent 30,375 individuals. Philip II's decision to abandon the town in 1559 even though it was the place of his birth brought about a fall—6,644 *vecinos* (29,898) in 1561 and 5,258 *vecinos* (23,661) in 1570—but the contraction proved temporary. The town added to its numbers until the final decade of the century. In 1591 the fiscal survey of that year reported 8,112 households, perhaps some 36,504 inhabitants. The rural hinterland followed the pattern set by the city. From a select sample of twenty-three villages it appears that the population expanded in the period 1530 to 1561 by 14.7 per cent. Over the next twenty years numbers increased by a mere 2 per cent. As with the town of Valladolid, rapid growth in the surrounding countryside was very much a phenomenon of the first half of the sixteenth century; the second half saw a consolidation rather than an increase in numbers.

The regions of Castile which remained outside the immediate orbit of a large town followed in broad terms the pattern of the urban centres. A case in point is the area known as La Bureba just north of Burgos through which, then as now, the main route from Burgos to the French frontier ran. La Bureba shared in the general expansion which marked Castile after 1530; and by 1561 it may have contained as many as 3,712 households, a figure roughly equivalent perhaps to 16,700 individuals. The region was severely hit by the plague of 1565–6, an outbreak which struck at the neighbouring Burgos and the more distant Aragonese town of Barbastro, but which does not appear to have affected other Iberian towns. The violence of the plague can be gauged from the fact that the town of Briviesca, the most significant urban centre of La Bureba, lost between 1,200 and 1,300 out of a population of 2,500. Severe though the losses were, continuing economic prosperity and the absence of further outbreaks of the plague meant that the population was able to recover in a short space of time. Numbers increased once more and reached their maximum between 1580 and 1585. At this point growth ceased. A brief period of stability followed; and this in turn gave way to a rapid decline after 1591. Within the limits of regional variation, La Bureba conforms to the Castilian demographic pattern. Roughly speaking, expansion of numbers characterized the first seven or eight decades of the century. A period of equilibrium then ensued which could vary in length according to local circumstances; and thereafter a significant contraction of population occurred over the whole of Castile during the last years of Philip II's reign.

The experience of the Castilian meseta as exemplified by the case of Valladolid or Medina del Campo was not representative of the other kingdoms, or, for that matter, the other regions controlled by the ruler of Castile. Each of the geographical provinces revealed peculiarities of detail in respect of its demographic expansion and subsequent decline. Cáceres demonstrates the point. It was one of the principal towns of Extremadura, a province renowned for the harshness of its climate and the poverty of the soil. The town and indeed the region had formed part of the Castilian crown since the thirteenth century. In 1557, the date of the first reliable survey, the town numbered 1,401 *vecinos* (6,305). Over the next twenty years the movement of population was virtually imperceptible. But in the period from 1584 to 1595 something in the nature of an explosion seems to have taken place: the town may have increased by as many as 211 *vecinos* or 950 new inhabitants. Over the next decade numbers began their retreat. In 1608 there were 1,571 *vecinos* (7,070); but this still marked a level well above that for most of the sixteenth century. Four decades on (1646) the number of households was down to 1,370 (6,165), a clear fall but still not far short of the figure registered a century before. As a case-history Cáceres is instructive for a variety of reasons. It shows that within the lands directly administered by the Castilian authorities the surge in numbers was not a universal phenomenon, at least during the first half of the sixteenth century. Furthermore the increase, when it did come, reached its high point nearly twenty years after the cities of the Castilian meseta; and finally the effective reduction in the size of population took place much later than in the lands north of the Tagus and with much less brutality.

The southern possessions of the Castilian monarchs shared in general the prosperity of the sixteenth century while managing to escape the full force of the disasters which brought the expansion of the central meseta to such an early and abrupt end. Without doubt the most dynamic of all the regions ruled from Madrid was the kingdom of Murcia. Here the increase in numbers, and economic expansion as a whole, was well under way by the first quarter of the sixteenth century. The most striking addition to the population occurred in the years from 1530 to 1561, an obvious parallel to the demographic vigour of Castile in the same period. The rising of the moriscos in Granada (1568–71) temporarily affected the province; but with the toughness that appears as the hallmark of the century numbers continued to rise. The decade 1586–96 set a limit to the movement. Up to this point Murcia appeared to have done little more than march in step with the Castilian regions of the interior. But then an unexpected development took place. The population, while no longer expanding, was not cut back to the same extent as its Castilian counterpart. When it did set in the decline in numbers occurred gradually, the process taking over two decades to reveal itself as unmistakable (1597–1620), and it was mild in comparison to events elsewhere. The 'decline' of the seventeenth century came in an attenuated form as far as Murcia and its hinterland were concerned. In this way the history of the town and its province adds confirmation to the general theory of a shift in economic strength from the interior of the peninsula to the peripheral zones during the course of the seventeenth century.

If Murcia provided what might be termed a 'southern' pattern it should also be pointed out that it was possibly the most buoyant of all the meridional centres. A more typical example could be found in the city of Córdoba. The town's prosperity depended on its agriculture and a textile industry which rivalled and at times surpassed that of Segovia. In accordance with a by now familiar story, the town's population, some 28,000 in 1530, moved swiftly forward over the next four decades. It attained its maximum point in 1571: 50,000–54,000; and then began to sink back slowly. So far, the Cordoban experience seemed to provide a carbon copy of events north of the Tagus. Twenty years later (1591) the population had drifted down to between 43,000 and 45,000; and by 1618 it had declined further, to between 31,000 and 34,000. Once again, in broad terms, little seems to differentiate Córdoba from one of its northern counterparts. Its population then stabilized at this point for the next twenty years before experiencing another reduction during the course of the plagues which struck the south in the middle of the seventeeth century. For purposes of comparison, Córdoba offers a hybrid version of the peninsula's demographic history. In the sixteenth century it expanded in much the same way as the Castilian cities; and the commencement of its decline again falls into the Castilian pattern. But subsequently the town held its numbers until the middle of the seventeenth century; and here its postponed loss is characteristic of the south rather than the north.

Of the other 'kingdoms' of *al-Andalus*, two conformed to the common pattern, while the third is a special case. On the basis of the partial evidence available, it appears that the population of the town and region of Jaén increased slowly, if at all, during the first decade of the sixteenth century. Its expansion began after 1510 and by the time of the census carried out between 1528 and 1536, the 'kingdom' comprised 31,888 households (143,495). By the time of the last census, 1591, the number of households had increased to 43,262 (194,679). In the course of the century the population had added 51,184 souls to its numbers, an increase of the order of 35.7 per cent; and not unexpectedly the most vigorous push had occurred between 1541 and 1561.

The dominant city of the south (and increasingly of the peninsula) was Seville. But as in the case of Burgos, this importance is not reflected in the quality of modern works on the subject. According to a recent account the 'kingdom' of Seville may have contained 355,000 inhabitants in 1534, a figure which increased to 549,000 in 1591. Information then becomes virtually unobtainable until the outbreak of plague in 1648. The epidemic had an immediate, disastrous, and lasting effect on the fortunes of the city. It represents for the capital of Andalucía a setback of comparable magnitude to the population loss undergone by Old Castile fifty years before. So great was its impact that the regular convoy system from Seville to the New World was temporarily suspended.

The exception to the general demographic increase of the sixteenth century was provided by the 'kingdom' of Granada. A recent authority puts the figure for the Nasrid state at around 300,000 in 1500. Over the next fifty years the populaton, so far from increasing as had been the case virtually everywhere else, drifted downwards. In 1561 numbers may have stood at 292,252, this after the most prolific decades for the Christian 'kingdoms'; and by the time of the last census (1591) the population had fallen far more sharply to 209,857. Explanations for the unrelieved fall are not hard to find. The oppression and subsequent rebellions of the Islamic communities (in 1499–1500 and again between 1568 and 1571) offer the fundamental reasons. The first rising encouraged those who could afford to leave to do so if they had not already taken the opportunity; the second was followed by the deportation of the Islamic population from the former Nasrid domain. The new settlers who took their place failed to restore the previous levels. The thirteen thousand Old Christian families who migrated to Granada after 1571 were too few in number; and they failed to adapt either to the countryside or the traditional economy.

Regional sentiment and the awareness of a separate identity has coloured the whole of Iberian history; and it could be argued that its pervasive influence is as evident in the economic field as it is in the political. The lands of the Aragonese crown (Aragon proper, the kingdom of Valencia, and the principality of Catalonia) had an economic rhythm and were subjected to demographic forces quite distinct to those which operated in Castile. Valencia ranks as the most intensely studied of these eastern regions. For this particular territory the 'long sixteenth century' made a belated appearance. The first signs of demographic growth were not in evidence until after 1550, a full hundred years behind Old Castile. But as if to make amends, the population increased rapidly in the period from 1563 to 1609. In terms of 'hearths' (*fuegos*) numbers went up from 64,075 in 1563 to 96,731 in

1609. If Valencia can be assumed at all typical, population on the eastern littoral (and perhaps further inland as well) began to increase much later than in Castile; and then, by way of compensation, it continued to grow after the turn of the century and did not experience the misfortunes of its western neighbour until the late 1620s.

The more northerly territories of the Aragonese crown, the principality of Catalonia and the region of Aragon itself, compared in terms of numbers with the kingdom of Valencia—all three hovered around the 300,000 mark—but differed in one important respect. They could draw on population resources beyond their borders. Since time immemorial the tide of migration had ebbed and flowed across the Pyrenees. As was often the case, apparent obstacles, the Pyrenees to the north, the Straits of Gibraltar to the south, formed not a barrier but a link to those on either side. In the sixteenth and early seventeenth century the tide ran strongly southwards. Large numbers from the poorer French provinces, the lower Pyrenees, Languedoc, and the Auvergne made the journey to Aragon and Catalonia, encouraged by the wages and the availability of land in areas linked so closely to their own by culture and language. Young, landless males formed a high proportion of these new immigrants, providing in many cases recruits for the rural proleteriat; and their efforts helped to revive both Aragonese and Catalan agriculture over the period 1540 to 1620. After 1620 the number of migrants fell off, partly, it has been suggested, because employers could no longer offer the wages which had drawn their predecessors. This influx from the French Midi had far-reaching consequences for Aragon and Catalonia while at the same time having a negligible impact upon Castile where the number of immigrants was never, in the early modern period, of significance.

Although it may be impossible to state with precision the particular reasons for the generalized growth in population during the sixteenth century, certain developments obviously favoured the process. The restoration of political stability by the Catholic Monarchs and its preservation by their successors provided an environment conducive to the expansion of numbers. In the case of Castile, a major impetus to demographic growth came from the prosperity of the wool trade, both the increase in the size of the flocks, hence the clip, and the production of cloth itself. The woollen trade, centred on Burgos, boomed in the late fifteenth century and its prosperity was not to be broken until after 1569. The role of industrial demand in promoting population expansion can be seen at its clearest in the case of Segovia. Here demand for woollen goods led to increased employment both in the countryside where the weaving of cloth had been long established and in the town itself where, at the height of the boom (1590) as many as six hundred looms were in operation. Industrial expansion in its rural and urban form as exemplified in Segovia lends weight to Malthus's theory that an increase in the opportunities for employment prompts a growth in population, an idea which has been taken up and amplified by modern demographers.

The area of land under cultivation was another obvious determinant of population. Throughout the sixteenth century land reclamation in its various forms proceeded apace the entire length of the peninsula. In the province of Murcia the acreage under cultivation was increased by approximately a quarter in the period from 1480 to 1621. Again in this particular instance drainage and improvement reached its height between 1510 and 1576, dates roughly comparable to those of the highest rates for population increase. The exploitation of marginal or common lands was another feature especially of the central decades of the sixteenth century, although this often proved a precarious and short-lived expedient undertaken to boost output in regions of high population density.

If the period of the early Habsburgs in Spain had been characterized by prosperity and general increase, the seventeenth century presented a strikingly changed prospect. Decline and a reduction in numbers occurred sooner or later throughout the entire peninsula; and the slide was not to be halted, or in some cases reversed, until the 1680s. Several factors explain the onset of this period of contraction. In the first place, Europe at the turn of the seventeenth century no longer demonstrated the economic buoyancy which had been the predominant feature of the previous century and a half. Secondly, the demands of the state in the form of increased taxation began adversely to affect the Castilian economy after 1588. The phenomenon of harsher fiscality, while not confined to the Iberian peninsula, may have inflicted more lasting damage than elsewhere. Then came the plague.

The 'Atlantic' plague, as it has recently been described, entered Castile through the port of Santander on the Cantabrian coast. Its appearance was first reported in 1598. It then spread throughout Old Castile, crossed the Tagus and by March 1599 had entered Seville. The latest account of the Atlantic epidemic claims that its impact was to be felt throughout the peninsula. It was not a localized outbreak confined to the northern provinces. Yet it was in these lands that the plague was to have its more dramatic and lasting effects. The Atlantic plague had, in the words of Bartolomé Bennassar, devastating consequences: 'It deprived Old Castile, the heartland of the monarchy, of its last trump—its richness in men.' Segovia, the great textile centre for the interior of Castile, may have lost as much as 10 per cent of its population in the period 1599–1602. Valladolid suffered even worse. Bennassar estimates that within the space of four months the region of Valladolid lost between 6,000 and 6,500 inhabitants, or approximately 18 per cent of its population. The neighbouring town of Palencia sustained yet higher losses: during the course of the outbreak the number of hearths within the city went down from 2,047 to 1,326, a reduction of some 35.2 per cent.

Other regions of the peninsula, if left untouched, might have made up for the victims of the Atlantic plague. But these, too, were struck, both during the course of the Atlantic plague and, more seriously, in subsequent decades. The 'Milanese' plague of 1629–31 fell principally on Catalonia and the adjoining province of Roussillon. Twenty years later the plague made its unwelcome return and this time it was the Levantine ports of Valencia and Alicante which were the points of entry. From Valencia and Alicante the disease swept northwards to Zaragoza and Huesca and southwards to the centres of what remained of Castilian prosperity, Málaga and Seville. A further series of 'high mortalities' which ravaged the eastern littoral from 1676 to 1685 completed the work of economic and demographic destruction. In brief, the population of the peninsula was first reduced by the Atlantic and Milanese plagues; and subsequent recurrences of disease prevented any speedy recovery of numbers.

However imprecise the figures for the population of the various Iberian kingdoms, a number of simple conclusions can be drawn. From first to last Castilian dominance in terms of population remained overwhelming. Hence Castile's position within the complex of Habsburg possessions was assured regardless of additional benefits such as an overseas empire. Secondly, as Ruiz Martín remarks, Castile's demographic superiority actually increased during the course of the sixteenth century. Castile, in terms of numbers alone, grew at a faster rate than any of its neighbours; and this dynamism, taken in conjunction with other advantages, explained, at least in part, the prolonged eclipse of the peripheral kingdoms.

Within Castile itself the balance of population shifted during the reign of the first Habsburgs. A steady drift to the south took place throughout the century, a migration deplored by those moralists who witnessed the abandonment of the land and thought they saw a surrender to the attractions and perils of urban life. Recent studies have suggested that by 1591 the population of Andalucía may have numbered 1,200,000. If the aggregate figure for Castile considered as a political unit and not as a geographical expression stood at slightly under six million—and Ruiz Martín puts it higher at 6,617,251—then Andalucía contained just over one-fifth of the subjects of the Castilian crown.

Castile's demographic vigour had implications both for domestic and international politics. It guaranteed the standing of Castile as the principal support of the Habsburg dynasty within the peninsula, and it may also explain the success of the Habsburgs during the sixteenth century in dealing with the other great power of the day, France. The population of Valois France, although huge by contemporary standards, did not increase to any notable extent. The economic and social causes of this demographic inertia remain obscure; but the Wars of Religion which broke out in 1561 certainly acted as a constraint. Ruiz Martín contends that Spain's primacy during the sixteenth century was partly attributable to Castile's expanding population. It was this dynamism which provided the Habsburg monarchy with the additional resources to pursue an adventurous foreign policy at a time when the principal check on the Habsburgs, France, failed to enjoy the benefit of comparable increases. In short, demographic growth can be considered as a determinant not merely of the equilibrium within the Iberian peninsula but also in terms of its wider ramifications over the European continent.

CHAPTER 18

The ethnic inheritance of Spain: the moriscos

THE moriscos represented Spain's Islamic past. They were descended from settlers who had crossed over into the peninsula during the centuries of Arab occupation; and even after the destruction of the last Arab state they had remained faithful to the religion and culture of Islam. In the course of the movement known as the Reconquest, the Islamic communities had been accommodated without undue friction into the Christian kingdoms. They formed, if nothing else, a valuable economic asset; and the Christian monarchs had proved generally lax or indifferent on the point of religion. The victorious states were fully capable of absorbing the indigenous populations, Islamic or Jewish. That, at any rate, was the appearance. By 1500, however, circumstances had clearly altered: the western Mediterranean, so far from being a busy thoroughfare between Europe and Africa, as it had been in the days of Nasrid Granada and Merinid Fez, was developing into a battleground between two distinct and hostile creeds; while Christian rulers themselves, influenced by new stresses within Europe, began to insist on religious and, by extension, cultural conformity. Relations between the Spanish monarchs and their Islamic subjects during the sixteenth century were characterized by growing intolerance and fear.

Morisco communities were to be found throughout the peninsula with the exception of Galicia and the Cantabrian coast. But the most significant concentrations were located in the states of the Aragonese crown, particularly in Valencia, and in Granada. The Levantine provinces had been one of the regions of densest Islamic settlement during the Middle Ages; while Granada's population had been reinforced during the thirteenth and fourteenth centuries by migrants from areas newly occupied by the Christians. Although the moriscos adhered to a common faith, Islam, history and geography determined that their individual experience would differ. At the turn of the sixteenth century there was little contact between the Grenadine

communities and their counterparts in Valencia or Aragon, and
certainly not in the political sphere. While their religion, and ultimately their fate, may have been the same, each of the major communities has to be studied in its own right.

The province of Granada easily surpassed any other region in terms
of political and strategic importance. The memory of political
independence was very recent; and the traditional social order,
although damaged, still remained intact. The generosity of the terms
granted by the Catholic Monarchs on the surrender of Granada in
January 1492 helps to explain the reasons. The Nasrid king, Boabdil,
received a vast appanage in the region of Alpujarras with his seat in the
town of Andarax; and the population at large was both confirmed in its
property rights and guaranteed, at the same time, the full exercise of
religion and custom. Even if military considerations figured prominently in the drawing-up of the capitulations—to storm Granada
would be costly and would diminish the value of the asset, the incorporation of Islamic territory formed a part of an age-old process; and
the Christian rulers, like the Arab invaders before them, were anxious
to disturb the existing society as little as possible.

Ferdinand of Aragon, if not his more pious consort Isabel, was
probably content to settle for minimal alterations in the government of
Granada, in the belief that time would bring about the conversion and,
with it, the ultimate assimilation of the moriscos. The first archbishop
of Granada, Hernando de Talavera, himself—significantly—of Jewish
origins, showed how this could be achieved. He insisted that his clergy
learn Arabic so that their preaching might be understood by its
intended audience; and he demonstrated sensitivity towards the life-
style and traditions of his flock. The way to integration lay through
understanding and tact. Given time, Talavera's method might have
worked; but, in the event, it was denied the chance. The primate of
Spain, Jiménez de Cisneros, took a personal interest in the work of
conversion; and initially he supported Talavera's patient approach.
But within eight years of Granada's surrender he, and many others,
had tired of subtle tactics. Instead he sanctioned the harassment of the
native population and arranged for the ceremonial burning of Arabic
books. The decision on the part of the Christian authorities to speed
up the process of conversion provoked an almost inevitable reaction.
Over a period from November 1499 to the early days of the following
year, a series of disturbances broke out in the mountainous area to the
south of the city, the region of the Alpujarras, in the Sierra Nevada and

as far away as the western parts of the bishopric of Málaga. Not of great military significance, these risings ushered in a new period in the history of relations between overlord and subject. Once the immediate danger had passed, the crown rescinded the guarantees extended in 1492. The Islamic population was presented with a choice between conversion to Christianity or, the stark alternative, emigration. Most chose to stay as they lacked the means, and possibly the will, to abandon their native soil. The decision to remain was taken by the authorities as an acceptance of Christianity. After 1500 the population of Granada was assumed to be Christian in its entirety, subject to the obligations and penalties of their new faith but denied, as events were to show, most of the privileges. The aftermath of the 'first revolt of the Alpujarras', the inflated title given to the unrest of these months, witnessed the end of any attempt at reconciliation and the introduction of a policy which permanently divided the communities.

The position of the morisco in Granada had also been undermined by developments from within the community. After the conquest, the Catholic Monarchs refrained from tampering with Islamic society. The ruling class had been left in full enjoyment of their property and standing. But some amongst the defeated could read the signs. Boabdil, wise if only in this, had left Granada in 1493; and during the same decade six thousand from amongst the principal families had followed him into exile. The consequences of the revolt of the Alpujarras encouraged any waverers who still had the means to take the same course. By the new century the moriscos had lost their natural leaders. The subsequent determination of the authorities to hunt down the *alfaquíes*, or religious instructors, compounded the loss. Those who remained after 1500 faced the Christian onslaught weakened by the emigration of their leaders and the persecution of their teachers.

From the annulment of the original capitulations to the great rebellion known as the second revolt of the Alpujarras (1568–71) relations between the authorities and the nominally Christian population deteriorated steadily. In effect these years saw the uneven struggle between two religions and two traditions, or, in the dramatic abbreviation sometimes used, a clash of the cultures.

The attempt to break down the beliefs and identity of morisco society took a number of forms. Official legislation embodied the more obvious attack. At regular intervals the crown published blanket decrees designed to suppress the morisco language and customs, in particular the use of distinctive dress. These efforts culminated in the decree of 7 December 1526: the emperor Charles V issued a set of regulations which, had they been carried out, would have swept away all the identifying symbols and customs of the Islamic community in Granada. The moriscos reacted with speed and skill. Intensive lobbying at court, directed in all probability at the house of Tendilla, lavish distribution of bribes, and the promise of a handsome subsidy to the exchequer, helped to stave off the evil day. In return for an immediate grant of ninety thousand ducats spread over six years, and an annual payment thereafter on a reduced scale, the emperor was persuaded to suspend the legislation; and it remained effectively in abeyance for the next forty years. The moriscos had gained their respite. Only in the 1560s did religious conviction prevail over financial sense.

Cultural pressure came to be applied spasmodically in some cases and systematically in others. Royal edicts had a noticeable sartorial content; and the intention was not, as in the case of sumptuary legislation elsewhere, to restrain expenditure. Clothing and jewellery, far from reflecting the fashion of the moment or the whim of the owner, had an essential part to play in the preservation of the Grenadan community. Their accumulation provided a simple and very effective means of saving. Over the generations the wealth of a family found its way into the traditional costumes and adornments of the womenfolk. The stock of garments and jewels determined the worth of a lineage. In addition, the personal effects of the women, and their dowries in particular, could not be touched by the Inquisition, a real benefit in the face of an institution which depended for its existence on confiscation. The habit of investing in clothes had economic repercussions. The weaving and finishing of silk was far and away the most important source of employment within the city of Granada; and those who were not occupied in the preparation of silk were involved in the production of garments made from silk. Christian efforts to compel the moriscos to change their traditional costume and adopt the dress of their overlords struck equally at the identity and economic foundations of the existing society; and for these reasons they were resented and disregarded.

Islamic society placed a high value on the notion of law, higher, in fact, than the Christian state. The difference, however, was not one of degree but fundamental principle; and in the case of Granada it was bound up with the role and function of the clan. This formed the central element of morisco society and law. A legal system based on the clan demands an exact and extensive knowledge of lineage and pedigree. The Arab patronymic, an object of much Christian legislation, identified the clan to which each individual belonged. Such knowledge was essential to the operation of Islamic justice. Legal disputes were resolved through arbitration. In the case of major crime, homicide, for instance, the settlement took the form of a blood payment, in money or in goods. The sanction applied to enforce an award, or, where this was not forthcoming, to pursue the malefactor, was the vendetta, the call to the whole clan to back up a claim or to hunt down the culprit. The aggrieved looked to their kin, and the aggressor looked to his. This form of justice based on arbitration, kinship, and the blood feud was, in theory at any rate, alien to the Christian tradition with its insistence on written codes and permanent courts. In Granada two systems of justice came into being, the one unofficial but valid for the majority, and the other recognized as the law of the land but shunned by the bulk of the inhabitants. The repeated attempt by the legislators to suppress the Arabic patronymic in favour of the Christian surname posed a serious threat to the integrity of Muslim society. If nothing else, it represented a challenge to Islamic law and its assumptions; and by endeavouring to remove the protection of the patronymic it placed the individual morisco in mortal peril among his own people. The rival legal systems also contributed directly to the breakdown of order. Those who resorted to the blood feud were treated as outlaws by the agents of the crown. To escape punishment they were forced to seek sanctuary in the mountains, the Alpujarras and the Sierra Nevada usually, where they swelled the already numerous bands of brigands, the much feared *monfíes*.

As the Christians were all too aware, the moriscos clung tenaciously to the basic precepts of Islam. Although they produced no original literature of their own after 1492, they preserved the sacred texts; and thus kept the faith alive. As late as 1579 the Holy Office in Aragon was complaining bitterly about the free circulation of the Koran in the face of all efforts to confiscate every copy. Algiers, it was widely suspected, provided the main source of supply. Muslim teaching also accommodated public or outward compliance to an alien creed under the doctrine of the *taqiyya*, a device more frequently associated with the heretical Shiites than the orthodox Sunni. Away from prying eyes in the fastness of the mountains, or behind closed doors in the Muslim ghettos, the indigenous population fulfilled as best it could the five basic requirements of the creed. This included the profession of faith and the performance daily of the five liturgical prayers. In addition the devout were expected to observe the periods of fast, Ramadan being the best known. They were further called upon to perform charitable works such as the ransoming of captives, and then, as a special mark of sanctity, to visit Mecca, although this became virtually impossible after 1530. Before praying, the faithful were required to carry out ritual ablution, even if this were only simulated. Where major pollution had occurred, they had to wash their bodies completely. Acquainted as they were with the Koranic requirements, the Christian authorities regarded the public baths with profound suspicion despite morisco assurances that they existed to enable butchers, tanners and the like to clean themselves. Mixed bathing, apparently, was not allowed.

Like the Mosaic code, the Koran gave instruction in matters of diet and social hygiene. The drinking of wine and the consumption of pork and its derivatives was forbidden. Observance of these and other taboos created a distinctive cuisine. The morisco diet contained a high proportion of fruit, vegetables, and meat, usually mutton or goat. Olive oil was used in the preparation. This diet, typical of the Mediterranean, went back to the days of Homer and beyond. The Christians, on the other hand, followed the habits and tastes of the inland meseta. They consumed much more grain and, of course, pork. Lard or butter was used in the cooking. To modern eyes, the difference might seem to be one of calories (and cholesterol); but for sixteenth-century man the distinction symbolized two faiths and two cultures. If food was one way of telling immediately who was an Old and who a New Christian, there were other tests. The slaughter of cattle with a knife and with the victim's head held towards the east was a sure indication; and another was the practice of circumcision which, although not mentioned in the Koran itself, was taken correctly to be an intrinsic rite of the faith.

However zealously the Christian authorities attempted to destroy what to them was an alien culture, they were unable to eradicate, at least in the short term, institutions and traditions developed over centuries of Islamic rule. In the province of Almería a modified version of Arabic law, referred to in the texts as the *ley malakita*, continued to govern relations between the landowner and his tenants (sharecroppers for the most part). Contracts based on this system were being drawn up as late as 1561, as if the Reconquest had never taken place. Other forms of social organization persisted long after the disappearance of the emirate. The *wata* had developed during the Middle Ages in the kingdom of Granada as in other parts of the Islamic world. The institution resembled an extended family and a client network. It included both those linked by ties of blood and those who had chosen to associate themselves with the particular group. The *wata* acted in defence of its members without regard to their individual origin. This form of 'good lordship', to borrow a term from English history, still flourished wherever the former Islamic ruling class had managed to retain its estates. The landlord, his family, his tenants, and even on occasions his slaves, were joined in a common bond for the preservation of their culture and their religion.

Isolated as they were from the mainstream of Islamic life, the moriscos of Granada and later their co-religionists of the eastern provinces conducted a lively and at times subtle polemic with those who sought to convert them. Unlike their Christian adversaries, morisco writers showed a profound knowledge of the opposing faith. Nor did they regard it as simply a degenerate variant of their own. They were also able to exploit a new source of criticism against the Roman church, the writings of the Reformers. Time and again morisco polemicists returned to the fundamental division between Islam and Christianity. To repeat the formula of the faith, there was only one God and He was both timeless and indivisible. The nature of God could not be separated in any way, as suggested by the Christian doctrine of the Trinity. To argue that God had a number of different manifestations was to err in the direction of polytheism.

The moriscos believed that Christ was indeed the Messiah, but only in the Islamic sense of 'He who is purified'. To them, Christ, a model believer, was the greatest of the earthly prophets; yet he remained for all that a mere mortal, not part of a God who by his very nature could not be divided. Morisco thinkers also took issue with the Christians over individual doctrines; and they trained their fire on the role of the papacy in the elaboration of many (erroneous) beliefs. Successive popes bore the blame for the distortion of the scriptures considered authoritative by both faiths. They and their associates had invented such untenable doctrines as that of Purgatory; and in their teaching on the nature of the Eucharist, the notion of God had been reduced to a travesty. The moriscos, and they were hardly alone in this, did not believe that God was present in the Host. What, they inquired, would happen if during the service of Holy Communion the consecrated wafer fell to the ground? Did God fall with it?

The moriscos found themselves subject to constant religious pressure, while being simultaneously penalized financially. They had to bear a number of discriminatory taxes. These were the *farda mayor*, which paid for the troops directly under the command of the Captain General, at this stage invariably a member of the house of Tendilla, and the *farda menor*, which was levied first to construct and then maintain a string of watch-towers along the Grenadine coast. Without these taxes, which the Old Christians for the most part successfully evaded, the Captain General would have been unable to maintain discipline amongst his troops; nor could have have hoped to keep his early warning system along the coast operational. The close financial bond explains why the house of Tendilla emerged as the natural protector of the morisco. Such a community interest between an alien minority and a baronial dynasty formed a striking and stable feature of Grenadine society; and it offers clear parallels with the case of both Aragon and Valencia.

The additional taxes demanded of the New Christians might have been patiently borne as simply another irritant. But taken in combination with other discriminatory measures they served to goad the Islamic community into a final effort to recover their independence. The Crown looked to the *fardas* to pay for the local security forces; and they used at the same time the silk industry, the mainstay of the local economy, as an important source for general expenditure. Both town and country were involved in the preparation of silk. The white mulberry on which the silkworm fed was cultivated in the Alpujarras. During the winter months, when communications with the outside world virtually ceased, the population of the mountain villages devoted themselves to the laborious task of unwinding the silk thread from the cocoon, spinning it, and packing the yarn for shipment to the city once the snow had melted. In Granada the weaving alone, according to K. Garrad, employed 4,000 and the marketing of the finished product a further 300. The prosperity of the town and the region hung on a silken thread.

In the course of the sixteenth century, the silk industry became a victim of a number of government measures, several fiscally inspired. An embargo was placed in 1552 on the sale of Grenadan silk outside the peninsula. This example of misguided consumer protection was not lifted until 1561. The financial embarrassment of the Habsburgs at the abdication of Charles V had a direct and adverse effect on the health of the industry. In 1557 the new king, Philip II, desperate for funds, raised the farm of the silk tax. The yield of the lease, usually held by merchants from Toledo, rose from 26 million maravedís

(69,333 ducats) to 42.5 million maravedís (113,333 ducats). Not content with this, the crown decided to repeat the strategem in 1565 when the farm was lifted to 53 million maravedís (141,333 ducats). Burdens of this order imposed on an industry already in trouble could not be absorbed without considerable hardship. The difficulties of the silk trade and the second revolt of the Alpujarras were tightly linked: the rebellion was planned in the silk-weaving quarter of Granada (the Albaicín) and it found its most determined supporters in the mountain villages of the Alpujarras.

If the crown looked to the moriscos to alleviate its wants, so, in time, did the Inquisition. During the first half of the century the local tribunal had not concerned itself unduly with the moriscos. In 1550 half of those punished in the *autos de fe* were moriscos, not a cause for satisfaction, but an approximate reflection of relative population densities. Thereafter the Holy Office began to direct its attentions to the Islamic community. Areas hitherto protected by neglect were visited for the first time; and offences hitherto considered minor were more severely judged. The level of recidivism may have increased amongst the moriscos increasingly sceptical about the benefits to be derived from their new faith. The cases tried by the Inquisition came to mirror these trends. In 1560 over 85 per cent of those punished by the tribunal were moriscos; and six years later the *auto de fe* had become an almost exclusively morisco affair, that community providing 92 per cent of the victims.

The threat to morisco property came not only from the Holy Office, which by its constitution was self-financing, but from a government-sponsored survey commissioned at the beginning of the 1560s. As part of a scheme to increase revenue, the crown dispatched a certain Dr Santiago to investigate title deeds to land. It was common knowlege that during the confusion of the Christian conquest much land had been usurped; and it was the government's intention to remedy this and turn it, belatedly, to their own profit. Dr Santiago began work in 1561 and his investigations alarmed both communities. Christian claims were often shaky, to say the least; while the moriscos could rarely produce the sort of written evidence of ownership acceptable in a Christian court. Appeals against Santiago's rulings very quickly snarled up the workings of the superior courts; and the whole operation created in the province the deepest sense of foreboding.

The cumulative pressure on the indigenous population had created by the mid 1560s a highly unstable situation. Rivalry between the authorities made this still more precarious. Conflict of jurisdictions formed a guiding principle of Habsburg rule; but in Granada the practice had been allowed to luxuriate riotously. The royal chancellery of Granada, established in 1505 and with jurisdiction over all lands south of the Tagus, represented the supreme civil authority, while military matters and internal security fell within the province of the Captain General. Not unexpectedly, the two were permanently at loggerheads, and they spent much of their time complaining to the king about infringements of jurisdiction. If this was not sufficient, the municipality of Granada had its own scores to settle with the Captain General. During the land grab which followed the conquest his ancestors had made off with the summer grazing lands of the city; and these had never been returned. Other powerful interests nurtured their own grievances either against the house of Tendilla, the principal butt of these antagonisms, or another sectional group. The Inquisition, never to be trifled with even by the mightiest in the land, clashed time and again with the Captain General over his treatment of the moriscos whom, for fiscal reasons if nothing else, he was anxious to protect. Conflicts of this type could be found throughout the Habsburg empire; but in the case of Granada in the mid-sixteenth century they led to the paralysis of government which made it impossible to react swiftly and effectively against an internal rising.

Towards the end of 1566 the central government decided to revive the legislation first drawn up in 1526 and subsequently shelved. As before, the intention was to suppress the continued use of Arabic or its patois variant, the patronymics, the clothing, the baths, and the other distinctive emblems of morisco life; but on this occasion the monarch and his advisers were not to be bought off. The Pragmática, or royal order, was officially proclaimed on 1 January 1567, to coincide with the anniversary of Granada's surrender. There could be no doubt that a new and even harsher era had begun.

As originally conceived, the rebellion had three main objectives. These were to elect a king, to raise the Alpujarras, and to capture the city of Granada. The driving spirit behind the rising was Farax aben Farax, a dyer's journeyman by trade, who had fled the city and taken refuge with the bandits. It was he who led the attack on Granada at the head of his *monfíes* in the early hours of 26 December 1568. The attempt failed because the Albaicín, the Muslim quarter, refused to rise and the Captain General's forces guarded the Alhambra. But elsewhere the rising did catch fire, in the valley of Lecrin and the

Alpujarras. The character of the rebellion was determined almost from its first moments; it was a rural movement and the outcome would be decided by ambush, the siege of mountain villages, and ultimately, mass deportation.

As Captain General, the count of Tendilla (or, to use his other style, the marquis of Mondéjar) took over immediate responsibility for the counter-insurgency measures. Had his vigorous campaign in the early months of 1569 been followed up, the rebellion might well have ended in that year, but deep-seated animosities within the Christian camp prevented a speedy end to the war. The chancellery of Granada refused to co-operate with Tendilla; while the court preferred to entrust military authority to yet another rival of the count, Pedro de Fajardo, marquis of los Vélez and *adelantado* of Murcia. The defeat of los Vélez on 3 May 1569 meant that the uprising developed into a war of attrition and devastation.

For their part, the morisco leaders were unable to mobilize their full potential. The failure initially to secure Granada deprived them of a capital and the resources of the Albaicín. When hatching the conspiracy, they had calculated on two things, Spain's involvement in the Low Countries and the pledge of support from the Ottoman empire. As it turned out, the sultan's forces were involved in the conquest of Cyprus and there was little to spare for so distant a sphere of operations as the western Mediterranean. The Barbary states sent small detachments, volunteers and adventurers, whose principal effect was to terrorize friend and foe alike.

Yet, as so often, the morisco cause was compromised above all by internal divisions. The life and death of the first king raised up by the rebels illustrated the point. The conspirators chose as their new ruler Hernando de Valor. He was picked for reasons of his wealth, the prestige of his uncle, Hernando de Valor el Zaguar, and his lineage. The family claimed descent from the Umayyad Caliphs, hence the name used by the new king after his coronation, Abenhumeya. The reign proved short. On 20 October 1570, he was deposed by his own guards. Just before his execution (he was throttled by rope) he explained that he had become king in order to avenge himself on those amongst his own people who had surrendered his father to royal justice. Now that his vengeance had been satisfied, he died a happy man. The feuds and vendettas which had figured so prominently in the history of Granada as an independent state continued to run their course unchecked down to the last hours of that society.

Hostilities came to an end in 1571. The second 'king' of the Alpujarras, elected before the eyes of Abenhumeya, and known as Abenaboo, was himself murdered on 11 March 1571. His assassin, a brigand with the nickname El Xeniz, hoped to secure a pardon and the release of his family. Isolated groups still remained at large; but by the beginning of the summer they too had been smoked out of their last strongholds in the caves of the Alpujarras.

Even before the end of operations, the Christian authorities indicated how the region was to be pacified. As early as March 1570 the deportation of the entire Muslim population had been decided. Since this required planning and co-ordination, the province was divided into seven zones, in each of which the morisco inhabitants were rounded up before deportation. The plan further envisaged marching the expelled communities to assembly points outside the province and their subsequent distribution, in much smaller groups, throughout the kingdom of Castile. Behind the scheme lay the idea that deportation and separation into smaller units would at last bring about the integration of the moriscos into Christian society. The first part of the operation went off more or less as anticipated. Five and a half thousand reached Seville, 6,000 Toledo, 12,000 Córdoba, and a further 21,000 Albacete. But the second stage of this operation was not put into effect. For this reason the exiled communities tended to congregate in the southern parts of Castile; and the total disintegration of their society was not achieved. In all it has been estimated that 80,000 were expelled from Granada, although how many failed to survive the rigours of deportation, hunger and typhus being two obvious ones, is impossible to determine.

In ways that were not realized at the time, the expulsion of the moriscos from Granada came to affect the future course of Habsburg policy and the destiny of other Islamic communities. The dispersal of the Grenadine exiles throughout Castile so far from eliminating the problem of their alien identity merely reinforced it. When the Christian authorities next considered a solution, it was designed to apply to all the moriscos of the peninsula. The deportation of one community in 1570 ended with the expulsion of all the communities in 1609.

In terms of settlement the moriscos of the states of Aragon were not as concentrated as their Grenadan counterparts. They had been under Christian rule for much longer; and their demographic homogeneity had been broken up by the arrival of Christian settlers. But certain areas, which had been densely populated during the centuries of Islamic rule, still retained their Muslim character. This was the case in the Sierra of the Albarracín and the valley of the Ebro. By the sixteenth century the morisco communities were associated with the dry uplands of the interior and the flood plains of the littoral. They constituted a rural proletariat, noted for their ability to farm the poor *secano* which had been avoided by Christian immigrants, and their willingness to work the malarial sugar plantations and rice fields of the coast. According to Joan Reglà, the areas of densest morisco occupation were the irrigated plains of Játiva and Gandía.

An analogy has been drawn between the condition of the moriscos of the eastern kingdom and the slaves of the Deep South. The similarities were strong: the moriscos were serfs, in all but name, and their status was emphasized by the payment of servile dues, mainly in labour (*zofras*) from which their Christian neighbours were exempt. The comparison can be taken still further. The moriscos worked the lands of the nobility, not those of the crown or the church. As a natural consequence, the nobles emerged as the protectors of their workforce anxious to shield them from outside interference if only to maintain their own rent rolls. The moriscos, for their part, came to regard their overlords partly as oppressors, which they were, and partly as their only defenders against a hostile world. The relationship between Christian masters and morisco serfs had its bizarre moments. On a visit to his estates in the valley of Guadalest, Sancho de Cardona, Admiral of Aragon, came across an abandoned mosque in the village of Azaneta. On Cardona's instructions, the mosque was rebuilt for the worship of his vassals and anyone else who cared to use it. Such eccentricity, insolent and admirable, caught the attention of the Inquisition who punished the challenge to their authority; and it drew from Philip II himself an order for the destruction of the mosque.

Until well into the sixteenth century the Aragonese moriscos lived unaffected by the events taking place elsewhere in the peninsula. They retained their freedom of worship when it had been withdrawn in Granada; and this privilege was to last until the rebellion known as the *Germanías* (1520–1). The *Germanías* were to the states of Aragon what the first revolt of the Alpujarras had been to the province of Granada. A reduction in the power of the nobility provided one of the aims of those who took part in the *Germanías*; and this meant, in the context, a change in the status of those who worked their lands. To bring this about, the rebels baptized the moriscos in their thousands.

According to legend, one of the principal ringleaders, Vicent Peris, had baptized the new converts with a broom and bucket, so great was the 'demand'. The Old Christians identified the morisco peon as both the victim and the ally of the seigneurial order which they were intent on destroying. To convert the serf was to attack the lord.

The *Germanías* ended the indifference from which the moriscos of the Aragonese crown had benefited. After weighty theological consideration, royal advisers decided that the conversion, however brought about, must stand. Thenceforth the Aragonese moriscos were to be deemed Christians and subject to all the obligations of their new faith.

Alarmed by the dramatic change in status and appalled by the prospect of the Inquisition, the Islamic quarters (*aljamas*) sent a deputation to Madrid to plead their case. A royal decree of 8 December 1525 ordering the imposition of Christianity without exception gave an added element of urgency. The Aragonese embassy, like the one from Granada which came shortly after, knew that Charles V was in dire financial straits; and they had authority to make an offer he was unlikely to refuse. They succeeded. After intensive lobbying by, amongst others, the Aragonese nobles, it was agreed that the Holy Office would not interfere in the lives of the newly converted for the next forty years; and in return for this immunity the *aljamas* paid 40,000 ducats into the exchequer. The bargain held; and, as in the case of Granada, the moriscos lived relatively unmolested until the advent of Philip II.

The change in policy towards Granada involved a similar alteration in the treatment of Valencia. In both cases this came about in the 1560s. Even without the adoption of more inflexible attitudes, the crown was responding to a number of factors, some recent in origin, others which reached back a long way. Operating out of such pirates' nests as Larache and Chercel, the corsairs, many of whom had fled from Andalucía or were descendants of émigrés, had raided the Spanish coast with virtual impunity since the days of the Catholic Monarchs. It was common knowledge that they obtained supplies and information from the morisco communities, which, on occasion, they helped to evacuate *en masse*. These descents on the coastal regions were minor when compared to a more recent development. The Ottoman fleets had swept effortlessly and apparently irresistibly across the Mediterranean; and if they succeeded in taking Malta, as they had with so many other island fortresses, this would unlock the whole of the western Mediterranean. To the planners in Madrid the morisco communities, whether they were in the mountains of Granada or the plains of Valencia, were just another element in the grand Islamic design which threatened to encircle and overwhelm Christian Spain.

In 1563, as a precautionary measure, the crown ordered the moriscos of Aragon to be disarmed. This had little effect. But the rising of the Alpujarras and the dispersal of the Grenadine communities was to transform the whole context of the problem. After 1571 the monarch and his advisers could not regard the moriscos as a series of isolated difficulties, separated by geography and tradition. The dispersal of the Grenadine survivors throughout Castile generalized the threat. Neither, as soon became evident, had resettlement brought about the anticipated dissolution of the society. Changes within the displaced communities kept the dangers, real or imagined, which they represented very much alive. In their new environment the moriscos, who had been farmers for the most part, were compelled to acquire different skills. The figure of the New Christian as a pedlar, tinker, or huckster now became a familiar one on the dusty tracks of the Castilian meseta. The mobility of the morisco trader enabled the émigré settlements to retain their links with their fellow exiles and, more alarmingly, to forge new ones with the principal enemies of Habsburg Spain.

In theory the moriscos settled on the domains of the Castilian crown did not form a separate caste. They were taken to be a part of the Christian population. In the states of the Aragonese crown it was different. There had been no deportation; and the morisco leaders, even after the imposition of Christianity, were able to present the view that their followers constituted a special category which could not be treated on the same basis as the Old Christians. The authorities, faced with a problem which seemed as intractable as it was old, never hit upon a consistent policy. They wavered continuously between coercion and conciliation.

Even those most hostile to the moriscos of Aragon conceded that little attempt had been made to instruct the nominally converted in the basics of the faith. Without such provision—a mandatory requirement, according to recent Tridentine legislation, for the Christians themselves—no genuine conversion could come about. In 1573 a scheme was launched to establish a network of parishes in areas of high morisco settlement. Lack of funds, and a demonstrable lack of enthusiasm, prevented the successful implementation of the plan. It was revived on a number of subsequent occasions; and it should be said to the credit of its advocates that, by the time of the final expulsion, a number of new parishes had been set up, notably in the bishopric of Segorbe.

If some royal counsellors had a dim awareness of the need to make special provision for their recalcitrant charges, others preferred more direct methods. With a confusion so characteristic of Castilian government, two juntas were set up in 1587 to discuss the morisco question, one to sit in Madrid, the other in Valencia. They were to advise on how best the moriscos might be instructed in the message of the Gospel. Their recommendations had a familiar ring: Arabic was to be suppressed, Christian-style clothing was to replace traditional costume, every Muslim community should employ a Christian midwife to ensure that the newly born were baptized correctly, and similarly a Christian butcher was to be at hand to see that the traditional Islamic methods of slaughter were not used. The Aragonese *aljamas* were gradually succumbing to the influence of Christian society and the clerical juntas may have hoped to accelerate the process of cultural disintegration.

The ecclesiastics who made up the two juntas favoured the application of continuous pressure. Some of their lay counterparts advocated an even more severe approach. In 1582 Philip II, newly installed in Lisbon, convened a junta to advise on the matter. Its membership included that staunch advocate of uncomplicated remedies, the duke of Alba. Perhaps as a result of his intervention, the junta concluded that the moriscos, and this meant the entire community, Grenadan, Castilian, Aragonese, and Valencian should be expelled at the earliest opportunity. The Jewish problem had been solved in this way; and given a similar situation with regard to the moriscos this was the appropriate cure. By the 1580s a consensus had emerged in government circles that expulsion offered the only remedy; yet an enterprise of this scale required careful planning and substantial forces. These did not become available until Spain had disengaged from its other commitments. As long as Philip and his successors found themselves at war with the Protestant powers no action could be taken.

This, however, did not stop the debate about the merits and demerits, the latter mostly, of the morisco presence. Some observers were struck to the point of indignation by the frugality of the community. The moriscos could build up savings even from their miniscule incomes. More significantly, commentators noticed a divergence in population patterns. The moriscos, debarred for the obvious reason of their background from the army and the church, did not suffer from the same losses as the Christian communities. They tended moreover to marry younger; for a morisco girl the mean age at first marriage might be eighteen years, on average two years less than her Christian counterpart. These observations fostered the impression, and in the absence of reliable statistics it could be nothing more, that a demographic race was under way and the moriscos stood every chance of winning.

In their assessment of the moriscos as a strategic liability, royal counsellors were on much firmer ground. It was common knowledge that the New Christians provided a ready-made network of informants for Spain's enemies, with an ideal courier service in the shape of the morisco muleteers. Jaime Bleda, whose length of service as a missionary amongst them was only matched by his antipathy towards his erstwhile flock, voiced a common opinion when he noted that 'The moriscos used to send embassies to the Grand Turk and to other princes hostile to the Christian faith. And they received and sheltered the corsairs and pirates of Algiers.' The Inquisition periodically uncovered conspiracies involving the moriscos. These uprisings, for the most part fanciful, incorporated a number of standard components. First, the moblization of an armed force of moriscos, then a landing either by the corsairs or the Ottoman navy, and finally collaboration with that arch-enemy of Catholic Spain, Henry of Navarre.

These fears were fed, in turn, by the virtually endemic disorders of what was an open frontier, the Pyrenees. In upper Aragon sectarian warfare raged between the Muslim inhabitants of the valleys, the town of Codo in particular, and the Old Christian herdsmen of the mountains with their stronghold in the Val d'Aran. Raids and counter-raids carried out by two embittered communities, the constant fear of invasion either by land, or by sea, or in combination kept the lands of the crown of Aragon in constant ferment.

Under Philip III (1598–1621) the problem was at last 'resolved'. At the beginning of the reign Juan de Ribera, archbishop of Valencia from 1569 to 1611 and the most influential churchman of the eastern provinces, recommended unequivocally that the moriscos should be expelled. After years of passionate, even intemperate, evangelization, this emotional man had reached the conclusion that without the measure Spain 'would be lost'; the conversion of the moriscos was a chimera. These views were presented by Ribera to the crown in two formal submissions, the first in 1601 and the second in the following year. The council of state, moved, perhaps, by Ribera's opinion, added its approval to the idea of expulsion in 1602.

What might have been accepted as official policy still had to be translated into practice. Before this took place, certain obstacles had to be overcome. The nobles of Aragon and Valencia had steadfastly opposed the expulsion of a workforce on whom their prosperity depended. Their attitude, taken in conjunction with Spain's overseas involvements, prevented anything being done during the reign of Philip II. Circumstances changed on the accession of a new king, Philip III. Peace was concluded with England in 1604; and a truce was signed with the Dutch in 1609. This eirenic policy, foreshadowed in the last years of the old reign, had been carried to a successful conclusion by Philip III's principal minister, Francisco Gómez de Sandoval, marquis of Denia and duke of Lerma. The termination of hostilities brought with it the prospect of reduced expenditure, not in the event realized, and a measure of freedom for domestic policy which, in the event, was exploited. Lerma had secured peace and thereby paved the way for the expulsion. But his contribution was far more direct. It was, in fact, central. Lerma was Valencian, not Castilian as his titles indicated. He had a knowledge of local conditions and had actually served as governor of Valencia from 1595 to 1597. As one of the leading magnates of the region he disposed of an extensive clientèle amongst the lesser nobility, and his views, or moods, always carried weight.

By 1608 Lerma had come to agree that the moriscos represented such a threat to state security that expulsion was the only solution. To win support for the measure from a class which had hitherto resolutely blocked it, Lerma offered a number of powerful inducements. Under the terms of the expulsion, the nobility acquired the lands and most of the chattels which had belonged to their morisco tenants. Of equal importance, they obtained a measure of relief on their debts. Several unusual features complicated the issue. In a number of instances morisco villages had stood surety for money advanced to their overlords; and there was no guarantee that Christian settlers would be willing to shoulder the same financial responsibility or, for that matter, that the villages would be repopulated at all. On a more general point, the expulsion of a morisco tenantry which made up, on some estates, the entire workforce, was certain to affect the income of the nobility; it reduced their ability to meet existing charges on their outstanding debts. To help the seigneurial class overcome these problems, the crown decreed a reduction in the interest to be paid on loans and mortgages. The measure did indeed improve the position of the nobility even if it prejudiced their creditors, rentiers for the most part drawn from the city, in a way and to a degree not anticipated.

The deportation of the entire morisco population began in 1609 and ended in 1611. As an exercise in planning and organization, it was an unqualified triumph. Apart from isolated disturbances in the Sierra of the Espadán, there was no opposition and no delay. Although there can be little certainty in the matter, the total of those expelled is widely believed to have been around 300,000. According to Henri Lapeyre, the morisco contingents numbered 61,000 from Aragon, 45,000 from the two Castiles, 30,000 from Aragon, 16,000 from Murcia, 3,000 from Granada (*sic*), and 1,000 from the Canary Islands. The province of Valencia occupied a special category. Lapeyre suggested that its morisco population numbered 135,000; whereas Joan Reglà opted for a looser estimate of anywhere between 117,000 and 170,000.

The impact of the expulsion was serious but not as catastrophic as has sometimes been portrayed. In demographic terms Habsburg Spain may have lost between 3 and 4 per cent of its population; significant, but not irreplaceable. By driving out the moriscos, the crown deprived Castile and Aragon of industrious horticulturalists, artisans, and muleteers and contributed thereby to the crippling scarcity of labour, with the corresponding increase in wage costs. But in this instance the crown exacerbated rather than initiated a trend. Only in the specific case of Valencia could the results of the expulsion be termed devastating. If Reglà's figures are to be credited, the region lost between 22 and 30 per cent of its total population. These numbers were not made good in the seventeenth century either by immigration or natural increase. Economically the consequences were as far-reaching. Juan de Ribera was presumably not the only Valencian to ask who, in the future, would make his shoes. If the impact of the expulsion was obvious in the towns, it was even more so in the country. The output of the sugar and rice plantations was severely curtailed by the sudden removal of much of the workforce. In the cases where the proprietors did manage to induce Christians to take over abandoned lands they very often lacked the skill of the previous tenants. Valencia's output of rice and sugar fell; and it was not until well into the eighteenth century, as a result of renewed demographic pressure, that the province became once again a major exporter of rice. For Spain the deportation of the Islamic communities in 1609 marked the end of an era, symbolic rather than economic in terms of its overall consequences. For Valencia the very reverse was the case. The measure reduced its population by a quarter and ensured that the depression of the seventeenth century would be deeper and more prolonged than for any other region of Spain.

CHAPTER 19

The church, the Inquisition, and the ordering of society

BOTH Ferdinand and Isabel considered the reform of the Iberian church as one of their main priorities; and both worked consistently to promote this end. Advancement to the higher reaches of the ecclesiastical establishment came to depend on learning and personal sanctity, not, as in the past, on noble blood and political connection. The queen's piety contributed a good deal to this change in recruitment, but it was also based on considerations of state. The Catholic Monarchs were intent on bringing to an end the era of warrior bishops and king-making primates.

To achieve an improvement in standards, Isabel turned to her own household and above all her confessor, Francisco Jiménez de Cisneros (1436–1517). A Franciscan friar at the outset, this remarkable man rose to be royal confessor, primate, and on two occasions regent of the kingdom. He provided the archetype of the Catholic reformer, living proof that the Iberian provinces of the Latin church were capable of internal regeneration. Cisneros began his mission by raising standards within his own order. He insisted on the observance—a key word throughout—of the founder's rule, without stirring up the dangerous question of poverty. His ability so impressed the papacy that he was instructed to proceed in the same way with the Dominican and Augustinian Orders. Although the work of Cisneros was not as effective in rooting out abuse as he would have wished, he did improve the reputation of the church in the eyes of the faithful. His particular concern with the Franciscans and then the other mendicant orders helped to preserve the esteem in which the friars were held; and this had important implications for the reception (and ultimate rejection) of Erasmian ideas.

The Catholic Reform also began to work its way through the monastic communities in the fifteenth century. Its chosen instrument was García Jiménez de Cisneros, cousin to the great cardinal and for much of his adult life abbot of Montserrat. The idea of monastic reform reached back to 1390, the year in which San Benito de Valladolid was established. This foundation became associated with the strict observance of St Benedict's Rule. It insisted that the monks remain perpetually confined within the walls of the monastery; and it also introduced the novelty of electing its head for a two-year term instead of for life, in the interests presumably of maintaining standards. García Jiménez de Cisneros brought the strict observance to Montserrat on his appointment as abbot. Although few Benedictine houses showed an immediate willingness to imitate the example, Montserrat acted as a beacon of reform; and its practice became standard throughout the order in the years after the Council of Trent.

The Catholic Monarchs conceived of the church not merely as an institution essential for salvation, theirs and that of their subjects, but an instrument of government which they were resolved to control. The process whereby the monarchy asserted its absolute rights over the spiritual estate could be traced back to 1486. In anticipation of the lands to be recovered from the infidel of Granada, the pope, Innocent VIII, authorized the Catholic Monarchs to nominate the incumbents to an ecclesiastical system which had yet to be established. The concession of 1486 laid the foundations of what became known as the *patronato real*, or royal right of presentation. Granada served as a model (and a justification) when the newly discovered lands in the Caribbean came to be organized on a diocesan basis. Ferdinand the Catholic worked patiently through his envoys in Rome to win papal confirmation for his rights over the colonial church. Unaware of what exactly was being granted away, Julius II confirmed the power to make all appointment to ecclesiastical office in the Americas under the terms of the historic bull *Univeralis Ecclesiae Regiminis* (28 July 1508). Adrian VI (1522–3) amplified these concessions by entrusting to the Castilian crown the responsibility for recruiting and dispatching the missionaries to the New World. This additional privilege was embodied in the bull *Exponi Nobis* (9 May 1522). The papacy soon came to regret what it had so generously bestowed on the monarchs of Castile, as it had in the case of the Inquisition; but it was unable to rectify the initial mistake. In terms of its manning and administration, the colonial church became the exclusive preserve of His Most Catholic Majesty.

Where the overseas church led, the peninsular one followed. Whatever the differences of origin, Charles V proved the faithful continuator of Ferdinand's policy in reducing the ecclesiastical powers to complete dependence on royal authority. Aided, some might say abetted, by his former tutor Adrian VI, the most pliant pope with whom he ever had dealings, Charles V made it his business to secure absolute right of nomination to the peninsular church. Adrian VI obliged with the bull *Eximiae Devotionis Affectus* (6 September 1523), by the terms of which Charles and his successors acquired the right to appoint to every ecclesiastical office. The powers of the monarchy over the domestic and the overseas church had been brought into harmony; and the bull which completed this annexation of authority on the part of the crown was popularly referred to not by its Latin title but by the word *Omnímoda*.

As a European figure, Charles V became closely identified with the promotion of internal reform within the Catholic church; and in this he was once more following in the path of his maternal grandparents. Externally, he emerged as the most constant advocate of a universal council which might lend weight to the reforms which were required so urgently; while internally, that is, within the peninsula itself, he gave every encouragement to the innovations which reformers of a previous generation, Cisneros amongst them, had been so anxious to promote. Great stress had been laid by these religious pioneers on the need to preach the Word of God to the faithful, and the obligation on the part of the bishop to reside in his diocese. During his returns to Spain, and as the short time allowed, Charles vigorously supported the programme of the Catholic reformers; and it is no accident that Spanish representatives at the Council of Trent became the earliest and most persistent advocates of the bishop's residence as a divine injunction. Castile could even boast of having produced a minor version of Gian Matteo Giberti, the reforming bishop of Verona, in the shape of Juan Pardo de Tavera (1472–1545), successively archbishop of Santiago and Toledo. The Constitutions of Tavera's diocesan synods came to be regarded as providing a model of how best to manage a bishopric, anticipating, like Gilberti's, the authoritative pronouncements of Trent on the subject.

Of all the Habsburgs Philip II had the most exalted notions of a king's responsibility for the moral well-being of his people. Throughout the whole course of his life he spared no effort to impose higher standards upon the church. Although he entertained misgivings about the implications of Trent for his temporal powers, he generally welcomed the legislation of the Council, insisting on the adoption of its dogmatic teaching and seconding the introduction of administrative improvements. The wind of reform blew more fiercely through the Iberian church. Many Spanish bishops had attended the last sessions of the Council (1562–3) when the Fathers had turned their attention to the restoration of episcopal power and the need for a clergy adequately trained. One of their number, Guillem Cassador, the bishop of Barcelona (1561–70), returned to his diocese determined to begin right away on the task of implementing the Tridentine reforms. In obedience to the injunction *Cum adolescentium aetas* (15 July 1563) the bishop set about the foundation of a seminary in his diocese for the training of a new priesthood. It took time before Guillem Cassador could persuade his subordinates of the urgent need, and still longer for him to wring the necessary resources out of the diocese. On 29 November 1567, four years after the closure of the council, the bishop laid the foundations of his seminary. Cassador's enthusiasm and success contrasted favourably with the record of bishops elsewhere in Europe. Not until a century and a half after Trent did every bishopric have a seminary for the training of its diocesan clergy. And his commitment to basic Tridentine reform marked him out from some of his Spanish contemporaries. In 1582 the primate of Spain, Gaspar de Quiroga, summoned a provincial council to meet in Toledo. For all the professions of reforming zeal and the enormous wealth at his disposal, Quiroga felt unable to release the funds required to set up a seminary in his own archdiocese; and, even more surprisingly, the king did not question his decision.

Philip II devoted particular attention to the supervision of the church. It formed part of his duties as trustee of the *patronato real*; and such activity also answered an emotional commitment on his part. He worked for hours considering the respective merits of candidates for ecclesiastical preferment, even minor posts; and his correspondence with his secretaries, particularly Mateo Vázquez de Leca, was full of such discussions. The king brought knowledge and talent to the job, the only task in which he deserved the epithet of prudent. His main concerns, as revealed by the voluminous records, was to ensure that his clergy should have reached a high standard of morals and education; and, the obverse side of the coin, he was particularly anxious to punish sexual lapses such as concubinage or, yet more heinous, solicitation, the abuse of female parishioners in the obscurity of the confessional.

At the same time Philip mixed moral with political considerations.

Just as his predecessors had wheedled out of the papacy a monopoly over appointments to the Iberian and the American church, so Philip negotiated tirelessly to sever the links which bound the Orders which were of foreign origin from their mother houses beyond the national borders. In 1561 he secured a separation of the Spanish province of the Cistercian Order from the jurisdiction of Cîteaux in France. The unsettled conditions of many European states may have offered a partial justification for such a policy; communications between the mother and daughter houses had become hazardous. But the ulterior purpose behind these diplomatic manœuvres at the papal court was hardly a secret. Philip intended reducing to an absolute minimum foreign influence over the Iberian church; and in this he largely succeeded.

The peculiar character of Philip's religious attitude, a mixture of fidelity to the Roman church and the jealous insistence on his regal powers, can be studied in the design of the Escorial. This palace (or mausoleum) fixed in stone and mortar the fundamental creed of its builder. The idea of commissioning a monument to recall a great victory reached back to the battle of las Navas de Tolosa (1212) and the subsequent foundation of las Huelgas, the royal convent just outside the walls of Burgos. In Philip's case the triumph he chose to commemorate was that of St Quentin (10 August 1557); and the immediate inspiration behind this project came from the Jeronimite monastery at Belém built by Manuel I of Portugal, Philip's maternal grandfather, as an offering to God for success in India.

A site was chosen for the new palace in November 1561, on a southern spur of the Sierra de Guadarrama; and the first stone was laid on 23 April 1563. The whole complex was completed on 13 September 1583, although it was another seventeen years before the interior fittings and decorations were finished to the requirements of the Escorial's founder. The palace was, in effect, an ensemble of buildings, each with its own function. Philip intended that the mortal remains of Charles V, his family, and their descendants (including himself) should find a last resting-place in the vaults of the Escorial. Royal corpses started to arrive in 1574 even though the pantheon had yet to be prepared. At the same time the Escorial was designed with the needs of the living very much to the fore. Whilst building was still in progress, the king, mindful of Tridentine teaching on the subject, gave orders for the opening of the seminary which had been included in the original plans. The hospital attached to the Escorial began its operations at roughly the same time; and here, once again, there existed a conscious reference to the pronouncements of Trent. The efficacy of good works had been reaffirmed by the Fathers; and the hospital became the place *par excellence* where the quality of charity might be best shown.

Yet it was in the overall design and decoration of the Escorial that Philip and his advisers sought to demonstrate their belief in the principal doctrines of the church. The complex contained forty-four altars in all; and the main altar of the basilica provided the spiritual as well as the architectural focus of the entire construction. The Protestants had stressed the pulpit and the sermon; Philip reaffirmed the altar and the Mass. His daily attendance at worship also underscored the position of the Holy Eucharist in the celebration of the cult. In countless other ways the detail and the routine of the palace restated traditional or Tridentine doctrines. Its dedication to St Lawrence expressed confidence in the veneration of saints; the Immaculate Conception of the Virgin Mary was proclaimed from many of the canvases which adorned the state and private rooms; and it housed one of the greatest collections of relics in Catholic Europe.

The Escorial also projected a political message. It contained a Gallery of Battles which recorded the triumph of Castilian arms over the infidel. Similar prominence was given to the victories secured in Philip II's name, St Quentin (1557), the Azores (1583) and the repulse of English pirates. Philip was not only the dutiful son of the Holy Church, Roman and Apostolic; he was also the defender of Christianity against its internal and external foes, as his father had been before him.

The general improvement in the standards of the church in Spain can be credited to the Catholic Monarchs; and their successors in effect followed in the path marked out by them. Ferdinand and Isabel were also the driving force behind the setting up of a new type of Inquisition which ensured that the Spanish kingdoms remained largely uncontaminated by heretical ideas. According to tradition, the Catholic Monarchs first became aware of the need to replace the episcopal Inquisition when they established residence in Seville over the winter of 1477-8. They saw with their own eyes, or so the account runs, the way in which Jewish converts to Christianity (the *conversos*) openly derided their new faith and continued to adhere instead to 'the law of Moses'. Within a year the Monarchs induced the pope, Sixtus IV, to publish the bull *Exigit Sincerae Devotionis*, in which the pontiff declared his intention to appoint two or three clerics of mature years chosen by the papal authorities to act as special inquisitors for the Spanish kingdoms. But by an oversight, the papacy allowed the Monarchs to make the nomination. It was a blunder of the first order. In 1480 Ferdinand and Isabel appointed two inquisitors with instructions to proceed without delay to Seville. Once installed, the pair worked with speed and devotion hunting down suspects; and six 'Judaizers' were burnt at the *auto de fe* held on 6 February 1481, the first of many such occasions. The bull *Exigit Sincerae Devotionis*, suitably interpreted, enabled the Spanish monarchs to eliminate, or terrify into conformity, the large number of Jewish recidivists who had flourished in the south since the days of the great pogrom (i.e. 1391); but its real significance went well beyond that. The crown asserted from the outset the right to select the inquisitors, something which it was never to relinquish. Try as they might, neither Sixtus IV or those who came after were able to recover what had been so heedlessly surrendered to the lay ruler.

Quite the opposite. Remorseless diplomatic pressure applied to a series of popes who were vulnerable or discreditable led to further concessions. In 1483 the Catholic Monarchs set up the Supreme Council of the Holy Inquisition, hereafter 'the Suprema', and nominated the membership. They secured, in addition, papal confirmation for their choice of Inquisitor General, Fray Tomás de Torquemada, a man whose name was to become over the years synonymous with the institution itself. This marked another irrevocable advance. From the beginning the Council of the Inquisition and the Inquisitor General served the king and not the pope. All those who sat on the Suprema owed their office to royal favour; and, naturally enough, they considered themselves first and foremost as crown servants. The Inquisition formed just one more aspect of conciliar government. Furthermore the terms under which the first Inquisitor General received his appointment in 1483 left few in any doubt as to the power which he and the Holy Office would exercise. Torquemada had authority in both Castile and Aragon, a jurisdiction which no other official could boast. The Inquisitor General alone could be regarded as a national officer whose writ ran the length of both kingdoms; and the crown was to remember this.

Within the lifetime of the Catholic Monarchs the Inquisition grew from a temporary body, constituted to deal with a specific problem, into one which had a permanent council and a number of regional tribunals. In the half century after Ferdinand's death it underwent considerable modification until it attained its 'classic' form under Fernando de Valdés, Grand Inquisitor from 1546 until 1566. During his presidency of the Suprema, Habsburg Spain was divided into fourteen districts, each with its own tribunal. At the outset these regional tribunals were peripatetic; but they soon came to settle in the principal town of the region. In the sixteenth century the Council kept the regional tribunals under strict supervision through periodic 'visits'. These were intended to check any propensity on the part of the local inquisitors to misuse their authority or to fall beneath what was considered a satisfactory standard. The tight subordination of the regional tribunals to the Council may also have enhanced the value of the Inquisition to the crown as a means of monitoring the provinces and controlling them. In the seventeenth century the grip of the Suprema slackened, a sign perhaps of the general deterioration in government.

As an institution the Inquisition soon gained an unsavoury reputation outside the peninsula, a notoriety which extended from the *Apology* of William the Silent to the imaginative fiction of Edgar Allan Poe. The hate and fear which it inspired derived from its method of operation. Its procedures were first established by Tomás de Torquemada in the 1480s and then modified extensively until the publication in 1561 of Valdés's *Instructions*. Fernando de Valdés can be regarded as both the architect and the lawgiver of the Holy Office. For their information the tribunals relied upon a network of local agents, the 'familiars', who, although not paid, enjoyed valuable privileges such as exemption from the billeting of troops. The inquisitors also encouraged the delation on the part of the general public. Once a sufficient number of depositions had been gathered, the machinery began to turn. A small group of assessors (the *calificadores*) examined the denunciations; and if they decided that there was a case to answer, the suspect was arrested and his goods immediately seized. A series of interrogations followed, during the course of which the defendant was closely questioned about his personal beliefs, his family background—had any of his relatives come before the Holy Office?—and he was invited to name those who wished him ill. In the early days of his detention the prisoner was at liberty to make a statement to the inquisitors as often as he wished. After the preliminary sessions the declarations of the accused and the testimony of the hostile witnesses were compared to determine whether or not a common body of truth existed. At this (late) stage the defendant was allowed the services of a lawyer, but only one of the tribunal's choosing. The officers of the Inquisition met once again at this point to decide how the case should proceed. If the prisoner were palpably innocent, he or she might be set at liberty—a rare occurrence. The inquisitors might call upon the defendant to admit to the offence of which he stood accused and to abjure his errors. Or, if they remained dissatisfied with what they had so far heard, they might opt for the use of torture. The decision to apply pain had to be taken unanimously; and any confession could only be considered in evidence if it were corroborated by the victim subsequently. Once the prisoner had been tortured, the inquisitors had to decide upon appropriate punishment. Where the accused had proved obdurate in the face of manifest guilt, he (or she) was handed over to the secular authorities. Should he recant before the *auto de fe*, he might be garrotted and spared the final agony. If he remained 'pertinacious' to the end, he would be burnt alive at the stake. The burning of living heretics always marked the high point of the festivities. But in the vast majority of cases those who passed before the Inquisition suffered punishment of a lesser order. To purge their errors the convicted had to appear in the *auto de fe* and perform thereby an act of public contrition. They might be flogged, imprisoned for a term, or compelled to wear a special cloak, the *sambenito*, carefully preserved after death so that the humiliation of one generation might be transmitted to the next.

By the standards of the age, the Holy Office was not particularly brutal. Possibly as few as 10 per cent of its victims underwent torture in an age when this was considered standard procedure. For the most part the inquisitors observed the *Instructions* drawn up by Torquemada and then Valdés to the letter. They often showed themselves shrewd in assessing malice in the denunciations, occasionally punishing it. But the fact remains that the philosophy and basis of its operations were barbarous. The onus lay with the accused to prove his innocence. The prisoner was never told the names of those who had borne witness against him, although he might diminish the impact of such testimony by declaring to the inquisitors the names of his enemies. Nor did the defendant have the right to appoint a lawyer: he could only avail himself of a nominee, and that when the proceedings were well advanced.

Cases were seldom dismissed even when innocence was obvious

because the tribunals were under constant financial pressure to confiscate, if not to convict. Attempts were made to stabilize the income
of the various tribunals; and in 1559 Fernando de Valdés secured an
important concession. Paul IV, not noted for his friendship towards
Spain, allowed the revenues of one canonry in every cathedral chapter
to be set aside for the upkeep of the Inquisition. This was something,
but it was not enough. To maintain themselves, and to earn the money
they had to remit to the Suprema, the regional tribunals depended
throughout on the seizure of property belonging to the accused. They
fed on their victims. When in 1609 the moriscos were expelled from
the peninsula, the tribunal of Valencia, the area of densest settlement,
faced ruin.

Several attempts were made to limit the power of the Inquisition. Its
wide competence troubled the popes, who sought at various periods to
reserve for their own courts certain categories of cases. But their
efforts were effectively blocked by the Spanish Inquisition and its
royal patron. They salvaged jurisdiction only in the instances where a
bishop stood accused; and this explains why the trial of Archbishop
Carranza was eventually transferred to Rome. The cortes of Aragon
tried in 1510, and again in 1512, to reduce the power of the Holy Office
which, it was thought, infringed the liberties of the realm, an instance
of obscurantism in the service of enlightenment. The cortes failed.
The Inquisition drew its strength not merely from the approval of
successive monarchs. It was genuinely popular. The Old Christian
inhabitants of the peninsula looked upon it as a means of tracking
down insincere converts to the faith, in particular families of Jewish
extraction who had embraced Christianity in the fourteenth and
fifteenth centuries and who in many cases had prospered economically
as merchants, doctors, royal advisers. It promised retribution for
worldly success obtained under false pretences. The Holy Office
operated in much the same way against the Islamic population of Granada and Valencia once they had been forced, nominally at any rate, to
abandon the religion of their forefathers, although its treatment of
moriscos tended to be less harsh than that meted out to Judaizers
unless treason happened to be involved. As an institution the Inquisition attracted the support as much from men of substance as from the
lower orders. Those with any claim to wealth competed for the honour
of being named a familiar as this was considered a mark of distinction
in much the same way as the English gentry strove to be included on
the commission of the peace. By the seventeenth century one tribunal,

that of Galicia, had been taken over by the local nobility; and this may have happened elsewhere.

In the course of its existence, which spanned more than three centuries, the Inquisition changed in character and purpose. Each tribunal moreover had its own history, determined for the most part by the conditions of the region it served. Some were active, others somnolent. The resurgence of Judaic practice led to the establishment of the first tribunal, in Seville, and its repression monopolized inquisitorial energies for the next decade (*c*.1480–*c*.1492). The expulsion of the Jews, ordered by the Catholic Monarchs on 31 March 1492, in theory ended this problem whereas, in fact, it merely transformed it. Thereafter the Inquisition began to concern itself with the various manifestations of the 'New Learning' in the peninsula. As early as 1519 it was alerted to the existence of the *alumbrados* or 'illuminated ones', a select group of pious layfolk. They met in the households of the nobility; the duke of Infantado was a noted patron; and, although miniscule in number, the 'illuminated ones' included a high proportion of *conversos* whose existence had so preoccupied the Holy Office in previous years. As with other sects, the main ideas of this group can be glimpsed only partially, and then through the eyes of its principal critic. In 1525 the Inquisition of Toledo published an edict denouncing a series of beliefs particularly associated with the Illuminist or *alumbrado* movement. Time passed: the tribunal stayed its hand. Four years later it felt ready to strike. The principal *alumbrados* were rounded up, including the main inspiration of the cell, Isabel de la Cruz, and the man primarily responsible for the diffusion of her ideas, Pedro Ruiz de Alcaraz. He was a lay preacher who was self-taught in matters of religion. He lived at the court of the marquis of Villena at Escalona (Toledo) where he received a stipend from his host. In drawing up charges against the Illuminists, the tribunal experienced considerable difficulties. Out of a total of forty-eight counts laid against the *alumbrados*, two related to heresies of a Beghard nature, two were for holding specifically Lutheran views, while the remainder qualified as tending to hersey, or, in extreme cases, as 'mad'. The Illuminists stressed the idea of abandonment to the will of God, they remained sceptical of the value of good works, and they emphasized the practice of internal prayer. Many of their cherished beliefs derived from theories current in the previous century; but some had been incorporated into Lutheran theology and became automatically highly suspect. Modern opinion holds that the Illuminists owed their inspiration in the main to the tradition of Franciscan spirituality, promoted by, amongst others, Cardinal Cisneros, and, before that, by the Devotio Moderna. The *alumbrados* were forced to atone for their errors at the *auto de fe* held in Toledo on 22 July 1529; and in return for this public admission of guilt their lives were spared. Their punishment served notice to all that the Inquisition intended to be less indulgent in the future to those who chose to experiment in religious affairs.

In defence of their orthodoxy the *alumbrados* had invoked the name of Desiderius Erasmus, one of the major literary figures of the age. Although he never set foot in the peninsula, his writings occupy a special place in the spiritual history of early modern Spain. Cardinal Jiménez de Cisneros was anxious that he should collaborate on the great textual enterprise, the Polyglot Bible, which, after interminable delays, first went on sale in 1522. Even though the Dutchman refused the offer (and the money) his works swept into Spain when the accession of Charles as king opened the floodgates to the art and thought of northern Europe. For a short while thereafter the intellectual life of the peninsula became truly cosmopolitan. When Charles V returned to Spain in 1522 after his coronation at Aachen, and his only meeting with Martin Luther, at the diet of Worms (1521), Erasmian ideas seemed assured of an honoured place in Spanish culture. The ruling élite of both church and state proved receptive to the call for the reform of Christian life; and his writings received the open approval of the highest in the land. In 1527 Alonso Manrique, the Inquisitor General no less, accepted the dedication of the *Enchiridion Militis Christiani* (The Handbook of the Christian Knight), held by many to be the author's most seminal work. Critics of Erasmus demanded a special conference to consider his orthodoxy in the hope that such a gathering would find against him. The experts met on 27 June 1527, and continued to deliberate until 13 August without reaching any conclusion. The storm had been weathered. Erasmus stood vindicated.

His triumph was short-lived. Neither Louvain nor that other guardian of orthodoxy, the Sorbonne, were sympathetic towards the Dutchman's approach. The mendicant orders, in the peninsula as elsewhere, resented the anticlerical flavour of much of his writings, for instance *The Praise of Folly* (1514), directed very often against them in particular. Spanish textual critics had little difficulty in showing that his editions of sacred texts were inferior at many points to those prepared by more careful scholars. Most damaging of all, Erasmus could be regarded as Luther's spiritual mentor, even if the two had subsequently fallen out. The arrest of Juan de Vergara by the Inquisition in 1533 signalled the withdrawal of official endorsement for Erasmus's publications. The Erasmian interlude, so much at odds with what was to follow, had lasted barely a decade.

Juan de Vergara (1492–1557) had shown phenomenal linguistic gifts from an early age. Cardinal Cisneros, always keen to employ talent of his sort, had secured his services for the preparation of the Polyglot Bible; and Vergara continued in the cardinal's household as private secretary. He acted in a similar capacity for William of Croy and Alonso de Fonseca, each, in their turn, occupants of the primatial see of Toledo. During the course of his duties he travelled abroad extensively; and he was present, along with other Spaniards, at the historic diet of Worms. Whilst a member of the imperial entourage Vergara, a man of letters in his own right, made a point of cultivating Erasmus's friendship; and on his return to his native land he attempted to mediate between the Dutchman and his detractors, while clearly acting as a propagandist for his views. Unfortunately, the Inquisition was beginning to have doubts about men like Vergara; and the latter foolishly supplied the Holy Office with the opportunity to act. Juan de Vergara attempted to communicate with his brother, Bernardino Tovar, who had been arrested on a charge of heresy. For his pains, he himself was seized on 23 June 1533, and arraigned on a series of charges. The twenty-two counts under which he stood indicted amounted to a blanket denunciation for the crimes of Illuminism, Erasmian sympathies, and Lutheranism. The accused defended himself ably by denying the first and last charges while pointing out that Erasmus had been courted by the emperor and pope alike. For all the skill of his advocacy, Vergara did not escape condemnation. On 21 December 1535, he stood, amongst other penitents, in the Zocodover square in Toledo to hear his sentence read out. He had been found guilty of suspected heresy and with having attempted to pervert the course of (inquisitorial) justice. The Holy Office used the trial of Juan de Vergara, erstwhile secretary to cardinals and a canon of Toledo (a post he was allowed to retain), as a means of proclaiming that it insisted on strict orthodoxy and that, in the context, it would no longer tolerate Erasmian deviations. In this it merely set a trend which others were happy to follow.

Charles V was one example. The repeated failure to arrive at a compromise with the Protestants in Germany had brought about in the emperor's mind a gradual disenchantment with the idea of compromise which Erasmus had put forward. Once he retired to his former Spanish kingdoms in 1556 he devoted the little that was left of his life to ensuring that the peninsula would not go the way of the Holy Roman Empire. At some point in the early 1550s the Holy Office had reached the conclusion that the preservation of the realm from Lutheranism should be its first priority. Emperor and Inquisition awaited the chance to act; and a number of 'revelations' provided just the incentive that was required. In 1558 one Julián Hernández was caught red-handed trying to smuggle into Seville two barrels full of heretical books. Almost at the same time a Protestant 'cell' grouped around Carlos de Seso had been flushed out in Valladolid. This northern circle included Agstín Cazalla, at one time a preacher at Charles V's court, and a member of the luckless family of whom four were burnt at the stake and a further two reconciled. These occurrences, omens perhaps of a deep-seated infection, galvanized the authorities. The regent, Doña Juana, her father the emperor, and the Holy Office itself believed that extraordinary measures must be taken in hand. To purge all traces of heresy two *autos de fe* were thought necessary for Valladolid. Both were more lavish than anything yet seen. The first took place before the regent and the court on 21 May 1559. The second, staged on 8 October 1559, was attended by Philip II himself, newly returned from the Low Countries. Carlos de Seso had been held over to grace this royal occasion; and Philip is reported, reliably in spirit if not in fact, as telling this malefactor, contumacious to the last, that he, Philip, would bring the firewood with his own hands if his son had proved as wicked as the condemned. Not to be outdone by its northern counterpart, Seville provided the location for two equally splendid *autos*. The first was held on 24 September 1559 and it was on this occasion that Julián Hernández, the foolhardy colporteur, went to the stake. A second *auto de fe*, which took place on 22 December 1560, renewed the impression and the warning of the first, lest anyone had forgotten. Supplementary burnings were carried out in Zaragoza and Murcia.

The *autos de fe* of 1559, part festive, part monitory, revealed much about the politics and the spirit of the age. It remains an open question whether or not those arrested in Valladolid and Seville were true Lutherans. Even if they did qualify for this description, these miniscule groups may not have posed a real threat to the integrity of the Catholic faith. The crisis of 1559 may have been engineered in part by the Inquisitor General, Fernando de Valdés. Valdés had shown recently a haughtiness bordering on the reckless in refusing to contribute to the special levies needed to finance the last stages of the war against Henry II of France. Now that peace had been concluded, a threat to religion might offer the only way to recover royal favour. Conceivably, Valdés exaggerated the importance of men like Carlos de Seso to avert imminent disgrace. Yet even if the *autos*, and the sensational arrest of Bartolomé Carranza, the archbishop of Toledo, on a charge of heresy, might have been in doctrinal terms of dubious validity, both symbolized the new trend. Habsburg Spain opted to preserve its chosen identity by orthodoxy at home and isolation from abroad.

The Holy Office exercised both a remedial and a preventive function; and in its efforts to eliminate possible sources of error it was responsible for the Spanish version of the Index. Adrian of Utrecht began the practice of censoring or prohibiting books thought to be prejudicial to the faith. In his capacity as Grand Inquisitor, he placed a total ban on the sale (and reading) of Luther's works in the peninsula (1521). As the theological controversies raged and the ideological gulf grew ever wider, the ecclesiastical authorities throughout Catholic Europe realized that a systematic approach must be adopted to the problem of evaluating books, and, if need be, proscribing them. In 1546 the university of Louvain published a list of writings deemed heretical; and a year later this same catalogue was reissued in Spain. The Council of the Inquisition reproduced this in 1551 with, for the first time, a number of purely Spanish additions. Had a copy of the supplement been preserved, it would have thrown light on an important aspect of intellectual history.

Members of the Suprema rapidly came to the conclusion that the reproduction of an Index compiled by an overseas university with a number of Spanish titles tacked on left a great deal to be desired. On 17 August 1559 the Grand Inquisitor, Fernando de Valdés, brought out the first authentic Spanish Index which varied in significant detail from its Italian counterpart. Out of some 670 works banned, only 170 were actually written in Castilian. The burden of prohibition lay most heavily upon liturgical works and numerous versions (in Latin and the vernacular) of the Bible: and this emphasis reflected contemporary fears in Catholic circles that editions of Holy Scripture, translations of the same, and works of piety which had not been examined and approved by the teaching church were a particularly virulent source of confusion and outright heresy. Although the Inquisitor General took expert advice in the preparation of the Index, consulting amongst others Melchor Cano, it showed none the less signs of haste in composition. This may have resulted from Valdés's need to placate his royal master with a display of energy; and it formed part of the general hysteria which gripped Spain in the mid-sixteenth century and from which Valdés hoped to profit.

Not content with the action of its own inquisitors, the crown passed a law which further reduced the choice of reading-matter to which the public might have access. The so-called 'Law of Blood' (13 September 1559) made the importation of books printed in the vernacular an offence punishable by death unless a special licence had been obtained beforehand from the Council of Castile. This measure has often been considered in conjunction with another royal order published a few weeks later which recalled to Spain all the king's subjects who were attending foreign universities and declared that in future study abroad would only be permitted under special authorization (22 November 1559). Philip and his advisers were intent upon restricting the links between Spain and the outside world; and in the course of time their efforts proved disastrously successful.

The Index of Valdés served one overriding purpose—to ban the more obvious works of heresy. Yet once the panic created by the discovery of the Spanish 'Lutherans' had abated, the Inquisition appreciated how imperfect an instrument it was. It was rough-hewn and crude. Something both more balanced and comprehensive was required. In 1572 work started on a new version, one which would draw on the skill of the greatest scholars from the universities; and eleven years later it was ready for the edification and protection of the faithful. The Index of Quiroga, very much the brainchild of the Theology Faculty at Salamanca, appeared in two parts: first a list of books whose consultation was totally forbidden (8 July 1583), and then, a year later, a catalogue of works from which certain passages were to be deleted. Subsequently, the Index was updated to take account of recent literature and any change in requirements on the part of the Catholic church. Each new version took its name from the Inquisitor General of the day. The Index of Sandoval y Rojas appeared in 1612; that of Zapata in 1632; and the most restrictive of all, the Index of Sotomayor, in 1640.

Each generation of inquisitors put a different gloss on the nature of their task. Those who drew up Indices of the sixteenth century saw their function as the outright suppression of heretical texts or the expurgation of books which took an anticlerical line. They showed little interest in lascivious or scabrous publications. In the seventeenth century, and probably under the influence of the Jesuit experts whom it consulted, the Inquisition construed its remit in broader terms. Passages were expunged from the text of the *Celestina* for the first time in 1632. Eight years later the Index of Sotomayor, as a general policy, banned or demanded the removal of paragraphs or parts deemed injurious to morals. From 1608 the Holy Office extended its competence to the fine arts; and it sought guidance in such matters from men like Francisco Pacheco, a painter and theorist of repute, even if better known to history as Velázquez's father-in-law.

The Inquisition realized that it would have to enforce the Index. It had to assume police functions. As a consequence its officials carried out periodic inspections of bookshops to discover if any forbidden titles were in stock. Agents of the Holy Office were stationed at the ports to board visiting ships and inspect their cargoes in case they included prohibited material.

As an institution the Holy Office supervised ordinary belief and guided artistic taste, functions reminiscent of authoritarian governments in the twentieth century. It also became a ministry for ethnic affairs, and again the parallel with modern times is striking. The growth of racial intolerance in the peninsula at the close of the Middle Ages created a problem peculiar to Spain and Portugal. During the pogroms of 1391 many Jews embraced Christianity to save their lives; and later persecutions whipped up by the antisemitic preaching of men such as St Vicente Ferrer swelled the number of converts. It has also been suggested this apostasy was encouraged by a strong philosophical tendency within the Jewish community itself. This new strain regarded formal belief, whether in Judaism or Christianity, as subordinate to the contemplation of the higher truths. If acceptance of Christianity meant physical protection for the individual, then, according to this school, it should be welcomed for providing just that—and nothing more.

Those who decided to abandon 'the law of Moses' for 'that of Christ' were regarded as lost forever by those who remained loyal to Judaism. They were also loathed by the Old Christians, who doubted the sincerity of their conversion and envied their worldly success. This prosperity was often reflected by the high standing of the New Christians at court, and their ability to intermarry with the nobility.

Those who had nothing to boast of except their Christian ancestry referred to their new brothers as *conversos* or *marranos*, the latter a word of dubious etymology, but clearly derogatory in intention. The antagonism felt towards the *conversos* by the majority creed might in time have diminished, and a merger might have taken place between the 'Old' and the 'New'. The reasons why this fusion did not come about are to be found in the hostility, or prejudice, of the non-noble orders.

In 1449 the king's principal minister, Alvaro de Luna, imposed a special levy on the city of Toledo and appointed a *converso*, Alonso Cota, as the main collector. The attempt provoked a riot which soon led to rebellion against John II himself. At the head of the insurgents stood Pero Sarmiento, the royal governor of the city no less. One of his first acts as rebel commander was to issue a *Sentencia-Estatuto* (5 June 1449) which excluded fourteen named citizens from all public office in Toledo. This notorious document justified such disqualification on the grounds that those cited were of Jewish ancestry and therefore automatically 'infamed', condemned by reason of their origins. In effect, the *Sentencia-Estatuto* gave expression to the idea that all candidates to public office had to possess 'purity of blood'—they must be of Old Christian stock.

Initially, and much to its credit, the papacy denounced the *Sentencia* as unchristian in the bull *Humani Generis Inimicus* (24 September 1449), although its action may in part have been a response to political pressure from the Castilian mission in Rome. Shortly after, however, Nicholas V withdrew the bull, this time certainly at the instigation of the king's representatives. John II, who had at first opposed the idea of racial purity, agreed to the *Sentencia-Estatuto* as a means of recovering Toledo. The example spread like a contagion as cathedral chapters and public bodies one after the other sought to impose similar restrictions on entry to their membership. There is even a suggestion that in 1482 the Basque province of Guipúzcoa debarred all *conversos* from settlement or marriage within its boundaries. By 1541 the cathedral chapters of Seville, Córdoba, and León, to mention only the more noteworthy, had amended their statutes so that all aspirants to canonries had to establish their 'purity of blood'. Ironically, the last redoubt of *converso* power within the church proved to be the chapter of the cathedral of Toledo. It required the implacable fervour of the archbishop, Juan Martínez de Guijarro (Silíceo), a cleric of peasant and therefore untainted ancestry, and the expenditure of at least 80,000 ducats, before the canons of the primatial see gave way. With the acceptance by the Toledan chapter of the new qualifications for election (29 July 1547), purity became mandatory, and remained so in Toledo until 1865.

The exclusion of the *converso* from public life powerfully affected the subsequent development of the state. About 300,000 strong at the turn of the sixteenth century according to one estimate, the *conversos* were primarily an urban class. If Castile were to acquire a strong bourgeoisie, they would be amongst its most active members. The terror unleashed by the Inquisition particularly during the 1480s and 1490s helped to demoralize a community which had a great deal to contribute commercially and intellectually to the Christian kingdoms. It has further been suggested that the Jews and after them the *conversos* were amongst the foremost patrons of vernacular literature, especially in Catalonia and Valencia. The Inquisition's pursuit of the *conversos* and its deep suspicion of vernacular translations of scriptural works prevented the growth and extension of Catalan and Valencian as the language of the ruling classes.

Some *conversos*, rebuffed in their attempts at assimilation into the Christian state, may have felt compelled to seek refuge in the beliefs of their forefathers. This reversion, which never took place on the scale alleged, prompted the Catholic Monarchs to revive the Inquisition. Refurbished with new powers, the Holy Office had the task of hunting out those who sought to deny their Christian baptism, an eternal contract in the eyes of the church, and return to the Judaic rite. The formal expulsion of the Jewish communities in that *annus mirabilis* 1492 exacerbated the *converso* problem. Many Jews had remained steadfast in their faith in spite of external pressures and the corrosion of morale from within. The decree of 31 March 1492 offered them the choice of conversion or emigration. Perhaps as many as 150,000 chose to leave the peninsula, whilst another 50,000 opted for Christianity. Those who stayed behind brought fresh recruits to the *converso* class.

For all these disabilities, the *conversos* might still have escaped into the mass of Christian society had it not been for developments in Portugal. Many of the Spanish Jews had sought shelter there on their expulsion. To please his Spanish in-laws, or so it was alleged, Manuel the Fortunate presented his Jewish subjects in 1497 with the familiar choice of accepting Christianity or leaving; and a considerable number decided to conform rather than start (or resume) their wanderings. Even as New Christians, those of Jewish extraction found the climate more propitious in Portugal than in the neighbouring kingdom. The Portuguese monarchy did not establish its own Inquisition until 1536. The New Christians, whether recent immigrants or long-term residents, flourished as never before, consolidating their prominent position in both government and trade. Some of their number developed extensive trading links with Jewish communities abroad, particularly in the Low Countries. Although hard to quantify as a phenomenon, it appears that after the annexation of Portugal in 1580 the Jewish *conversos* joined with their countrymen in flooding the neighbouring kingdom and, of equal significance, Spain's colonial possessions. By the 1630s, or so it was claimed, Portuguese merchants of *converso* extraction had established a ring for the supply of slaves to Peru—and this was just one area of their activities. Under the count-duke of Olivares, Philip IV's leading minister from 1621 to 1643, the Habsburgs extended official protection to a consortium of New Christian bankers of Lusitanian origin; and used them to displace the Genoese as the main suppliers of credit to the monarchy after 1627. This influx of Portuguese *conversos* into Castile and her colonies after 1580 formed an important element in the development of trade and public finance. Yet it was of even greater consequence for the social history of the peninsula. Up to 1580, it has been argued, the Castilian *conversos* stood a chance of achieving full integration into Christian society; after that date any hope of assimilation vanished. The prominence, ubiquity, and success of the Portuguese New Christians revived all the prejudice against their class. Such feelings found a reflection in the work of the Inquisition which throughout the seventeenth and well into the eighteenth century continued to hunt down crypto-Jews. The various tribunals demonstrated a degree of harshness to those suspected of Judaism not matched in its treatment of other offenders, an indication, perhaps, that the *converso* was looked upon, above all others, as the real enemy of the faith.

The Inquisition interpreted its function in several ways. It stood, first and foremost perhaps, as the guardian of orthodoxy against the internal menace of crypto-Judaism and the external threat of Protestantism. But by the third quarter of the sixteenth century the Holy Office could be reasonably satisfied that the former had been contained, though liable to erupt at any moment, and the latter no longer posed a serious threat to the body of the faithful. Foreign sailors might be arrested for what they said when drunk in a tavern; but their remarks were hardly likely to influence—or even be understood by—

the natives. While retaining their traditional brief to eradicate heresy, the various tribunals began to act more as the custodians of morals. They developed a pronounced interest in matrimonial and sexual affairs. Those guilty of bigamy could expect to answer for their crime to the Holy Office. In Galicia the tribunal of Santiago de Compostela, founded as late as 1574, worked energetically to eliminate a number of popular misconceptions, amongst these the idea that 'simple fornication'—that is, sexual relations between the unmarried—was lawful. It showed the same vigour in seeking to disabuse the faithful of the notion that consorting with prostitutes was no sin. In its intrusion into the domain of private conduct, the Galician example was probably typical of other tribunals.

The Council of Trent had set great store by the teaching of the faithful. It was the bishop's duty to ensure that his flock understood at least the rudiments of Catholic doctrine; hence the establishment of seminaries, amongst other measures. The Inquisition, in the shape of its regional tribunals, aided the episcopal authorities by taking on what might be termed catechetical responsibilities. In the archdiocese of Toledo a programme was launched in the days of Archbishop Carillo (1446–82) to make certain that every communicant understood the meaning of the four basic prayers, the Credo, the Pater Noster, the Ave Maria, and the Salve Regina. In its periodic visits to the archdiocese the inquisitors both encouraged the scheme and monitored its progress. Amongst those who could read, a minority admittedly, the tribunal discovered over the period 1575–1650 that 86 per cent of those questioned comprehended the significance of these fundamental texts. The Inquisition acted as an agent, admittedly as a junior partner, in the internal Christianization of Catholic Europe.

Conclusion

T HE Middle Ages witnessed the creation of several Christian states in the Iberian peninsula. Although bound by a common purpose—the Reconquest—and a common religion, each developed its own tradition and either its own language or dialect. There was every reason for believing that they would continue to preserve their separate identities, as, indeed, in an attenuated form, they have to this day.

Widely interpreted as the beginnings of modern Spain, the marriage of Isabel to Ferdinand in 1469 did not appear so momentous to contemporaries. The spouses married for mutual convenience. Both anticipated difficult successions, the more so in the case of Isabel since she hoped to oust the rightful heiress. Dynastic unions for short-term ends were hardly new, even across the barrier of language. Bohemia would be linked with the crown of Hungary; while Poland, the most promiscuous kingdom in Europe, sold its favour at one time or another to France, Sweden, and the electorate of Saxony.

The Catholic Monarchs approved the plan to join their realms to Portugal as this would have called into being a federation of states justified both in terms of economic interest and geographical proximity. The attempt to bring about such a union failed on two occasions, but only by a narrow margin. When it became obvious that the succession would pass to a cadet member of the family, Ferdinand of Aragon did everything humanly possible to detach Aragon from Castile. He knew that his daughter, Juana, was in no fit state to rule; and he detested his son-in-law, Philip of Burgundy. Chance in its commonest form, death, thwarted all his efforts. Ferdinand in old age was incapable of producing an heir to outlive him. It was a sad conclusion to so lusty a career.

Even then the separation of the kingdoms might still have come about. The young archduke, Ferdinand of Austria, had passed his entire life at his grandfather's court; and he was certainly more popular than his elder brother, Charles, who had yet to set foot in the peninsula. Ferdinand of Aragon made no bones about his own preference. He wanted his namesake to inherit the lands of the Aragonese crown, if not those of Castile; and many in his court inclined to the same view. The regent appointed after the king's death, Cardinal-Archbishop Jiménez de Cisneros, stood foursquare against such a plan. For good or for ill, he had made up his mind to keep the kingdoms united on behalf of a youth he never lived to see. All attempts to place the archduke on the throne of Aragon came to nothing; and the cardinal's success in maintaining the union of the crown against all opposition makes him, and not the Catholic Monarchs, the true architect of modern Spain.

Charles of Ghent took formal possession of his Iberian inheritance without encountering any resistance. The nature of that bequest was decided during the first of the emperor's many journeys abroad. The distinctive features of the Habsburg state emerged in the aftermath of victory over the *comunero* and *Germanía* movements. This applied as much to economic as to political trends. The nobility, who unaided had defeated the urban militias, were quite prepared to see the Iberian kingdoms plunged into the turmoil of imperial adventures, correctly anticipating employment and enrichment for themselves and heedless of what the ultimate price might be. The defeat of the towns also confirmed the status of Castile as a primary producer. Calls for the protection of nascent industries could be safely dismissed; and all ideas of building a quality textile industry behind tariff walls abandoned. The wool clip continued to be sold on the open market to the highest bidder, a situation which brought most benefit to the rent rolls of the aristocracy and the ecclesiastical foundations.

The strategic interests of his Iberian kingdoms shifted fundamentally during Charles's reign, and not for the better. Before his accession, Castile and Aragon had been regional powers, each pursuing, with the odd lapse, policies which corresponded to immediate interest. Under the emperor, Castile assumed a continental role, with all that this meant in terms of additional obligation and expenditure. The military instrument—the tercio—which had been forged during the Italian wars of Ferdinand the Catholic came to be deployed in distant European theatres. The Spanish infantry played a decisive part in the battle of Mühlberg (1547). Had this represented an isolated foray into imperial affairs, the campaign might have become yet another glorious page in the annals of the Spanish tercios. In fact, it symbolized much more. Whatever the internal differences, the Habsburgs continued to visualize themselves as a single family with a shared purpose informed by a common faith. For the best part of a century Castile remained committed to the preservation of Austria as a major power in central Europe. Mühlberg and Metz represented the beginning of a policy which was to end at the White Mountain (1620) and Nördlingen (1634).

The attachment of Castile to the maintenance of the Austrian Habsburgs imposed a grievous, and unnecessary, burden upon the kingdoms of the peninsula. Yet this was not the only distortion in the pattern of Castilian interests which took place under Charles V. In a moment when emotion may have clouded judgement, the emperor willed the Netherlands upon his eldest son, Philip II. Given the distance between Castile and the Low Countries, given the fractious spirit of the nobility, given the religious and cultural complexities, the prospects for upholding Habsburg suzerainty were highly doubtful. The only type of regime likely to survive was one based on devolution in government and moderation in religion. Nothing could have been further from Philip's mind. He sought tight supervision of the Low Countries in terms of administration; and he did wish to make windows into men's souls. The king of Spain opted at the outset for centralization and strict orthodoxy. He preserved the confessional purity of his subjects at the cost of seven out of the original seventeen provinces. By the time he was prepared to concede the demand for political autonomy by installing his daughter and her husband as the rulers of the Low Countries (1598), the lands north of the great rivers had been lost forever. Worse still, in an attempt to re-impose his authority on the whole of the Netherlands, Philip was drawn deeper and deeper into French affairs, and a conflict he could not hope to win.

Castile bore the cost of the military campaigns in the Low Countries and, indeed, elsewhere. From 1572 onwards Philip II regularly spent on his armies in the Netherlands a multiple of Castile's annual income. Even when the scale of operations had been reduced, the amount earmarked for the Low Countries exceeded all reasonable limit. On 26 August 1593, royal auditors estimated that total expenditure for the calendar year 1594 would reach the figure of 6,113,496 ducats, and of this 3,999,996 ducats were allocated for use in the Netherlands. The Army of Flanders absorbed, according to the official projection, 65.4 per cent of the state's budget.

During the course of Philip II's reign the cost of warfare, in the Seventeen Provinces and in other theatres, far outstripped the income of the monarchy. To cover the shortfall the government had to borrow as never before. Genoa stood on hand to satisfy these unprecedented requirements. For approximately seventy years the 'old nobility' from the Ligurian republic answered the call for credit. As bankers the Genoese raised initially part, if not all, of their working stock in the Italian peninsula and, probably, southern Germany; but they soon grew adept at tapping the savings of Castilian depositors, a feat apparently beyond the ingenuity of the royal exchequer. Important though the Genoese were for the history of banking, their virtuosity prejudiced the well-being of the kingdom. Before 1560 those with surplus funds had a tradition of sinking them into loans for agricultural improvement (*censos*); after this date investors preferred the higher interest paid on state bonds (*juros*), issued primarily to pay for armies overseas. The savings of Castile—together, in all likelihood, with those of other Mediterranean countries—were drained off to finance war in the Low Countries. They were lost forever to the domestic economy.

The struggle by land and sea in northern Europe represented only one amongst many Habsburg commitments. Under Philip II the Indies received a form of government which lasted, with minor alterations, to the early nineteenth century. As colonial administrators, the Castilians were second to none; but unlike their rivals, they failed to exploit all the economic opportunities presented by empire. The settlements in the New World reproduced the principal features of the Castilian economy. They remained primary producers and extractors of metal. The profits of these transatlantic possessions flowed to countries more advanced than the motherland. It could not have been otherwise. Castile had no textile industry—or any other, for that matter—sufficiently developed to meet colonial demand. Supplies had to be obtained elsewhere. It was left to the Flemish, the French, and later the English to profit from the opening of the new and potentially limitless market. The failure of the *comuneros* was decisive. Under the early Habsburgs Castile, first amongst the European powers, asserted and then retained its control over lands separated by thousands of miles of sea. The metropolitan government also adjusted psychologically to its new responsibilities by accepting that its obligations were as much American as European. But it showed itself incapable of imposing a trading monopoly and excluding all competitors.

For a variety of reasons, the Castilian monarchs were also unable to preserve the diverse cultural tradition of the peninsula which had contributed so greatly to its prosperity in the Middle Ages. Already in the fifteenth century this chilling of the spirit was unmistakeable. Recent converts to Christianity were hounded from public office after 1449; and ever harsher forms of discrimination, some official, some social, applied against them. Toledo led the way; but other towns and corporations were willing enough to follow the example. Those who had chosen to remain faithful to the Jewish faith were expelled in 1492, the year of Columbus's first voyage to America—a venture partly financed with Jewish money. The Iberian kingdoms paid dearly for their intolerance. The trading community, never large in Castile, was further reduced; and in the sixteenth century, if not before, such tasks as it might have fulfilled were taken over by foreign entrepreneurs, the Genoese prominent amongst them. Castile's economic inadequacy stemmed as much from the decimation of the bourgeoisie as its treason.

The failure to comprehend grew if anything more pronounced under the Habsburgs. In Granada the morisco community produced a valuable export, silk; and in Valencia its counterpart made the land productive and the orchards bloom. In 1570–1 the silk industry was permanently damaged as a result of the policy of deportation adopted to break up the morisco population. In Valencia the mass expulsion of the Islamic workforce which took place in 1609 represented a disaster of the first order for the region, a fact which the patriarch Ribera, at one time a leading advocate of their removal, lived just long enough to acknowledge.

This constriction of the spirit applied almost as much to the Christians as it did to the minorities. However splendid the monuments of the Counter-Reformation, however noble the austerity of its mystics, as a movement it brought little benefit to Castile. The example of Archbishop Carranza, and a number of lesser mortals, acted as a timely reminder to the curious not to engage in loose theological speculation. The Index, while applied selectively at the outset, expanded into a general form of censorship which discouraged inquiry and innovation. More poorly endowed in terms of natural resources than her neighbours, Castile could ill afford to suppress the talent of its people.

During the sixteenth century Castile found itself in the forefront of European warfare and diplomacy. This prominence rested on two factors. The first was the relative freedom with which the early Habsburgs could tax the non-privileged orders of the kingdom. Until

1575 royal demands did not impose an undue strain: after that date, and as a consequence of the widening commitments in northern Europe, the crown became much harsher with its subjects. In 1590, to reconstruct its fleet, the monarch taxed for the first time consumption, by the introduction of the *millones*. Originally designed as an emergency measure, the levy rapidly developed into a permanent burden, and one periodically adjusted to take account of the monarchy's uncontrolled requirement for additional funds. By 1635 the *pecheros* (commoners) of Castile may have paid in real terms three times as much tax as their forefathers in 1575, in a time, moreover, of general economic malaise. The fiscal demands of Charles V and Philip II, in his early years, had not been excessive; and they coincided with a period of growth and demographic buoyancy. The exactions of the monarchy in the second half of Philip's reign became progressively harder to meet as the expansionary times of previous decades reached their end by 1590, if not by 1570.

The acquisition of Portugal confirmed the status of Castile as a great power, although both parties to the bargain were disappointed in their expectations. But the cause of Habsburg pre-eminence in the latter part of the sixteenth century is to be found elsewhere. The last Valois did not show the same authority or overweening ambition as their progenitors, Francis I or Henry II. Even if they had, the endemic civil wars effectively limited their freedom of action. As long as France remained prey to internecine strife, the Habsburg position could not be challenged. Yet this was a temporary state of affairs, unless, that is, France were dismembered. Such a solution crossed Philip's mind on several occasions. As it was, even at the end of eight civil wars, France under Henry IV brought its Habsburg rival back in 1598 to the position from which both sides had started in 1559. With perhaps double the population of Castile and a sounder agriculture, France was more likely to emerge the victor in any protracted conflict. Once the Bourbons had curbed their nobility and eliminated the Huguenot Commonwealth, then the Habsburg powers knew that France would resume its traditional role as a counterbalance to their pretensions. The greatness of Spain was predicated on the eclipse of France. As soon as this abnormal state had been corrected, the most Castile could hope for was to postpone its demotion.

Bibliography

A number of general introductions exist; John Lynch: *Spain under the Habsburgs*, vol. 1: *Empire and Absolutism, 1516—1598*; vol. 2: *Spain and America, 1598—1700* (Oxford, 1964, 1969), and John Elliott: *Imperial Spain, 1469—1716* (London, 1963) are two works which have long held the field as the standard accounts; and they should be read together, as their respective merits complement each other. Two more recent English contributions come from the pen of R. A. Stradling: *Europe and the Decline of Spain. A Study of the Spanish System, 1580—1720* (London, 1981); and Henry Kamen: *Spain, 1469—1714. A Society of Conflict* (London, 1983).

The history of Spain has also provided the inspiration for a work unique in the twentieth century and one which should be read as much for its literary merits as its historical insights, Fernand Braudel: *The Mediterranean and the Mediterranean World in the Age of Philip II* (2 vols, London, 1972–3). The Iberian peninsula also looms large in another great work from the same hand, idem: *Civilization and Capitalism, 15th—18th Century* (3 vols, London, 1981–4). Much can be learned about a country from the study of its daily life; and here, once again, the French historians have led the way. See the vivid recreation in Marcelin Defourneaux: *La Vie quotidienne en Espagne au siècle d'or* (Paris, 1964); and for life in the new colonies, Georges Baudot: *La Vie quotidienne dans l'Amérique espagnole de Philippe II, XVIe siècle* (Paris, 1981). Also of interest are Pedro Herrera Puga: *Sociedad y delincuencia en el Siglo de Oro* (Granada, 1971); Manuel Fernández Alvarez: *La sociedad espanola en el Siglo de Oro* (Madrid, 1984); and Claude Chauchadis: *Honneur, morale et société dans l'Espagne de Philippe II* (Paris, 1984).

Until the last decade it has been customary to look upon 'Spain' as a unified state without regard to its different regions. This reflected more the needs of successive regimes in the twentieth century than the historical realities of the sixteenth or the seventeenth century. This tendency has now been reversed, to the benefit of all concerned. Collected histories of at least six regions, or former 'kingdoms', are in progress; and many others are being planned. Those now available include *Historia de Castilla y León* (10 vols, Bilbao, 1982–); *Historia de Asturias* (10 vols, Castrillón, 1977–); *Historia general del País Vasco* (12 vols, San Sebastián, 1980–); *Historia de Andalucía* (8 vols, Madrid, 1980–1); *Historia de la Región Murciana* (10 vols, Murcia, 1980–); and *Historia de Granada* (3 vols, Granada, 1983).

Geographical setting

The geographical background can be studied at several levels. Spanish schoolchildren had the advantage of using the excellent J. Vicens Vives and Sobrequés Vidal: *España geográfica. Curso de geografía* (London, 1965). In French there is a good example of how beneficial the series 'Que sais-je?' can be, Michel Drain: *Géographie de la péninsule ibérique* (Paris, 1968). For a discussion in English, J. M. Houston: *The Western Mediterranean World* (3rd edn, London, 1971). More modern in its themes and approach is Catherine Delano-Smith: *Western Mediterranean Europe. An Historical Geography of Italy, Spain and Southern France* (New York, 1979). Spanish geographers have produced their own accounts which are scholarly, clear, and beautifully illustrated. See M. de Terán, L. Solé Sabaris *et al.*: *Geografía general de España*, vol. 1 (2nd edn, Barcelona, 1979); and Juan Vila Valenti: *La Península ibérica* (Barcelona, 1980). The authoritative description remains H. Lautensach: *Die Iberische Halbinsel* (Munich, 1964, Spanish trans., Barcelona, 1967). I found myself returning time and again to the masterly presentation in Naval Intelligence Division: BR 502 Geographical Handbook Series. *Spain and Portugal*, vol. 1: *The Peninsula* (London, 1941). Rainfall patterns have been discussed in Inocencio Font Tullot: *Climatología de España y Portugal* (Madrid, 1983).

The Catholic Monarchs

English readers have at their disposal J. F. O'Callaghan: *A History of Medieval Spain* (London, 1975); and, should more detail be required, J. N. Hillgarth: *The Spanish Kingdoms, 1250–1516*, vol. 2 (Oxford, 1978). For an interpretation of the entire course of Spanish medieval history, Angus MacKay: *Spain in the Middle Ages* (London, 1977), to which should be added the same author's 'Ritual and Propaganda in Fifteenth Century Castile' in *Past and Present* 107 (May 1985).

The reign of the Catholic Monarchs has been described ably by Joseph Perez: *L'Espagne des Rois catholiques* (Paris, 1971), and brilliantly by M. A. Ladero Quesada: *Historia de América latina*, vol. 1: *España en 1492* (Madrid, 1978)—probably the finest short treatment of the fifteenth century at present available. Students also have the benefit of two recent surveys Luis Suárez Fernández (ed.): *Los Trastámara y la unidad española (1369–1517)* (Madrid, 1982), volume 5 in a new series, *Historia general de España y América*. Secondly, Pilar Azcarate Aguilar-Amat: *Baja edad media: Los Trastámara, Historia de Castilla y León*, vol. 4 (Valladolid, 1984) which is more an attempt at popularization.

The Catholic Monarchs have been the subject of biographies by, amongst others, Tarsicio de Azcona: *Isabel la Católica. Estudio crítico de su vida y reinado* (Madrid, 1964); Felipe Fernández-Armesto: *Ferdinand and Isabella* (London, 1975); and Jaime Vicens Vives: *Fernando II de Aragón* (Zaragoza, 1962) for the early years of Isabel's consort.

The last Islamic emirate has been treated sympathetically in M. A. Ladero Quesada: *Granada. Historia de un país islámico (1232—1571)* (Madrid, 1969), and has been given greater coverage in Rachel Arié: *España musulmana (siglos VIII— XV)* (Barcelona, 1982). The 'reforms' of the Catholic Monarchs can be better appreciated from the work of Antonio Alvarez de Morales: *Las Hermandades. Expresión del movimiento comunitario en España* (Valladolid, 1974), and Angus MacKay: *Money, Prices and Politics in Fifteenth-Century Castile* (London, 1981) which presents a clear analysis and a convincing interpretation.

The emperor Charles V

The fullest modern treatment of the entire region is provided by Pierre Chaunu: *L'Espagne de Charles V* (2 vols, Paris, 1973). A Spanish survey which can still be consulted is Manuel Fernández Alvarez: *La España del Emperador Carlos V (1500—1558; 1517—1556)* (Madrid, 1966) which forms vol. 18 of the *Historia de España*, gen. ed. Ramón Menéndez Pidal.

The political situation in Castile on the eve of Charles's arrival is well presented in Excmo. Sr. Conde de Cedillo: *El Cardenal de Cisneros, gobernador del reino* (Madrid, 1921). Additional information is provided in Manuel Giménez Fernández: *Bartolomé de las Casas*, vol. 1: *Delegado de Cisneros para la reformación de las Indias* (Seville, 1953). The unfavourable impression created by Charles and his entourage on their appearance in Castile provides the subject of Andreas Walther: *Die Anfänge Karls V* (Leipzig, 1911). The rising of the *comuneros* has been narrated by H. L. Seaver: *The Great Revolt in Castile* (Boston, 1928). But the most convincing analysis comes from Joseph Perez: *La Révolution des 'comunidades' de Castile (1520—21)* (Bordeaux, 1970), which, for all its length, reads easily. An intelligent reconstruction of these same events can be found in Stephen Haliczer: *The Comuneros of Castile. The Forging of a Revolution, 1475—1521* (Wisconsin, 1981). One region at the heart of the rising has been studied in Luis Fernández Martín S.I., *El Movimiento comunero en los pueblos de Tierra de Campos* (León, 1979). The career of a turbulent cleric who ended his days on a gibbet has been recounted by Alfonso M. Guilarte: *El Obispo Acuña. Historia de un comunero* (Valladolid, 1979) while the political implications of the rising have been explored in Juan Ignacio Gutiérrez Nieto: *Las comunidades como movimiento antiseñorial* (Barcelona, 1973). The latter has also examined the antecedents to the urban rebellion in two important articles, 'Semántica del término "comunidad" antes de 1520. Las asociaciones juramentadas de defensa' in *Hispania* 136 (1977); and 'En torno al problema de la significación del termino "comunidad" en 1520' in *V Simposio Toledo Renacentista (Toledo 24—26 Abril 1975)*, vol. 2 (Madrid, 1980). For the military aspects of these events, José Miranda Calvo: *Reflexiones militares sobre las comunidades de Castilla* (Toledo, 1984).

The uprising in the eastern provinces has been studied by Ricardo García

Cárcel on several occasions. See his *Moriscos i Agermanats* (Valencia, 1974), *Las Germanías de Valencia* (Barcelona, 1975), *La revolta de les Germanies* (Valencia, 1981). The consequences are spelt out in the relevant chapters of Joan Reglà, Joan Fuster, Sebastian García Martínez *et al*. (eds): *Història de País Valencià*, vol. 3: *De les Germanies a la Nova Planta* (Barcelona, 1975). For Catalonia and the reasons for its (enforced) tranquillity, Eulàlia Duran; *Les Germanies als països catalans* (Barcelona, 1982).

For modern assessments of Charles V, and a general review of the literature, three recent contributions form the best starting-point. Alfred Kohler: 'Karl V' in *Neue Deutsche Biographie*, vol. 11 (Berlin, 1977); Heinrich Lutz: 'Karl V—Biographische Probleme' in Grete Klingenstein, H. Lutz *et al*. (eds): *Biographie u. Geschichtswissenschaft* (Vienna, 1979); and idem: 'El Imperio Romano-Germánico y España en la época de Carlos V' in *Actas del Simposio sobre Posibilidades y limites de una historiografía nacional* (Madrid, 1984). The best biographies are those of Karl Brandi: *Charles V* (London, 1939) and Ghislaine de Boom: *Charles V, prince des Pays-Bas* (Brussels, 1952) to which might be added Henri Lapeyre: *Charles-Quint* (Paris, 1971) and Royal Tyler: *The Emperor Charles V* (London, 1938).

For interpretations of Charles's policies see Ramón Menéndez Pidal: *Idea imperial de Carlos V* (Buenos Aires, 1941). This should be followed by the 'classic' account of Peter Rassow in a series of works which include *Die Kaiser-Idee Karls V dargestellt an der Politik der Jahre 1528—1540* (Berlin, 1932), *Die politische Welt Karls V* (Munich, 1942), *Karl V. Der letzte Kaiser des Mittelalters* (Göttingen, 1957), *Die geschichtliche Einheit des Abendlandes* (Cologne, 1960). A different reading, more troubled and nuanced, has been submitted by Heinrich Lutz in his *Christianitas Afflicta. Europa, das Reich, u. die päpstliche Politik im Niedergang der Hegemonie Karls V (1552—1556)* (Göttingen, 1964).

The female members of the Habsburg family, most of whom had tragic lives, have attracted a sympathetic biographer who has the additional skill of being able to recreate the atmosphere of the courts over which they presided. See Ghislaine de Boom: *Eléonore d'Autriche, Reine de Portugal et de France* (Brussels, 1943); idem: *Marguerite d'Autriche* (Brussels, 1945); idem: *Marie de Hongrie* (Brussels, 1956).

The Emperor's dealings with his brother are described in two articles. Ernst Laubach: 'Karl V, Ferdinand I. u. die Nachfolge im Reich' in *Mitteilungen des Österreichischen Staatsarchiv* 29 (1976) and Christian Thomas: ' "Moderación del Poder". Zur Entstehung des geheimen Vollmacht für Ferdinand I. 1531' in *Mitteilungen des Österreichischen Staatsarchiv* 27 (1974).

Since German affairs do figure so prominently it is essential to have some acquaintance of their main outlines. For this see Bernd Moeller: *Deutschland im Zeitalter der Reformation* (Göttingen, 1977) and Heinrich Lutz (ed.): *Das Römisch-Deutsche Reich im politischen System Karls V* (Munich–Vienna, 1982).

Individual commitments and specific problems can be studied through

Giancarlo Sorgia: *La politica nord-africana di Carlo V* (Padua, 1963). The historic choice before the Emperor in 1544 has been well laid out in Federico Chabod: '¿Milan o los Paises Bajos? Las discusiones en España sobre la "Alternativa" de 1544' in *Carlos V (1500—1558)*. *Homenaje de la Universidad de Granada* (Granada, 1958), an article published in at least two other places. The Italian possessions have formed the subject of G. Coniglio: *Il regno di Napoli al tempo di Carlo V. Amministrazione e vita economico-sociale* (Naples, 1951), and by the same author *Aspetti della società meridionale nel secolo 16°* (Naples, 1978). Federico Chabod: *Lo stato e la vita religiosa a Milano nell' epoca di Carlo V* (Turin, 1971) collects together three previous studies; and it has far more to say than Vincente de Cárdenas y Vincent: *La herencia imperial de Carlos V en Italia: el Milanesado* (Madrid, 1978).

For the disastrous campaign which spelt the end for Charles see Gaston Zeller: *Le Siège de Metz par Charles-Quint (oct.—déc. 1552)* (Nancy, 1943). For the circumstances of the abdication nothing has ever surpassed L. P. Gachard: *Retraite et mort de Charles-Quint au monastère de Yuste* (3 vols, Brussels, 1854), which assembles the relevant documents and offers the best interpretation.

The discovery and settlement of the New World

The history of Latin America in colonial times has undergone a resurgence, attributable in part to its contemporary importance in world affairs. In English a distinguished collection of surveys is available. They range from the masterly Clarence H. Haring: *The Spanish Empire in America* (New York, 1947); Charles Gibson: *Spain in America* (New York, 1966); J. H. Parry: *The Spanish Seaborne Empire* (London, 1966) to the modern James Lockhart and Stuart B. Schwartz: *Early Latin America. A History of Colonial Spanish America and Brazil* (Cambridge, 1983); Leslie Bethell (ed.), *The Cambridge History of Latin America*, vols 1–2, *Colonial Latin America* (Cambridge, 1984), and Lyle McAlister: *Spain and Portugal in the New World, 1492—1700* (Minneapolis, 1984). None of the more recent studies supersedes the older ones; they merely indicate the shifts in historical interest.

Summaries in other languages have been provided by M. Hernández Sánchez-Barba: *Historia de América* (3 vols, Madrid, 1981); Guillermo Céspedes del Castillo: *América hispánica (1492—1898)* (Barcelona, 1983); Francisco Morales Padrón: *Historia del descubrimiento y conquista de América* (4th edn, Madrid, 1981); Manuel Lucena Salmoral (gen. ed.): *Historia general de España y América*, vol. 7, *El descubrimiento y la fundación de los reinos ultramarinos hasta fines del siglo XVI* (Madrid, 1982).

The French contribution can be measured from Pierre Chaunu: *Conquête et explorations des Nouveaux Mondes* (Paris, 1969); Marianne Mahn-Lot: *Una aproximación histórica a la conquista de la América española* (Barcelona, 1977); and Bartolomé Bennassar: *La América española y la América portuguesa, siglos XVI—XVIII* (Madrid, 1980).

For an eastern European view, the underrated Tibor Wittman: *Historia de América Latina* (2nd edn, Budapest, 1980); and I. P. Maguidóvich: *Historia del descubrimiento y exploración de Latinoamérica* (Moscow, 1965), which has useful maps. On the background to the discoveries the literature is overwhelming. A start can be made with Michel Mollat: *Les Explorateurs du XIIIᵉ au XVIᵉ siècle. Premiers régards sur des mondes nouveaux* (Paris, 1984). Charles Verlinden: *The Beginnings of Modern Colonization* (Ithaca, N. Y., 1970) has a valuable discussion on Ferdinand van Olmen and his attempt to sail westward. A far-ranging examination of the problems can be found in Bibiano Torres Ramírez and José Hernández Palomo (eds): *Andalucía y América en el siglo XVI. Actas de las II Jornadas de Andalucía y América* (2 vols, Seville, 1983).

Navigational problems can be looked at through José María López Piñero: *El arte de navegar en la España del Renacimiento* (Barcelona, 1979); José María Martínez-Hidalgo: *Columbus' Ships* (Barre, Mass., 1966, Spanish trans. Barcelona, 1969). Luis de Albuquerque: *Curso de história de náutica* (Coimbra, 1970). Much information is also available in A. Teixeira da Mota (ed.): *A Viagem de Fernão de Magalhães e a questão das Molucas* (Lisbon, 1975).

Two books written from a partisan viewpoint make important contributions: Manuel Fernandes Costa: *As navegações atlânticas no séc. XV* (Lisbon, 1979); and idem: *O descobrimento da América e o tratado de Tordesilhas* (Lisbon, 1980), by stressing what Columbus learned from his Portuguese associates.

On the financing of the voyages and the development of the early trade, Jacques Heers: 'Los genoveses en la sociedad andaluza del siglo XV: orígenes, grupos, solidaridades' in *Actas del II Coloquio de Historia Medieval. Andalucía (Sevilla 8/10 Abril, 1981)* (Seville, 1982); Hermann Kellenbenz: 'Die Finanzierung der spanischen Entdeckungen' in *Vierteljahrsschrift für Sozial- u. Wirtschaftsgeschichte*, 69(2) (1982); Jacques Heers: 'Le Rôle des capitaux internationaux dans les voyages de découvertes aux XVᵉ et XVIᵉ siècles' in *Aspects internationaux de la découverte océanique aux XVᵉ et XVIᵉ siècles. Actes du Cinquième Colloque international d'Histoire maritime* (Paris, 1966); Enrique Otte: 'Das Genuesische Unternehmertum und Amerika unter den Katholischen Königen' in *Jahrbuch für Geschichte Lateinamerikas* 2 (1965), and idem: 'Träger u. Formen der wirtschaftlichen Erschliessung Lateinamerikas im 16. Jhdt.' in *Jahrbuch für Geschichte Lateinamerikas* 4 (1967); Ruth Pike: *Enterprise and Adventure. The Genoese in Seville and the Opening of the New World* (Ithaca, N. Y., 1966).

On the subject of Christopher Columbus only a small selection can be offered. Jacques Heers: *Christophe Colomb* (Paris, 1981) is good on the Italian aspect, but less sure in Spanish matters. The most penetrating short studies remain Charles Verlinden: *Kolumbus. Vision u. Ausdauer* (Göttingen, 1962) which is particularly alive to the medieval features of his outlook, as expressed, for instance, in the Capitulations of Santa Fe, and Richard Konetzke: *Entdecker u. Eroberer Amerikas* (Frankfurt-am-Main, 1963) which is possibly the finest work of this distinguished scholar. Two recent books throw light on the Admiral's inspiration and motives: Alain Milhou: *Colón y su mentalidad mesiánica en el ambiente franciscanista español* (Valladolid, 1983) and Juan Pérez de Tudela y Bueso: *Mirabilis in altis. Estudio crítico sobre el orígen y significado del proyecto descubridor de Cristobal Colón* (Madrid, 1983). A life of the second Admiral of the Ocean Sea is in progress: Luis Arranz: *Don Diego de Colón, Almirante, Virrey y Gobernador de las Indias*, vol. 1 (Madrid, 1982). On the construction of the maritime links, consult the leisurely and splendid narrative of Clarence H. Haring: *Trade and Navigation between Spain and the Indies in the time of the Habsburgs* (Cambridge, Mass., 1918). Then, for the institutional aspects, Ernst Schäfer: *El Consejo Real y Supremo de las Indias* (2 vols, Seville, 1935–47). Emigration can be studied from José Luis Martínez: *Pasajeros de Indias. Viajes transatlánticos en el siglo XVI* (Madrid, 1983). The best contemporary account of the passage comes from Joseph de Veitia Linaje: *Norte de la contratación de las Indias Occidentales* (Seville, 1672; repr. Madrid, 1981).

For experience of colonization and the early settlements, Eduardo Aznar Vallejo: *La integración de las Islas Canarias en la Corona de Castilla (1478–1520)* (Seville–La Laguna, 1983); Felipe Fernández-Armesto: *The Canary Islands after the Conquest. The making of a colonial society in the early sixteenth century* (Oxford, 1982). Then, for the first white presence in the Americas, Ursula Lamb: *Fray Nicolás de Ovando. Gobernador de las Indias (1501–1509)* (Madrid, 1956); I. A. Wright: *The Early History of Cuba, 1492–1586* (New York, 1916); Frank Moya Pons: *La Española en el siglo XVI (1493–1520)* (2nd edn, Santiago, Dominican Rep., 1973); Eugenio Fernández Méndez: *Las encomiendas y esclavitud de los indios de Puerto Rico, 1508–1550* (5th edn, San Juan, 1976).

For Aztec society, the general setting has been provided by R. C. Padden: *The Hummingbird and the Hawk: Conquest and Sovereignty in the Valley of Mexico, 1503–1541* (New York, 1970), and (a historical figure in his own right) Jacques Soustelle: *L'Univers des Aztèques* (Paris, 1979). Christian Duverger: *La Fleur létale. Economie du sacrifice aztèque* (Paris, 1979). George A. Collier, Renato I. Rosaldo, and John D. Wirth: *The Inca and Aztec States, 1400–1800. Anthropology and History* (New York–London, 1982). H. R. Harvey and Hanns J. Prem (eds): *Explorations in Ethnohistory. The Indians of Central Mexico in the Sixteenth Century* (Albuquerque, N. M., 1984). A fine account of the warrior mentality can be found in I. Clendinnen: 'The Cost of Courage in Aztec Society' in *Past and Present* 107 (May 1985).

The more important of the narratives relating to the conquest of America are in the process of publication in cheap and attractive editions. They form part of the twenty-volume series Crónicas de América (Madrid, 1984–6). Individual titles are referred to in the subsequent text.

No definitive biography of Hernán Cortés exists. The conqueror's own version of events was delivered in his letters to Charles V. For these, A. R.

Pagden (ed.): *Hernán Cortés. Letters from Mexico* (Oxford, 1972). For the most famous contemporary account, Bernal Diaz del Castillo: *Historia verdadera de la conquista de Nueva' España*, ed. M. León-Portilla, Crónicas de América (Madrid, 1984). C. Harvey Gardiner: *Naval Power in the Conquest of Mexico* (Austin, Tex., 1956) reveals one aspect of Cortés's resource. His personal gain is described by G. Michael Riley: *Fernando Cortés and the Marquesado in Morelos, 1522–1547* (Albuquerque, N. M., 1973). Most of Cortés's lieutenants were brave, tough, and highly unlikeable. For the careers of two, C. Harvey Gardiner: *The Constant Captain. Gonzalo de Sandoval* (Carbondale, Ill., 1961) and John Eoghan Kelly: *Pedro de Alvarado, conquistador* (Princeton, 1932). For the literature which they may have heard, if not actually read, I. A. Leonard: *Books of the Brave* (Cambridge, Mass., 1949).

On the extension of the frontier, A. Grove Day: *Coronado's Quest* (Berkeley, 1940); J. Lloyd Mecham: *Francisco de Ibarra and Nueva Vizcaya* (Durham, N. C., 1927); Philip Wayne Powell: *Soldiers, Indians and Silver: The Northward Advance of New Spain, 1550–1600* (Berkeley, 1952); idem: *Mexico's Miguel de Caldera. The Taming of America's First Frontier (1548–1597)* (Tucson, Ariz., 1977).

The establishment of royal government has been examined by Arthur Scott Aiton: *Antonio de Mendoza: First Viceroy of New Spain* (New York, 1927); J. H. Parry: *The Audiencia of New Galicia in the Sixteenth Century* (Cambridge, 1948); Mª Justina Sarabia Viejo: *Don Luis de Velasco: Virrey de Nueva España, 1550–1564* (Seville, 1978); Antonio F. Garcia-Abasolo: *Martín Enríquez y la reforma de 1568 en Nueva España* (Seville, 1983); Guillermo Porras Muñoz: *El gobierno de la ciudad de Mexico en el siglo XVI* (Mexico, DF, 1982). For the isthmus, Mª del Carmen Mena García: *La sociedad de Panama en el siglo XVI* (Seville, 1984).

Ranching and mining formed the twin pillars of New Spain's economy. These two activities have been examined in two brilliant works, François Chevalier: *La Formation des grands domaines au Méxique* (Paris, 1952) and its revision for the Spanish edition published in Mexico, 1976; and the complementary study by P. J. Bakewell: *Silver Mining and Society in Colonial Mexico, Zacatecas 1546–1700* (Cambridge, 1971). The same author has contributed a chapter on mining in colonial Spanish America which can be found in the *Cambridge History of Latin America* (1984). For later developments, José F. de la Peña: *Oligarquía y propriedad en Nueva España, 1550–1624* (Mexico, DF, 1983); Francisco de Solano: 'La tenencia de la tierra en Hispanoamérica. Proceso de larga duración. El tiempo virreinal' in *Revista de Indias* 43 (1983). For a specific problem which nearly destroyed the colony, L. B. Simpson: *The Encomienda in New Spain* (Berkeley, 1950). For the subsequent history of mining (mainly in the seventeenth century), Robert C. West: *The Mining Community in Northern New Spain. The Parral Mining District* (Berkeley, 1949).

The fate of the indigenous peoples under the new dispensation can hardly be described adequately. The first, and undoubtedly most famous, attempt is

Bartolomé de las Casas: *Brevísima relación de la destrucción de las Indias*, ed. André Saint-Lu (2nd edn, Madrid, 1984). Modern calculations of population loss have been influenced by W. W. Borah and S. F. Cook: *The Aboriginal Population of Central Mexico on the Eve of the Spanish Conquest* (Berkeley, 1963); but a useful corrective has come from A. Zambardino: 'Mexico's Population in the Sixteenth Century: Demographic Anomaly or Mathematical Illusion?' in *Journal of Interdisciplinary History* 11 (1980). If Zambardino is right, then his findings invalidate most of the views expressed in William M. Denevan (ed.): *The Native Population of the Americas in 1492* (Madison, 1976). How the Indians fared under their new masters has been graphically depicted by Charles Gibson: *The Aztecs under Spanish Rule* (Stanford, 1964) and Nancy M. Farriss: *Maya Society under Colonial Rule. The Collective Enterprise of Survival* (Princeton, 1984).

The defence of the colonial monopoly from European intruders has attracted a voluminous literature. Antonio Rumeu de Armas: 'Franceses y españoles en el Atlántico en tiempos del Emperador' in *Charles-Quint et son temps* (Paris, 1959); Frédéric Mauro: 'Monopole ibérique et ambitions françaises' in F. Braudel (ed.): *Le Monde de Jacques Cartier: l'aventure au XVIᵉ siècle* (Montreal–Paris, 1984); Henry Folmer: *Franco-Spanish Rivalry in North America, 1524—1763* (Glendale, Calif., 1953); C.-A. Julien: *Les Français en Amérique* (Paris, 1946). Other interlopers are discussed in Paul E. Hoffman: *The Spanish Crown and the Defense of the Caribbean, 1535—1585* (Baton Rouge, La., 1980); Eugene Lyon: *The Enterprise of Florida. Pedro Menéndez de Avilés and the Spanish Conquest of 1565—68* (Gainesville, Fla., 1976); K. R. Andrews: *The Spanish Caribbean: Trade and Plunder, 1530—1630* (London, 1978); idem: *Drake's Voyages* (London, 1967); idem: *Trade, Plunder and Settlement: maritime enterprise and the genesis of the British Empire* (Cambridge, 1984). For the system of static defence, José Mañas Martínez (gen. ed.): *Puertos y fortificaciones en América y Filipinas* (Madrid, 1985) with the *Actas* of the corresponding symposium also published in Madrid, 1985. The career of the master builder has been examined in Diego Angulo Iñiguez: *Bautista Antonelli: Las fortificaciones americanas del siglo XVI* (Madrid, 1942), which can be supplemented by Juan Manuel Zapatero: *Historia de las fortificaciones de Cartagena de Indias* (Madrid, 1979). The sixteenth-century history of this town has received ample coverage from María del Carmen Gómez Pérez: *Pedro de Heredia y Cartagena de Indias* (Seville, 1984) and María del Carmen Borrego Plà: *Cartagena de Indias en el siglo XVI* (Seville, 1983).

Pierre and Huguette Chaunu: *Séville et l'Atlantique (1504—1650)* (Paris, 1955–60) dominates all research and, one might be tempted to think, the actual trade itself. Its 8 volumes will blunt the enthusiasm of all but the keenest. Fortunately, the principal author has taken to explaining his own work, as in *Histoire de l'Amérique latine* (7th edn, Paris, 1976) and *Séville et l'Amérique, XVIᵉ— XVIIᵉ siècles* (Paris, 1977). Eufemio Lorenzo Sanz: *Comercio de España con*

América en la época de Felipe II (2 vols, Valladolid, 1979) makes good use of the archives at Simancas. Valuable studies of particular aspects can be found in Guillermo Lohmann Villena: *Les Espinosa: une famille d'hommes d'affaires en Espagne et aux Indes à l'époque de la colonisation* (Paris, 1968); Enrique Otte: *Las perlas del Caribe: Nueva Cádiz de Cubagua* (Caracas, 1977); Georges Scelle: *La Traite negrière aux Indes de Castille* (Paris, 1906); Rolando Mellafe: *Breve historia de la esclavitud en América latina* (Mexico, DF, 1973). Memorable portraits of the obscure and the unscrupulous, all the better for being in their own words, are presented in James Lockhart and Enrique Otte (eds): *Letters and People of the Spanish Indies* (Cambridge, 1976).

The exploitation of Latin America as a third world country has been much dwelt on by historians, and, latterly, western bankers. Much good sense has been spoken by Herbert S. Klein in his 'Ultimas tendencias en el estudio de la hacienda hispanoamericana' in *Papeles de Economía Española* 20 (Madrid, 1984). For other views, A. R. Barbosa Ramírez: *La estructura económica de la Nueva España (1519—1810)* (Mexico, DF, 1977); Alejandra Moreno Toscano and Enrique Florescano: *El sector externo y la organización espacial y regional de México (1521—1910)* (Puebla, 1977); Marcelo Carmagnani: *Ensayos sobre el desarrollo económico de México y América Latina (1500—1975)* (Mexico, DF, 1979). A restrained presentation of the 'exploitative' view can be found in Stanley J. and Barbara H. Stein: *The Colonial Heritage of Latin America* (New York, 1970). Less inhibited expressions come from Hans Jürgen Puhle (ed.): *Lateinamerika—Historische Realität u. Dependencia Theorien* (Hamburg, 1976) and Carlos Sempat Assadourian: *El sistema de la economía colonial* (Lima, 1982).

In comparing the Spanish with the English colonial experience I have perhaps relied too much on Ralph Davis: *English Merchant Shipping and Anglo-Dutch Rivalry in the Seventeenth Century* (London, 1975) and Samuel F. Manning: *New England Masts and the King's Broad Arrow* (London, 1980).

How the white man imposed his religion, his language, and his customs— the process of acculturalization, in the jargon—has stimulated some outstanding work. Pierre Ricard: *The Spiritual Conquest of Mexico* (Berkeley, 1966, from the original, Paris, 1933) has come in for criticism in recent years; but its status as a classic remains undiminished. I much enjoyed G. Kubler: *Mexican Architecture in the Sixteenth Century* (2 vols, New Haven, 1948) which has almost as much to say about the missions as it does about the subject of the title. Two further works from a vast output might also be consulted: Johann Specker: *Die Missionmethode in Spanisch-Amerika im 16. Jhdt.* (Beckenried, 1953) and José María Kobayashi: *La educación como conquista* (Mexico, DF, 1974).

The Inca empire has exercised a permanent fascination for western historians. Edward P. Lanning: *Peru before the Incas* (New York, 1967) gives an account of the geography and the earlier civilizations. Henry F. Dobyns and

Paul L. Doughty: *Peru. A Cultural History* (New York, 1976) continues the story after the arrival of Pizarro.

The Instituto de Estudios Peruanos has sponsored much of the best research carried out in recent times and some of the findings have been presented in Juan Mejía Baca (ed.): *Historia del Perú* (5th edn, Barcelona, 1984). Vols 1–4 deal with the period under discussion. Several native historians are to be singled out for the excellence of their work. Franklin Pease G.Y.: *Los últimos Incas del Cuzco* (Lima, 1972); idem: *El dios creador andino* (Lima, 1973); idem: *Del Tawantinsuyu a la historia del Perú* (Lima, 1978). Franklin Pease's introduction to Felipe Guamán Poma de Ayala: *Nueva coronica y buen gobierno* (2 vols, Caracas, 1980) should also be consulted. The late Raúl Porras Barrenechea was another great interpreter of the chronicles. See his *Crónistas del Perú (1528—1650)* (Lima, 1962) and *Mito, tradición e historia del Perú* (2nd edn, Lima, 1969). Further contributions have been made by John V. Murra: *Formaciones económicas y políticas del mundo andino* (Lima, 1975); and idem: *La organización económica del estado inca* (Mexico, DF, 1978); and Jürgen Golte: *La racionalidad de la organización andina* (Lima, 1980).

Most of what is known about Francisco Pizarro has been gathered and published (posthumously) by Raúl Porras Barrenechea in his *Pizarro* (Lima, 1978). An account of the initial conquest, old but serviceable, has been provided by Philip Ainsworth Means: *The Fall of the Inca Empire* (London, 1932). Whether or not men like Pizarro and Almagro would have dealt honestly with one another is open to doubt. Josep M. Barnadas: *Charcas. Orígenes históricos de una sociedad colonial, 1535—1565* (La Paz, 1973) explains a basic cause of conflict—the search for profitable *encomiendas*.

On the establishment of a European society, James Lockhart: *Spanish Peru, 1532—1560* (Madison, 1968). On the dour and brutal man who established effective royal control for the next two centuries, Roberto Levillier: *Don Francisco de Toledo, supremo organizador del Perú: su vida, su obra (1515—1582)* (Madrid, 1935). Arthur Franklin Zimmerman: *Francisco de Toledo. Fifth Viceroy of Peru, 1569—1581* (Caldwell, Idaho, 1938) is another solid piece of research. For an example of his great survey of the Andean viceroyalty Noble David Cook (ed.): *Tasa de la visita general de Francisco de Toledo* (Lima, 1975). For a review of this and later periods, Raúl Porras Barrenechea: *El Perú virreinal* (Lima, 1973). In the context of white society a wayward but stimulating article deserves notice: David E. Vassberg: 'Concerning Pigs, the Pizarros, and the Agro-Pastoral Background of the Conquerors of Peru' in *Latin American Research Review* 13 (3) (1978).

The fate of the Indian population, assailed by a force they could not under-stand, has been described by John Hemming: *The Conquest of the Incas* (rev. edn, London, 1983) and Nathan Wachtel: *The Vision of the Vanquished* (Brighton, 1977). For regional studies, Steve J. Stern: *Peru's Indian Peoples and the Challenge of Spanish Conquest* (Madison, 1982) and Karen Spalding:

Huarochirí: An Andean Society under Inca and Spanish Rule (Stanford, 1984). The demographic implosion has been soberly traced in Noble David Cook: *Demographic Collapse. Indian Peru, 1520–1620* (Cambridge, 1981).

As a principal point of contact between white and Indian societies, mining provoked, at least in part, the reduction in numbers. It also became the main pillar of the colonial economy. On the subject, consult D. A. Brading and Harry E. Cross: 'Colonial Silver Mining: Mexico and Peru' in *Hispanic American Historical Review* 52 (1972). Then two surveys of the entire field, Alvaro Jara: *Tres ensayos sobre economía hispanoamericana* (Santiago de Chile, 1966); Carlos Sempat Assadourian *et al.*: *Minería y espacio económico en los Andes.Siglos XVI–XX* (Lima, 1980). Much can be gained about how silver was extracted from Bernhard Neumann: *Die Metalle. Geschichte, Vorkommen, und Gewinnung* (Halle a/S., 1904). The output of the Peruvian mines has been established by Peter J. Bakewell: 'Registered Silver Production in the Potosí District, 1550–1735; in *Jahrbuch für Geschichte Lateinamerikas* 12 (1975). How the refined ore was brought from the mountains to the coast is studied by Gwendolin B. Cobb: 'Supply and Transportation for the Potosí Mines, 1545–1640' in *Hispanic American Historical Review* 29 (1949).

Peru was also able to cover its own requirements for mercury. On this grim subject, Arthur Preston Whitaker: *The Huancavélica Mercury Mine* (Cambridge, Mass., 1941) and Guillermo Lohmann Villena: *Las Minas de Huancavélica en los siglos XVI y XVII* (Seville, 1949).

For the generally unsuccessful attempt to win the uplands over to Christianity, Pierre Duviols: *La Lutte contre les religions autochtones dans le Pérou colonial* (Lima, 1971). Antonine Tibesar: *Franciscan Beginnings in Colonial Peru* (Washington, DC, 1953) decribes how Pizarro, in contrast to Cortés, was unable to attract highly motivated clergy to the newly conquered lands.

Peru and the mines have tended to monopolize the attention of European historians. But other regions should be considered. Alvaro Jara: *Guerra y sociedad en Chile* (Santiago de Chile, 1971) portrays a society starved of resources and always open to Indian attack. Germán Colmenares: *Historia económica y social de Colombia, 1537–1719* (3rd edn, Bogotá, 1983) examines the mineral wealth of this region which attracted the attention of those eager to emulate the most celebrated conquistadores. José María Vargas OP: *Historia de Ecuador—Siglo XVI* (Quito, 1977) looks at just such an adventurer, Sebastian de Belalcázar. If one reverts to an older tradition, R. B. Cunningham Graham produced a series of biographies devoted to such men as Gonzalo Jiménez de Quesada and Pedro de Valdivia.

Those interested in the translation of commerical organizations and techniques to the American trade might consult R. S. Smith: *The Spanish Guild Merchant. A History of the Consulado, 1250–1700* (Durham, N. C., 1940); Manuel Basas Fernández: *El Consulado de Burgos en el Siglo XVI* (Madrid, 1963); and the excellent Teófilo Guiard y Larrauri: *Historia del Consulado y Casa de Contratación de Bilbao y del comercio de la villa* (2 vols, Bilbao, 1913–14). The latter points out that Bilbao had already organized a system of *flotas* for trading with its principal partners. Seville's convoy system owed much to Bilbao's experience of trading to the French ports and the Low Countries.

On the intellectual repercussions of the Discoveries the literature is enormous. It has been reviewed by J. H. Elliott: *The Old World and the New, 1492–1650* (Cambridge, 1970). For the champion of Indian rights, see Marcel Bataillon and André Saint-Lu: *Las Casas et la défense des Indiens* (Paris, 1971) and for a good biography, Marianne Mahn-Lot: *Bartolomé de las Casas et le droit des Indiens* (Paris, 1982). Those wishing to continue research into the career of the repentant planter should look at his Utopian scheme for establishing racial harmony: André Saint-Lu: *La Vera Paz. Esprit évangélique et colonisation* (Paris, 1968); and idem: *Las Casas indigéniste* (Paris, 1982). Lewis Hanke has made a permanent contribution to the field. His principal arguments are laid out in his *La lucha española por la justicia en la conquista de América* (2nd edn, Madrid, 1967). Another cleric and his contribution to Indian rights is remembered in D. Ramos, A. García *et al.: Francisco de Vitoria y la escuela de Salamanca. La ética en la conquista de América* (Madrid, 1984).

Anthony Pagden: *The Fall of Natural Man. American Indians and the Origins of Comparative Ethnology* (Cambridge, 1982) is strong on Dominican theology. Giuliano Gliozzi: *Adamo e il nuovo mondo. La nascita dell'antropologia come ideologia coloniale: dalle genealogie bibliche alle teorie razziali (1500–1700)* (Florence, 1977) surveys a broad canvass and deserves wider recognition.

At the furthest extremity of empire, a link in the trade between Mexico and China, the last of the overseas conquests, the Philippine Islands. The modern study is Nicholas P. Cushner: *Spain in the Philippines* (Quezon City, 1971). And for an example of how history should be written, William Lytle Schurz: *The Manila Galleon* (New York, 1959).

The reign of Philip II

Biographies of Philip II come, like sunspots, in cycles. The latest irruption occurred in the mid-1970s and produced a number of usable accounts. See Geoffrey Parker: *Philip II* (London, 1979); Peter Pierson: *Philip II of Spain* (London, 1975); and V. Vázquez de Prada: *Felipe II* (Barcelona, 1978). But several earlier studies have yet to be surpassed. Charles Bratli: *Philippe II, roi d'Espagne* (Paris, 1912) had the merit of evaluating the printed accounts of contemporaries and near-contemporaries. The author was also amongst the first systematically to exploit the archive of Simancas. But the most satisfying treatment to date remains that of Ludwig Pfandl: *Philip II. Gemälde eines Lebens u. einer Zeit* (Munich, 1936). Pfandl understood the society of the golden age as few others while paying due attention to the earlier part of Philip's life, particularly his relations with his Austrian cousins.

On specific aspects of Philip's life, José María March: *Niñez y Juventud de*

Felipe II (2 vols, Madrid, 1941–2). His relations with his family are discussed in L. P. Gachard: *Don Carlos et Philippe II* (2nd edn, Paris, 1867). This also provides the most balanced assessment of Don Carlos's brief career. Whether the heir to the throne was martyr or miscreant has provoked a blistering controversy. Two doughty polemicists took opposing views. Viktor Bibl: *Der Tod des Don Carlos* (Vienna–Leipzig, 1918) led to Felix Rachfahl: *Don Carlos: kritische Untersuchungen* (Freiburg-im-Breisgau, 1921). From an unfortunate son to an unfortunate queen. Agustín G. de Amezúa y Mayo: *Isabel de Valois. Reina de España (1546–1568)* (3 vols, Madrid, 1949) gives details of her medical history—migraine, haemorrhoids, and miscarriages. A life of her successor, Anne of Austria, would have an equally sombre story to tell.

The king revealed something of himself in his letters to his daughters. L. P. Gachard: *Lettres de Philippe II à ses Filles*. . . (Paris, 1884) relates his impressions from the journey to Portugal. Erika Spivakovsky (ed.): *Felipe II. Epistolario familiar. Cartas a su hija, la infanta doña Catalina (1585–1596)* (Madrid, 1975) begin with some warmth, and include his views on obstetrical practices, but they become terser towards the end. The diplomatic corps attached to the court have left numerous accounts of the king. Once again L. P. Gachard: *Rélations des ambassadeurs venétiens sur Charles-Quint et Philippe II* (Brussels, 1856). The full series can be studied from Luigi Firpo (ed.): *Relazioni di ambasciatori veneti al Senato*, vol. 8, *Spagna (1497–1598)* (Turin, 1981). The French court was kept informed even if relations did wax and wane. See Beccarie de Pavie (Raimond), baron de Fourquevaux: *Dépêches de M. de Fourquevaux, ambassadeur du roi Charles IX en Espagne, 1565–72* (3 vols, Paris, 1896–1904); Albert Mousset: *Un résident de France en Espagne au temps de la Ligue (1583–1590). Pierre de Ségusson* (Paris, 1908). Other, this time more personal, accounts are provided by Alfredo Morel-Fatio and Antonio Rodríquez Villa (eds): *Relación del viaje hecho por Felipe II en 1585 a Zaragoza* (Madrid, 1876); and, a partial reprint of the same material, J.-P. Devos: *Description de l'Espagne par Jehan Lhermite et Henri Cock, humanistes belges* (Paris, 1969). P. Félix G. de Olmedo (ed.): *Don Francisco Terrones del Caño: instrucción de predicadores* (Madrid, 1946) discusses the writings of Philp II's favourite preacher, one much admired for the simplicity of his style and accorded the rare privilege of preaching to his sovereign as the latter moved his bowels. An entertaining, if at times too laudatory, account of the king can be found in Baltasar Porreño: *Dichos y hechos del Señor Rey Don Felipe II* (Valladolid, 1863). Fidel Pérez Mínguez: *Psicología de Felipe II* (Madrid, 1925) can still be consulted profitably.

For the monument associated above all with Philip II (and the Counter-Reformation), George Kubler: *Building the Escorial* (Princeton, 1982) to be read in conjunction with the review by John Bury in *Burlington Magazine* 124 (1982). A recent anniversary gave rise to *El real monasterio de El Escorial. Estudios en el IV centenario de la terminación* (El Escorial, 1984). But the best account to date, and unlikely to be improved upon, is Cornelia von der Osten Sacken: *San Lorenzo el Real de El Escorial. Studien zur Baugeschichte u. Ikonographie* (Munich, 1979). For the artistic currents of the period see Fernando Checa: *Pintura y escultura del Renacimiento en España, 1450—1600* (Madrid, 1983); Juan Rivera: *Juan Bautista de Toledo y Felipe II. La implantación del clasicismo en España* (Valladolid, 1984); Rosa López Torrijos: *La mitología en la pintura española del Siglo de Oro* (Madrid, 1985). For a great painter who failed to find favour see the catalogues to the splendid exhibitions of *El Greco de Toledo* (Madrid, 1982) and *El Toledo de El Greco* (Toledo, 1982). The reader is also referred to Jonathan Brown (ed.): Studies in the History of Art 11: *Figures of Thought: El Greco as Interpreter of History, Tradition, and Ideas* (Washington, DC, 1982); and Jonathan Brown and José Manuel Pita Andrade (eds): Studies in the History of Art 13: *El Greco: Italy and Spain* (Washington, DC, 1984). I am grateful to Dr Carole Rawcliffe for both pointing out these last two works—and buying them for me.

The history of Castilian administration has yet to receive the treatment it warrants. The best general survey remains J. Gounon-Loubens: *Essais sur l'administration de la Castille au XVIe siècle* (Paris, 1860). A century later, J. Vicens Vives produced his masterly 'The Administrative Structure of the State in the Sixteenth and Seventeenth Centuries', reprinted in Henry J. Cohn (ed.): *Government in Reformation Europe, 1520—1560* (London, 1971). I. A. A. Thompson: *War and Government in Habsburg Spain, 1560—1620* (London, 1976) vigorously argues a case which rests on the attempt of royal officials to exercise direct control over the machinery of the administration.

Internal government can be regarded as a virtual *terra incognita*. Pedro Molas Ribalta: *Consejos y audiencias durante el reinado de Felipe II* (Valladolid, 1984) promises more than it delivers. The later Middle Ages have fared slightly better than the early modern period in that the student can consult David Torres Sanz: *La administración central castellana en la baja edad media* (Valladolid, 1982) and Salustiano de Dios: *El Consejo Real de Castilla (1385—1522)* (Madrid, 1982). The only monograph devoted to an administrative tribunal in the sixteenth century is Joaquín José Salcedo Izu: *El Consejo Real de Navarra en el siglo XVI* (Pamplona, 1964). Additional material can also be gathered from Laura Fernández Vega: *La Real Audiencia de Galicia. Organo de gobierno en el Antiguo Régimen* (3 vols, La Coruña, 1982). How the courts of appeal operated can be studied from María Antonia Varona García: *La Chancillería de Valladolid en el reinado de los Reyes Católicos* (Valladolid, 1981). An examination of the *corregidor* offers a promising line of future research. The subject can be approached from the excellent Benjamín González Alonso: *El corregidor castellano (1348—1808)* (Madrid, 1970). This should be read together with the vade-mecum of the royal agent, Gerónimo Castillo de Bovadilla: *Política para corregidores y señores de vasallos en tiempo de paz y guerra* (Madrid, 1978, repr. of 1704 edn) and the essay dedicated to Castillo de Bovadilla which can be found in Francisco Tomás y Valiente: *Gobierno e instituciones en la España del Antiguo Régimen* (Madrid, 1982).

For the personnel of government J. A. Escudero: *Los secretarios de Estado y del Despacho, 1474–1724* (2nd edn, Madrid, 1976) makes available a useful series of biographies. A. González Palencia: *Gonzalo Pérez. Secretario de Felipe II* (2 vols, Madrid, 1964) throws light on the early years of the reign. On the man who shaped the administration and made it Castilian in outlook, Diego de Espinosa, there is virtually nothing. Scraps of information are contained in José Luis de Orella y Unzué: 'El Cardenal Diego de Espinosa, consejero de Felipe II, y el monasterio de Iranza . . .' in *Principe de Viana* 140–1 (1975). Philip II's private secretary, whom he inherited from the cardinal, forms the subject of A. W. Lovett: *Philip II and Mateo Vázquez de Leca: the Government of Spain (1572–92)* (Geneva, 1977). Martin Philippson: *Ein Ministerium unter Philip II. Kardinal Granvella am spanischen Hofe (1579–1586)* is a first-class study of how Granvelle masterminded the annexation of Portugal. Gregorio Marañon: *Antonio Pérez* (9th edn, Madrid, 1977) deals with the colourful career of a secretary who, for a time, held his master spellbound. Angela Delaforce: 'The Collection of Antonio Pérez, Secretary of State to Philip II' in *Burlington Magazine* 124 (1982) indicates the breadth of his tastes. For his political associate but hardly comrade-in-arms—she was too much of a snob for that—Gaspar Muro: *Vida de la Princesa de Eboli* (Madrid, 1877).

On the external aspects of Philip's reign, consult Henri Lapeyre: *Las etapas de la política exterior de Felipe II* (Valladolid, 1973); A. Domínguez Ortiz: *Notas para una periodización del reinado de Felipe II* (Valladolid, 1984); and Ernest Belenguer i Cebrià: *La problemática del cambio político en la España de Felipe II* (Barcelona, 1980).

For relations with Italy, H. G. Koenigsberger: *The Practice of Empire* (Ithaca, 1969). The founder of the Savoyard state, and a protégé of the Spanish court, provides the subject of Carlo Moriondo: *Testa di Ferro. Vita di Emanuele Filiberto di Savoia* (Milan, 1981). C. Riley: 'The State of Milan in the Reign of Philip II' (D.Phil. thesis, Oxford, 1977), although primarily concerned with religious matters, has much to say on more general problems. Further south, Spanish rule is examined in R. Villari: *La rivolta antispagnola a Napoli. Le origini (1585–1647)* (Bari, 1967, Spanish trans., Madrid, 1979). Another Spanish possession has received exhaustive treatment in a work which heralded a great tradition in French scholarship, Lucien Febvre: *Philippe II et la Franche-Comté* (Paris, 1912).

Islam and Habsburg Spain

The starting-point for any discussions of the relations between the Great Powers of the sixteenth century is Fernand Braudel: *The Mediterranean and the Mediterranean World in the Age of Philip II* (2 vols, London, 1972–3) which began life as a study of the Holy League. The transformation of the North African interior is dealt with by, amongst others, Charles-André Julien: *Le Maroc face aux impérialismes, 1415–1956* (Paris, 1978). For the creation of the Algerian state and the careers of ʿAruj and Khair al-Din Barbarossa see J. M. Abun-Nasr: *A History of the Maghrib* (Cambridge, 1971). These two have also received a lively and sympathetic treatment in Ernle Bradford: *The Sultan's Admiral* (London, 1969); while the same author's *The Great Siege. Malta 1565* (London, 1961) has become a classic. Another biography of a corsair is provided by Gustavo Valente: *Vita di Ochiali* (Milan, 1960).

For the Spanish response to the Ottoman threat, a trio of works: C. Fernández Duro: *Armada española desde la unión de Castilla y de Aragón* (Madrid, 1895–1903), vols 1–2; F.-F. Olesa Muñido: *La Organización naval de los estados mediterráneos y en especial de España durante los siglos XVI y XVII* (2 vols, Madrid, 1968); and the careful account of a major disaster, Charles Monchicourt: *L'Expédition espagnole de 1560 contre l'île de Djerba* (Paris, 1913).

The factors leading to the battle of Lepanto have been excellently recounted in a book which deserves a wider audience Michel Lésure: *Lépante: la crise de l'empire ottoman* (Paris, 1972). For the history of the way in which the frontier between the religions became fixed, Andrew C. Hess: *The Forgotten Frontier. A History of the Sixteenth Century Ibero-African Frontier* (Chicago, 1978), a book rich in suggestion even if hard evidence is sometimes lacking. The general problems of the Turkish empire in this period have been illuminated by Donald E. Pitcher: *An Historical Geography of the Ottoman Empire* (Leiden, 1972) and two articles from the doyen of Ottoman studies, Ömer Lûfti Barkan. See the latter's 'The Price Revolution of the Sixteenth Century: a Turning Point in the Economic History of the Near East' in *International Journal of Middle East Studies* 6 (1975); and 'L'Empire ottoman face au monde chrétien au lendemain de Lépante' in Guido Benzoni (ed.): *Il Mediterraneo nella seconda metà del '500 alla luce di Lepanto* (Florence, 1974).

The government of the Netherlands

In the English-speaking world no account is likely to replace J. L. Motley: *The Rise of the Dutch Republic* (London, 1855); P. Geyl: *The Revolt of the Netherlands* (London, 1932) has been adopted as the definitive interpretation of modern times. Geoffrey Parker: *The Dutch Revolt* (London, 1977) looks at the events from both Spanish and Dutch sides. Recent literature has been assessed by G. de Bruin: 'Un fuoco nascosto o un fuoco spento? I. La storiografia sulla rivolta dei Paesi Bassi dopo il 1945' in *Rivista Storica Italiana* 95 (Sept. 1983). The best general account, and one which it must be hoped will be translated into English, is S. Groenveld, H. L. Ph. Leeuwenberg, N. E. H. Mout, W. M. Zappey: *De Kogel door de Kerk? De Opstand in de Nederlanden, 1559–1609* (2nd edn, Zutphen, 1983).

Other surveys worthy of note are: Robert van Roosbroeck: *Die Geschichte Flanderns* (Jena, 1942). Horst Lademacher: *Geschichte der Niederlanden* (Darmstadt, 1983). G. Janssens: 'Van de komst van Alva tot de Unies, 1567–1579' in

Algemene Geschiedenis der Nederlanden vol. 6, *Nieuwe Tijd* (Haarlem, 1979) provides a careful factual account. For interpretation I have based my account on J. J. Woltjer: 'Der niederländische Bürgerkrieg u. die Gründung der Republik der Vereinigten Niederlande (1555–1648)' in Joseph Engel (ed.): *Handbuch der Europäischen Geschichte*, vol. 3 (Stuttgart, 1971); J. W. Smit: 'The Netherlands Revolt' in G. A. M. Beekelaar *et al.*: *Vaderlande Verleden in Veelvoud* (The Hague, 1975) or in Robert Forster and Jack P. Greene (eds): *Preconditions of Revolution in Early Modern Europe* (Baltimore–London, 1970); and a masterpiece of understanding and compression, Heinz Schilling: 'Der Aufstand der Niederlande: Bürgerliche Revolution oder Elitenkonflikt?' in H.-U. Wehler (ed.): *200 Jahre amerikanische Revolution u. moderne Revolutionsforschung* (Göttingen, 1976).

Guy E. Wells: 'Antwerp and the Government of Philip II' (Ph.D. thesis, Cornell, 1982) offers an interesting interpretation of the circumstances surrounding the grant of the Novennial Aid. The religious situation has been efficiently summarized in Léon-E. Halkin: *La Réforme en Belgique sous Charles-Quint* (Brussels, 1957) and M. Dierickx: *L'Erection des nouveaux diocèses aux Pays-Bas* (Brussels, 1967). The state of the Low Countries during the early period of opposition has been well related by Felix Rachfahl in his two studies: *Margaretha von Parma. Statthalterin der Niederlande (1559–1567)* (Munich–Leipzig, 1898) and his (incomplete) 3-volume work *Wilhelm van Oranien* (Halle–The Hague, 1906–24). The progress of the reformed faith can be followed through the pioneering work of J. J. Woltjer: *Friesland in Hervormingstijd* (Leiden, 1962). The many interpretations of 1566 have been alluded to in Robert van Roosbroeck: 'Wunderjahr oder Hungerjahr? Antwerpen, 1566' in Franz Petri (ed.): *Kirche u. gesellschaftlicher Wandel in deutschen u. niederländischen Städten der Werdenden Neuzeit* (Vienna, 1980).

The prince of Orange and his shifting attitude to events have to be studied in their own right. Robert van Roosbroeck: *Wilhelm von Oranien. Der Rebell* (Göttingen, 1959) is sympathetic in tone; and it has been joined by A. Th. van Deursen and H. de Schepper: *Willem van Oranje. Een Strijd voor Vrijheid en Verdraagzaamheid* (Weesp, 1984). The 400th anniversary of his death stimulated many journals into devoting special numbers to his career. The best collection came from *Bijdragen en Mededelingen Betreffende de Geschiedenis der Nederlanden* 99 (1984) which contained K. W. Swart: 'Wat bewoog Willem van Oranje de strijd tegen de Spaanse overheersing aan te binden?' and Volker Press: 'Wilhelm von Oranien, die deutsche Reichsstände u. der niederländische Aufstand'. The themes discussed in these respective articles can be followed up in R. H. Bremmer: *Reformatie en Rebellie. Willem van Oranje, de Calvinisten en het Recht van Opstand* (Wever, 1984) and the rewarding study: Rolf Glawischnig: *Niederlande, Kalvinismus u. Reichsgrafenstand, 1559–1584. Nassau-Dillenburg unter Graf Johann VI* (Marburg, 1973).

The indefatigable J. J. Woltjer has discussed such topics as the prince's attitude towards religious toleration on a number of occasions. See his 'De Politieke Betekenis van de Emdense Synod' in D. Nauta *et al*.: *De Synode van Emden, Oktober 1571* (Kampen, 1971); and his: 'Willem van Oranje en de godsdienstige pluriformiteit' in A. Alberts and J. E. Verlaan (eds): *Apologie van Willem van Oranje. Hertaling en Evaluatie na vierhonderd jaar, 1580—1980* (Amsterdam, 1980). Two other contributions from the same author should also be consulted. First his 'De Vrede-makers' in *Tijdschrift voor Geschiedenis* 89 (1976), and then his inaugural lecture: *Kleine oorzaken, grote gevolgen* (Leiden, 1975).

The two implacable enemies of the prince, apart from Philip himself, were Granvelle and Alba. The former has been studied in M. van Durme: *Antoon Perrenot: Bisschop van Atrecht, Kardinaal van Granvelle, minister van Karel V en Filips II (1517—1586)* (Brussels, 1953); and the latter in William S. Maltby: *Alba. A Biography of Fernando Alvarez de Toledo, third Duke of Alba (1507—1582)* (Berkeley, 1983). The prince acquired a cause, and owed his salvation, to Alba's fiscal miscalculations. These form the subject of Ferdinand H. M. Grapperhaus: *Alva en de Tiende Penning* (Zutphen, 1984).

For the establishment of an independent state, so different from the hopes and expectations of the 1560s, see J. C. Boogman: 'The Union of Utrecht: its Genesis and Consequences' in *The Low Countries History Yearbook/Acta Historica Neerlandica* 12 (1979); Horst Lademacher: *Die Stellung des Prinzen von Oranien als Statthalter in der Niederlanden von 1572 bis 1584* (Bonn, 1958); and Leo Delfos: *Die Anfänge der Utrechter Union, 1577—1587* (Berlin, 1941). For history as told from the localities, C. C. Hibben: *Gouda in Revolt. Particularism and Pacificism in the Revolt of the Netherlands* (Utrecht, 1983); R. Reitsma: *Centrifugal and Centripetal Forces in the Early Dutch Republic. The States of Overijssel, 1566—1600* (Amsterdam, 1982) and Charlie R. Steen: *A Chronicle of Conflict. Tournai, 1559—67* (Utrecht, 1985).

The definitive military history of the Spanish Reconquest has been told in the magisterial volumes of Leon van der Essen: *Alexandre Farnèse, prince de Parme, gouverneur général des Pays-Bas (1512—92)* (Brussels, 1933-7). The inexorable rise (with the occasional dip) in expenditure can be traced through the accounts of the successive paymasters who served in the Netherlands. For a study of these Geoffrey Parker: *The Army of Flanders and the Spanish Road, 1559—1659* (Cambridge, 1972). The same author has collected his articles on this and allied themes in *Spain and the Netherlands, 1559—1659* (London, 1979). The instrument of Spain's fearsome reputation has been examined in detail. See René Quatrefages: *Los tercios españoles (1567—77)* (Madrid, 1979); and for a less successful attempt to assert a presence by sea, Magdalena Pi Corrales: *España y las potencias nórdicas. 'La otra Invencible' 1574* (Madrid, 1983).

Portugal and the Habsburgs

A reliable and well-written guide to Portuguese history has been made available recently: Joaquim Veríssimo Serrão: *História de Portugal*, vol. 3, *(1495—1580)*

(2nd edn, Lisbon, 1980) and vol. 4, *(1580—1640)* (Lisbon, 1979). In English the best account takes the form of a work on colonial history, C. R. Boxer: *The Portuguese Seaborne Empire* London, 1969) which is both scholarly and entertaining. Two collections drawn from C. R. Boxer's many articles are warmly recommended: *From Lisbon to Goa, 1500—1750. Studies in Portuguese Maritime Expansion* (London, 1984) and *Portuguese Conquest and Commerce in Southern Asia, 1500—1750* (London, 1985).

For the general setting, two works of outstanding merit: António Sérgio: *Introdução geográfico-sociológica a história de Portugal* (5th edn, Lisbon, 1982) and João Lúcio de Azevedo: *Epocas de Portugal económico-esboços de história* (Lisbon, 1929). Much information can be derived from another pioneering work: Manuel Nunes Dias: *O capitalismo monárquico Português (1415—1549)* (Coimbra, 1963). The reader will find his endurance tested by V. Magalhães Godinho: *L'Economie de l'empire portugais aux XVe et XVIe siècles* (Paris, 1969) which remains, nevertheless, essential. Another book relevant to economic matters is F. Mauro: *Le Brésil du XVe à la fin du XVIIIe siècle* (Paris, 1977).

An attempt, unconvincing for the most part, to argue that a shift took place in Portuguese interests in the mid-sixteenth century has been made by Francisco Sales Loureiro: *D. Sebastião. Antes e despois de Alcácer Quibir* (Lisbon, 1978). For the disastrous reign of the boy king the soundest interpretation is that of J. M. de Queiroz Vellosa: *D. Sebastião, 1554—1578* (3rd edn, Lisbon, 1945). For a clear description of the event which lost the king his life and Portugal her independence see E. Bovil: *The Battle of Alcazar* (London, 1952). The brief interlude between the death of D. Sebastian and the accession of Philip II forms the subject of a two-volume study. J. M. de Queiroz Vellosa: *O reinado do Cardeal Henrique* (Lisbon, 1946) and *O interregno dos governadores e o breve reinado de D. António* (Lisbon, 1953). A lengthier account of the prior's undistinguished career occurs in Joaquim Veríssimo Serrão: *O reinado de D. António, prior de Crato*, vol. 1, *(1580—2)* (Coimbra, 1956). To appreciate the skill of Habsburg diplomats on the eve of Portugal's absorption, and the subsequent achievements of the local boy made good, Alfonso Danvila y Burguero: *Don Cristóbal de Moura, primer marqués de Castel Rodrigo (1538—1613)* (Madrid, 1900). For Portugal in the last years of the sixteenth century, Francisco Caeiro: *O Arquiduque Alberto de Austria. Vice-rei e Inquisidor Mor de Portugal, Cardeal Legado do Papa, Governador e despois Soberano dos Países Baixos* (Lisbon, 1961).

Attention should also be drawn to Charles L. Redman: *Qsar es Seghir (Alcácer Ceguer): a 15th- and 16th-century Portuguese colony in North Africa* (Lisbon, 1981); António de Oliveira: *A vida económica e social de Coimbra de 1537 a 1640* (2 vols, Coimbra, 1971–2); Joaquim Antero Romero Magalhães: *Para o estudo do Algarve económico durante o século XVI* (Lisbon, 1970); António Cruz: *A vida económica e social do Porto nas vésperas de Alcácer Quibir* (Porto, 1967); Maria Angela V. da Rocha Beirante: *Santarém quinhentista* (Lisbon, 1981); and the contribution of

Helder Fernando Parreira de Sousa Lima: 'Os Açores na economia atlântica' in *Instituto Histórico da Ilha Terceira* 34 (1976) (Angra do Heroismo).

On the links with the Castilian colonies, see Gonçalo de Reparaz: *Os portugueses no vice-reinado do Peru (séculos XVI e XVII)* (Lisbon, 1976) and the fundamental work of Alice Piffer Canabrava: *O comercio português no Rio da Prata (1580—1640)* (São Paulo, 1944).

The Grand Design

Much of the literature for this section has been noted elsewhere.

For guidance in French history I have relied on two excellent works separated in time by nearly eighty years, Ernest Lavisse: *Histoire de la France*, vol. 16.i: *La Réforme et la Ligue—L'Édit de Nantes (1559—1598)* (Paris, 1904) and Hubert Méthivier: *L'Ancien Régime* (Paris, 1981).

On the prelude to the Religious Wars two biographies offer an introduction, I. Cloulas: *Henri II* (Paris, 1985) and idem: *Catherine de Médicis* (Paris, 1979). For the later stages of the conflict, Yves Cazaux: *Henri IV ou la Grande Victoire* (Paris, 1977); Arlette Lebigre: *La Révolution des curés. Paris, 1588—1594* (Paris, 1980); Elie Barnavi: *Le Parti de Dieu. Etude sociale et politique des chefs de la Ligue parisienne (1585—1594)* (Brussels–Louvain, 1980). Mark Greengrass: *France in the Age of Henry IV: the Struggle for Stability* (London, 1984) concentrates more on the period after 1598. Howell A. Lloyd: *The Rouen Campaign, 1590—1592* (Oxford, 1973) deals with a campaign which settled the eventual outcome of the war.

English affairs are well covered by Garret Mattingly: *The Spanish Armada* (London, 1959); and R. B. Wernham: *After the Armada* (Oxford, 1984). The technicalities of ship design are discussed in David Watkin Waters: *The Elizabethan Navy and the Armada of Spain* (Greenwich, 1975).

The parties and the prolonged negotiations which led to the termination of hostilities form the subject of a detailed monograph, Arthur Erwin Imhof: *Der Friede von Vervins, 1598* (Aarau, 1966).

The eastern kingdoms

The series Colección Aragón has published a number of historical studies. These include G. Colás Latorre and J. A. Salas Ausens: *Aragón bajo los Austrias* (Zaragoza, 1977); María Luisa Ledesma Rubio and María Isabel Falcón Pérez: *Zaragoza en la baja edad media* (Zaragoza, 1977); Jesús Lalinde Abadía: *Los fueros de Aragón* (Zaragoza, 1976); and Luis González Antón: *Las cortes de Aragón* (Zaragoza, 1978). The collective work *Aragón en su historia* (Zaragoza, 1980) also testifies to a new sense of regional pride.

On the reign of Ferdinand the Catholic, two essays, Fernando Solano Costa: *Fernando el Católico y el ocaso del Reino Aragonés* (Zaragoza, 1979); and Guillermo Redondo Veintemillas and Luis Orera Orera: *Fernando II y el Reino de Aragón* (Zaragoza, 1980). Also relevant, José Angel Sesma Muñoz: *La*

Diputación del Reino de Aragón en la época de Fernando II (1479–1516) (Zaragoza, 1977) and Angel Alcalá Gálvez: *Orígenes de la Inquisición en Aragón* (Zaragoza, 1984).
The standard work on the kingdom in the early Habsburg period is Gregorio Colás Latorre and José Antonio Salas Ausens: *Aragón en el siglo XVI. Alteraciones sociales y conflictos políticos* (Zaragoza, 1982). But however good the modern authorities, they will never supersede the marqués de Pidal: *Historia de las alteraciones de Aragón en el reinado de Felipe II* (3 vols, Madrid, 1862) which in its turn draws on the indispensable works of Lupercio Leonardo de Argensola: *Información de los sucesos de Aragón en los años de 1590 y 1591 en que se admiten los yerros de algunos autores* (Madrid, 1808), Gonçalo de Céspedes y Meneses: *Historia apologética en los sucesos del Reyno de Aragón y su ciudad de Çaragoça, años de 91 y 92* (Zaragoza, 1622), and Vicencio Blasco de Lanuza: *Historias eclesiásticas y seculares de Aragón* (2 vols, Zaragoza, 1622). Antonio Pérez is a central figure, and the best biography to date remains Gregorio Marañon: *Antonio Pérez* (Madrid, 1954). A useful collection of documents has been made available in Gregorio Marañon: *Los procesos de Castilla contra Antonio Pérez* (Madrid, 1947).

Some information about the state of Aragon has been presented in Carlos Riba: *El Consejo Supremo de Aragón en el reinado de Felipe II* (Valencia, 1914). The rural economy of the kingdom is unexplored territory; but a start has been made in G. Colás Latorre: *La agricultura aragonesa en los siglos XVI y XVII* (Zaragoza, 1980). For the perennial curse of the mountains, banditry, see the interesting, if at times confused, A. Melón y Ruiz de Gordejuela: *Lupercio Latrás y la guerra de moriscos y cristianos en Aragón a fines del siglo XVI* (Zaragoza, 1917), for the life of a brigand who served the count of Villahermosa, then on the Invincible Armada, and ended his days by being strangled in Segovia for treason. The medieval antecedents to the rural disorders of the sixteenth century have been discussed in Esteban Sarasa Sánchez: *Sociedad y conflictos sociales en Aragón: siglos XIII–XV* (Madrid, 1981).

The principality of Catalonia

The period under discussion is dealt with by Josep M. Salrach and Eulàlia Duran: *Història dels Països Catalans* vols 1 and 2 (Barcelona, 1982). These form part of a 3-volume set under the direction of A. Balcells. Jean Vilar: *La Catalogne dans l'Espagne moderne*, vol. 1 (Paris, 1962) is indispensable. Shorter introductions are provided by Jaume Vicens i Vives: *Els Trastàmares (segle XV)* (Barcelona, 1956) and Joan Reglà: *Els virreis de Catalunya* (Barcelona, 1956). Joan Bada: *Situació religiosa de Barcelona en el segle XVI* (Barcelona, 1970) presents a good account of how the principality was governed.

As for individual topics, overseas expansion has been discussed in Jesús Lalinde Abadía: *La corona de Aragón en el Mediterráneo medieval (1229–1479)* (Zaragoza, 1979). The civil war has attracted a detailed modern study,

Santiago Sobrequés i Vidal and Jaume Sobrequés i Callicó: *La guerra civil catalana del segle XV* (2 vols, Barcelona, 1973), while the economic recovery, or *redreç*, is examined by Manuel J. Peláez: *Catalunya després de la guerra civil del segle XV* (Barcelona, 1981). Two older works on the period make an essential contribution Jaime Vicens Vives: *Política del Rey Católico en Cataluña* (Barcelona, 1940) and idem (Jaume Vicens i Vives): *Ferran II i la Ciutat de Barcelona, 1479–1516* (3 vols, Barcelona, 1936–7).

The 'isolation' of Catalonia under Philip II and the attempt to seal the border with France is a preoccupation of Catalan historians. The most interesting study is Joan Reglà: *Bandolers, pirates i hugonots a la Catalunya del segle XVI* (Barcelona, 1969) which is a re-working of the same author's *Felip II i Catalunya* (Barcelona, 1956). The thesis is overstated, but the book remains the best study of the principality in the period. For the growth of banditry, Lluis María Soler y Terol: *Perot Roca Guinarda. Història d'aquest bandoler* (Manresa, 1909), which is unusually sensitive to the character of vendetta society.

Important aspects of political life have been discussed by Jaume Sobrequés Callicó: *Pactisme a Catalunya* (Barcelona, 1982) and Joan B. Culla Clara *et al.*: *Catalunya i la Generalitat al llarg de la nostra història* (Barcelona, 1983).

For an area which seldom appears in historical accounts, consult Onofre Vaquer: *Aspectes sòcio-econòmics de Manacor al segle XVI* (Mallorca, 1978).

Sicily and Naples absorbed much of the energy of the Aragonese kingdom. Italian historians have been active in the field. See Carmelo Trasselli: *Da Ferdinando il Cattolico a Carlo V: l'esperienza siciliana, 1475–1525* (Catanzaro, 1982), Aurelio Cernigliaro: *Sovranità e feudo nel regno di Napoli, 1505–1557* (2 vols, Naples, 1983), and, for a slightly later period, Giuseppe Coniglio: *Il viceregno di don Pietro de Toledo (1532–53)* (2 vols, Naples, 1984).

The Habsburg financial system

The best introduction to the whole question is Richard Ehrenberg: *Das Zeitalter der Fugger* (3rd edn, 2 vols, Jena, 1922). Several attempts have been made to translate this book, into both French and English, but none has proved satisfactory. Two other works warmly recommended are Jakob Van Klaveren: *Europäische Wirtschaftsgeschichte Spaniens im 16. u. 17. Jhdt.* (Stuttgart, 1960) and Konrad Haebler: *Die wirtschaftliche Blüte Spaniens im 16. Jhdt. u. ihr Verfall* (Berlin, 1881). There are some grievous mistakes in the latter (the state bankruptcy of 1574 – *sic*), yet it remains an impressive achievement for its time. More recent studies include Modesto Ulloa: *La hacienda real de Castilla en el reinado de Felipe II* (2nd edn, Madrid, 1977) and the pioneering Ramón Carande: *Carlos V y sus banqueros* (2nd edn, Barcelona, 1983), this a recast version of his earlier 3-volume study of the same title. Information on the taxation system is provided by Miguel Artola: *La hacienda del Antiguo Régimen* (Madrid, 1982) and in another work whose theme is primarily agricultural, David E. Vassberg: *Land and Society in Golden Age Castile* (Cambridge, 1984).

For studies of individual themes Henri Lapeyre: *Simon Ruiz et les asientos de Philippe II* (Paris, 1953) and (admittedly less relevant to financial matters), idem: *Une famille de marchands: les Ruiz* (Paris, 1953). There exists a fine study of a fair, the merchant community which served it, and the type of transaction conducted (mainly commercial) in Falah Hassan Abed Al-Husein: 'Trade and Business in Old Castile. Medina del Campo, 1500–1575' (Ph.D. thesis, University of East Anglia, 1982). For a rather limited investigation into the origins of the Exchequer, Esteban Hernández Esteve: *Creación del Consejo de Hacienda de Castilla (1523–25)* (Madrid, 1983).

Much work has been done on various aspects of financial history in this period. It has to be hunted down in periodicals and conference proceedings that are not always accessible. The importance of the Netherlands to imperial finance at an early stage has been made plain by F. Braudel: 'Les Emprunts de Charles-Quint sur la place d'Anvers' in *Charles-Quint et son temps* (Paris, 1959). Felipe Ruiz Martín has devoted a string of articles to a discussion of economic subjects, amongst them the role of the Genoese. See his 'Rasgos estructurales de Castilla en tiempos de Carlos V' in *Moneda y Crédito* 96 (1966) — a review of Carande which ended up as an article in its own right; 'Economía y sociedad en la España de Carlos V' in *Doce consideraciones sobre el mundo hispano-italiano en tiempos de Alfonso y Juan de Valdés*, Publicaciones del Instituto Español de Lengua y Literatura de Roma (Salamanca, 1979); 'Los hombres de negocios genoveses de España durante el siglo XVI' in H. Kellenbenz (ed.): *Fremde Kaufleute auf der Iberischen Halbinsel* (Cologne, 1970); 'Un expediente financiero entre 1560 y 1575: la Hacienda de Felipe II y la Casa de Contratación de Sevilla' in *Moneda y Crédito* 92 (1965); 'La finanzas españolas durante el reinado de Felipe II' in *Cuadernos de Historia* 2 (1968) — this is the best study to date of Philip's financial management; 'Crédito y banca, comercio y transportes en la etapa del capitalismo mercantil' in *Actas de las I Jornadas de Metodología Aplicada de las Ciencias Históricas* vol. 3 (Santiago de Compostela, 1975); 'Procedimientos crediticios para la recaudación de los tributos fiscales en las ciudades castellanas durante los siglos XVI y XVII. El caso de Valladolid' in *Dinero y Crédito (siglos XVI al XIX)* (Madrid, 1978); 'Gastos ocasionados por el sostenimiento de la guerra: Repercusiones económicas que se experimentaron en España' in *Domanda e Consumi. Livelle e strutture (nei secoli XIII–XVIII)*, Istituto Internazionale di Storia Economica F. Datini (Florence, 1978). For another series of articles, this time on the management of state bankruptcies, see A. W. Lovett: 'Juan de Ovando and the Council of Finance (1573–1575)' in *Historical Journal* 15 (1972); 'The Castilian Bankruptcy of 1575' in *Historical Journal* 23 (1980); 'The General Settlement of 1577: an aspect of Spanish finance in the early modern period' in *Historical Journal* 25 (1982). A discussion of the background to financial administration together with a number of contemporary submissions can be found in Margarita Cuartas Rivero: *Arbitristas del siglo XVI* (Madrid, 1981).

State bonds (*juros*) and their emission have been examined by Alvaro Castillo Pintado in another series of articles. See his 'Los juros de Castilla. Apogeo y fin de un instrumento de crédito' in *Hispania* 23 (1963); 'Dette flottante et dette consolidée de 1557 à 1600' in *Annales E.S.C.* 18 (1963); 'Population et "richesse" en Castille durant la seconde moitié du XVIe siècle' in *Annales E.S.C.* 20 (1965); ' "Decretos" y "Medio Generales" dans le système financière de la Castille. La crise de 1596' in *Mélanges en l'Honneur de Fernand Braudel. Histoire économique du monde méditerranéen, 1450–1650*, vol. 1 (Paris, 1973); 'El Mercado del dinero en Castilla a finales del siglo XVI. Valor nominal y curso de los juros castellanos en 1594' in *Anuario de Historia Económica y Social Año III* (1970, 3). Also of interest from the viewpoint of taxation is José Martínez Caados: 'Las cortes de Castilla en el siglo XVI' in *Revista de la Universidad de Madrid*, vol. 6, 24 (1957). I. A. A. Thompson: 'Crown and Cortes in Castile, 1590–1665' in *Parliaments, Estates and Representation*, vol. 2,1 (1982) gives an indication of the new thinking on the role and nature of the Castilian Cortes. Much information on the Cortes and taxation should become available with the publication of the papers presented to *I. Congreso Internacional del Instituto de Estudios Castellanos 'Cortes de Castilla y León' (s. XII a XVII) 10–14 Marzo 1986*.

The economic history of Spain

The two basic texts are Jaime Vicens Vives: *Manual de historia económica de España* (Barcelona, 1959 rep. many times, English trans., Princeton, 1969). More recently there has appeared the admirable V. Vázquez de Prada: *Los Siglos XVI y XVII* (Madrid, 1978) which forms the third volume in the series *Historia económica y social de España*, gen. ed. V. Vázquez de Prada.

On the specific topic of the woollen industry nothing will ever supersede Julius Klein: *The Mesta* (Cambridge, Mass., 1920, many reprints). Interest has been revived in the subject over the last few years. A summary of recent literature, and a contribution in its own right, can be found in Charles J. Bishko: 'Sesenta años despues. La Mesta de Julius Klein a la luz de la investigación subsiguiente' in *Historia. Instituciones. Documentos*, vol. 8 (1981). The fundamental contributions of modern times come from two historians. Jean-Paul le Flem: 'Las cuentas de la Mesta (1510–1709)' in *Moneda y Crédito* 121 (June 1972); idem: 'Miguel Caxa de Leruela, défenseur de la Mesta' in *Mélanges de la Casa de Velázquez*, vol. 9 (1973); and the same author's introduction to Miguel Caxa de Leruela: *Restauración de la abundancia de España* (Madrid, 1975), a contemporary seventeenth-century text well worth reading in itself. Another valuable contribution to the history of the Mesta which enables certain conjectures to be submitted to practical test can be found in Guy Lemeunier: 'Les Extremeños, ceux qui viennent de loin. Contribution à l'étude de la transhumance ovine dans l'est castillan (XVIe–XIXe siècles)' in *Mélanges de la Casa de Velázquez*, vol. 13 (1977). Le Flem's work can be complemented by that of Felipe Ruiz Martín: 'Pastos y ganaderos en Castilla: la Mesta (1450–1600)' in Mario Spallanzani (ed.): *La lana come materia prima* (Florence, 1974). Istituto Internazionale di Storia Economica F. Datini. Atti della Prima Settimana di Studio (18–24 Aprile, 1969). Not all Ruiz Martín's arguments are fully worked out, or totally convincing; but the piece remains a seminal contribution.

On the history of the textile trade the basic study is P. Iradiel Murugarren: *Evolución de la industria textil castellana en los siglos XIII–XVI* (Salamanca, 1974). It should be supplemented by the equally informative Angel García Sanz: *Desarrollo y crisis del Antiguo Régimen en Castilla la Vieja. Economía y sociedad en tierras de Segovia, 1500–1814* (Madrid, 1977); Jean-Paul le Flem has also contributed to the subject in his 'Vraies et fausses splendeurs de l'industrie textile ségovienne (vers 1460–vers 1650)' in Mario Spallanzani (ed.): *Produzione, commercio e consumo dei panni di lana (nei secoli XII–XVIII)* (Florence, 1976). Henri Lapeyre has followed the theme in his 'Les exportations de laine de Castille sous le règne de Philippe II' in *La lana come materia prima* (op. cit. above) and his *Comercio exterior de Castilla a través de las aduanas de Felipe II* (Valladolid, 1981).

The sale of crown lands, a subject which bears directly on the woollen industry, has received treatment in David E. Vassberg: *La venta de tierras baldías. El comunitarismo agrario y la corona de Castilla durante el siglo XVI* (Madrid, 1983). Germane to the subject is José M. Mangas Navas: *El régimen comunal agrario de los concejos de Castilla* (Madrid, 1981).

For the fluctuations in prices the essential work remains Earl J. Hamilton: *American Treasure and the Price Revolution in Spain* (Cambridge, Mass., 1934) and the essential criticism Jorge Nadal Oller: 'La revolución de los precios españoles en el siglo XVI. Estado actual de la cuestión' in *Hispania* 19 (1959). A brilliant, and simple, explanation of inflation can be found in *History Today* 33 (April 1983): 'Inflation: who wins?' (various authors).

Demographic change

It is virtually impossible to separate demographic from economic history, since the first is an essential component of the second. Jorge Nadal: *La población española* (5th edn, Barcelona, 1984) provides a sure guide to the specific theme of demography; and this can be supplemented by Felipe Ruiz Martín: 'La población española al comienzo de los tiempos modernos' in *Cuadernos de Historia* (Anejos de Revista Hispania) 1 (1967); idem: 'Demográfia eclesiástica hasta el siglo XIX' in *Diccionario de historia eclesiástica de España*, vol. 2 (Madrid, 1972); and Bernard Vincent: 'Récents travaux de démographie historique en Espagne (XIVᵉ–XVIIIᵉ siècles)' in *Annales de Démographie Historique* (1977). For general surveys José Larraz: *La época del mercantilismo en Castilla (1500–1700)* (Madrid, 1943) still has useful things to say. But the most sophisticated analysis, one based on the research of a lifetime, comes from Jean-Paul Le Flem: 'El siglo XVI. Un crecimiento inacabado. El tiempo de las ilusiones', in *La Frustración de un Imperio (1476—1714)*, *Historia de España*, ed. Manuel Tuñón de Lara, vol. 5 (Barcelona, 1982). Two other contributions to interpretation should be noticed. Angel García Sanz: 'Castilla la Vieja y León durante el Antiguo Régimen: sociedad y política en los siglos XVI, XVII y XVIII' in Julio Valdeón *et al*. (eds): *Iniciación a la historia de Castilla—León* (Burgos, 1980); and Gonzalo Anes: 'El sector agrario en la España Moderna' in *Papeles de Economía Española* 20 (1984). Conferences on the topic have proliferated, as was only to be expected. Of these, two might be mentioned: Emilio Sáez *et al*. (eds): *La ciudad hispánica durante los siglos XIII al XVI* (Madrid, 1985); and *Congreso de historia rural, siglos XV al XIX* (Madrid, 1984).

Monographs should be grouped together by regions. The meseta has been relatively well investigated. See Noël Salomon: *La vida rural castellana en tiempos de Felipe II* (Madrid, 1973), and A. Molinié-Bertrand: *Au siècle d'or. L'Espagne et ses hommes. La population du royaume de Castile au XVI* siècle* (Paris, 1985) for the general view. The best two local studies are Bartolomé Bennassar: *Valladolid au siècle d'or* (Paris-The Hague, 1967) and Angel García Sanz: *Desarrollo y crisis del Antiguo Régimen en Castilla la Vieja. Economía y sociedad en tierras de Segovia, 1500—1814* (Madrid, 1977). Almost as good is F. Brumont: *Campo y campesinos de Castilla la Vieja en tiempos de Felipe II* (Madrid, 1984), which is an extended (and translated) version of his earlier book (New York, 1977) on the Bureba, a region just north of Burgos. Other studies with important findings to contribute include Alberto Marcos Martín: *Auge y declive de un núcleo mercantil y financiero de Castilla la Vieja. Evolución demográfica de Medina del Campo durante los siglos XVI y XVII* (Valladolid, 1978); and María del Carmen González Muñoz: *La población de Talavera de la reina (siglos XVI—XX)* (Toledo, 1974). It is also to be hoped that the example of Luis Antonio Ribot García *et al*. (eds): *Valladolid, Corazón del mundo hispánico. Siglo XVI, Historia de Valladolid*, vol. 3 (Valladolid, 1981) will be followed by others dealing with major urban centres—Burgos is an obvious choice. Essays dealing with the region can be found in *Pasado histórico de Castilla y León*, vol. 2: *Edad moderna* (Valladolid, 1984).

The records of southern Spain are unusually rich, or the region has been luckier in its historians. The area boasts the finest regional history yet to appear, Antonio Domínguez Ortiz (ed.): *Historia de Andalucía*, vol. 4, *La Andalucía del Renacimiento* (Madrid, 1980). There exists a useful collection of essays, Antonio Malpica Cuello, José María Ruiz Povedano *et al*. (eds): *Andalucía en el siglo XVI* (Granada, 1981); and the inescapable conference *Actas II Coloquios. Historia de Andalucía. Córdoba, noviembre 1980. Andalucía moderna* (2 vols, Córdoba, 1983).

In a wider sweep other works should be considered, such as Angel Rodríguez Sánchez: *Cáceres: Población y comportamientos demográficos en el siglo XVI* (Cáceres, 1977); Manuel Sánchez Martínez and Juan Sánchez Caballero: *Una villa giennense a mediados del siglo XVI: Linares* (Jaén, 1975); Carla Rahn Phillips: *Ciudad Real, 1500—1750. Growth, Crisis, and Readjustment in the Spanish*

Economy (Cambridge, Mass., 1979); José E. López de Coca Castañer: *La Tierra de Málaga a fines del siglo XV* (Granada, 1977); F. Cortés Cortés: *La Población de Zafra en los siglos XVI y XVII* (Badajoz, 1984); E. Cabrera Muñoz: *El condado de Belalcázar (1444—1518)* (Córdoba, 1977); Antonio González Gómez: *Moguer en la baja edad media (1248—1538)* (Huelva, 1977); Manuel Acien Almansa: *Ronda y su serranía en tiempos de los Reyes Católicos* (3 vols, Málaga, 1979); Pedro Ponce Molina: *El espacio agrario de Fondón en el siglo XVI* (Fondón, ?1983); idem: *Agricultura y sociedad de El Ejido en el siglo XVI* (El Ejido, 1983); Antonio Moreno Ollero: *Sanlúcar de Barrameda a fines de la edad media* (Cádiz, ?1983). Antonio L. Cortés Peña and B. Vincent: *La época moderna, siglos XVI al XVII, Historia de Granada*, vol. 3 (Granada, 1983).

The major city of the south, indeed of the kingdom, has received the serious attention it merits, although much remains to be done. See Antonio Collantes de Terrán Sánchez: *Sevilla en la baja edad media* (Seville, 1977); Gregorio García-Baquero López: *Estudio demográfico de la parroquia de San Martín de Sevilla (1551—1749)* (Seville, 1982); and Antonio Herrera García: *El Aljarafe sevillano durante el Antiguo Régimen* (Seville, 1980). The former capital of Muslim Spain has attracted the talents of a first-rate historian, José Ignacio Fortea Pérez: *Córdoba en el siglo XVI. Las bases demográficas y económicas de una expansión urbana* (Córdoba, 1981); a résumé was published under the same title (Salamanca, 1979).

The eastern kingdoms have also been relatively well served in terms of modern research. J. Nadal and E. Giralt: *La Population catalane de 1553 à 1717* (Paris, 1960); Ricardo García Cárcel: *Población, jurisdicción y propriedad del obispado de Girona, siglos XIV—XVII* (Gerona, 1976); Josep Iglésies: *El Fogatge de 1553* (2 vols, Barcelona, 1979) for the principality. Aragon is beginning to produce monographs, José Antonio Salas Ausens: *La población de Barbastro en los siglos XVI y XVII* (Zaragoza, 1981); Gregorio Colás Latorre: *La Bailía de Caspe en los siglos XVI y XVII* (Zaragoza, 1978) to which might be added the same author's 'La transformación de la superficie agraria aragonesa en el siglo XVI' in *Congreso de historia rural. Siglos XV al XIX* (Madrid, 1984). Valencia has benefited from a particularly active school of local historians. See Francisco Pons Fuster: *Aspectos económicos-sociales del condado de Oliva (1500—1750)* (Valencia, 1981); Antoni Furió: *Camperols dels País Valencià. Sueca, una comunitat rural a la tardor de l'Edat Mitjana* (Valencia, 1982); and two fine studies which complement one another, Eugenio Císcar Pallarés: *Tierra y señorío en el país valenciano (1570—1620)* (Valencia, 1977), and James Casey: *The Kingdom of Valencia in the Seventeenth Century* (Cambridge, 1979). To these should be added Juan Bautista Vilar: *Orihuela, una ciudad valenciana en la España moderna* (3 vols, Murcia, 1981).

The adjoining region of Murcia has been scrutinized by Francisco Chacón Jiménez in a variety of publications: *Murcia. Un modelo económico en el mundo mediterráneo durante el siglo XVI* (Murcia, 1978); *Murcia en la centuria del quinientos* (Murcia, 1980); and the publication he edited with others, *Historia de la Región Murciana*, vol. 5: *La época de la expansión (1500–1590)* (Murcia, 1981). French historians have also worked on this topic. Guy Lemeunier: 'La coyuntura murciana: población y producción en el Siglo de Oro (1500–1650)' in *Cuadernos de Historia* 10 (1983); and the joint publication Mª Teresa Pérez Pocazo and Guy Lemeunier: *El proceso de modernización de la región murciana* (Murcia, 1984).

Northern studies are also beginning to show signs of progress. Margarita Cuartas Rivero: *Oviedo y el principado de Asturias a fines de la edad media* (Oviedo, 1983); Mª del Carmen González: *Galicia en 1571. Población y economía* (La Coruña, 1982); and Juan Eloy Gelabert González: *Santiago y la tierra de Santiago de 1500 a 1640* (La Coruña, 1982). The Basque provinces can be approached via Julio Caro Baroja (ed.): *Historia general del País Vasco*, vol. 6 (Bilbao–San Sebastian, ?1982). Then E. Enciso: *Laguardia en el siglo XVI* (Vitoria, 1959)—a somewhat dated book that comes equipped with a Nihil Obstat, whereas Alfredo Floristán Imízcoz: *La merindad de Estella en la edad moderna: los hombres y la tierra* (Pamplona, 1982) employs the latest techniques. Much economic and demographic information can be obtained from Santiago Lasaosa Villanua: *El 'Regimiento' municipal de Pamplona en el siglo XVI* (Pamplona, 1979).

The plagues which devastated Castile at the end of the sixteenth century have been placed in a general framework by Bernard Vincent in his 'La peste atlántica de 1596–1602' in *Asclepio* 28 (1979). Bartolomé Bennassar: *Recherches sur les grands épidémies dans le nord de l'Espagne à la fin du XVI*ᵉ *siècle* (Paris, 1969) deals with the same theme, as does the at times wordy Vicente Pérez Moreda: *Las crisis de mortalidad en la España interior. Siglos XVI–XIX* (Madrid, 1980).

Further information on sixteenth-century economic history can be obtained from Linda Martz: *Poverty and Welfare in Habsburg Spain: the example of Toledo* (Cambridge, 1983); Enrique Lorente Toledo: *Gobierno y administración de la ciudad de Toledo y su término en la segunda mitad del siglo XVI* (Toledo, 1982); Alfonso María Guilarte: *El régimen señorial en el siglo XVI* (Madrid, 1962); Bartolomé Clavero: *Mayorazgo. Propriedad feudal en Castilla (1369–1836)* (Madrid, 1974); Peter Clark (ed.): *The European Crisis of the 1590s* (London, 1985), which contains articles by James Casey on Spain: 'A Failed Transition', and I. A. A. Thompson on 'The Impact of War'.

The moriscos

Fernand Braudel: *The Mediterranean and the Mediterranean World* (2 vols, London, 1972–3) has a short passage (2. 780–98) which provides a penetrating insight into the 'clash of the cultures', a phrase which the author helped to popularize, if he did not invent it. Amongst the first to write seriously on the theme was Manuel Danvila y Collado: *La expulsión de los moriscos españoles— conferencias pronunciadas en el Ateneo de Madrid* (Madrid, 1889); and he was followed by Pascual Boronat y Barrachina: *Los moriscos españoles y su expulsión.*

Estudio histórico-crítico (2 vols, Valencia, 1901) which, for all its prejudice, remains the most original work on the subject. A more sympathetic view is present in another classic, H. C. Lea: *The Moriscos of Spain: their Conversion and Expulsion* (London, 1901). An early example of research into customs and beliefs is to be found in Pedro Longás: *Vida religiosa de los moriscos* (Madrid, 1915). Like so many of the older works, it is irreplaceable. As a group the moriscos have proved a constant source of inspiration to historians, with the result that the moderns are quite the equals of the ancients. Two works summarize (and make a contribution to) recent literature, Juan Reglà: *Estudios sobre los moriscos* (Valencia, 1964); and then Antonio Domínguez Ortiz and Bernard Vincent: *Historia de los moriscos* (Madrid, 1978). One should also add the memorable study in cultural history which illuminates the whole question, Louis Cardaillac: *Morisques et chrétiens: un affrontement polémique* (Paris, 1977).

Monographs on the different morisco communities abound. Amongst the best are Julio Caro Baroja: *Los moriscos del reino de Granada* (2nd edn, Madrid, 1976); Tulio Halperin Donghi: *Un conflicto nacional: moriscos y cristianos viejos en Valencia* (Valencia, 1980); Rafael Benítez Sánchez-Blanco: *Moriscos y cristianos en el condado de Casares* (Córdoba, 1982); Juan Aranda Doncel: *Los moriscos en tierras de Córdoba* (Córdoba, 1984); Dolors Bramon: *Contra moros i jueus. Formació i estratègia d'unes discriminacions al País Valencià* (Valencia, 1981). Ramon Robres Lluch: *San Juan de Ribera. Patriarca de Antioquia, arzobispo y virrey de Valencia, 1532–1611* (Barcelona, 1960). Ribera, a man unbalanced in his judgement, first advised comprehension, and ended by advocating expulsion. Joan Reglà, Joan Fuster, Sebastian García Martínez, Trini Simò, Josep Climent (eds): *Història de País Valencià*, vol. 3 (Barcelona, 1975) has much to say on the moriscos of Valencia. After 1571 Valencia became the focus of Christian concern. Some of the reasons are indicated in Sebastián García Martínez: *Bandolerismo, piratería y control de moriscos en Valencia durante el reinado de Felipe II* (Valencia, 1977). All surviving morisco communities suffered increasingly from the predations of the Holy Office. For this development, Ricardo García Cárcel: *Orígenes de la Inquisición española. El tribunal de Valencia, 1478–1530* (Barcelona, 1976) and idem: *Herejía y sociedad en el siglo XVI. La Inquisición de Valencia, 1530–1609* (Barcelona, 1980); Mercedes García-Arenal: *Inquisición y moriscos. Los procesos del Tribunal de Cuenca* (Madrid, 1978); Peter Dressendörfer: *Islam unter der Inquisition. Die Morisco Prozesse in Toledo, 1575–1610* (Wiesbaden, 1971), the latter being a work based on records now kept in Halle (GDR).

The great study on the morisco community of Granada before 1570 has never been published—an enterprising university press might consider the project— K. Garrad: 'The Second Revolt of the Alpujarras' (Cambridge Ph.D. thesis, 1956). My account of the silk industry is taken from this source. The same author has published a useful contemporary document 'The Original Memorial of Don Francisco Núñez Muley' in *Atlante* 2 (London, 1954). A classic of its time, well worth reading, is Diego Hurtado de Mendoza: *Guerra de Granada* (Madrid,

1970) which has appeared in the *Clásicos Castalia* 22, with a rather unsavoury introduction by Bernardo Blanco González. For the study of another morisco community, Nicolás Cabrillana: *Almería morisca* (Granada, 1982). L. P. Harvey: 'The Literary Culture of the Moriscos, 1492–1609' (2 vols, Oxford D.Phil. thesis, 1958) gives an outstanding account of the development of morisco spiritual life under persecution. The same author has contributed an article 'The Survival of Arabic Culture in Spain after 1492' to *La Signification du Bas Moyen Âge dans l'histoire de la culture du monde musulman* (Aix-en-Provence, 1978). Some of Harvey's conclusions have been confirmed by Jacqueline Fournel-Guerin: 'La Livre et la civilisation écrite dans la communauté morisque aragonaise (1540–1620)' in *Mélanges de la Casa de Velázquez*, vol. 15 (1979).

For the last moments of Islam in the peninsula, Francisco Chacón Jiménez: 'El problema de la convivencia. Granadinos, mudéjares y cristianos viejos en el reino de Murcia, 1609–1614' in *Mélanges de la Casa de Velázquez*, vol. 18/1 (1982); and Encarnación Gil Saura: 'La expulsión de los moriscos en Alzira. Aspectos económicos (1609–1616)' in *Estudis. Revista de Historia Moderna* 9 (1981/2). Jaime Bleda (Predicador General de la Orden de Predicadores, Calificador de la Inquisicion de Valencia): *Crónica de los moros de España* (Valencia, 1618) is worth consulting for the way in which it conveys the (unpleasant) flavour of the times.

Felipe Ruiz Martín has made a significant contribution to this field of study as do so many others. Consult his 'Movimientos demográficos y económicos en el Reino de Granada durante la segunda mitad del siglo XVI' in *Anuario de Historia Económica y Social* I (1968).

The morisco problem has lent itself readily to treatment by conference. See *Les Morisques et leur temps* (Table Ronde Internationale, Montpellier 4–7 juillet, 1981) (Paris, 1983); *Actas I Congreso de Historia de Andalucía (Diciembre de 1976)*, in particular *Andalucía Medieval* vol. 2 (Córdoba, 1978), and *Andalucía Moderna*, vols 1–2, *Siglos XVI–XVII* (Córdoba, 1978).

Church, Inquisition, and society

Church history has benefited, like much else, from the renaissance of the last two decades. The subject can be first approached through a collective work, Ricardo García-Villoslada (ed.): *Historia de la Iglesia en España*, vol. 3 (2 parts): *La iglesia en España de los siglos XV y XVI* (Madrid, 1980). For those with strong theological tastes, Melquíades Andrés Martín: *La teología española en el siglo XVI* (2 vols, Madrid, 1976).

On the reforms of the fifteenth century—the internal movement for the regeneration of the church—consult García M. Colombás: *Un reformador benedictino en tiempo de los Reyes Católicos García Jiménez de Cisneros, Abad de Montserrat* (Montserrat, 1955), an excellent work which explains what the Observance really meant. Another study of the Catholic Reform, Joaquín

Ortega Martín: *Un reformador pretridentino: Don Pascual de Ampudia, Obispo de Burgos (1496—1512)* (Rome, 1973). Along more conventional lines, P. Tarsicio de Azcona: *La elección y reforma del episcopado español en tiempo de los Reyes Católicos* (Madrid, 1960) and José García Oro: *Cisneros y la reforma del clero español en tiempo de los Reyes Católicos* (Madrid, 1971). The Holy Office seemed to many the embodiment of Habsburg Spain. The modern work which, when complete, will hold the field for many years is Joaquín Pérez Villanueva and Bartolomé Escandell Bonet (eds): *Historia de la Inquisición en España y América*, vol. 1: *El conocimiento científico y el proceso histórico de la Institución (1478—1834)* (Madrid, 1984). Henry Kamen: *The Spanish Inquisition* (London, 1976) provides a clear summary of the literature and proposes an interesting thesis. Henry Charles Lea: *A History of the Inquisition in Spain* (London, 1906–7) will always be read with respect because it made the first scientific use of the documents on which all subsequent work has been based. The French school has, as might be assumed, made a distinguished contribution. See Bartolomé Bennassar: *L'Inquisition espagnole, XVe—XIXe siècles* (Paris, 1979). The conference threatens to take over as the principal means of communicating the fruits of research here as elsewhere. See Joaquín Pérez Villanueva (ed.): *La Inquisición Española. Nueva visión, nuevos horizontes* (Madrid, 1980) and Angel Alcalá (ed.): *Inquisición española y mentalidad inquisitorial (Ponencias del Simposio internacional sobre Inquisición, Nueva York 1983)* (Barcelona, 1984). For a basic reader, Miguel Jiménez Monteserín: *Introducción a la Inquisición española* (Madrid, 1980).

On the different tribunals, Ricardo García Cárcel: *Orígenes de la Inquisición española. El Tribunal de Valencia (1478—1530)* (Barcelona, 1976); idem: *Herejía y sociedad en el siglo XVI. La Inquisición en Valencia (1530—1609)* (Barcelona, 1980). Iñaki Reguera: *La Inquisición española en el País Vasco (El tribunal de Calahorra, 1513—1570)* (San Sebastián, 1984). Jordi Ventura: *Inquisició espanyola i cultura renaixentista al País Valencià* (Valencia, 1978) has value even if the case is overstated. For a neighbouring tribunal Eufémia Fort i Cogul: *Catalunya i la Inquisició* (Barcelona, 1973). On the all-important consideration of finance, J. Martínez Millán: *La hacienda de la Inquisición (1478—1700)* (Madrid, 1984).

Relations between the papacy and Madrid were always close, if not invariably cordial. See John Lynch: 'Philip II and the Papacy' in *Transactions of the Royal Historical Society* 5th series, 2 (1961); Gaetano Catalano: 'Controversie giurisdizionali tra chiesa e stato nell'età di Gregorio XIII e Filippo II' in *Atti della Accademia di Scienze Lettere e Arti di Palermo* (Palermo, 1955). Antonio Rouco-Varela: *Staat u. Kirche im Spanien des 16. Jhdts.* (Munich, 1965). Antonio Molina Melía: *Iglesia y estado en el Siglo de Oro español. El pensamiento de Francisco Suárez* (Valencia, 1977).

For the intellectual influence of northern Europe on Spain Marcel Bataillon: *Erasmo y España. Estudios sobre la historia espiritual del siglo XVI* (2nd edn, Mexico, DF, 1966), and idem: *Erasmo y erasmismo* (Barcelona, 1977), to cite but two titles from a vast output. For the trial of Juan de Vergara, that standard-bearer of Erasmian ideas, John E. Longhurst: *Luther's Ghost in Spain* (Lawrence, Kansas, 1969). Those who may have derived inspiration from this movement have been studied by Antonio Márquez in his *Los Alumbrados* (Madrid, 1972), and, for the later period, Antonio Huerga in his *Historia de los Alumbrados (1570—1630)* (2 vols, Madrid, 1978). For a bishop and inquisitor of Erasmian times see Augustin Redondo: *Antonio de Guevara (1480?—1545) et l'Espagne de son temps* (Geneva, 1976).

Luther was probably more reviled and feared in the Iberian peninsula than any other contemporary figure. In reality his influence was oblique rather than direct. The point is made in the basic study of Augustin Redondo: 'Luther et l'Espagne de 1520 à 1538' in *Mélanges de la Casa de Velázquez*, vol. 1 (1965). On the theme, consult Melquíades Andrés Martín: *Reforma española y reforma luterana* (Madrid, 1975).

Orthodoxy became defined much more carefully; and those who erred were punished accordingly. For the most exalted victim of the growing intolerance, José Ignacio Tellechea Idígoras: *El Arzobispo Carranza y su tiempo* (2 vols, Madrid, 1968). This is a collection of discrete studies rather than a structured biography. The same author has provided a further set of articles in book form, *Tiempos recios. Inquisición y heterodoxias* (Salamanca, 1977). Another figure, less prominent but intellectually more eminent, who fell foul of the Holy Office has stimulated interest: María Paz Aspe Ansa: *Constantino Ponce de la Fuente. El hombre y su lenguaje* (Madrid, 1975) and José Ramón Guerrero: *Catecismos españoles del siglo XVI. La obra catequética del Doctor Constantino de la Fuente* (Madrid, 1969).

Even though the age saw the flowering of Spanish mysticism the Inquisition took an unsympathetic view in general. See Enrique Llamas Martínez: *Santa Teresa de Jesús y la Inquisición española* (Madrid, 1972). Efrén de la Madre de Dios and Otger Steggink: *Tiempo y vida de Santa Teresa* (Madrid, 1968). E. W. Trueman Dicken: *The Crucible of Love. A Study of the Mysticism of St Teresa of Jesus and St John of the Cross* (London, 1963)—a book which can be read by anyone with pleasure. For a general survey of the mystic tradition, Melquíades Andrés Martín: *Los recogidos. Nueva visión de la mística española (1500—1700)* (Madrid, 1976).

The Council of Trent marks a turning-point in the history of all the states which remained loyal to Rome. Antonio Marín Ocete: *El Arzobispo Don Pedro Guerrero y la política conciliar española en el siglo XVI* (2 vols, Madrid, 1970) looks at a Spanish representative who took part in the debates. A collective work examines various aspects of the Council's impact, *Miscelánea conmemorativa del Concilio de Trento (1563—1963). Estudios y Documentos* (Madrid–Barcelona, 1965). At regional level, José Ignacio Tellechea Idígoras: *La reforma tridentina en San Sebastián* (San Sebastián, 1974). The artistic effects of conciliar rulings on

Iberian art have been measured in a short work I much liked, Cristina Cañedo-Argüelles: *Arte y teoría. La contrarreforma y España* (Oviedo, 1982). Censorship, if at first in a surgical form, was another bequest of the Council. How it was imposed (and why) can be pieced together from José Luis G. Novalín: *El Inquisidor General Fernando de Valdés (1483–1568)* (2 vols, Oviedo, 1968–71); a general survey, Antonio Márquez: *Literatura e Inquisición en España (1478–1834)* (Madrid, 1980), followed by Virgilio Pinto Crespo: *Inquisición y control de ideología en la España del siglo XVI* (Madrid, 1983); and ending with two articles, J. M. de Bujanda: 'La Littérature castillane dans l'Index espagnol de 1559' in Augustin Redondo (ed.): *L'Humanisme dans les lettres espagnoles* (Paris, 1979), and the illuminating P. E. Russell: 'El Concilio de Trento y la literatura profana: Reconsideración de una teoría' in his collected essays *Temas de 'la Celestina'* (Barcelona, 1978).

On the Jewish communities in the peninsula a general review can be found in José María Monsalvo Antón: *Teoría y evolución de un conflicto social. El antisemitismo en la corona de Castilla en la baja edad media* (Madrid, 1985). For an interpretation which carries conviction, even if it is controversial, Benzion Netanyahu: *The Marranos of Spain from the late XIVth to the early XVIth Century* (New York, 1966). Josep M. Solá-Solé, Samuel G. Armistead, Joseph H. Silverman (eds): *Hispania Judáica. Studies on the History, Language and Literature of the Jews in the Hispanic World* (Barcelona, 1980) contains essays which are polemical and often, in my view, perverse. For studies of individual communities, Haim Beinart: *Trujillo. A Jewish Community in Extremadura on the Eve of the Expulsion from Spain* (Jerusalem, 1980) and idem: *Conversos on Trial. The Inquisition in Ciudad Real* (Jerusalem, 1981). On the expulsion itself, Maurice Kriegel: 'La Prise d'une décision: l'expulsion des juifs d'Espagne en 1492' in *Revue Historique* 280 (1978). Specifically on the *converso* problem, Eloy Benito Ruano: *Los orígenes del problema converso* (Barcelona, 1976); Albert Sicroff: *Les Controverses des statuts de 'pureté de sang' en Espagne du XVᵉ au XVIIᵉ siècle* (Paris, 1960); Antonio Domínguez Ortiz: *Los judeoconversos en España y América* (Madrid, 1971). A convincing reading of the *converso* problem in the sixteenth century is offered by I. S. Révah: 'Les Marranes' in *Revue des Etudes Juives* 118 (1960); and a review of the recent writings can be found in Bruce A. Lorence: 'The Inquisition and the New Christians in the Iberian Peninsula: main historiographic issues and controversies' in *The Sephardi and Oriental Heritage* (Jerusalem, 1982).

The records of the Inquisition have proved a mine of information on popular beliefs and social mores. This has been demonstrated by Jaime Contreras: *El Santo Oficio de la Inquisición de Galicia (poder, sociedad, y cultura)* (Madrid, 1982) which, for all its length, holds the reader's attention throughout. The value of another major study which has yet to appear can be gauged from Jean-Pierre Dedieu: 'Les Inquisiteurs de Tolède et le visite du district. La sédentisation d'un tribunal (1550–1630)' in *Mélanges de la Casa de*

Velázquez 13 (1977) and ' "Christianisation" en Nouvelle Castille. Catéchisme, messe et confirmation dans l'archevêché de Tolède, 1540–1650' in *Mélanges de la Casa de Velázquez* 15 (1977).

Major contributions to the study of religion in Spain during this period have come from William A. Christian: *Local Religion in Sixteenth-Century Spain* (Princeton, 1981), and Gustav Henningsen: *The Witches' Advocate. Basque Witchcraft and the Spanish Inquisition* (Reno, Nev., 1980). Religion also affected profoundly the training of the young, and for this subject Julia Varela: *Modos de educación en la España de la contrarreforma* (Madrid, 1983). M. Ricardo Sáez is at present studying the educational record (the *probanzas*) of the clergy; and this should reveal much about the general level of education in the early modern period.

The following appeared after the completion of this book: Jeffrey A. Cole: *The Potosí Mita, 1573—1700. Compulsory Indian Labor in the Andes* (Stanford, 1985); Ricardo García Cárcel: *Historia de Cataluña. Siglos XVI—XVII* (2 vols, Barcelona, 1985); Pegerto Saavedra: *Economía, Política y Sociedad en Galicia: La provincia de Mondoñedo, 1480—1830* (Madrid, 1985).

Glossary

audiencia   Legal tribunal to be found in both the Iberian peninsula and America. It had extensive powers of government and was frequently in conflict with the viceroy.

alumbrado   A member of the Illuminist groups, influenced by Franciscan spirituality and Erasmian teachings.

brazo   One of the 'estates' of Aragonese or Catalan representative assemblies.

calificador   Assessor who determined whether the Inquisition should proceed against a suspect.

Casa de Contratación   Principal body regulating trade to the New World.

comunero   One who took part in the rising of the Castilian towns, 1520–1.

converso   (Or New Christian.) A Jew who had converted to Christianity. Applied to descendants of the same.

corregidor   Representative of the crown in all the important towns, who presided as of right over the municipal council.

cortes   The representative institution of Castile to which seventeen towns sent delegates. After the conquest of Granada, eighteen towns were authorized to attend.

corts   The Catalan representative institution.

cruzada   Tax originally granted by the papacy to pay for campaigns against Islamic kingdoms.

Diputación (Diputació)   Small standing committee drawn from the estates which met when the Catalan or Aragonese cortes were not in session.

encomendero   See *encomienda*.

encomienda   Grant entitling holder to the labour and produce of a stated number of Indians. The grant was limited in terms of years and did not imply any right to land. The beneficiary was known as an *encomendero*.

escusado   Tax granted to monarch by the papacy.

farda mayor/menor   Taxes levied on the moriscos of Granada for the upkeep of coastal defences.

firma   An appellant invoking protection of the Aragonese Justiciar (q.v.) would pledge not to abscond before the case had been heard. *Firma* referred to his surety or bail.

fuego   A hearth. Employed as a unit of taxation.

fuero   Constitutional right.

hermandad   Literally, 'brotherhood'. Specifically used of an association of Castilian cities under the Catholic Monarchs.

junta Small group of leading advisers (with no official standing but often great influence), which might include experts on a specific topic (e.g. finance).

juros State bonds (as opposed to *censos* which were used for private debt).

Justiciar The legally appointed guardian of Aragonese rights. Appointed for life until 1592.

mayorazgo Strict entail. Legal device most frequently used by the nobility.

Mesta The body which controlled movement of flocks to and from winter pasture.

millones Tax voted in 1590 granting king eight million ducats over six years.

manifestado One who had appealed to the court of the Aragonese Justiciar and was lodged in the Justiciar's prison pending an outcome to his case.

monfies Bandits who infested the mountains of Granada. Usually morisco in origin.

paria Tribute paid by emirs of Granada to Christian kings.

presidio A garrison, usually along N. African coast.

procurador Representative of town which sent delegates to Castilian cortes.

remensa Applied to peasants of Old Catalonia subject to the 'six bad uses'.

repartimiento The assignment of Indians to a colonist. Linked with phenomenon of *encomienda* (q.v.).

resguardo The additional securities extracted by bankers from the crown when making loans.

servicio In two forms, the ordinary and extraordinary. Tax voted to the king by Castilian cortes usually at beginning of the session.

síndico Elected representative of county of Ribagorza.

stadholder Royal representative in some of the provinces of the Low Countries.

subsidio Tax granted at the beginning by papacy to king.

tercio Characteristic square formation of Spanish infantry, first developed in the Italian wars at the outset of the sixteenth century.

vecino A householder. Often in the context of a unit for taxation or military purposes.

Index